Tolley's
Tax Computations
1990/91

by
David Smailes FCA
Stephen Savory PhD
Robert Wareham BSc(Econ) FCA

Tolley Publishing Company Limited
A UNITED NEWSPAPERS PUBLICATION

Published by
Tolley Publishing Company Ltd
Tolley House
2, Addiscombe Road
Croydon Surrey CR9 5AF
England
081–686 9141

Photoset by Promenade Graphics, Cheltenham

Printed and bound in Great Britain by
Mackays of Chatham PLC, Chatham, Kent

ISBN 0 85459 494–9

About This Book

Tolley's Tax Computations is a companion publication to Tolley's Income Tax, Tolley's Corporation Tax, Tolley's Capital Gains Tax, Tolley's Inheritance Tax and Tolley's Value Added Tax. Many of our subscribers have shown interest in worked examples of the legislation explained in the above five annual books but the format of these does not allow for all the appropriate examples to be included. This book has therefore been specially designed to complement these main annuals although the book may also be used independently. There are five parts, one for each tax. Each part contains chapters arranged in alphabetical order by subject to assist reference, and the chapter headings follow those of the main annuals so that the reader can easily find the related worked examples. Most of the computations have explanatory notes. A table of statutes and an index are also included. This edition has been fully updated to take account of the provisions of the Finance Act 1990 and other relevant information up to 1 September 1990.

Comments on this annual publication and suggestions for improvements and additional computations are always welcome.

TOLLEY PUBLISHING CO LTD

Contents

Contents

Contents

VALUE ADDED TAX

Abbreviations and References

ABBREVIATIONS

AAA	=	Allowable Aggregate Amount
ACT	=	Advance Corporation Tax
BDV	=	Budget Day Value
b/f	=	brought forward
C & E	=	Customs and Excise
C/A	=	Court of Appeal
CAA	=	Capital Allowances Act
CCAB	=	Consultative Committee of Accountancy Bodies
C/D	=	Chancery Division
c/f	=	carried forward
CFC	=	Controlled Foreign Company
CGT	=	Capital Gains Tax
CGTA	=	Capital Gains Tax Act 1979
CT	=	Corporation Tax
CTT	=	Capital Transfer Tax
CY	=	Current Year
DTR	=	Double Tax Relief
ESP	=	Expected Selling Price
FA	=	Finance Act
F(No 2)A	=	Finance (No 2) Act
FIFO	=	First In, First Out
FII	=	Franked Investment Income
FY	=	Financial Year
H/L	=	House of Lords
HMIT	=	Her Majesty's Inspector of Taxes
IBA	=	Industrial Buildings Allowance
ICTA	=	Income and Corporation Taxes Act
IRPR	=	Inland Revenue Press Release
IHT	=	Inheritance Tax
IHTA	=	Inheritance Tax Act 1984
IT	=	Income Tax
LIFO	=	Last In, First Out
NBV	=	Net Book Value
PAYE	=	Pay As You Earn
PR	=	Personal Representative
PY	=	Previous Year
RAV	=	Reckonable Aggregate Value
Reg	=	Regulation
s	=	section
SC/S	=	Scottish Court of Session
Sch	=	Schedule
Sec	=	Section
SI	=	Statutory Instrument
TMA	=	Taxes Management Act 1970
VAT	=	Value Added Tax
VATA	=	Value Added Tax Act 1983
WDA	=	Writing-down Allowance
WDV	=	Written-down Value

Abbreviations and References

REFERENCES

STC   = Simon's Tax Cases, (Butterworth & Co (Publishers) Ltd, 88 Kingsway, WC2B 6AB)

TC   = Official Tax Cases, (H.M. Stationery Office, P.O. Box 276, SW8 5DT)

BOOKS

Tolley's Tax Annuals
The following are companion publications to this book with the same alphabetical format and cross-referencing system. They are each detailed guides to the tax they cover and include the provisions of the Finance Act 1990 and other relevant information up to 26 July 1990.

Tolley's Income Tax 1990/91. £22.95
Tolley's Corporation Tax 1990/91. £18.95
Tolley's Capital Gains Tax 1990/91. £19.95
Tolley's Inheritance Tax 1990/91. £16.95
Tolley's Value Added Tax 1990/91. £19.95

Income Tax

1   Allowances and Tax Rates

Cross-reference. See also 11.1 MARRIED PERSONS for transfer of married couple's allowance, and transitional reliefs following the introduction of independent taxation with effect from 6 April 1990.

1.1   **AGE-RELATED ALLOWANCES** [*ICTA 1988, ss 257(2)–(5), 257A(2)–(5); FA 1988, s 33; SI 1990/677*]

(A)

In 1990/91, a single man, whose 65th birthday fell on 1 April 1991, received earnings of £11,600 and bank deposit interest of £1,500 net. His tax position is as follows.

	£	£
Earnings		11,600
Bank deposit interest	1,500	
Add notional tax at $\frac{25}{75}$ × 1,500	500	2,000
		13,600
Deduct		
Personal allowance	3,670	
Less Reduction for excess		
$\frac{1}{2}$ (13,600 – 12,300)	650	3,020
Taxable income		£10,580
Tax on £10,580 at 25%	2,645	
Less notional tax suffered	500	£2,145

Notes

(*a*)   The taxpayer is entitled to the age-related personal allowance by virtue of his being 65 or over *at any time* within the year of assessment.

(*b*)   Bank deposit interest (or building society interest) which is deemed to have suffered tax at the composite rate must be grossed up at basic rate to determine the figure to be included in total income and thus the figure by reference to which the age-related personal allowance is restricted.

(*c*)   If total income had been £30 greater, the age-related personal allowance would have been reduced by a further £15 ($\frac{1}{2}$ × £30) to £3,005. It could not be reduced below this figure, regardless of the amount of extra income, as this is the normal personal allowance.

(B)

In 1990/91, a single woman, aged 78, receives UK income of £10,000, comprising state and occupational pension, and foreign income from property of £3,000 on which foreign tax of £750 has been paid.

	£	£
Tax on total income		
Earnings		10,000
Income from property (foreign tax £750)		3,000
		13,000
Deduct		
Personal allowance	3,820	
Less Reduction for excess $\frac{1}{2}$ (13,000 – 12,300)	350	
		3,470
Taxable income		£9,530
Tax on £9,530 at 25%		£2,382.50

Tax on total income, excluding foreign income		
Earnings		10,000
Deduct Personal allowance		3,820
Taxable income	.	£6,180
Tax on £6,180 at 25%		£1,545.00

Note

(*a*) The difference between the computations is £837.50. As the foreign tax is less than this, full credit of £750 is available against UK tax payable. If the foreign tax was £900, the credit would be limited to £837.50 and the balance of £62.50 would be unrelieved. [*ICTA 1988, s 796(1)*].

(C)

Mr and Mrs Brown are a married couple aged 75 and 70 respectively at 6 April 1990. Mr Brown's total income for 1990/91 before deductions amounts to £14,800 and Mrs Brown's to £13,000, all consisting of untaxed income. Mr Brown pays private medical insurance premiums of £375 (net), covering both himself and his wife, under an eligible contract certified under *FA 1989, s 56*.

3

IT 1.1   Allowances and Tax Rates

Taxable income and tax payable is calculated as follows

	Mr Brown £	Mrs Brown £
Total income before deductions	14,800	13,000
Deduct private medical insurance (gross) note(c)	500	—
	14,300	13,000
Deduct personal allowances (see below)	(3,005)	(3,320)
married couple's allowance (see below)	(2,000)	—
Taxable income	£9,295	£9,680
Tax payable at 25%	2,323.75	2,420.00
Add tax retained from medical insurance	125.00	—
Net liabilities	£2,448.75	£2,420.00

Calculation of allowances

Unrestricted personal allowances		3,820	3,670
Deduct $\frac{1}{2}$ × £2,000/700 (i.e. excess over £12,300)		1,000	350
		2,820	£3,320
Add back amount required to restore to level of normal allowance		185	
		£3,005	
Unrestricted married couple's allowance		2,185	
Deduct $\frac{1}{2}$ × £2,000 =	£1,000		
Less restriction in personal allowance (£1,000 − £185)	815	185	
		£2,000	

Notes

(a)   The restriction in the married couple's allowance is by reference to the husband's income only.

(b)   The restriction of the married couple's allowance is itself restricted by the reduction in the personal allowance. *[ICTA 1988, s 257A(5); FA 1988, s 33]*.

(c)   If the husband were under 75 and the wife 75 or over, the husband would still qualify for the highest rate of married couple's allowance for the over 75s. The personal allowance is, however, calculated by reference to the individual claimant's age.

(d)   With effect for 1990/91 and later years, relief is available for private medical insurance premiums under eligible contracts insuring the over 60s. Relief is given to the person paying the premium whatever his own age. Basic rate relief is given at source and higher rate relief by reducing total income. *[FA 1989, ss 54–57]*.

(e)   See 11.1(C) MARRIED PERSONS for transitional relief available where in 1989/90 the husband received age allowance by virtue of his wife's age.

4

1.2 **ADDITIONAL PERSONAL ALLOWANCE, WIDOW'S BEREAVEMENT ALLOWANCE**
[*ICTA 1988, ss 259, 260, 262; FA 1988, s 30, 3 Sch 7*]

In 1990/91, Mr Hare and Mrs Rabbit, a widow whose husband died in early 1989/90, commence to live together as man and wife. They have total income of £25,000 and £14,000 respectively and each has a qualifying child, within *ICTA 1988, s 259(5)*. Mr Hare has a daughter aged 11 and Mrs Rabbit a son aged 9. Both children live with the couple.

The couple's tax position is as follows.

	Mr Hare	Mrs Rabbit
	£	£
Total income	25,000	14,000
Deduct personal allowances	(3,005)	(3,005)
widow's bereavement allowance		(1,720)
additional personal allowance	(1,720)	
Taxable income	£20,275	£9,275
Tax at 25%	£5,068.75	£2,318.75

Notes

(*a*)   Mrs Rabbit would have been entitled to widow's bereavement allowance for 1989/90 also. She remains so entitled for the year following her husband's death, having not re-married before the beginning of that year.

(*b*)   By virtue of *ICTA 1988, s 259(4A)* as introduced with effect from 1989/90 by *FA 1988, s 30*, the couple are entitled to only one additional personal allowance between them, this being in respect of the youngest child. It is assumed that Mr Hare will claim the allowance, in respect of Mrs Rabbit's son, as this is the most tax efficient method in that the allowance reduces his income to below £20,700, the point at which he would pay tax at the higher rate of 40%. They may, however, divide the allowance between them (*ICTA 1988, s 260*) in whatever proportions they decide.

IT 1.3 Allowances and Tax Rates

1.3 **RELIEF FOR CLASS 4 NATIONAL INSURANCE CONTRIBUTIONS** [*ICTA 1988, s 617(5)*]

A single man under 65, who has been trading for many years, has assessable Schedule D, Case I profits of £8,600 for the year ended 30 June 1989. In 1990/91 he receives UK dividends of £4,500.

	£	£
His taxable income for 1990/91 is		
Schedule D, Case I profits (PY basis)		8,600
UK dividends	4,500	
Tax credits	1,500	
		6,000
		14,600
Deduct Relief for Class 4 NIC		
Schedule D, Case I profits	8,600	
Deduct Lower limit of profits	5,450	
	£3,150	
Class 4 NIC £3,150 at 6.3%	£198.45	
Whereof 50%		99
Total income		14,501
Deduct Personal allowance		3,005
Taxable income		£11,496

Notes

(*a*)   50% of the Class 4 NIC paid for the year of assessment is deductible in computing total income of that year. It is not a trading or professional expense to be deducted in computing the Schedule D, Case I or II profit.

(*b*)   For 1990/91, Class 4 NIC is charged at 6.3% on profits between £5,450 and £18,200.

2   Business Expansion Scheme

[*ICTA 1988, ss 289–312; CGTA 1979, s 149C*]

2.1   CONDITIONS FOR RELIEF

(A)

Mr Jones is resident and ordinarily resident in the UK. In 1988/89 he subscribes for ordinary shares in two unquoted UK resident companies, both of which were incorporated in the UK.

A Ltd was formed by some people in Mr Jones' neighbourhood to provide a free local newspaper. 40,000 ordinary £1 shares were issued at par in August 1988 and the company started trading in September 1988. Mr Jones subscribed for 1,600 of the shares.

B Ltd, which is controlled by an old friend of Mr Jones, has acquired the rights to manufacture a new type of industrial cleaning solvent and requires additional finance. Mr Jones subscribed for 8,000 ordinary £1 shares at a premium of £1.50 per share in October 1988, thereby increasing the company's issued share capital to 25,000 ordinary £1 shares.

Mr Jones will obtain a deduction from his total income in 1988/89 as follows

	£	
A Ltd	1,600	
B Ltd	—	note (b)
	£1,600	

Notes

(a)   Mr Jones is entitled to relief on the full amount of his investment in A Ltd regardless of the amount of relief claimed by other investors.

(b)   Mr Jones is not entitled to relief against his income for his investment of £20,000 in B Ltd. As a result of the share issue he owns more than 30% of the issued ordinary share capital and is therefore regarded as connected with the company and denied relief.

(c)   It is assumed that Mr Jones makes no claim under *ICTA 1988, s 289(6)* to carry back relief to 1987/88. See note (a) to (B) below.

(B)

In 1989/90 Mr Jones subscribes for shares in three more unquoted UK trading companies.

C Ltd is a local company engaged in the manufacture of car components. It issues a further 200,000 ordinary £1 shares at £1.80 per share in June 1989 (having raised its original share capital other than under the business expansion scheme) and Mr Jones subscribes for 5,000 shares costing £9,000, increasing his stake in the company to 2%. He had originally held 9,000 shares, acquired by purchase at arm's length in May 1987 for £10,800.

D Ltd has been trading as a hotel and restaurant for several years and requires an injection of capital to finance an extension to the restaurant. Mr Jones and two other individuals each subscribe for 20,000 ordinary £1 shares at par in November 1989. The balance of 80,000 shares are held by Mr Jones' sister and niece.

IT 2.1 Business Expansion Scheme

E Ltd is an electronics company controlled by two cousins of Mr Jones. The company is seeking extra capital to enable it to expand and take advantage of new computer technology. Mr Jones, who already owns 1,000 ordinary £1 shares, sub-scribes for 20,000 ordinary £1 shares at par in December 1989 which increases his stake in the company to 20%.

If he makes the necessary claims Mr Jones will obtain a deduction from his total income as follows

1988/89

C Ltd	note (a)	£4,500

1989/90

		£
C Ltd		4,500
D Ltd	note (b)	16,667
E Ltd	note (c)	18,833
		£40,000

Notes

(a) Since the C Ltd shares were issued before 6 October 1989, Mr Jones may elect to carry back half the relief, subject to an overriding maximum of £5,000, to the preceding tax year. The relief will be given in addition to that previously claimed for 1988/89 (see (A) above). If Mr Jones had previously claimed relief of say £38,000 in 1988/89 the amount carried back would be restricted to £2,000 as relief in any one year may not exceed £40,000 (see also note (c) below). [*ICTA 1988, ss 289(6)(7), 290(2)*].

(b) It is found that more than one half of the assets of D Ltd are land and build-ings. Relief is restricted to claims in total of £50,000. The restriction is applied rateably and thus each of the three individuals will be granted relief on 50,000/60,000 of the amount subscribed. [*ICTA 1988, ss 294–296*].

(c) Relief in any one year may not exceed £40,000. The example assumes that the E Ltd claim will be restricted in this way, relief having already been given for the earlier C Ltd and D Ltd claims.

(C)

In June 1990, Mr Jones sells 3,000 ordinary £1 shares in C Ltd, in an arm's length transaction, for £7,500.

The position is then as follows

Income Tax

1988/89

	£
Relief given in respect of shares sold in June 1990 (2,500 shares at £1.80 per share)	4,500
Consideration received $\left(\dfrac{2,500}{3,000} \times £7,500\right)$	6,250
Excess of consideration over relief	£1,750
Relief withdrawn — Schedule D, Case VI assessment	£4,500

1989/90 £
Relief given in respect of shares sold in
June 1990   (500 shares at £1.80 per share) 900

Consideration received $\left(\dfrac{500}{3,000} \times £7,500\right)$ 1,250

Excess of consideration over relief £350

Relief withdrawn — Schedule D, Case VI assessment £900

Capital Gains Tax

1990/91 £
Disposal proceeds 7,500
Cost of shares sold (4,500 + 900) 5,400

Unindexed gain 2,100
Indexation allowance (June 1989 to June 1990) 529

Chargeable gain £1,571

Notes

(*a*) Relief is withdrawn in full as Mr Jones has made a gain on the disposal without having held the shares for the relevant five-year period. Relief is withdrawn by means of a Schedule D, Case VI assessment for the year for which it was originally given.

(*b*) Where relief has been given in each of two consecutive years of assessment by virtue of the carry-back provisions in *ICTA 1988, s 289(6)(7)*, any withdrawal of relief is made primarily for the first of those years rather than the second. [*ICTA 1988, s 307(1)*].

(*c*) Where a holding consists of shares some of which have attracted relief and some of which have not, any disposal is treated as relating first to the shares for which relief has been given and not withdrawn. [*ICTA 1988, s 299(3)*]. For capital gains tax purposes, shares for which relief has been given and not withdrawn are not subject to normal identification rules and are therefore not pooled. [*CGTA 1979, s 149C(4)*]. It is understood that the Revenue look at the position immediately *before* any disposal, so in this example, the 3,000 shares sold are shares on which relief has been given and not withdrawn. They are not therefore pooled with the 9,000 shares already held.

IT 2.1   Business Expansion Scheme

(D)
In December 1990 Mr Jones disposes of 3,000 ordinary £1 shares in D Ltd to his sister for £1,500 when the market value was £2,000.

The position is then as follows

Income Tax

1989/90   £
Relief given in respect of shares sold in

December 1990 $\left(\dfrac{3,000}{20,000} \times £16,667 \right)$ 2,500

Consideration received   1,500

Relief withdrawn   note (*a*)   £(2,500)

Schedule D, Case VI assessment   £2,500

Capital Gains Tax

1990/91   £
Deemed disposal proceeds   note (*b*)   2,000
Cost   3,000

Unindexed loss   1,000
Indexation allowance (November 1989 to December 1990), say   330

Allowable loss   £1,330

Notes
(*a*)   If the disposal had been at arms's length, for £2,000, the relief withdrawn would have been limited to the consideration received and would thus have been £2,000, leaving £500 remaining. There would have been no allowable loss as the shares would be exempt from capital gains tax, relief having been given and not fully withdrawn.
On a disposal not at arm's length, the relief withdrawn is not limited by the consideration received.

(*b*)   For CGT purposes the disposal to a connected person is deemed to take place at market value.

(E)
In November 1993 Mr Jones sells his 1,600 shares in A Ltd for their market value of £1,000.

Income Tax
As Mr Jones has held the shares for the relevant five-year period there is no withdrawal of relief.

Capital Gains Tax
As there is no withdrawal of income tax relief on the disposal, the shares are exempt from capital gains tax. [*CGTA 1979, s 149C(2)*].

2.2   **RESTRICTION OF RELIEF BY REFERENCE TO PERMITTED MAXIMUM**
[*ICTA 1988, s 290A; FA 1988, s 51; SI 1990/862*]

G Ltd, an unquoted company engaged in confectionery manufacture, decides to expand and issues, on 1 June 1990, 400,000 £1 ordinary shares at £2 per share. There have been no previous issues in the preceding six months. 50,000 of the new shares are subscribed for other than by individuals and the remaining 350,000 by individuals qualifying for business expansion relief. Mr Smith subscribes for 20,000 shares and duly claims and receives relief of £40,000. On 1 June 1991, G Ltd sets up a new subsidiary which enters into a joint venture with an unconnected company for the purpose of developing a proposed new brand of low calorie chocolate.

Restriction of relief
As a result of the joint venture within the relevant period of three years from date of issue, the relief available as a result of the 1 June 1990 issue is restricted as follows.

	£
Total amount raised	800,000
Deduct: amounts not eligible for relief	100,000
	700,000

Permitted maximum (originally £750,000) but now

$$\frac{£750,000}{1+1} = \quad \text{note } (c) \qquad\qquad 375,000$$

Excess over permitted maximum	£325,000

	£
Relief originally claimed by Mr Smith	40,000

Revised relief available $\dfrac{375,000}{700,000} \times £40,000 =$ 21,429

Relief withdrawn for 1990/91	£18,571

Notes
(a)   Any amounts raised from eligible shares issued in the period of six months ending with the date of the current issue or, if longer, the period from the preceding 6 April to the date of the current issue would fall to be aggregated with the amount raised from the current issue in deciding if and to what extent the permitted maximum is exceeded. [*ICTA 1988, s 290A(1)(2)*].

(b)   Shares issued other than to individuals qualifying for relief are disregarded. [*ICTA 1988, s 290A(3)(a)*].

(c)   The denominator of the fraction is 1 plus the number of companies involved in the venture apart from the company in question or any of its subsidiaries. [*ICTA 1988, s 290A(4)*].

(d)   The available relief is apportioned on a pro rata basis between qualifying individuals. [*ICTA 1988, s 290A(5)*].

(e)   The permitted maximum was increased from £500,000 to £750,000 with effect from 1 May 1990 by *SI 1990/862*.

3 Capital Allowances

3.1 BASIS PERIODS [*CAA 1990, s 160*]

(A) Commencement of business. Overlapping periods. No election under *ICTA 1988, s 62*

S commenced business on 1.5.88 preparing accounts annually to 30 April. The following expenditure was incurred

	Plant £	Motor Car £
Period 1.5.88 – 5.4.89	10,000	4,000 (no private use)
Period 6.4.89 – 30.4.89	2,000	
Period 1.5.89 – 30.4.90	7,500	
Period 1.5.90 – 30.4.91	6,000	

An item of plant was sold for £500 (original cost £1,000) on 27.4.89.

Profits will be assessed as follows
1988/89 Period 1.5.88 – 5.4.89 (actual)
1989/90 Year ended 30.4.89 (first 12 months)
1990/91 Year ended 30.4.89 (preceding year)
1991/92 Year ended 30.4.90 (preceding year)
1992/93 Year ended 30.4.91 (preceding year)

The capital allowances are

	Pool £	Pool for cars £	Total allowances £
1988/89 (basis period 1.5.88 – 5.4.89)			
Plant	10,000		
Motor car		4,000	
	10,000	4,000	
Allowances			
WDA 25% × $\frac{11}{12}$	(2,292)	(917)	£3,209
WDV at 5.4.89	7,708	3,083	
1989/90 (basis period 6.4.89 – 30.4.89)			
Plant	2,000		
Disposals	(500)		
	9,208	3,083	
Allowances			
WDA 25%	(2,302)	(771)	£3,073
WDV at 5.4.90	6,906	2,312	
1990/91 (no basis period)			
Allowances			
WDA 25%	(1,727)	(578)	£2,305
WDV at 5.4.91	c/f 5,179	c/f 1,734	

	Pool	Pool for cars	Total allowances
	£	£	£
	b/f 5,179	b/f 1,734	
1991/92 (basis period 1.5.89 – 30.4.90)			
Plant	7,500		
	12,679	1,734	
Allowances			
WDA 25%	(3,170)	(434)	£3,604
WDV at 5.4.92	9,509	1,300	
1992/93 (basis period 1.5.90 – 30.4.91)			
Plant	6,000		
	15,509	1,300	
Allowances			
WDA 25%	(3,877)	(325)	£4,202
WDV at 5.4.93	£11,632	£975	

Notes

(a) The period 1.5.88–5.4.89 falls into the profits basis periods for 1988/89, 1989/90 and 1990/91. It will therefore form the capital allowances basis period for the first year, 1988/89.

(b) The period 6.4.89–30.4.89 falls into the profits basis periods for both 1989/90 and 1990/91. Again, for capital allowances, the overlap will fall into the earlier year, 1989/90.

(c) In 1988/89, $\frac{11}{12}$ths of a full year's writing-down allowance will be given because the business was in operation for only eleven months of that period.

(B) Commencement of business. Overlapping periods. Election under *ICTA 1988*, *s 62*

Further analysis of S's capital expenditure (see (A) above) revealed the following

	Plant	Motor Car
	£	£
Period 1.5.88 – 5.4.89	10,000	4,000
Period 6.4.89 – 30.4.89	2,000	
Period 1.5.89 – 5.4.90	6,000	
Period 6.4.90 – 30.4.90	1,500	
Period 1.5.90 – 5.4.91	3,000	
Period 6.4.91 – 30.4.91	3,000	

Following an election under *ICTA 1988, s 62*, profits will be assessed for the first five years as follows

1988/89	Period 1.5.88 – 5.4.89 (actual)
1989/90	Period 6.4.89 – 5.4.90 (actual)
1990/91	Period 6.4.90 – 5.4.91 (actual)
1991/92	Year ended 30.4.90 (preceding year)
1992/93	Year ended 30.4.91 (preceding year)

IT 3.1 Capital Allowances

The capital allowances are

	Pool £	Pool for cars £	Total allowances £
1988/89 (basis period 1.5.88 – 5.4.89)			
Plant	10,000		
Motor car		4,000	
	10,000	4,000	
Allowances			
WDA 25% × $\frac{11}{12}$	(2,292)	(917)	£3,209
WDV at 5.4.89	7,708	3,083	
1989/90 (basis period 6.4.89 – 5.4.90)			
Plant	8,000		
Disposals	(500)		
	15,208	3,083	
Allowances			
WDA 25%	(3,802)	(771)	£4,573
WDV at 5.4.90	11,406	2,312	
1990/91 (basis period 6.4.90 – 5.4.91)			
Plant	4,500		
	15,906	2,312	
Allowances			
WDA 25%	(3,977)	(578)	£4,555
WDV at 5.4.91	11,929	1,734	
1991/92 (no basis period)			
Allowances			
WDA 25%	(2,982)	(434)	£3,416
WDV at 5.4.92	8,947	1,300	
1992/93 (basis period 6.4.91 – 30.4.91)			
Plant	3,000		
	11,947	1,300	
Allowances			
WDA 25%	(2,987)	(325)	£3,312
WDV at 5.4.93	£8,960	£975	

Notes

(a)   The period 1.5.89 – 5.4.90 falls into the profits basis periods for both 1989/90 and 1991/92. It will therefore fall into the capital allowances basis period for the earlier year, 1989/90.

(b)   The period 6.4.90 – 30.4.90 falls into the profits basis periods for both 1990/91 and 1991/92. It will therefore fall into the capital allowances basis period for the earlier year, 1990/91.

(c)   The period 1.5.90 – 5.4.91 falls into the profits basis periods for both 1990/91 and 1992/93. Again, for capital allowances, it will fall into the basis period of the earlier year, 1990/91.

14

(C) Cessation of business. Interval between basis periods. No Inland Revenue adjustment under *ICTA 1988, s 63*

T ceased trading on 30.9.91 having prepared accounts annually to 30 June. The following expenditure and disposals arose

	Expenditure (Plant) £	(Disposal Proceeds) £
Period 1.7.87 – 30.6.88	1,800	(2,000)
Period 1.7.88 – 30.6.89	4,000	(300)
Period 1.7.89 – 30.6.90	1,700	—
Period 1.7.90 – 5.4.91	800	(200)
Period 6.4.91 – 30.9.91	400	(250)

Profits of the closing years will be assessed as follows

1989/90   Period 1.7.87 – 30.6.88 (preceding year)
1990/91   Period 1.7.88 – 30.6.89 (preceding year)
1991/92   Period 6.4.91 – 30.9.91 (actual)

The capital allowances are

	Pool £	Total allowances £
WDV at 5.4.89 (say)	2,600	
1989/90 (basis period 1.7.87 – 30.6.88)		
Additions	1,800	
Disposals	(2,000)	
	2,400	
Allowances		
WDA 25%	(600)	£600
WDV at 5.4.90	1,800	
1990/91 (basis period 1.7.88 – 5.4.91)		
Additions	6,500	
Disposals	(500)	
	7,800	
Allowances		
WDA 25%	(1,950)	£1,950
WDV at 5.4.91	5,850	
1991/92 (basis period 6.4.91 – 30.9.91)		
Additions	400	
Disposals	(250)	
	6,000	
Value at 30.9.91 (say) note (*b*)	(3,000)	
Balancing allowance	£3,000	£3,000

IT 3.1 Capital Allowances

Notes

(*a*)   The interval between the profits basis periods (1.7.89–5.4.91) will fall into the capital allowances basis period for the earlier year, 1990/91, since the business is permanently discontinued in the later year, 1991/92. [*CAA 1990, s 160(3)(c)*].

(*b*)   The value of assets remaining at the date of cessation will consist of
   (i)   the proceeds on disposal of any assets sold subsequently, and
   (ii)   the market value of any assets appropriated for personal use.
   [*CAA 1990, s 26(1)(e) (f)*]

(D) Cessation of business. Interval between basis periods. Inland Revenue adjustment under *ICTA 1988, s 63*

Further analysis of T's capital expenditure (see (C) above) reveals

	Expenditure (Plant) £	(Disposal Proceeds) £
Period 1.7.87 – 30.6.88	1,800	(2,000)
Period 1.7.88 – 30.6.89	4,000	(300)
Period 1.7.89 – 5.4.90	900	—
Period 6.4.90 – 30.6.90	800	—
Period 1.7.90 – 5.4.91	800	(200)
Period 6.4.91 – 30.9.91	400	(250)

Profits are such that the Inland Revenue make an adjustment under *ICTA 1988, s 63* and the final three years are assessed as follows

1989/90	Period 6.4.89 – 5.4.90	(actual)
1990/91	Period 6.4.90 – 5.4.91	(actual)
1991/92	Period 6.4.91 – 30.9.91	(actual)

The capital allowances are

	Pool £	Total allowances £
WDV at 5.4.89 (say)	2,600	
1989/90 (basis period 1.7.87 – 5.4.90)		
Additions	6,700	
Disposals	(2,300)	
	7,000	
Allowances		
WDA 25%	(1,750)	£1,750
WDV at 5.4.90	c/f £5,250	

16

		Pool	Total allowances
		£	£
1990/91 (basis period 6.4.90 – 5.4.91)	b/f	5,250	
Additions		1,600	
Disposals		(200)	
		6,650	
Allowances			
WDA 25%		(1,663)	£1,663
WDV at 5.4.91		4,987	
1991/92 (basis period 6.4.91 – 30.9.91)			
Additions		400	
Disposals		(250)	
		5,137	
Value at 30.9.91 (say)		(3,000)	
Balancing allowance		£2,137	£2,137

Note

(*a*)   Since the assessment for 1988/89 would have remained based on the year ended 30.6.87, the interval between profits basis periods is 1.7.87 – 5.4.89. Since the trade did not cease in the following year (1989/90), the interval will be deemed to be part of the basis period for that year. [*CAA 1990, s 160(3)(b)*].

3.2   **SUCCESSIONS** [*CAA 1990, ss 77, 78, 152, 157, 158*]

A change of partnership occurred on 1.9.90 when A and B, who had been partners for a number of years, admitted C as a partner. Accounts had been prepared to 31 August annually and revealed the following expenditure on and disposals of machinery and plant.

	Expenditure	(Disposal Proceeds)
	£	£
Period 1.9.88 – 31.8.89	2,000	(1,000)
Period 1.9.89 – 5.4.90	7,200	(1,200)
Period 6.4.90 – 31.8.90	1,000	—
Period 1.9.90 – 5.4.91	5,000	(300)

The market value of the assets at 1.9.90 totalled £10,000. In no case did an asset's market value exceed its cost.

The capital allowances treatment in the year of the change will depend on whether or not the partnership change was treated as (*a*) cessation and commencement [*ICTA 1988, s 113(1)*] or (*b*) continuation [*ICTA 1988, s 113(2)*].

17

IT 3.2   Capital Allowances

Cessation and commencement
(i) No election under *CAA 1990, s 77(3)*

	Pool	Total allowances
	£	£
Old partnership (period 6.4.90 – 31.8.90)		
1990/91 WDV forward at 5.4.90 (say)	7,500	
Additions	1,000	
Market value	(10,000)	
	(1,500)	
Balancing charge	1,500	£(1,500)
New partnership (period 1.9.90 – 5.4.91)		
1990/91 Additions	15,000	
Disposals	(300)	
	14,700	
Allowances		
WDA $\frac{7}{12}$ × 25%	(2,144)	£2,144
WDV at 5.4.91	£12,556	

Note
(*a*)   The capital allowances will be on an actual basis. See 3.1 above.

(ii) Election under *CAA 1990, s 77(3)*

	Pool	Total allowances
	£	£
Old partnership (period 6.4.90 – 31.8.90)		
1990/91 WDV forward at 5.4.90 (say)	7,500	
Additions	1,000	
	8,500	
Deemed sale proceeds	(8,500)	
Balancing charge	Nil	Nil
New partnership (period 1.9.90 – 5.4.91)		
1990/91 Additions	13,500	
Disposals	(300)	
	13,200	
Allowances		
WDA $\frac{7}{12}$ × 25%	(1,925)	£1,925
WDV at 5.4.91	£11,275	

Notes
(*a*)   Under *CAA 1990, s 77(3)–(8)*, for successions occurring after 29 July 1988, machinery and plant passing to the successor is deemed to have been sold by the predecessor to the successor at such a price as to leave no balancing allowance or balancing charge. If no election is made under *section 77(3)*, the machinery and plant is treated as sold to the successor at open market value. [*Sec 78(1)*]. Similar rules apply for other assets. [*Sec 152(1)*].

(*b*)   An election under *CAA 1990, s 77(3)* may be made only between connected persons, as defined by *section 77(5)*, must be made jointly by predecessor and successor and must be made within two years of the succession, i.e. by 1 September 1992 in this example.

(*c*)   For certain assets other than machinery and plant, a similar election is available under *CAA 1990, s 158* for certain transfers between connected persons.

Continuation

If the partners elect under *ICTA 1988, s 113(2)*, the capital allowances for 1990/91 would be calculated as follows.

	Pool	Total allowances
	£	£
WDV at 5.4.90 (say) note (*a*)	2,250	
1990/91 (basis period 1.9.88 – 31.8.89)		
Additions	2,000	
Disposals	(1,000)	
	3,250	
Allowances		
WDA 25%	(813)	£813
WDV at 5.4.91	£2,437	
Allocated		
Old partnership ($\frac{5}{12}$ths)		339
New partnership ($\frac{7}{12}$ths)		474
		£813

Note

(*a*)   The written-down value brought forward is that at the end of the basis period for 1989/90 which in this case is the period 1.9.87 – 31.8.88. In the previous examples, all additions and disposals up to 5.4.90 would have been taken into account and thus, the written-down value was a different figure.

IT 3.3   Capital Allowances

3.3   **AGRICULTURAL BUILDINGS ALLOWANCES** [*CAA 1990, ss 122–133*]

(A) Calculation of allowances

Farmer Jones prepares accounts annually to 30 June and has incurred the following expenditure

		£
12.1.86	Extension to farmhouse	12,000
3.6.87	Construction of cattle court	15,000
26.4.89	Erection of barn	10,000
31.5.90	Replacement barn for that acquired on 26.4.89 which was destroyed by fire. The insurance proceeds totalled £15,000	20,000

The agricultural buildings allowances are as follows

Date of expenditure	Cost	Residue brought forward	Allowances Initial 20%	WDA	Residue carried forward
	£	£	£	£	£
1986/87 (basis period — year to 31.3.86)					
12.1.86	4,000	note (*d*)	800	(10%) 400	2,800
1987/88 (basis period — 1.4.86 to 30.6.86)					
12.1.86	4,000	2,800		400	2,400
1988/89 (basis period — year to 30.6.87)					
12.1.86	4,000	2,400		400	2,000
3.6.87	15,000			600	14,400
	£19,000	£2,400		£1,000	£16,400
1989/90 (basis period — year to 30.6.88)					
12.1.86	4,000	2,000		400	1,600
3.6.87	15,000	14,400		600	13,800
	£19,000	£16,400		£1,000	£15,400
1990/91 (basis period — year to 30.6.89)					
12.1.86	4,000	1,600		400	1,200
3.6.87	15,000	13,800		600	13,200
26.4.89	10,000			400	9,600
	£29,000	£15,400		£1,400	£24,000

Date of expenditure	Cost	Residue brought forward		WDA	Residue carried forward
	£	£		£	£

(i) No election for a balancing adjustment

1991/92 (basis period—year to 30.6.90)

Date of expenditure	Cost	Residue brought forward		WDA	Residue carried forward
12.1.86	4,000	1,200		400	800
3.6.87	15,000	13,200		600	12,600
26.4.89	10,000	9,600		400	9,200
31.5.90	20,000			800	19,200
	£49,000	£24,000		£2,200	£41,800

(ii) Election for a balancing adjustment

1991/92 (basis period—year to 30.6.90)

Date of expenditure	Cost	Residue brought forward		WDA	Residue carried forward
12.1.86	4,000	1,200		400	800
3.6.87	15,000	13,200		600	12,600
31.5.90	20,000			800	19,200
	£39,000	£14,400		1,800	£32,600

Balancing charge

	£	
Proceeds (restricted to cost)	10,000	
Written-down value	9,600	
Balancing charge		400
Net allowances		£1,400

Notes

(a)   The current provisions, applicable to expenditure incurred after 31 March 1986, are in *CAA 1990, ss 123–133*. The provisions relating to expenditure incurred before 1 April 1986 are in *CAA 1990, s 122*.

(b)   For expenditure after 31 March 1986 the basis period by reference to which allowances are given is the period used in assessing profits to income tax (or the chargeable period for corporation tax).

(c)   Balancing adjustments arise, under *CAA 1990, s 128*, only if an election is made under *section 129*. Thus on the destruction of the barn costing £10,000, allowances will continue to be available, in the absence of an election, until the expenditure has been exhausted. Allowances can also be claimed on the replacement asset in the normal way. The destruction of the barn and the receipt of insurance monies will give rise to a chargeable gain, but this may be postponed by a claim for rollover relief under *CGTA 1979, s 21(4)* or *s 115*. If the election is made, a balancing charge or allowance is computed as shown. Balancing adjustments do not apply in respect of expenditure incurred before 1 April 1986.

(d)   Only a maximum of one-third of capital expenditure on a farmhouse qualifies for allowances. [*CAA 1990, s 124(1)(a)*].

21

IT 3.3 Capital Allowances

(B) Transfers of allowances on sale etc.

X is a farmer making up accounts to 30 June. Part of the land he farms as a tenant of Y. On this land the following expenditure is incurred:

			£
23.1.88	Farmhouse extension	(paid by Y)	15,000
5.2.88	Barn	(paid by X)	10,000
1.5.88	Cattle pens	(paid by X)	2,000
1.11.89	Drainage	(paid by X)	12,000

On 31.12.90, X assigns the lease to Z, a neighbouring farmer making up accounts to 30 April. Payment for the lease includes £11,750 for the drainage, £5,000 for the barn and £200 for the cattle pens. On 1.6.91, Z demolishes the cattle pens receiving £100 for scrap. X and Z agree to elect jointly for the sale of the cattle pens to be treated as a balancing event. Z elects for the demolition of the cattle pens to be treated as a balancing event.

The following allowances are due to X, Y and Z

X
1989/90 (basis period—year to 30.6.88)

Date of expenditure	Cost	Residue brought forward	Allowances WDA 4%	Residue carried forward
	£	£	£	£
5.2.88	10,000		400	9,600
1.5.88	2,000		80	1,920
	£12,000		£480	£11,520

1990/91

Date of expenditure	Cost	Residue brought forward	Allowances WDA 4%	Residue carried forward
5.2.88	10,000	9,600	400	9,200
1.5.88	2,000	1,920	80	1,840
	£12,000	£11,520	£480	£11,040

1991/92

Date of expenditure	Cost	Residue brought forward	Allowances WDA 4%	Residue carried forward
5.2.88	10,000	9,200	400	8,800
1.5.88	2,000	1,840	80	1,760
1.11.89	12,000		480	11,520
	£24,000	£11,040	£960	£22,080

1992/93

Date of expenditure	Cost	Residue brought forward	Allowances WDA 4%	Residue carried forward
5.2.88	10,000	8,800	$(400 \times \frac{1}{2})$ 200	8,600
1.5.88	2,000	1,760	Balancing event	
1.11.89	12,000	11,520	$(480 \times \frac{1}{2})$ 240	11,280
	£24,000	£22,080	see note (a) 440	£19,880

Balancing event

Residue of expenditure brought forward	1,760	
Proceeds of sale	200	
Balancing allowance to X		1,560
Total allowances to X		£2,000

Y

Y's allowances (on the farmhouse extension) as landlord are given by way of discharge or repayment of tax and amount to £200 (£15,000 × $\frac{1}{3}$ × 4%) for 1987/88, being the year of assessment in which the expenditure was incurred, and each subsequent year up to and including 2011/2012.

Z

1992/93 (basis period — year to 30.4.91)

Date of expenditure	Cost	Residue brought forward		Allowances WDA 4%	Residue carried forward
	£	£		£	£
5.2.88 (1.1.91 – 30.4.91)	10,000	8,600	($\frac{4}{12}$ × £400)	133	8,467
1.5.88 (Acquired 1.1.91)	200	note (b)		9	191
1.11.89 (1.1.91 – 30.4.91)	12,000	11,280	($\frac{4}{12}$ × £480)	160	11,120
	£22,200	£19,880		£302	£19,778

1993/94

5.2.88	10,000	8,467		400	8,067
1.5.88	200	191		Balancing event	
1.11.89	12,000	11,120		480	10,640
	£22,200	£19,778		880	£18,707

Balancing event

Residue of expenditure	191		
Scrap proceeds	100		
Balancing allowance to Z		91	
Total allowance to Z		£971	

Notes

(a) X and Z may jointly elect for balancing adjustments on the cattle pens, barn and drainage. As no election is made in respect of the barn and drainage the writing-down allowances are given to X for the period 1.7.90 to 31.12.90, claimed in 1992/93. Z can claim allowances from 1.1.91 to 30.4.91 in 1992/93 and full allowances in 1993/94 et seq.

(b) As an election for a balancing adjustment was made on the cattle pens, Z claims allowances on the residue of expenditure £1,760 less balancing allowance given to X of £1,560. The allowances are due to Z from 1.1.91 for the remainder of the writing-down period running from 6.4.89 to 5.4.2014, i.e. $23\frac{1}{4}$ years. The allowance for each year is £200 divided by $23\frac{1}{4}$, which is approximately £9.

(c) See 1989/90 and earlier editions for transfers of allowances in respect of expenditure incurred before 1 April 1986.

3.4   **CEMETERIES AND CREMATORIA** [*ICTA 1988, s 91*]

GE, who operates a funeral service, owns a cemetery for which accounts to 31 December are prepared. The accounts to 31.12.90 reveal the following

(i)	Cost of land representing 110 grave spaces sold in period	£3,400
(ii)	Number of grave spaces remaining	275
(iii)	Residual capital expenditure on buildings and other land unsuitable for interments	£18,250

The allowances available are   £

(*a*)   Item (i)   3,400

(*b*) $\dfrac{110}{110 + 275} \times £18,250$ 5,214

£8,614

Note

(*a*)   £8,614 will be allowed as a deduction in computing GE's Schedule D, Case I profits for the accounting period ending on 31 December 1990.

3.5   **DREDGING** [*CAA 1990, ss 134, 135*]

D is the proprietor of an estuary maintenance business preparing accounts to 30 June. Expenditure qualifying for dredging allowances is incurred as follows:

	£
Year ended 30.6.87	4,000
Year ended 30.6.88	5,000

On 2 January 1991, D sells the business to an unconnected third party. The Revenue do not revise the 1988/89 and 1989/90 assessments under *ICTA 1988, s 63*.

The allowances available are

Date of Expenditure	Cost	Residue brought forward	Allowances WDA 4%	Residue carried forward
	£	£	£	£
1988/89 (basis period — year ended 30.6.87)				
1987	4,000	—	160	3,840
1989/90 (basis period — 1.7.87 – 5.4.90)				
1987	4,000	3,840	160	3,680
1988	5,000	—	200	4,800
			£360	
1990/91 (basis period — 6.4.90 – 2.1.91, nine months)				
1987	4,000	3,680	$(\frac{9}{12})$ 120	3,560
1988	5,000	4,800	$(\frac{9}{12})$ 150	4,650
			270	£8,210
Balancing allowance note (a)			8,210	
Total allowances			£8,480	

Note

(a)   On a permanent discontinuance of the trade, including a sale other than one falling within *CAA 1990, s 157(1)*, a balancing allowance is given and is equal to the residue of expenditure after deducting writing-down allowances for the final year of assessment. There are no provisions for a balancing charge or a transfer of allowances to a purchaser.

IT 3.6 Capital Allowances

3.6 **INDUSTRIAL BUILDINGS** [*CAA 1990, ss 1–21*]

(A) Writing-down allowances and balancing changes and allowances

Prior to commencing business on 1 June 1987, P incurred the following expenditure

		£
10.1.87	Plot of land	5,000
20.2.87	Clearing and levelling site	2,000
20.4.87	Construction of factory	50,000
		£57,000

The factory remained in use for a qualifying purpose and on 1.5.90 it was sold to Y for £55,500, being £43,500 for the factory and £12,000 for the land. P drew up accounts annually to 31 May.

The allowances available to P

Year of assessment			Residue of expenditure £
1987/88	Qualifying expenditure		52,000
	Writing-down allowance	4% of £52,000	(2,080)
1988/89–	Writing-down allowance		
1990/91	for 3 years	4% of £52,000 × 3	(6,240)
			43,680
1991/2	Writing-down allowance		—
	Sale proceeds		(43,500)
	Balancing allowance		£180

The allowances available to Y

Date of first use	1.6.87
Date of purchase by Y	1.5.90
Number of years remaining	22 years 1 month
Residue of expenditure	£43,500

Y is therefore entitled to writing-down allowances of £1,970 p.a. until total allowances reach £43,500.

Notes

(*a*) Writing-down allowances are first due in 1987/88, being P's first chargeable period, but are *not* restricted to the length of the basis period (which runs from 1 June 1987 to 5 April 1988).

(*b*) No allowances are due on the cost of the land.

(*c*) Provided that the factory was used by Y for a qualifying purpose he would be entitled to writing-down allowances on the residue of expenditure after sale (being the residue immediately prior to sale, less the balancing allowance due to P) over the number of years still remaining to 25 years from first use (22 years 1 month).

Capital Allowances

(B) Non-qualifying purposes and balancing adjustments [*CAA 1990, s 4(5)–(9)*]

A, B and C entered into partnership in 1971 and prepare accounts annually to 31 March. The partnership incurred £40,000 of expenditure in 1975 on the construction of a building which was brought into use as an industrial building on 1 April 1975. After four years of use for a qualifying industrial purpose, it was used for three years for non-qualifying purposes after which the original qualifying activity was resumed until the building was destroyed by fire.

The fire occurred on 1 October 1989 with an insurance recovery of (i) £50,000 (ii) £35,000. The partnership's 1990/91 industrial buildings allowance position will be as follows

1989/90 Balancing charge £

(i) *Proceeds exceed cost*		
Actual allowances given	note (*a*)	37,600
Balancing charge		£37,600

(ii) *Proceeds less than cost*		
Net cost (£40,000 – £35,000)		5,000
Reduction $\dfrac{3y}{14y\ 6m}$	note (*b*)	(1,034)
Adjusted net cost		3,966
Allowances given	note (*a*)	37,600
Excess		£33,634
Balancing charge		£33,634

Notes

(*a*) Allowances given in previous years are

	£
Initial allowance £40,000×50%	20,000
Writing-down allowances £40,000 × 4% × 11	17,600
	£37,600

Writing-down allowances would not have been given for the three years when the building was used for a non-qualifying purpose.

(*b*) In example (ii), the net cost is reduced by the proportion which the period of non-qualifying use bears to the total period of ownership.

rd of non-industrial part [*CAA 1990, s 18(4)(7)*]

who prepares accounts annually to 31 December, incurred expenditure
on the construction of a new factory. Of this amount, £60,000 related to
ɔn of office accommodation. H brought the factory into use for his trade
1988. Because of the expansion of his business, H requires additional
storage and office accommodation and he incurs expenditure of £56,000 on the construction of an extension in November 1990. £9,000 of this cost relates to the office extension.

The allowances available to H are

Year of assessment	Qualifying expenditure £	Residue brought forward £	Writing-down allowance (4%) £	Residue carried forward £
1989/90	170,000	—	6,800	163,200
1990/91	170,000	163,200	6,800	156,400
1991/92	170,000	156,400	6,800	149,600
	56,000	—	2,240	53,760
	60,000	—	2,400	57,600

Note

(*a*)   After completion of the extension, the non-industrial proportion of the building is under 25% (£69,000 out of £286,000) so that allowances are due on the full cost of the extension. Additional allowances are available for expenditure on the original office accommodation, but only for the basis period of the change and subsequent basis periods.

(D) Buildings in enterprise zones [*CAA 1990, ss 1, 6, 21*]

In December 1987, J, a builder, incurs expenditure of £400,000 on the construction of a building in a designated enterprise zone. In June 1988, he sells the building unused to K for £800,000 including £200,000 for the land. In July 1988, K leases the building to a trader who immediately brings it into use as a supermarket. K claims an initial allowance of £50,000. In August 1990, he sells the building for £1 million including £250,000 for the land.

The allowances available to K are

Year of assessment			£	Residue of expenditure £
1988/89	Qualifying expenditure			600,000
	Initial allowance (maximum 100%)		50,000	
	Writing-down allowance	25% of £600,000	150,000	
	Total IBA due		200,000	(200,000)
1989/90	Writing-down allowance		150,000	(150,000)
				250,000
1990/91	Writing-down allowance		—	—
	Sale proceeds			(750,000)
				£500,000
	Balancing charge (restricted to allowances claimed)			£350,000

Notes

(*a*)   K's qualifying expenditure would normally be the lesser of cost of construction and the net price paid by him for the building. [*CAA 1990, s 10(1)(2)*]. However, on purchase from a builder, whose profit on sale is taxable as a trading profit, his qualifying expenditure is equal to the net price paid for the relevant interest (excluding the land). [*CAA 1990, s 10(3)*].

(*b*)   K's allowances as a non-trader will be given by way of discharge or repayment of tax primarily against letting income from buildings qualifying for IBA's. He could have claimed a 100% initial allowance in 1988/89 if he had so wished. There is no provision for claiming a reduced writing-down allowance.

(*c*)   Allowances for buildings in enterprise zones are given for commercial buildings as well as industrial buildings.

(*d*)   The purchaser can, providing the building continues to be used for a qualifying purpose, claim writing-down allowances over the remainder of the 25-year writing-down period — see (A) above. His qualifying expenditure is restricted to £600,000, i.e. the residue of expenditure (£250,000) plus the balancing charge on K.

3.7   **MACHINERY AND PLANT** [*CAA 1990, ss 22–83*]

Cross-reference. See also 23.4(B) SCHEDULE E below.

(A) Writing-down allowances, motor cars, partial non-business use, acquisitions from connected persons and balancing charges
A is in business as a builder and demolition contractor and his accounts for the year ended 30.6.90 reveal the following additions and disposals

	£
Additions	
Plant	
Dumper Truck	5,000
Excavator	32,000
Bulldozer	20,000
	£57,000
Fittings	
Office furniture	£2,000
Motor Vehicles	
Land Rover	6,000
Van	5,000
Car 1 (used by A)	8,200
Car 2 (used by staff)	2,000
	£21,200

Disposals	Cost £	NBV £	Proceeds £
Excavator	32,000	32,000	30,000
Digger loader	15,000	3,000	4,000
Car (Audi)	5,200	3,000	4,200
Fittings	3,500	500	300
	£55,700	£38,500	£38,500

The dumper truck was bought second-hand from Q, brother of A, but had not been used in a trade. The truck had originally cost Q £6,000, but its market value at sale was only £2,000.

The excavator was sold without having been brought into use. The bulldozer and car 2 were both acquired from P, father of A and had originally cost P £25,000 and £3,500 respectively. Both assets had been used for trading purposes. In neither case did the price paid by A exceed the market value.

The Audi sold and the new car 1 are both used for private motoring by A. Private use has always been 30%.

The capital allowances for 1991/92 are

	Pool	Car pool	Motor Vehicles		Total allowances
	25%	25%	Audi	Car 1	
	£	£	£	£	£
WDV forward at 6.4.91 (say)	8,500		3,900		
Additions					
Plant (excavator) note (*a*)	2,000				
Plant (dumper truck) note (*b*)	2,000				
Plant (bulldozer) note (*c*)	20,000				
Fittings	2,000				
Motor vehicles (Land Rover, van)	11,000				
Motor vehicles (cars) note (*d*)		2,000		8,200	
Disposals					
Plant (digger)	(4,000)				
Fittings	(300)				
Audi			(4,200)		
	41,200	2,000	(300)	8,200	
Allowances					
WDA note (*e*)	(10,300)	(500)		(2,000)	12,800
30% private use restriction					
(Car 1)					(600)
Balancing charge			300		
Less 30% private use			(90)		
			£210		(210)
WDV forward	£30,900	£1,500	£6,200		
Total allowances					£11,990

Notes

(*a*)   Writing-down allowances are available even though an asset is disposed of without being brought into use, always provided that the original expenditure was incurred *for the purposes of the trade*. Where disposal takes place in the same period as acquisition, the addition to the Pool is effectively the excess of cost over disposal value. [*CAA 1990, ss 24(2), 25(1)*].

(*b*)   Qualifying expenditure on the dumper truck is restricted to the lowest of
   (i)   open market value;
   (ii)   capital expenditure incurred by the vendor (or, if lower, by a person connected with him);
   (iii) capital expenditure incurred by the purchaser.
   [*CAA 1990, ss 75, 76(2)*].

(*c*)   Qualifying expenditure on the bulldozer is restricted to the disposal value brought into account in the vendor's computations. [*CAA 1990, s 75(1)*]. As the vendor is a connected person this would be open market value but for the fact that the purchaser is himself entitled to claim capital allowances on the acquisition. [*CAA 1990, s 26(1)(b)*]. A's qualifying expenditure is thus equal to the amount paid by him for the asset. The same applies to the purchase of Car 2.

(d)   Car 1, by virtue of its costing over £8,000 is not pooled. [*CAA 1990, s 34(2)*]. Car 2 is separately pooled by virtue of *CAA 1990, s 41(1)(c)(2)*. See note (c) above as regards the amount of qualifying expenditure to be brought into account in respect of Car 2.

(e)   The writing-down allowance on A's new car is restricted to £2,000 before adjustment for private use. [*CAA 1990, s 34(3)*].

(B) Reduced claim for writing-down allowances and relief for personal pension plan contributions [*CAA 1990, s 24(3)*]

Q's adjusted profits for the year ended 30.9.89 were agreed at £13,000 in May 1990. His capital allowances for 1990/91 comprised writing-down allowances of £8,900. He made a contribution of £820 to a personal pension plan in June 1990. He was aged 36 and unmarried at the beginning of 1990/91. An assessment for 1990/91 was issued in August 1990 as follows

	£	£
Profits		13,000
Less		
Writing-down allowances		8,900
		4,100
Relief for pension contribution (20% × £4,100)	820	
Personal allowance	3,005	3,825
Taxable		£275

Q married on 10 October 1990.

Q then submits a revised income tax computation as follows

	£	£
Profits		13,000
Less		
Writing-down allowances (restricted)		8,315
		4,685
Relief for pension contribution	820	
Personal allowance	3,005	
Married couple's allowance £1,720 × $\frac{6}{12}$	860	4,685
		—

Notes

(a)   Had Q not restricted his claim for writing-down allowances, £585 of his personal reliefs would have been lost.

(b)   Following the restricted claim to writing-down allowances, a higher personal pension contribution could be made, i.e. £937 (20% of £4,685). This would however result in wasted personal reliefs. Q may therefore restrict his claim to capital allowances to a greater extent in order to relieve in full the premium he wishes to pay.

The optimum position would be as follows

	£
	£
Profits	13,000
Less	
Writing-down allowances (restricted)	8,169
	4,831
Relief for pension contributions	
maximum £4,831 × 20%	(966)
Personal reliefs	(3,865)
	—

(*c*) Strictly, an individual should claim only the allowances which he requires (as compared with a company where allowances are given in full unless disclaimed). However, a reduced claim, as in this example, will normally be allowed where circumstances change after an assessment has been agreed (Revenue Statement of Practice SP A26).

(C) Short-life assets [*CAA 1990, ss 37, 38*]
A, who prepares trading accounts to 30 June each year, buys and sells machines as follows

	Cost	Date of acquisition	Disposal proceeds	Date of disposal
Machine 1	£20,000	10.4.90	£10,000	1.10.91
Machine 2	£25,000	15.5.90	£4,000	1.12.94

A elects under *CAA 1990, s 37* for both machines to be treated as short-life assets. His pool of qualifying expenditure brought forward at the beginning of 1990/91 is £80,000.

A's capital allowances are as follows

	Pool £	Machine 1 £	Machine 2 £	Allowances £
1991/92 (basis period 1.7.89–30.6.90)				
WDV at 6.4.91	80,000			
Additions		20,000	25,000	
WDA	(20,000)	(5,000)	(6,250)	£31,250
	60,000	15,000	18,750	
1992/93 (basis period 1.7.90–30.6.91)				
WDA	(15,000)	(3,750)	(4,688)	£23,438
	45,000	11,250	14,062	
1993/94 (basis period 1.7.91–30.6.92)				
Disposal		(10,000)		
Balancing allowance		£1,250		1,250
WDA	(11,250)		(3,515)	14,765
				£16,015
	c/f £33,750		c/f £10,547	

	Pool £	Machine 2 £	Allowances £
	b/f 33,750	b/f 10,547	
1994/95 (basis period 1.7.92–30.6.93)			
WDA	(8,437)	(2,637)	£11,074
	25,313	7,910	
1995/96 (basis period 1.7.93–30.6.94)			
WDA	(6,328)	(1,978)	£8,306
	18,985	5,932	
1996/97 (basis period 1.7.94–30.6.95)			
Transfer to pool	5,932	(5,932)	
	24,917	—	
Disposal	(4,000)		
	20,917		
WDA	(5,229)		£5,229
WDV c/f	£15,688		

Notes

(*a*)   Only machinery and plant which is not specified in *CAA 1990, s 38* is eligible to be treated as short-life assets.

(*b*)   Where separate identification of short-life assets is impracticable, a form of pooling may be adopted (Revenue Statement of Practice SP 1/86).

3.8   **LEASING OF MACHINERY AND PLANT** [*CAA 1990, ss 39–50*]

(A) Separate pooling [*CAA 1990, s 41*]

L has a leasing business preparing accounts annually to 30 June. In the year to 30.6.90, his expenditure included the following

		£
(i)	Machine 1, leased to M Ltd, a UK resident company for the purposes of its trade	20,000
(ii)	Machine 2, leased to N, a UK resident individual, for private use	8,000
(iii)	Machine 3, leased to P, a non-UK resident, for his overseas trade	16,000
(iv)	Fixtures and fittings for use in L's business	2,000
(v)	Motor car used by L entirely for business	6,000

At 6 April 1991, there is a written-down value brought forward in L's machinery and plant pool of £40,000.

His capital allowances for 1991/92, assuming no capital expenditure for the year to 30 June 1990 other than as listed above, are as follows

	Main pool	Cars	Separate pool Assets leased outside UK
	£	£	£
WDV b/fwd	40,000		
Additions	30,000	6,000	16,000
	70,000	6,000	16,000
WDA 25%	17,500	1,500	
WDA 10%			1,600
WDV c/fwd	£52,500	£4,500	£14,400

Total allowances (£17,500 + £1,500 + £1,600) = £20,600

Notes

(*a*)   Machines 1 and 2 go into the general pool for machinery and plant, as do the fixtures and fittings. Machine 3 goes into a separate pool under *CAA 1990, s 41* by virtue of its falling within *section 42* (assets leased outside the UK). The car also goes into this separate pool by virtue of *section 41(1)(c)*.

(*b*)   Although the car and Machine 3 form part of the same pool, it is in practice sub-divided into two pools as different rates of writing-down allowances apply. The allowance for Machine 3 is restricted to 10% under *section 42(2)*.

(B) Recovery of excess relief [*CAA 1990, s 46*]

L, who has a 30 September accounting date, incurred expenditure of £16,000 in March 1988 on a machine leased to Q Ltd, a company trading in the UK. In October 1990, Q Ltd terminated the lease and L then leased the machine, with effect from November 1990, to P Ltd, a company resident in Panama, for the purposes of its trade there.

A balancing charge arises in 1992/93 (basis year ended 30.9.91) as follows

Actual allowances

	£	Total allowances £
Expenditure (year ended 30.9.88)	16,000	
WDA 25% for 1989/90	4,000	4,000
	12,000	
WDA 25% for 1990/91	3,000	3,000
	9,000	
WDA 25% for 1991/92	2,250	2,250
	6,750	
WDA 25% for 1992/93	1,688	1,688
Residue of expenditure	£5,062	
	Total allowances claimed	£10,938

IT 3.8 Capital Allowances

Notional allowances

	£	Total allowances £
Expenditure (year ended 30.9.88)	16,000	
WDA 10% for 1989/90 note (*a*)	1,600	1,600
	14,400	
WDA 10% for 1990/91	1,440	1,440
	12,960	
WDA 10% for 1991/92	1,296	1,296
	11,664	
WDA 10% for 1992/93	1,166	1,166
	£10,498	

Notional allowances £5,502

Balancing charge, equal to the excess of actual allowances over
notional allowances, for 1992/93   note (*b*)   £5,436

L will then be deemed to have incurred expenditure of £10,498 (equal to the residue of expenditure plus the balancing charge) in the year to 30.9.92 i.e. the year following that in which the change of use arose, and will then be entitled to writing-down allowances of 10% for 1993/94 and following years. The expenditure will constitute, or form part of, a separate pool for the purposes of *CAA 1990, s 41*.

Notes

(*a*)   Notional writing-down allowances are restricted to 10% by virtue of *CAA 1990, s 42*, notwithstanding the fact that the machine was used for a qualifying purpose up to October 1990. It is used as mentioned in *section 42(1)* at some time in the requisite period (as defined in *section 40*).

(*b*)   In practice, the machine would originally have been included in the general pool for machinery and plant. For the purpose of calculating the balancing charge, it is assumed to have been the only item of machinery and plant qualifying for writing-down allowances. In 1992/93, a disposal value equal to the residue of expenditure (£5,062) must be deducted from the pool.

3.9   **MINERAL EXTRACTION** [*CAA 1990, ss 98–121*]

X has for some years operated a mining business with two mineral sources, G and S. Accounts are prepared to 30 September. On 31 December 1989 the mineral deposits and mineworks at G were sold at market value to Z for £80,000 and £175,000 respectively. A new source, P, was purchased on 30 April 1990 for £170,000 (including land with an undeveloped market value of £70,000) and the following expenditure incurred before the end of the accounting period ended 30 September 1990.

	£
Machinery and plant	40,000
Construction of administration office	25,000
Construction of mining works which are likely to have little value when mining ceases	50,000
Staff hostel	35,000
Winning access to the deposits	150,000
	£300,000

During the year to 30 September 1990, X incurred expenditure of £20,000 in seeking planning permission to mine a further plot of land, Source Q. Permission was refused.

Residue of expenditure brought forward
(based on accounts to 30 September 1989)

Mineral exploration and access	– Source G	170,000
	– Source S	200,000
Mineral assets	– Source G	95,250
	– Source S	72,000

The mineral extraction allowances due for 1991/92 (base year to 30.9.90) are

Source G	£	£
Mineral exploration and access		
WDV at 6.4.91	170,000	
Proceeds	175,000	
Balancing charge	£5,000	(5,000)
Mineral assets		
WDV at 6.4.91	95,250	
Proceeds	80,000	
Balancing allowance	£15,250	15,250

Source S		
Mineral exploration and access		
WDV at 6.4.91	200,000	
WDA 25%	(50,000)	50,000
WDV at 5.4.92	£150,000	
Mineral assets		
WDV at 6.4.91	72,000	
WDA 10%	(7,200)	7,200
WDV at 5.4.92	£64,800	
		c/f £67,450

IT 3.9 Capital Allowances

		b/f £67,450
Source P		
Mineral exploration and access		
Expenditure	150,000	
WDA 25%	(37,500)	37,500
WDA at 5.4.92	£112,500	
Mineral assets		
Expenditure	100,000	
WDV 10%	(10,000)	10,000
WDV at 5.4.92	£90,000	
Mining works		
Expenditure	50,000	
WDA 25%	(12,500)	12,500
WDV at 5.4.92	£37,500	
Source Q		
Mineral exploration and access		
Expenditure	20,000	
WDA 25%	(5,000)	5,000
WDV at 5.4.92	£15,000	
Total allowances (net of charges)		£132,450

Notes

(a) The current scheme of allowances was introduced by *FA 1986* for expenditure incurred after 31 March 1986. The residue of expenditure at 31 March 1986 under the old scheme was treated as incurred on 1 April 1986 and thus brought within the new scheme. See the 1987/88 and 1986/87 editions for an illustration of both the old scheme and the transitional provisions. The current provisions are now in *CAA 1990, Part IV*.

(b) Allowances are not due on either the office or staff hostel although the hostel may qualify for industrial buildings allowances under *CAA 1990, s 18 (1)(4)(5)*. Machinery and plant qualify for allowances under *CAA 1990, Part II* rather than for mineral extraction allowances.

(c) Abortive expenditure on seeking planning permission is qualifying expenditure by virtue of *section 105(6)* as if it were expenditure on mineral exploration and access.

(d) The undeveloped market value of land is excluded from qualifying expenditure and from disposal receipts under the new code. [*Secs 110, 112*]. Under transitional provisions, undeveloped market value is not deducted from disposal receipts in respect of expenditure which attracted allowances under the old scheme. [*Sec 119(3)(d)*].

(e) Expenditure on the acquisition of mineral assets, which includes expenditure on the acquisition of, or of rights in or over, both the site of a source and of mineral deposits, qualifies for a 10% writing-down allowance. The other types of expenditure illustrated in this example qualify for a 25% writing-down allowance. [*Secs 98(5), 105(1)(7)*].

3.10   **PATENT RIGHTS** [*ICTA 1988, ss 520–523, 528, 533(1)–(6)*]

P, who prepares accounts to 31 December, acquires three new patent rights for trading purposes

	Date	Term	Cost
Patent 1	20.2.86	20 years	£6,800
Patent 2	19.4.89	15 years	£4,500
Patent 3	5.1.90	5 years	£8,000

On 1.10.88 P sold his rights under patent 1 for £5,000 and on 1.4.90 he sold part of the rights under patent 2 for £2,000.

The allowances for each patent are

Patent 1

Expenditure	6,800
1987/88	
WDA $\frac{1}{17}$ × £6,800	(400)
	6,400
1988/89	
WDA $\frac{1}{17}$ × £6,800	(400)
	6,000
1989/90	
Disposal proceeds	(5,000)
Balancing allowance	£1,000

Patents 2 and 3	Pool	WDA
1990/91	£	£
Expenditure (patent 2)	4,500	
WDA 25%	(1,125)	£1,125
	3,375	
1991/92		
Expenditure (patent 3)	8,000	
Disposal proceeds (patent 2)	(2,000)	
	9,375	
WDA 25%	(2,344)	£2,344
WDV forward	£7,031	

Note

(a)   The system of giving allowances was changed for expenditure incurred after 31 March 1986. The spreading of expenditure over a maximum of 17 years is replaced by a writing-down allowance on a reducing balance basis.

IT 3.11 Capital Allowances

3.11 SCIENTIFIC RESEARCH [CAA 1990, ss 136–139]

C is in business manufacturing and selling cosmetics, and he prepares accounts annually to 30 June. For the purposes of this trade, he built a new laboratory adjacent to his existing premises, incurring the following expenditure

		£
April 1988	Laboratory building	50,000
June 1988	Technical equipment	3,000
March 1989	Technical equipment	4,000
June 1989	Plant	2,500
August 1990	Extension to existing premises comprising 50% further laboratory area and 50% sales offices.	30,000

In July 1989 a small fire destroyed an item of equipment originally costing £2,000 in June 1988; insurance recoveries totalled £3,000. In March 1990, the plant costing £2,500 was sold for £1,800.

The allowances due are
1989/90

		£
Laboratory building		50,000
Technical equipment		3,000
Plant	note(a)	700
		£53,700

1990/91

Technical equipment	£4,000

1991/92
No allowance due, but balancing adjustment of £2,000 arises.

1992/93

Extension	note (d)	£15,000

Notes

(a) As the plant was sold prior to 1990/91, the year in which an allowance would have been obtained, no allowance is due for that year. Instead, an allowance (£700) based on the excess of the cost (£2,500) over sale proceeds (£1,800) is made for the year of assessment in which the sale took place.

(b) The destruction of the equipment in the year to 30.6.90 results in a balancing adjustment limited to the allowance originally given. Thus the deemed trading receipt is assessable in 1991/92.

(c) A capital gain of £1,000 (£3,000 − £2,000) will also have arisen. However, the gain will be exempt from capital gains tax under the chattels exemption. [CGTA 1979, s 128].

(d) Capital expenditure incurred after 26 July 1989 which is only partly for scientific research is apportioned on a just basis to arrive at the amount qualifying for allowances. [CAA 1990, s 137(4)].

4   Deceased Estates

[ICTA 1988, ss 695–702]

4.1   ABSOLUTE INTEREST

C died on 5 July 1988 leaving his estate of £400,000 divisible equally between his three children. The income arising and administration expenses paid in the administration period which ends on 25 January 1991 are as follows

	Period to 5.4.89 £	Year to 5.4.90 £	Period to 25.1.91 £
Income (gross)	30,000	15,000	5,000
Tax at basic rate payable by executors	7,500	3,750	1,250
	22,500	11,250	3,750
Administration expenses relating to revenue	1,500	750	300
	£21,000	£10,500	£3,450
Each child's share	£7,000	£3,500	£1,150
Grossed-up at basic rate	£9,333.33	£4,666.67	£1,533.33

Note

(*a*)   Each beneficiary would receive tax certificates (Forms R185E) showing the gross amount of his entitlement and the basic rate tax paid by the executors for each of the three periods.

IT 4.2   Deceased Estates

4.2   **LIMITED INTEREST**

Mrs D died on 5 January 1989 leaving her whole estate with a life interest to her husband and then the capital to her children on his death. The administration of the estate was completed on 7 February 1991. Mr D received payments on account of income of £1,200 on 30 September 1989, £2,000 on 31 December 1990 and £861 on 30 March 1991.

The actual income of the estate was	Gross £	Tax £	Net £
1988/89	600	150	450
1989/90	2,500	625	1,875
1990/91 (to 7 February 1991)	2,800	700	2,100
	£5,900	£1,475	£4,425

The amounts to be included in D's tax returns would initially be

1988/89	Nil	Nil	Nil
1989/90	1,600.00	400.00	1,200
1990/91	3,814.67	953.67	2,861
	£5,414.67	£1,353.67	£4,061

Following completion of the administration, the income accruing in the period from 6 January 1989 to 7 February 1991 would have to be allocated on a day-to-day basis over the entire administration period of 25 months.

1988/89	90/763 × £4,061	638.69	159.67	479.02
1989/90	365/763 × £4,061	2,590.24	647.56	1,942.68
1990/91	308/763 × £4,061	2,185.74	546.44	1,639.30
		£5,414.67	£1,353.67	£4,061.00

Note

(*a*)   There is no difference in total income following reallocation (although this would not have been the case had there been a change in the basic rate), but the substantial difference in the allocation amongst the three tax years affected may materially affect D's tax liabilities. It will depend on the level of his other income and on availability of reliefs.

5   Double Tax Relief

[*ICTA 1988, ss 788–816*]

5.1   A UK resident has the following income, allowances and UK tax liability for the year 1990/91 before double tax relief

	£
Earned income	
UK directorship	12,650
USA directorship (foreign tax £1,500)	6,000
Dutch partnership (foreign tax £3,750)	7,500
	26,150
Unearned income	
UK dividends and tax credits	5,000
Foreign dividends (foreign tax £300)	2,000
Total income	33,150
Deduct	
Personal reliefs	4,725
Taxable income	£28,425
Tax on £20,700 at basic rate (25%)	5,175
7,725 at 40%	3,090
Tax liability before double tax relief	£8,265

The maximum double tax relief is obtained by progressively taking relief under *ICTA 1988, s 796(2)* for each foreign source with the source with the highest rate of foreign tax being eliminated first.

	£	£	£
Taxable income from all sources	28,425	28,425	28,425
Deduct Foreign income			
Dutch Partnership	(7,500)	(7,500)	(7,500)
USA Directorship	—	(6,000)	(6,000)
Dividends	—	—	(2,000)
	£20,925	£14,925	£12,925
Tax thereon	5,265	3,731	3,231
Tax on income before eliminating foreign source under review	8,265	5,265	3,731
Tax attributable to that source (A)	£3,000	£1,534	£500
Foreign tax suffered (B)	£3,750	£1,500	£300
Double tax relief i.e. lesser of (A) and (B)	£3,000	£1,500	£300

The UK income tax liability after credit for double tax relief is		
As computed before double tax relief		£8,265
Deduct Double tax relief		4,800
		£3,465

6   Herd Basis

[*ICTA 1988, s 97, 5 Sch; Revenue pamphlet IR9(1984)*]

6.1   A farmer acquires a dairy herd and elects for the herd basis to apply. The movements in the herd and the tax treatment are as follows

Year 1	No	Value
		£
Mature		
Bought @ £150	70	10,500
Bought in calf @ £180		
(Market value of calf £35)	5	900
Immature		
Bought @ £75	15	1,125

Herd Account		£
70	Friesians	10,500
5	Friesians in calf (5 × £(180 − 35))	725
75	Closing balance	£11,225

Trading Account	£
5 Calves (5 × £35)	175
15 Immature Friesians	1,125
Debit to profit and loss account	£1,300

Year 2	No	Value
		£
Mature		
Bought @ £185	15	2,775
Sold @ £200 note (*a*)	10	2,000
Died	3	—
Immature		
Born	52	—
Matured @ 60% of market value of £200 note (a)	12	1,440

Herd Account			£
75	Opening Balance		11,225
	Increase in herd		
15	Purchases	2,775	
12	Transferred from trading stock	1,440	
27		4,215	
(13)	Replacement cost £4,215 × 13/27	2,029	
14	Non-replacement animals cost		2,186
89	Closing balance		£13,411

44

Trading Account | £
Sale of 10 mature cows replaced | (2,000)
Transfer to herd — 14 animals | (2,186)
Cost of 13 mature cows purchased to replace those
sold/deceased ($\frac{13}{15} \times$ £2,775) | 2,405

Net credit to profit and loss account   note (*b*) | £(1,781)

Year 3

	No	Value £
Mature		
Jerseys bought @ £250	70	17,500
Friesians slaughtered @ £175	52	9,100
Immature		
Friesians born	20	—
Matured		
Friesians @ 60% of market value of £190 note (*a*)	15	1,710

Herd Account			£
89	Opening Balance		13,411
	Increase in herd		
18	Jerseys		4,500
	52 Improvement Jerseys @	£250	
	less Market value of Friesians (say)	185	
	52 @	65	3,380
	Transfer from trading stock		
15	Friesians		1,710
122	Closing balance		£23,001

Trading Account | £
Compensation | (9,100)
Transfer to herd | (1,710)
Purchase of replacements   note (*c*) (52 × £185) | 9,620

Net credit to profit and loss account | £(1,190)

Year 4
The farmer ceases dairy farming and sells his whole herd.

	No	Value £
Mature		
Jersey sold @ £320	70	22,400
Friesians sold @ £200	52	10,400
Immature		
Friesians sold @ £100	65	6,500

IT 6.1   Herd Basis

Herd Account

	£
Opening balance	23,001
52 Friesians	
70 Jerseys	
(122) Sales	(32,800)
– Profit on sale note (*d*)	£(9,799)

Trading Account

	£
Sale of 65 immature Friesians	(6,500)
Credit to profit and loss account	£(6,500)

Notes

(*a*)   The use of 60% of market value is by agreement between the National Farmers' Union and the Revenue. Alternatively, the actual cost of breeding or purchase and rearing could be used.

(*b*)   As the cost of rearing the 12 cows to maturity will already have been debited to the profit and loss account, no additional entry is required to reflect that cost. Due to the fact that the animals were in opening stock at valuation and will not be in closing stock, the trading account will in effect be debited with that valuation.

(*c*)   The cost of the replacements is restricted to the cost of replacing like with like.

(*d*)   Provided these animals are not replaced by a herd of the same type within five years the proceeds will be tax-free.

7   Interest on Unpaid Tax

[*TMA 1970, ss 69, 86, 88, 88A, 90, 91; F(No 2)A 1975, s 46; FA 1989, ss 156, 158–161, 178, 179*]

7.1   A received three estimated assessments dated 13.11.90

	Year of assessment	Tax charged £
Schedule A	1990/91	4,000
Taxed income (higher rates)	1989/90	12,750
Schedule D, Case I	1990/91	7,000

Each assessment was appealed against and events thereafter were as follows

Schedule A assessment
A applied to postpone £1,600 of tax which HMIT agreed to on 17.12.90.
He paid the balance of £2,400 on 23.2.91.
The appeal was determined on 12.8.91 and a revised assessment showing tax payable of £3,450 was issued on 15.8.91.
A paid the remaining balance of £1,050 on 3.10.91.

The dates of consequence are
(i)	Due date of payment had there been no appeal	1 January 1991
(ii)	Revised due date of payment of amount not postponed and date from which interest runs	16 January 1991 (30 days after HMIT's agreement)
(iii)	Due date of determined balance (£1,050)	14 Sept 1991 (30 days after date of revised assessment)
(iv)	Date from which interest will run on determined balance	1 July 1991 (the reckonable date)

The interest charge is as follows

£2,400 for 38 days (16.1.91 to 23.2.91)
£1,050 for 94 days (1.7.91 to 3.10.91)

Note
(*a*)   The rate of interest applying from 6 November 1989 is 13%. [*SI 1989/1297*]. (IRPR 26.10.89).

Taxed income assessment
A applied to postpone £5,000 of tax which HMIT agreed to on 28.12.90.
He paid the balance of £7,750 on 23.2.91.
The appeal was determined on 11.3.91 and a revised assessment showing tax payable of £8,500 was issued on 11.3.91.
A paid the remaining balance of £750 on 26.4.91.

IT 7.1   Interest on Unpaid Tax

The dates of consequence are

(i)   Due date of payment had there been no appeal — 13 December 1990 (30 days after issue of assessment)

(ii)   Revised due date of payment of amount not postponed and date from which interest runs — 27 January 1991

(iii)   Due date of determined balance (£750) — 10 April 1991 (30 days after date of revised assessment)

(iv)   Date from which interest will run on determined balance — 10 April 1991 (the reckonable date)

The interest charge is as follows

£7,750 for 27 days (27.1.91 to 23.2.91)
  £750 for 16 days (10.4.91 to 26.4.91)

Schedule D assessment
A applied to postpone £1,500 of tax which HMIT agreed to on 28.12.90, leaving £5,500 payable in two instalments, the first of which was paid on 23.2.91.
The second instalment was paid on 1.7.91.
The appeal was determined on 23.8.91 and a revised assessment showing tax payable of £7,800 was issued on 26.8.91.
A paid the remaining balance of £2,300 on 23.9.91.

The dates of consequence are

(i)   Due dates of payment had there been no appeal — One half on 1 Jan 1991. One half on 1 July 1991

(ii)   Revised due dates of payment of amount not postponed and dates from which interest will run — One half (£2,750) on 27 January 1991 (30 days after HMIT's agreement). One half on 1 July 1991

(iii)   Due date of determined balance (£2,300) — 25 September 1991 (30 days after date of revised assessment)

(iv)   Date from which interest will run on determined balance — 1 July 1991

The interest charge is as follows

£2,750 for 27 days (27.1.91 to 23.2.91)
£2,300 for 84 days (1.7.91 to 23.9.91)

Note
(a)   On determination of the appeal, the tax payable is £800 greater than that charged by the original assessment. However, interest will accrue as if the tax had been charged by the original assessment. [*TMA 1970, s 86(3)(3A); FA 1989, s 156(1)*].

7.2   B received the following assessments dated 15.11.90

	Year of assessment	Tax charged £
Schedule D, Case III	1989/90	3,250
Schedule D, Case III (estimate)	1990/91	12,000
Taxed income (higher rates – estimate)	1989/90	925

Schedule D, Case III 1989/90

The assessment was agreed and tax of £3,250 paid on 13.1.91.

The only date of consequence is
(i)   Due date of payment and date from which   15 December 1990
        interest runs   (30 days after date of
                                                                                    assessment)

The interest charge is as follows

£3,250 for 29 days (15.12.90 to 13.1.91)

Schedule D, Case III 1990/91

B appealed and applied to postpone £6,000 of tax which HMIT agreed to on 21.12.90.
He paid the balance of £6,000 on 20.1.91.
The appeal was determined on 23.7.91 when a revised assessment was issued showing tax of £10,500.
B paid the remaining balance on 31.8.91.

The dates of consequence are
  (i)   Due date of payment had there been no appeal   1 January 1991
  (ii)   Revised due date of payment of amount not   20 January 1991
          postponed and date from which interest runs   (30 days after HMIT's
                                                                                    agreement)

(iii)   Due date of determined balance (£4,500)   22 August 1991 (30 days
                                                                                    after date of revised
                                                                                    assessment)

(iv)   Date from which interest will run on the   1 July 1991 (the
          determined balance   reckonable date)

The interest charge is as follows

£4,500 for 61 days (1.7.91 to 31.8.91)

IT 7.3   Interest on Unpaid Tax

Taxed income assessment 1989/90
B appealed and applied to postpone £225 of tax which HMIT agreed to on 21.12.90.
He paid the balance of £700 on 30.5.91.
The appeal was determined on 15.4.91 when a revised assessment was issued showing tax of £900.
B paid the balance due (£200) on 30.5.91.

The dates of consequence are

(i)	Due date of payment had there been no appeal	15 December 1990 (30 days after assessment)
(ii)	Revised due date of payment of amount not postponed and date from which interest runs	20 January 1991 (30 days after HMIT's agreement)
(iii)	Due date of determined balance (£200)	15 May 1991 (30 days after date of revised assessment)
(iv)	Date from which interest will run on determined balance	15 May 1991 (the reckonable date)

The interest charge is as follows

£700 for 130 days (20.1.91 to 30.5.91)
£200 for 15 days (15.5.91 to 30.5.91).

Notes

(*a*)   The reckonable date is the date on which the tax is due, unless that date falls after the Table date. In that case, the reckonable date is the later of the Table date and the date on which the tax would have been due in the absence of any appeal. The Table date is

for income tax under Schedule A or D	1 July following tax year
for higher rate tax on taxed income and for capital gains tax	1 June after end of next tax year

For assessments under Schedule E, the reckonable date is always the date on which the tax is due.

(*b*)   Where the tax charged by an assessment is increased on settlement of the appeal, interest on the extra tax runs from the date it would have run from had it been charged by the original assessment. This is also the date from which interest on any postponed tax will run. [*TMA 1970, s 86; FA 1989, s 156(1)*].

7.3   C negligently omitted to include details of untaxed interest on his income tax returns. His returns were subsequently discovered to be incomplete and the following omitted income was agreed, in August 1990, to be assessable on C with tax due as shown

	Income £	Tax £
1986/87	2,500	1,500
1987/88	4,800	2,760
1988/89	4,875	1,950

Because of C's failure to make a full return, he is liable to interest under *TMA 1970, s 88* and a penalty under *TMA 1970, s 95* (see notes *(a)–(d)*). Interest due from the normal due date for payment (1 January in the year of assessment) to 1.9.90, the expected date for payment, is calculated using the following rates

9.5% p.a. from 6.11.86 to 5.4.87
9% p.a. from 6.4.87 to 5.6.87
8.25% p.a. from 6.6.87 to 5.9.87
9% p.a. from 6.9.87 to 5.12.87
8.25% p.a. from 6.12.87 to 5.5.88
7.75% p.a. from 6.5.88 to 5.8.88
9.75% p.a. from 6.8.88 to 5.10.88
10.75% p.a. from 6.10.88 to 5.1.89
11.5% p.a. from 6.1.89 to 5.7.89
12.25% p.a. from 6.7.89 to 5.11.89
13% p.a. from 6.11.89

Interest due is thus

	£
1986/87	
Interest on £1,500 from 1.1.87	562
1987/88	
Interest on £2,760 from 1.1.88	789
1988/89	
Interest on £1,950 from 1.1.89	382
	£1,733

Notes

(a)   For returns delivered and failures occurring after 26 July 1989, interest under *TMA 1970, s 88* arises in respect of tax lost through any error in a return or failure to make a return. Previously, interest arose only in cases of fraud, wilful default or neglect. [*TMA 1970, s 88(1); FA 1989, s 159(2)*].

(b)   If the possibility of a *section 88* interest charge for failure to make a return is to be avoided, the Revenue should be notified of income from a new source by 31 October following the end of the tax year in which it arose. (Revenue Statement of Practice SP 6/89).

(c)   For errors or omissions made fraudulently or negligently in returns submitted after 26 July 1989, the maximum penalty, in addition to interest, is the amount of tax lost. [*TMA 1970, s 95; FA 1989, s 163*]. Previously, the penalty could be as much as twice the tax lost in cases of fraud, and there was also a fixed penalty of £50.

(d)   The Inland Revenue will mitigate the penalty depending on factors such as disclosure, co-operation and the reason for the omission.

(e)   The Inland Revenue publish Interest Factor tables for use as ready reckoners in calculating interest on tax, and these are updated as rates change.

8   Interest Payable

[ICTA 1988, ss 353–358, 366–379; FA 1988, ss 41–44; FA 1989, s 46; FA 1990, s 71]

8.1   RELIEF FOR INTEREST PAID
(A) Interest payable on purchase of property

An individual pays interest on the following loans

(i) A building society mortgage of £18,000 on his main residence (R) which he acquired in 1976. He moved to house (S) on 6.10.89 (see (iii) below) after selling house (R) on 5.8.89 when he repaid the loan. Interest on the loan had been at 13% since 1.4.89. The loan was within the MIRAS scheme in 1989/90.

(ii) A building society mortgage of £8,000 on a bungalow which he bought in 1982 for occupation, rent-free, by his widowed mother. It was within the MIRAS scheme in 1989/90 and 1990/91. On 5.10.90 the bungalow was sold, following the mother's death shortly beforehand, and the mortgage repaid. Interest paid amounted to £300 (net), £490 (net) and £420 (net) for the periods 6.4.89 to 5.9.89, 6.9.89 to 5.4.90 and 6.4.90 to 5.10.90 respectively.

(iii) On 6.9.89 he took out a £26,000 mortgage with the same society towards the purchase of a house (S) which he and his family moved into on 6.10.89. It was within the MIRAS scheme in 1989/90 and 1990/91 with net interest paid amounting to £1,350 in 1989/90, £1,155 for the period 6.4.90 to 5.10.90 and £1,365 for the period 6.10.90 to 5.4.91, and gross interest of £330 and £280 paid for the first two of those periods respectively.

(iv) An advance from a bank of £5,000 to finance an extension to house S. This loan carried interest at 17%, payable monthly in arrears, from 1.4.90, the date it was taken out, and was not brought within the MIRAS scheme.

Relief for the interest paid against total income will be as follows for the years 1989/90 and 1990/91

		Interest
1989/90	£	£
6.4.89 – 5.9.89		
Overall limit on property loans	30,000	
Interest paid under deduction of tax		
House (R)	(18,000)	585
Mother's home	(8,000)	300
Limit not utilised	£4,000	
		£885
Gross interest paid on loans within MIRAS		
(relieved against total income for higher rate purposes)		
(£885 + tax £295)		£1,180
Basic rate relief given at source		£295

	£	Interest £
6.9.89 – 5.4.90		
Overall limit on property loans	30,000	
Interest paid under deduction of tax		
Mother's home	8,000	£490
Amount of mortgage qualifying for relief	£22,000	
Interest payable on £22,000 for seven months		£1,350
Gross interest paid on loans within MIRAS (relieved against total income for higher rate purposes) (£490 + £1,350 + total tax £613)		£2,453
Basic rate relief given at source		£613
1989/90 summary Interest relieved against total income for higher rate purposes £1,180 + £2,453		£3,633
Basic rate tax relief given at source £295 + £613		£908
Interest unrelieved on £4,000 for seven months		£330

1990/91

6.4.90 – 5.10.90		
Overall limit on property loans	30,000	
Interest paid under deduction of tax		
Mother's home	8,000	£420
Amount of mortgage qualifying for relief	£22,000	
Interest payable on £22,000 for six months		£1,155
Gross interest paid on loans within MIRAS (relieved against total income for higher rate purposes) (£420 + £1,155 + total tax £525)		£2,100
Basic rate relief given at source		£525
6.10.90 – 5.4.91		
Overall limit on property loans	30,000	
Interest paid under deduction of tax		
House (S)	26,000	£1,365
Limit not utilised	£4,000	
Gross interest paid on loan within MIRAS (relieved against total income for higher rate purposes) (£1,365 + tax £455)		£1,820
Basic rate relief given at source		£455

IT 8.1 Interest Payable

1990/91 summary
Interest relieved against total income for higher rate purposes
£2,100 + £1,820   £3,920

Basic rate tax relief given at source
£525 + £455   £980

Interest unrelieved on £4,000 for six months   280
Interest unrelieved on £5,000 at 17%   850

Total interest unrelieved   £1,130

Notes

(a)   Prior to 6 April 1987, lenders could choose whether to bring the qualifying
      proportion of limited loans (those which take the borrower over the tax relief
      limit) within MIRAS; MIRAS applies automatically, up to the tax relief
      limit, to all loans made after 5.4.87 by the same qualifying lender. [*ICTA
      1988, s 373*]. Thus, in this example, only £22,000 of the £26,000 mortgage is
      within the MIRAS scheme up to 5 October 1989 with interest on the remain-
      ing £4,000 payable gross.

(b)   Interest paid after 5 April 1988 on home improvements loans made after that
      date does not qualify for tax relief (and, consequently, cannot be within the
      MIRAS scheme). [*ICTA 1988, s 355(2A)–(2C); FA 1988, s 43*]. Interest on
      such loans made before 6 April 1988 continues to be deductible but subject to
      the £30,000 overall maximum.

(c)   Interest on the bungalow occupied by the widowed mother continues to
      qualify for relief after 5 April 1988 (notwithstanding the abolition of such
      relief by *FA 1988, s 44*) as the loan was made before 6 April 1988 *and* the loan
      qualified immediately before that date by reason of the property being used
      as the dependent relative's main residence.

(B) Interest payable on purchase of property — residence basis [*ICTA 1988,
ss 356A, 356C, 356D; FA 1988, s 42*]

On 1 October 1990, Mr Romeo and Miss Juliet took out a joint mortgage for
£64,000 for the purchase of a London flat to be used as their main residence. Gross
interest paid in 1990/91 amounts to £4,800.

Interest relief for 1990/91
Mr Romeo
Amount on which interest is payable   £32,000

Sharer's limit − £30,000 (qualifying maximum) ÷ 2 =   £15,000

Interest paid   £2,400

Relief restricted to £2,400 × $\dfrac{15,000}{32,000}$ =   £1,125

Miss Juliet
Identical calculation – relief restricted to   £1,125

Notes

(a)   In the case of a joint loan, the total amount thereof is divided by the number of parties thereto in arriving at the amount on which each pays qualifying interest. [*ICTA 1988, s 356D(8); FA 1988, s 42*].

(b)   The residence basis, whereby the qualifying maximum (£30,000) applies to a residence rather than to a borrower, applies to payments of qualifying interest made after 31 July 1988 with the exception of interest on certain loans made, or treated as made, before 1 August 1988. [*ICTA 1988, s 356C; FA 1988, s 42*].

(C) Residence basis — adjustment of sharer's limits

Three friends, A, B and C, decide to pool their resources and buy a house to be shared as their main residence. Each contributes his own savings and obtains a mortgage to fund the balance of his one-third share of the purchase price. The mortgages are all taken out in May 1990 and the amounts thereof, and interest paid thereon for 1990/91, are as follows

	Mortgage £	Interest payable £
A	7,000	1,050
B	14,000	2,100
C	16,000	2,400

Each has a sharer's limit of £10,000 (£30,000 ÷ 3). As A's limit exceeds the amount on which he pays interest, the excess is divided between B and C each of whose limits falls short of the amount on which he pays interest. B and C have shortfalls of £4,000 and £6,000 respectively, a total shortfall of £10,000, so A's excess of £3,000 is divided between them as follows

$B - \frac{4}{10} \times £3,000 = £1,200$ (revised sharer's limit £11,200)

$C - \frac{6}{10} \times £3,000 = £1,800$ (revised sharer's limit £11,800)

A's sharer's limit is reduced to £7,000.

Interest relief for 1990/91 is then calculated as follows

$A - \dfrac{7,000}{7,000} \times £1,050 =$ £1,050

$B - \dfrac{11,200}{14,000} \times £2,100 =$ £1,680

$C - \dfrac{11,800}{16,000} \times £2,400 =$ £1,770

(D) Interest payable on purchase of property — married couples [*ICTA 1988, s 356B; FA 1988, 3 Sch 14*]

Mr and Mrs Lloyd, a married couple living together, have a joint mortgage of £40,000 on which interest of £6,000 (gross) is paid in 1990/91. They have total income (before deducting mortgage interest relief) of £28,675 and £10,000 respectively and are entitled to no other reliefs apart from their personal allowances and married couple's allowance.

IT 8.1 Interest Payable

(i) No election under *ICTA 1988, s 356B(1)(a)*

	Mr Lloyd £	Mrs Lloyd £
Total income	28,675	10,000
Deduct mortgage interest:		
$£6,000 \times \dfrac{30,000}{40,000}$	(2,250)	(2,250)
personal allowances	(3,005)	(3,005)
married couple's allowance	(1,720)	
Taxable income	£21,700	£4,745

	Mr Lloyd	Mrs Lloyd
Tax payable:		
£20,700 @ 25%	5,175.00	
£4,745 @ 25%		1,186.25
£1,000 @ 40%	400.00	
	5,575.00	1,186.25
Add tax deducted under MIRAS		
£2,250 @ 25%	562.50	562.50
	£6,137.50	£1,748.75
Total tax payable	£7,886.25	

(ii) Election under *ICTA 1988, s 356B(1)(a)*

Mr and Mrs Lloyd jointly elect that the allowable interest of £4,500 be split £3,250 to Mr Lloyd and £1,250 to his wife.

	Mr Lloyd £	Mrs Lloyd £
Total income	28,675	10,000
Deduct mortgage interest	(3,250)	(1,250)
personal allowances	(3,005)	(3,005)
married couple's allowance	(1,720)	
Taxable income	£20,700	£5,745

	Mr Lloyd	Mrs Lloyd
Tax payable @ 25%	5,175.00	1,436.25
Add tax deducted under MIRAS:		
£3,250 @ 25%	812.50	
£1,250 @ 25%		312.50
	£5,987.50	£1,748.75
Total tax payable	£7,736.25	
Tax saving as result of election	£150.00	

Note

(*a*)   Under *ICTA 1988, s 356B* as substituted for 1990/91 and subsequent years by *FA 1988, 3 Sch 14*, husband and wife may jointly elect to allocate interest (and the sharer's limits) between them in whatever proportions they choose. This applies even where the mortgage is in the name of and the interest is paid by only one spouse. In the absence of an election, interest on a joint loan is divided equally.

(E) Interest payable on purchase of property — interest added to capital [*ICTA 1988, s 357*]

A, B, C and D all have loans which were used to purchase their main residences. The following are the relevant figures

	Original loan outstanding throughout 1990/91	Interest added to capital at 31.3.90	Interest paid in 1990/91
	£	£	£
A	30,000	1,000	4,100
B	30,000	1,010	4,101
C	29,500	1,000	4,050
D	33,000	1,000	4,400

In 1990/91 tax relief for loan interest paid will be given as follows

A $\dfrac{31,000}{31,000} \times £4,100$ £4,100

B $\dfrac{30,000}{31,010} \times £4,101$ £3,967

C $\dfrac{30,500}{30,500} \times £4,050$ £4,050

D $\dfrac{30,000}{34,000} \times £4,400$ £3,882

Notes

(*a*)   In determining whether the £30,000 limit has been exceeded, up to £1,000 of interest which has been added to capital is to be ignored.

(*b*)   B obtains relief for interest paid on only £30,000 of the loan because the loan, when interest added to capital, exceeds £30,000 and the interest so added exceeds £1,000.

(*c*)   C obtains relief on the full interest paid (and therefore obtains greater relief than B who paid more interest).

(*d*)   D also only obtains relief for interest on borrowings of £30,000. Although interest added to capital was only £1,000, his original loan already exceeded £30,000 and the capitalised interest does not have to be taken into account to determine whether the £30,000 limit is exceeded.

IT 8.1 Interest Payable

(F) Relief for interest payable on bridging loan

E encounters problems in selling his main residence after purchasing a new property and has to pay interest on the following loans

(i) A building society mortgage of £25,000 on his main residence (M) which he acquired in 1982. Interest on the loan had been at 14% since 1.4.90. The loan was within the MIRAS scheme for 1990/91. He moved to his new house (N) on 6.5.90 (see (iii) below) but was unable to sell house (M) until 4.11.90 when he repaid the loan.

(ii) A bridging loan of £65,000 was taken out for the period 6.5.90 to 4.11.90 to finance the purchase of (N). Interest of 16% was charged on the loan for the full term.

(iii) On 5.11.90 he took out a £35,000 mortgage on house (N) (in place of the bridging loan). The rate of interest on that mortgage is 14%. The new loan was within the MIRAS scheme for 1990/91.

Relief for the interest paid against total income for the year 1990/91 will be as follows

	Interest £
1990/91	
6.4.90 – 4.11.90	
Interest paid under deduction of tax House loan (M) £25,000	£1,531
Interest paid gross Bridging loan £65,000	
Relief $\dfrac{30,000}{65,000} \times (£65,000 \text{ at } 16\% + \frac{6}{12})$	2,400
(£2,400 is relieved against total income for basic rate purposes)	
Gross interest paid on loan within MIRAS: £1,531 $\times \dfrac{100}{75}$	2,041
Interest relieved against total income for higher rate purposes	£4,441
Basic rate tax relief given at source on loan within MIRAS (£2,041 − £1,531)	£510
5.11.90 – 5.4.91	
Interest paid under deduction of tax New house (N) (restricted to £30,000)	£1,312
Gross interest paid on loan within MIRAS (relieved against total income for higher rate purposes)	£1,750
Basic rate tax relief given at source on loan within MIRAS	£438

1990/91 Summary

Interest relieved against total income for higher rate purposes:
£4,441 + £1,750   £6,191

Basic rate tax relief given at source on loans within MIRAS: £510 + £438   £948

Note
(*a*)   Relief for interest paid on the bridging loan on the second house (N) is
        granted as if the first loan on house (M) did not exist and is subject to a separate £30,000 limit. This applies only to interest payable within twelve months
        (or such longer period as the Revenue may allow) from the making of the
        bridging loan. [*ICTA 1988, s 354(5)(6)*].

(G) Interest payable on purchase of property — small taxable income
G's assessable Schedule D, Case I profits for 1990/91 have been agreed in the sum
of £3,400. He pays interest on a £15,000 loan taken out to acquire his home from a
company which is not a qualifying lender under the MIRAS scheme. In 1990/91 he
pays interest of £2,100 on this loan. He is a single person with no other income and
pays a personal pension scheme contribution of £100.

G will be assessed in 1990/91 as follows	£	£
Trading profits		3,400
Deduct Loan interest	2,100	
Personal pension scheme contribution	100	
Personal allowance (part)	1,200	3,400
Taxable income		—

If G had borrowed from a lender within the MIRAS scheme, in addition to the
assessment on his trade and profits as above, he would receive an assessment charging basic rate tax as follows

	£
Interest paid under deduction of basic rate tax	2,100.00
Deduct Balance of personal allowance (£3,005 − £1,200)	1,805.00
	£295.00
Tax at 25% payable by G	£73.75
Tax retained by G out of interest paid (£2,100 at 25%)	£525.00
Net tax benefit to G	£451.25

Note
(*a*)   The potential recovery of basic rate tax deducted by G but not covered by tax
        paid by him on his income is removed by *ICTA 1988, s 369(4)* to the extent
        that he has unused personal reliefs. It is obviously to G's advantage to be
        within the MIRAS scheme.

IT 8.1 Interest Payable

(H) Property let at a commercial rent [*ICTA 1988, s 355(1)(b)(4)*]

Mr Abel purchased a cottage for letting purposes on 1 December 1987 and took out a loan of £15,000 at a fixed interest rate of 13% payable monthly in advance.

From 1.12.87 to 5.4.88	the property is redecorated.
From 6.4.88 to 31.10.88	it is let commercially.
From 1.11.88 to 5.4.89	it is vacant but available for letting.
From 6.4.89 to 5.4.90	it is occupied rent-free by friends.
From 6.4.90 to 30.11.90	it is let commercially and sold to the tenants at the end of that period.

1987/88
There is no letting income and the relief for interest paid of £812 is carried forward to the following year.

1988/89
Relief is due against letting income for the interest paid of £1,950 during the year and £812 brought forward.

1989/90
The property is not available for letting and no relief is due for the interest paid.

1990/91
The property is not available for letting throughout a 52-week qualifying period and no relief is due for the interest paid, despite the fact that the property was let for more than 26 weeks. If the disposal date had been deferred until 6 April 1991 and the property either let, available for letting or under repair between 1 December 1990 and 6 April 1991, the interest paid would have been deductible providing there was sufficient letting income in 1990/91 to cover it.

9   Life Assurance Policies

9.1   LIFE ASSURANCE RELIEF [*ICTA 1988, ss 266, 274*]

Life assurance premiums totalling £1,400 are paid in 1990/91 by a married woman on pre-14 March 1984 qualifying life policies in respect of her own life and that of her husband. Her income amounts to £11,000 and she pays mortgage interest of £2,180 (gross).

Calculation of limit of admissible premiums

	£
	11,000
Deduct Mortgage interest	2,180
	£8,820
Limit is greater of $\frac{1}{6}$ thereof (£1,470) and £1,500	£1,500
Gross premiums paid £1,400 $\times \dfrac{100}{87.5}$	£1,600
Income tax relief on payments made £1,600 $\times$ 12½%	200
Admissible premium relief £1,500 $\times$ 12½%	188
Income tax relief clawed back	£12

Notes

(*a*)   See the 1987/88 or earlier editions for an example of the clawback of relief where a qualifying policy is surrendered within four years. As no relief is given for policies taken out after 13 March 1984, it follows that those provisions do not apply to surrenders after 12 March 1988.

(*b*)   Depending on the husband's tax position, it may be possible to avoid a clawback in the above example by allocating some of the mortgage interest to the husband (by joint election under *ICTA 1988, s 356B* — see 8.1(D) INTEREST PAYABLE above), but other factors may influence the decision.

9.2　**LIFE ASSURANCE GAINS AND NON-QUALIFYING POLICIES** [*ICTA 1988, ss 539–552*]

Top-slicing relief

A single policyholder realises, in 1990/91, a gain of £1,200 on a ten-year policy which she surrenders after 2½ years. Her other income for 1990/91 comprises earned income of £21,320 and unearned income of £2,285.

The tax chargeable on the gain is calculated as follows

	Normal basis £	Top-slicing relief claim £
Policy gain	1,200	600
Earnings	21,320	21,320
Unearned income	2,285	2,285
	24,805	24,205
Personal allowance	3,005	3,005
	£21,800	£21,200

Tax applicable to policy gain
Higher rate

£1,100 at 40%	440.00	—
£500 at 40%	—	200.00
	440.00	200.00
Deduct		
Basic rate		
£1,100 at 25%	275.00	—
£500 at 25%	—	125.00
		£75.00
Appropriate multiple 2 × £75.00		£150.00
Tax chargeable lower of	£165.00　and	£150.00

Notes

(*a*)　Tax is calculated by treating the policy gain as the top slice of income.

(*b*)　Under the top-slicing relief calculation, the total policy gain is divided by the number of complete years the policy has run (two) and the resulting tax multiplied by the same factor.

(*c*)　Following abolition of all but one of the higher rates after 5 April 1988, top-slicing relief is beneficial only where the policy gain takes the taxpayer into the higher rate band, as in this example.

(*d*)　After 25 March 1982, if a qualifying policy is replaced by a new qualifying policy on a different life or lives then, if certain conditions are met, no chargeable event occurs on the surrender of the earlier policy. [*ICTA 1988, 15 Sch 20*].

(*e*)　Gains on offshore policies may, in certain circumstances, be charged to basic rate tax in addition to higher rate tax. [*ICTA 1988, s 553, 15 Sch Pt III*]. Similar rules apply to gains on policies issued by friendly societies as part of their tax exempt life or endowment business. [*ICTA 1988, s 547(7)*].

9.3   **PARTIAL SURRENDERS OF LIFE POLICIES ETC.** [*ICTA 1988, s 546*]

A policy is taken out on 4.2.86 for a single premium of £15,000. The contract permits periodical withdrawals.

(i)   The policyholder draws £750 p.a. on 4 February in each subsequent year.

There is no taxable gain because at the end of each policy year the 'reckonable aggregate value' (RAV) does not exceed the 'allowable aggregate amount' (AAA).

	£
At 3.2.90 withdrawals have been	2,250 (RAV)
Deduct 4 × $\frac{1}{20}$ of the sums paid in	3,000 (AAA)
	No gain

(ii)   On 20.7.90 the policyholder withdraws an additional £3,500.

	£
At 3.2.91 withdrawals have been	6,500 (RAV)
Deduct 5 × $\frac{1}{20}$ of the sums paid in	3,750 (AAA)
Chargeable 1990/91	£2,750

(iii)   The policyholder makes no withdrawal on 4.2.91 but with effect from 4.2.92 increases his annual withdrawals to £1,000.
In the year 1992/93 the position is

	£	£
At 3.2.93 withdrawals have been		7,500
Deduct Withdrawals at last charge		6,500
		1,000 (RAV)
Deduct 7 × $\frac{1}{20}$ of the sums paid in	5,250	
less amount deducted at last charge	3,750	
		1,500 (AAA)
		No gain

Notes

(*a*)   No charge will arise until 1995/96 as long as annual withdrawals continue at the level of £1,000.

(*b*)   Reckonable aggregate value is the total of all surrenders, withdrawals etc. for each policy year since commencement *less* the total of such values which have been brought into account in earlier chargeable events.

(*c*)   Allowable aggregate amount is the total of annual fractions of one-twentieth (with a maximum of 20 twentieths) of the premiums, lump sums etc. paid for each policy year since commencement *less* the total of such fractions which have been brought into account in earlier chargeable events.

(*d*)   A policy year is a year ending 12 months from the commencement of the policy or from an anniversary thereof.

10   Losses

10.1   SET-OFF OF TRADING LOSSES ETC. AGAINST OTHER INCOME [*ICTA 1988, s 380*]

(A)

A married man carries on a trade which prepares accounts to 5 April each year. In the year 1990/91 he receives a salary of £6,000 and investment income of £3,000 and sustains a loss of £17,000 in the trade. In the year ended 5 April 1990 he made a trading profit of £6,000. His wife has earned income of £7,300 and the husband makes a payment of £375 (net) to a charity under a four-year deed of covenant. He makes a claim for relief for the loss under *ICTA 1988, s 380(1)*.

The assessable income for 1990/91 is calculated as follows

		£
Husband —	salary	6,000
	trading profits	6,000
	investment income	3,000
		15,000
Deduct charges (gross)		500
		14,500
Loss relief under *Sec 380(1)*		14,500

Losses forward	
Loss for 1990/91	17,000
Utilised	14,500
	£2,500

Notes

(*a*)   For 1989/90 and earlier years, a trading loss made by one spouse would normally be set off against the income of both spouses, although a claim could be made to restrict the relief to the income of the spouse making the loss. For losses relieved in 1990/91 and later years, one spouse's losses can never be set off against the other's income.

(*b*)   The unrelieved loss of £2,500 could either be carried forward against future trading profits under *Sec 385* or relieved against other income for 1991/92 under *Sec 380 (2)* (see also (B) below).

(*c*)   A loss relieved under *Sec 380* must be relieved against all income of the year in question even though this will waste personal reliefs. In the above example, the unused married couple's allowance could be transferred to the wife (see 11.1(A) MARRIED PERSONS below) but the loss-maker's personal allowance is wasted. See also 3.7(B) CAPITAL ALLOWANCES above for restriction of capital allowances to leave sufficient income in charge to cover personal reliefs. Alternatively, capital allowances may be excluded from the loss relief claim (see also 10.2 below).

(*d*)   Where annual charges paid under deduction of tax exceed taxable income the tax deducted on the excess will be collected by an assessment under *ICTA 1988, s 350*. In the above example, the husband will therefore be liable for the income tax deducted from his annual charges, i.e. £500 at 25% = £125.

(B)

Y, a single man, has been carrying on a trade for some years and prepares accounts to 31 December each year. His results as adjusted for tax for the three years to 31.12.90 are as follows

	Trading profit/(loss) £		Other income £
31.12.88	10,000	1989/90	5,000
31.12.89	(20,000)	1990/91	7,000
31.12.90	(3,000)		

The assessments for 1989/90 and 1990/91 are as follows

1989/90

	£	£
Trading income — year ended 31.12.88		10,000
Other income		5,000
Total income		15,000
Deduct Claim under *Sec 380(1)*, see below		15,000
		—

1990/91

	£	£
Trading income — year ended 31.12.89		—
Other income		7,000
Total income		7,000
Deduct Claim under *Sec 380(2)*	5,000	
Claim under *Sec 380(1)*	2,000	
		7,000
		—

Utilisation of losses

1989/90

	£
Loss available under *Sec 380(1)*	20,000
Deduct Utilised in 1989/90	15,000
Available for carry forward	£5,000

1990/91

	£
Loss available under *Sec 380(2)*	5,000
Add Loss available under *Sec 380(1)*	3,000
Total loss available against other income	8,000
Deduct Utilised in 1990/91	7,000
Loss available for carry forward under *Sec 380(2)* or *Sec 385*	£1,000

Notes

(a)   In the year 1990/91 *Sec 380(2)* losses are utilised before *Sec 380(1)* losses, the result being that the unused balance may be carried forward under *Sec 380(2)* or *Sec 385*.

IT 10.2 Losses

(*b*) It would be advantageous not to make a claim under *Sec 380(1)* in respect of the loss sustained in 1990/91. Y's taxable income for that year, which would be reduced to £2,000 by a claim under *Sec 380(2)*, would be covered by his personal allowance. The loss available for a claim under *Sec 380(2)* for 1991/92 or for carry forward under *Sec 385* would increase to £3,000.

10.2 TREATMENT OF CAPITAL ALLOWANCES [*ICTA 1988, s 383*]

A carries on a trade for which accounts are prepared to 31 December each year. The results for the two years ended 31.12.90 are as follows

Year	Sch D, Case I profit £
31.12.89	25,000
31.12.90	4,500

	Capital Allowances £
1990/91	10,000
1991/92	6,100

The assessment for 1990/91 would be as follows

	£
Case I profit — year ended 31.12.89	25,000
Deduct Capital allowances	10,000
Adjusted Case I profit	15,000
Deduct Claim under *Sec 380(1)*	1,600
Taxable income	£13,400

Utilisation of losses under *Sec 380(1)*

Loss available for 1990/91 1991/92 assessment	£
Case I profit — year ended 31.12.90	4,500
Deduct Capital allowances	4,500
	—

Available for claim under *Sec 380(1)* Capital allowances	£1,600

Notes

(*a*) The claim under *Sec 380* is only in respect of the non-effective capital allowances, i.e. those to which effect has not been given in the taxing of the trade.

(*b*) It is not obligatory to include capital allowances in a *Sec 380* claim, or, as in this example, to create a loss by taking capital allowances into account. If A's income had been lower, he might have wasted personal reliefs by claiming the relief of £1,600. See also 3.7(B) CAPITAL ALLOWANCES above as regards restriction of capital allowances to leave sufficient income in charge to cover personal reliefs.

10.3   LOSSES IN EARLY YEARS OF A TRADE

(A) Losses carried back three years [*ICTA 1988, s 381*]

A married woman opened a health food cafe on 1 June 1988. The first three years produce losses of £9,000, £4,000 and £1,000 and the year to 31.5.92 a profit of £2,000 as adjusted for tax. In addition there were running costs of the premises before opening of £550. Capital allowances for the first three years of assessment are

	£
1988/89	4,000
1989/90	3,000
1990/91	2,250

Other income is as follows

	Own Investment Income £	Husband's Salary £	Husband's Investment Income £	Total £
1985/86	2,600	6,500	250	9,350
1986/87	2,800	7,000	250	10,050
1987/88	3,000	8,100	270	11,370
1988/89	1,200	8,200	220	9,620
1989/90	50	10,100	100	10,250

Losses are allocated as follows

	£
1988/89 ($\frac{10}{12}$ of 31.5.89)	7,500
1989/90 ($\frac{2}{12}$ of 31.5.89 + $\frac{10}{12}$ of 31.5.90)	4,833
1990/91 ($\frac{2}{12}$ of 31.5.90 + $\frac{10}{12}$ of 31.5.91)	1,500

In addition, £550 is available as a loss in 1988/89 — see note (*d*).

Loss relief under *ICTA 1988, s 381* is available as follows

	1988/89 £	1989/90 £	1990/91 £
Case I loss	8,050	4,833	1,500
Capital allowances	4,000	3,000	2,250
	£12,050	£7,833	£3,750

Set against total income			
1985/86	9,350	—	—
1986/87	2,700	7,350	—
1987/88	—	483	3,750
	£12,050	£7,833	£3,750

Notes

(*a*)   It would be possible to exclude the amount of capital allowances from the claims for loss relief.

(*b*)   It would be possible to restrict the loss claims to the wife's income only. (Relief claimed against income for 1990/91 and subsequent years would be available *only* against her income.)

(c) Although some of the losses arose after 5 April 1990, after which independent taxation of husband and wife came into force, relief claimed against income for 1989/90 and earlier years is still given against joint income, subject to a claim for restriction as mentioned in (b) above.

(d) Expenditure incurred in the five years before trading commences which would be deductible if incurred while trading is treated as a loss for the first year of assessment of the trade. For trades commenced before 1 April 1989, the relevant period was three years. [*ICTA 1988, s 401; FA 1989, s 114*].

(B) Losses carried forward [*ICTA 1988, s 385*]

R commenced trading on 1 October 1988 and makes up accounts to 30 June. In the nine months ended 30 June 1989 he incurred a loss of £3,900 and in the year ended 30 June 1990 he made a profit of £6,000. No election is made under *ICTA 1988, s 62.*

R's assessable profits will be as follows

	£	£
1988/89		
Period 1.10.88–5.4.89		Nil
1989/90		
Period 1.10.88–30.9.89 (first 12 months)		
Period 1.10.88–30.6.89	(3,900)	
Period 1.7.89–30.9.89 ($\frac{3}{12}$ × £6,000)	1,500	
	£(2,400)	Nil
1990/91		
Period 1.10.88–30.9.89 (as 1989/90)		Nil
1991/92		
Period 1.7.89–30.6.90	6,000	
Deduct Sec 385 loss relief (see below)	(900)	
		£5,100

If R makes a claim to carry losses forward under *ICTA 1988, s 385* loss relief will be given as follows

	£	£
1988/89		
Loss arising in year		
£(3,900) × $\frac{2}{3}$ =£(2,600)		
Loss carried forward		(2,600)
1989/90		
Losses required to reduce assessment to nil	1,500	
Deduct loss arising in period	(1,300)	
	200	
Deduct loss brought forward	(200)	200
	—	
Loss carried forward		£(2,400)

	£	£
Loss brought forward		(2,400)
1990/91		
Losses required to reduce assessment to nil	1,500	
Deduct loss brought forward	(1,500)	1,500
	—	
Loss carried forward		(900)
1991/92		
Profits assessable (see above)	6,000	
Deduct loss brought forward	(900)	900
	£5,100	—

Note

(a)   The loss at 6 April 1989 of £2,600 is reduced by the amount of relief given in computing the assessable profits for 1989/90 and 1990/91 and only the balance not so used is available for carry forward to 1991/92 under *ICTA 1988, s 385*. (*CIR v Scott Adamson, 17 TC 679* and *Westward Television Ltd v Hart, 45 TC 1*).

(C) Losses carried forward—interaction of *Sec 380* **and** *Sec 385*

If R in (B) above had made a claim to relieve the loss of £2,600 incurred in 1988/89 against his other income for that year, the position would have been as follows

	£	£
1988/89		
Loss arising in year	(2,600)	
Loss relieved against other income under		
Sec 380	2,600	
Loss carried forward	Nil	—
1989/90		
Profit arising in period	1,500	
Deduct loss arising in period	(1,300)	
Assessable profits		£200
1990/91 (as 1989/90)		
Assessable profits		£200
1991/92		
Assessable profits		£6,000

Notes

(a)   No *Sec 385* relief is due for 1989/90 or later years as the loss is relieved by the *Sec 380* claim in 1988/89 and by aggregation with profits in 1989/90 and 1990/91.

(b)   The overall taxable income of £3,800 (£6,400 less £2,600 loss claim) is £1,300 less than that in (B) above as relief for £1,300 has been given twice by aggregation.

10.4 TERMINAL LOSSES [*ICTA 1988, s 388*]

A carries on a trade and prepares accounts to 31 December each year. A ceases to trade on 30.9.90 and the results for the four years and nine months to date of cessation are as follows

Period	Trading Profit/(loss) £
31.12.86	3,500
31.12.87	5,000
31.12.88	600
31.12.89	(1,200)
30.9.90	(1,500)

Year of assessment	Capital Allowances £	Non-Trade Annual Payments £
1987/88	1,800	300
1988/89	1,500	300
1989/90	1,800	—
1990/91	1,600	—

The terminal loss available would be as follows

1990/91 $\frac{6}{9} \times$ £1,500			1,000
Capital allowances			1,600
1989/90 $\frac{3}{9} \times$ £1,500		500	
$\frac{3}{12} \times$ £1,200		300	800
Capital allowances			
$\frac{6}{12} \times$ £1,800	note (*a*)		900
			£4,300

The assessments for these years are as follows

Year	Assessment	£	*Sec 388* Relief £	Revised £
1987/88	Profits	3,500		
	Capital allowances	1,800		
		£1,700	800	£900
1988/89	Profits	5,000		
	Capital allowances	1,500		
		£3,500	3,200	£300
1989/90	Profits	600		
	Capital allowances	600		
		—		Nil
1990/91		Nil		Nil
			£4,000	(see below)

70

Terminal loss as above		£4,300
Less: Utilised in 1988/89		3,200
		1,100
Less: Deduction for non-trade charges	note(*c*)	300
		800
Less: Utilised in 1987/88		800
		Nil

Notes

(*a*)   The capital allowances of £900 for 1989/90 which are included in the terminal loss do not have to be restricted as only £600 of the total of £1,800 is set against the 1989/90 assessment. If £1,000 had been required to offset the 1989/90 assessment the 1989/90 capital allowances included in the terminal loss would have been restricted to £800.

(*b*)   The years 1988/89 and 1989/90 would not be revised to actual as income is greater on a preceding year basis. One quarter of the loss for the year ended 31.12.89 is therefore included as terminal loss relief.

(*c*)   The profits available for set-off against *Sec 388* loss relief are reduced by the annual payments which were paid out of income subject to tax. As they were non-trade charges, the terminal loss available against income of prior years is similarly reduced. [*Sec 388(5)*].

(*d*)   A could obtain more relief if he made a claim under *Sec 380(1)* for 1988/89 and then made a reduced claim for *Sec 388* terminal loss relief as follows

	£
Sec 380 relief 1988/89	
Profit for the year ended 31.12.88	600
Capital allowances (1989/90)	1,800
	£1,200

The terminal loss available would then be

	£
As calculated above	4,300
Deduct 1989/90 Capital allowances relieved under *Sec 380*	900
	£3,400

The position would then be

Year	Assessments	*Sec 380* relief	*Sec 388* relief	Revised
	£	£	£	£
1987/88	1,700		1,100	£600
1988/89	3,500	1,200	2,000	£300
1989/90	Nil			Nil
1990/91	Nil			Nil
		£1,200	£3,100	(see below)

Terminal loss as above	£3,400
Less: Utilised in 1988/89	2,000
	1,400
Less: Deduction for non-trade charges	300
	1,100
Less: Utilised in 1987/88	1,100
Balance	Nil

10.5 **LOSSES ON SHARES IN UNQUOTED TRADING COMPANY** [*ICTA 1988, ss 574–576*]

(A)

X is a semi-retired business executive. Over the years he has acquired several shareholdings in unquoted companies and he has suffered the following losses

(i) 500 shares in A Ltd which X subscribed for in June 1984, following his retirement from employment with A Ltd, at a cost of £25 per share. The market value at the date of purchase by X was £45.

The company went into liquidation in June 1990 and the inspector agreed that the shares may be regarded as of negligible value at that date. It is estimated there will be proceeds of £1 per share. The indexation factor from June 1984 to June 1990 is 0.420.

(ii) X subscribed for 500 shares in B Ltd in 1983 at £10 per share. B Ltd traded as a builder until 1986 when it changed its trade to that of buying and selling land. X received an arm's length offer for the shares of £3 per share in May 1990 which he accepted.

(iii) In 1973 X subscribed for 2,000 shares in C Ltd at £50 per share. In 1978 his aunt gave him a further 1,000 shares. The market value of the shares at that date was £60 per share. Their value at 31 March 1982 was £70 per share.

The company has been a trading company since 1973 but has fallen on hard times recently. A company offered X £20 per share in June 1989. X accepted, and sold 1,500 as he considered it to be a fair price. The indexation factor from March 1982 to June 1989 was 0.453. X elects under *FA 1988, s 96(5)* for assets held at 31 March 1982 to be regarded as having been acquired at market value on that date for the purpose of computing capital gains tax.

(iv) In 1985, X subscribed for 1,000 shares in D Ltd, a qualifying trading company, at £15 per share. In 1990/91, he sells the shares at their then market value of £17 per share. Indexation relief is at, say, 35%.

The treatment of these losses in relation to income tax would be as follows

(i) Loss claim — *ICTA 1988, s 574*, 1990/91 or 1991/92

	£
Proceeds	500
Cost of subscription	12,500
Loss before indexation	12,000
Indexation £12,500 × 0.420	5,250
Allowable loss	£17,250

(ii)   No loss claim under *ICTA 1988, s 574* as company is excluded under *Section 576(4)(5)*; loss of £3,500 (£5,000 – £1,500) (subject to indexation) available against chargeable gains.

(iii) Disposals are first identified with the most recent acquisitions — see note (*b*)

Date	Qualifying shares	Other shares
1973	2,000	
1978		1,000
1988	(500)	(1,000)

Loss claim — *ICTA 1988, s 574* for 1989/90 or 1990/91

	£
500 shares at 31.3.82 value	35,000
Disposal proceeds	10,000
Loss before indexation	25,000
Indexation £35,000 × 0.453	15,855
Allowable loss	£40,855

Capital loss — 1989/90	
1,000 shares at 31.3.82 value	70,000
Disposal proceeds	20,000
Loss before indexation	50,000
Indexation £70,000 × 0.453	31,710
Allowable loss	£81,710

(iv) Loss claim — *ICTA 1988, s 574*, 1990/91 or 1991/92

Proceeds	17,000
Cost of subscription	15,000
Unindexed gain	2,000
Indexation £15,000 × 0.350	5,250
Allowable loss	£3,250

Notes

(*a*) In (i) above, X's acquisition of the shares in A Ltd is not deemed to have been made for a consideration equal to the market value as there was no corresponding disposal and consideration is lower than the market value. [*CGTA 1979, s 29A(2)*]. Relief is given under *ICTA 1988, s 574(1)* on the allowable loss for CGT purposes. As X subscribed for the shares following his retirement, the £10,000 shortfall would probably be regarded as a payment on retirement and exempt from income tax under what is now *ICTA 1988, s 188*. The CGT base cost would therefore be actual cost of £12,500. If, however, the shares had been acquired during employment and a benefit subject to income tax of £10,000 had arisen, the base cost for CGT purposes would have been £22,500.

(*b*) *FA 1988, s 96* which introduced re-basing to 31 March 1982 applies for the purposes of capital gains tax only. It is therefore believed not to apply for the purposes of *ICTA 1988, s 576(1)* which requires disposals to be matched with acquisitions on a last in/first out basis in determining the extent to which a loss qualifies for relief against income under *Sec 574*.

IT 10.5 Losses

(B)
Assume the losses available under *Sec 574* in (A) above. The income of X and his wife is as follows

		1989/90	1990/91
		£	£
X	Trading income/(loss)	(4,000)	35,000
	Other income	14,000	16,000
Wife	Earned income	1,200	1,100
	Other income	1,400	1,450

The losses of £17,250, £40,855 and £3,250 on the disposals of shares in A Ltd, C Ltd and D Ltd respectively, available under *Sec 574*, could be set off as follows

1989/90

			£	£
X	Investment income			14,000
Deduct	Loss claim *ICTA 1988, s 574*	(C Ltd)		14,000
				—

1990/91

			£	£
X	Trading income			35,000
Deduct	Loss claim *ICTA 1988, s 385*			(4,000)
	Other income			16,000
				47,000
Deduct	Loss claims *ICTA 1988, s 574*	(C Ltd)	26,855	
		(A Ltd)	17,250	
		(D Ltd)	2,895	
				47,000
				—

Losses carried forward to 1991/92
Income tax
ICTA 1988, s 574 (D Ltd)(£3,250 − £2,895)   £355

Notes
(*a*)   Where relief is given for 1989/90 or earlier years, it is given against joint income of husband and wife. The claim can, however, be restricted to the income of the spouse incurring the loss. It is assumed that the restriction is claimed for 1989/90 in this example as the wife's income will be covered by personal reliefs. Relief given in 1990/91 and subsequent years is given only against the income of the spouse incurring the loss.

(*b*)   Relief under *Sec 574* is given in priority to loss relief under *ICTA 1988, ss 380, 381*.

(*c*)   If the loss on D Ltd shares of £355 is not utilised in 1991/92, it will revert to a loss for capital gains tax purposes, and will then be offset against any chargeable gains for 1990/91, the year of disposal, with any excess being carried forward against subsequent gains.

11   Married Persons

11.1   INDEPENDENT TAXATION FROM 1990/91

(A) Married couple's allowance [*ICTA 1988, ss 257A, 257B; FA 1988, s 33*]

Mr Grey is a sole trader and made a small trading loss in his accounting year ended 30 April 1989 which forms the basis period for the 1990/91 Schedule D assessment. The loss is relieved under *ICTA 1988, s 380* against other income for 1989/90. Mr Grey has been married for some years. He has investment income of £3,100 gross for 1990/91 and his wife has a salary of £15,000 and investment income of £2,000 gross. In addition to their other investment income, Mr and Mrs Grey receive interest of £750 in 1990/91 from a bank deposit account in their joint names. Mr Grey makes an investment of £500 on 1 November 1990, which qualifies for business expansion relief. Mr Grey elects under *ICTA 1988, s 257B* to transfer the unused balance of his married couple's allowance for 1990/91 to his wife.

Taxable income for Mr and Mrs Grey is computed as follows

	Mr Grey		Mrs Grey	
	£	£	£	£
Schedule D, Case I		Nil		—
Schedule E		—		15,000
Gross investment income		3,100		2,000
Bank deposit interest note(*d*)	375		375	
Add notional tax credit	125	500	125	500
		3,600		17,500
Less business expansion relief		500		—
Total income		3,100		17,500
Deduct personal allowance		3,005		3,005
		95		14,495
Deduct married couple's allowance (maximum £1,720)		95	note (*c*)	1,125
Taxable income		Nil		£13,370

Notes

(*a*)   With effect for 1990/91 and subsequent years, husband and wife are taxed as separate persons. Their income is not aggregated and they are each responsible for their own returns and tax liabilities. They each receive a personal allowance of the same amount as if they were single people.

(*b*)   The husband is entitled to a married couple's allowance. If it exceeds his total income after all other deductions, he may elect to transfer the unused balance to his wife.

(*c*)   In determining a person's total income after all other deductions for the purpose of (*b*) above, deductions for business expansion scheme relief, loan interest paid under the MIRAS scheme, pension contributions paid under deduction of tax and private medical insurance (under *FA 1989, s 54*) paid under deduction of tax are disregarded. Thus, in this example, Mr Grey's total income after other deductions is not £95 but £595 (adding back the business expansion relief of £500). The excess married couple's allowance transferable to Mrs Grey is £1,125 (£1,720 – £595) and £500 of the married couple's allowance is wasted. Effectively, Mr Grey has not received any relief for his business expansion scheme investment as his and his wife's income tax position would have been exactly the same if he had not made the investment.

(d)   With certain exceptions, income from property held in their joint names is to be divided equally between husband and wife. [*FA 1988, s 34*]. Certain gifts and settlements of property between spouses, being property from which income arises, are not valid transfers of income. [*ICTA 1988, ss 674A, 683, 685(4A)–(4C); FA 1989, ss 108, 109*]. These provisions apply where the donor retains an interest in the property. Outright gifts comprising both income and capital should not be caught.

(B) Transitional relief: transfer of husband's excess allowances [*ICTA 1988, s 257D; FA 1988, s 33*]

The facts are as in (A) above except that Mr Grey has no investment income of his own and doesn't make the business expansion scheme investment. Assume that no wife's earnings election was in force for 1989/90 and that Mr Grey received personal allowances in that year of £7,160 (comprising married person's allowance of £4,375 and wife's earned income relief of £2,785). Mr Grey makes a claim under *ICTA 1988, s 257D* for his 'excess allowances' to be set off against his wife's income.

Taxable income is calculated as follows

	Mr Grey £	Mrs Grey £
Schedule D, Case I	Nil	—
Schedule E	—	15,000
Gross investment income including joint bank deposit interest	500	2,500
	500	17,500
Deduct personal allowance	500	3,005
	Nil	14,495
Deduct married couple's allowance		1,720
		12,775
Deduct excess allowances transferred (see below)		1,935
Taxable income	Nil	£10,840

Excess allowances are calculated as follows	£	£
Husband's allowances for 1989/90		7,160
Less the aggregate of		
husband's total income for 1990/91		
note (*c*)	500	
wife's allowances for 1990/91		
(£3,005 + £1,720)	4,725	
		5,225
Excess allowances		£1,935

Notes

(*a*)   Mr Grey has lost £2,505 of his personal allowance due to his income being too low. If his and his wife's income had been aggregated in 1990/91, he would have received the full married man's allowance and wife's earned income relief. The transfer of £1,935 to Mrs Grey compensates the couple for the loss of allowances but not to the extent of increases in 1990/91 levels of allowances over those for the previous year. An election to transfer excess allowances also has effect as an election to transfer married couple's allowance.

(*b*)   This transitional relief under *section 257D(1)(2)* is available in 1990/91 only, but where it is claimed, further transitional relief may be available under *section 257D(5)–(7)* in subsequent years in which the husband has excess allowances as long as there was no intervening year for which it was not obtained.

(*c*)   A person's total income for the purposes of the excess allowances calculation is before deduction of personal allowances, business expansion scheme relief, loan interest under MIRAS, pension contributions paid under deduction of tax and private medical insurance (under *FA 1989, s 54*) paid under deduction of tax.

IT 11.1 Married Persons

(C) Elderly couples: transitional relief [*ICTA 1988, s 257E; FA 1988, s 33*]
Mr and Mrs Scarlet are a married couple aged 60 and 66 respectively at 5 April
1988. For 1989/90, they had income of £6,000 and £5,000 per annum respectively
and Mr Scarlet claimed age allowance of £5,385 by virtue of his wife's age. For the
purposes of this example, it is assumed that income, allowances and limits increase
by 10% per annum.

Taxable income for the years 1990/91–1992/93 is as follows

	Mr Scarlet £	Mrs Scarlet £
1990/91		
Income	6,600	5,500
Deduct personal allowances note (*a*)	(3,400)	(3,670)
married couple's allowance	(2,145)	
Taxable income	£1,055	£1,830
1991/2	£	£
Income	7,260	6,050
Deduct personal allowances note (*a*)	(3,400)	(4,037)
married couple's allowance	(2,360)	
Taxable income	£1,500	£2,013
1992/93	£	£
Income	7,986	6,655
Deduct personal allowances note (*a*)	(4,440)	(4,440)
married couple's allowance	(2,596)	
Taxable income	£950	£2,215

Notes

(*a*)   Were it not for transitional relief under *section 257E*, the husband's personal
allowance for 1990/91 would be £3,005. His combined personal allowance
and married couple's allowance for 1990/91 would then be £5,150 (£3,005 +
£2,145) which is less than his 1989/90 allowance of £5,385. This brings the
transitional provisions into play and his personal allowance is fixed at the
1989/90 level for a single person over 65. It remains fixed at this level until
such time as he is entitled to age allowance by virtue of his own age which in
this example is the year 1992/93.

(*b*)   See also 1.1(C) ALLOWANCES AND TAX RATES above for a general example on
age-related allowances for married couples.

11.2 WHEN THE MARRIAGE ENDS

Mr X died on 5 October 1990. His business had assessable profits of £16,000 for the year ended 30 June 1990 and £9,000 for the previous year. He had no other income. Mrs X received wages of £3,000 from her husband's business to 5 October and continued the business thereafter. She receives a lump sum widow's payment of £1,000 and a widow's pension of £1,220 to 5 April 1991.

1990/91	£	£
Mr X		
Earned income		
Profits (Sch D, Case I on preceding year basis)		
½ of £9,000		4,500
Deduct Personal reliefs		
Personal allowance	3,005	
Married couple's allowance (restricted)	1,495	
		4,500
Taxable Income		Nil
Mrs X		
Earned income		
Profits (Sch D, Case I on preceding year basis)		
½ of £9,000		4,500
Wages		3,000
Widow's pension (Sch E — actual)		1,220
		8,720
Deduct Personal reliefs		
Personal allowance	3,005	
Married couple's allowance (balance)	225	
Widow's bereavement allowance	1,720	
		4,950
Taxable Income		£3,770

Notes

(a) Under Inland Revenue extra-statutory concession A7, the continuation basis applies to a widow(er) continuing a deceased spouse's business, unless the discontinuance basis is claimed.

(b) The transfer of the unused married couple's allowance to the wife (see also 11.1(A) above) is dependent on a claim to that effect being made by the husband's executors.

(c) The wife's personal reliefs are all available against income arising both before and after the husband's death.

(d) Widow's bereavement allowance will also be available in 1991/92 if Mrs X does not remarry before 6 April 1991. [*ICTA 1988, s 262; FA 1988, 3 Sch 7*].

(e) The lump sum widow's payment, available where the husband dies after 10 April 1988, is not chargeable to income tax. [*ICTA 1988, s 617(1)(2)*].

11.3   **MAINTENANCE PAYMENTS** [*ICTA 1988, ss 347A–349, 351; FA 1988, ss 36, 38–40*].

(A) Court Orders before 15 March 1988

Mr Smith separated from his wife on 31 October 1987. In 1990/91 he has assessable Schedule D, Case I profits of £19,000 and dividends of £3,750. He pays gross mortgage interest of £2,500 on a loan which is within the MIRAS scheme. Under a court order dated 5 March 1988, Mr Smith pays £20 per week maintenance directly to his son, Paul, aged 17, who lives with Mrs Smith, and £70 per week maintenance to Mrs Smith. On 1 June 1989, the payments to Mrs Smith are increased by the Court to £80 per week. In 1990/91, Mrs Smith has part-time earnings of £2,500. Paul Smith has no other income.

	£	£
1990/91		
Mr Smith		
Earned income		19,000
Unearned income		
Dividends	3,750	
Add Tax credits	1,250	
		5,000
		24,000
Deduct Mortgage interest	2,500	
Maintenance payments — son	1,040	
Maintenance payments — wife note (*a*)	3,640	
Relief for Class 4 NIC note (*d*)	402	
		7,582
		16,418
Deduct personal allowance		3,005
Taxable income		£13,413

Tax liability		
£13,413 at 25%		3,353.25
Add Tax retained on mortgage interest payments (£2,500 at 25%)		625.00
		3,978.25
Deduct Tax suffered at source on investment income (£5,000 at 25%)		1,250.00
		£2,728.25

	£	£
Mrs Smith		
Earned income		2,500
Maintenance note (*a*)	3,640	
Deduction note (*a*)	1,720	
		1,920
		4,420
Deduct personal allowance note (*e*)		3,005
Taxable income		£1,415

Tax liability
£1,415 at 25%   £353.75

	£
Paul Smith	
Maintenance note (*c*)	1,040
Deduct personal allowance (restricted)	1,040
Taxable income	Nil
Tax payable/repayable	Nil

Notes

(*a*)   After 5 April 1989, all maintenance payments then falling due are made gross and there are rules to limit the tax relief and the amount chargeable on the recipient to the relief obtainable and the amount forming part of the recipient's income for 1988/89. The recipient may then deduct from the amount otherwise chargeable an amount equal to the married couple's allowance for the year, providing the payments are from a divorced or separated spouse. [*FA 1988, s 38, 3 Sch 33*].

(*b*)   The payer may elect to have payments treated under the rules for post-14 March 1988 Court Orders and maintenance agreements illustrated in (B) below. [*FA 1988, s 39*]. This would normally be beneficial only where his relief would otherwise be less than £1,720 (for 1990/91).

(*c*)   As the maintenance payments of £20 per week are paid directly to Mr Smith's son the gross amount forms part of the son's income, not Mrs Smith's.

(*d*)   Relief for Class 4 NIC is 50% of the maximum contribution of £803.25. [*ICTA 1988, s 617(5)*].

(*e*)   Mrs Smith may also be entitled to the additional personal allowance in respect of Paul if all the conditions of *ICTA 1988, s 259* are satisfied.

(*f*)   See the 1988/89 edition for an illustration of the position for that year.

IT 11.3 Married Persons

(B) Court Orders after 14 March 1988

Mr Green separated from his wife in June 1989 and, under a Court Order dated 15 July 1990, pays maintenance of £300 per month to his ex-wife and £100 per month to his daughter, payments being due on the first of each calendar month commencing 1 August 1990. Mr Green has earned income of £17,000 and dividends of £3,750 for 1990/91. He re-marries on 6 October 1990.

	£	£
1990/91		
Mr Green		
Earned income		17,000
Unearned income		
Dividends	3,750	
Add Tax credits	1,250	5,000
		22,000
Deduct Maintenance payments – wife		
(£2,700 paid) note (*a*)		1,720
		20,280
Deduct personal allowance	3,005	
married couple's allowance £1,720 × $\frac{6}{12}$ note (*d*)	860	3,865
Taxable income		£16,415

Tax liability		
£16,415 at 25%		4,103.75
Deduct Tax suffered on investment		
income (£5,000 at 25%)		1,250.00
Tax payable (before allowing for deductions at source under PAYE)		£2,853.75

Notes

(*a*) Relief for maintenance payments to a divorced or separated spouse is restricted to an amount equal to the married couple's allowance for the year. No relief is due for other maintenance payments. [*ICTA 1988, ss 347A; 347B; FA 1988, s 36, 3 Sch 13*].

(*b*) Maintenance payments are exempt from tax in the hands of the recipients.

(*c*) All maintenance payments are made without deduction of tax.

(*d*) Tax relief for maintenance payments does not affect entitlement to the married couple's allowance either in the year of re-marriage or in later years. The allowance for the year of re-marriage is restricted in the normal way under *ICTA 1988, s 257A(6)*.

(*e*) These rules affect maintenance payments under Court Orders and maintenance agreements made after 14 March 1988 except for Court Orders applied for before 15 March 1988 and made by 30 June 1988 and Orders which vary previous Orders made before 15 March 1988; these fall within the rules in (A) above.

11.4 **SEPARATE TAXATION OF WIFE'S EARNINGS** [*ICTA 1988, ss 287, 288*]

Mr and Mrs White are in partnership sharing profits equally. In 1989/90 the business had an assessable profit of £26,000 and each paid Class 4 NIC of £501. Mr and Mrs White have investment income of £6,300 and £1,000, respectively. Mrs White pays gross mortgage interest of £1,000 to a lender who is within the MIRAS scheme.

	(i) Without an election	(ii) With an election under *ICTA 1988, s 287*	
	Husband	Husband	Wife
Partnership profits (Sch D, Case I)	£	£	£
	26,000	13,000	13,000
Investment income	7,300	7,300	—
	33,300	20,300	13,000
Deduct Mortgage interest	1,000	—	1,000
	32,300	20,300	12,000
Deduct Relief for Class 4 NIC	502	251	251
	31,798	20,049	11,749
Deduct			
Personal allowance — married 4,375			
Wife's earnings allowance 2,785			
Personal allowance — single		2,785	2,785
	7,160		
Taxable Income	£24,638	£17,264	£8,964

Tax Payable							
£20,700	£17,264	£8,964	at 25%	5,175	4,316	2,241
3,938			at 40%	1,575	—	—
£24,638	£17,264	£8,964		6,750	4,316	2,241

Add Tax retained on mortgage interest payments (£1,000 at 25%)	250	—	250
	7,000	4,316	£2,491
		2,491	
	£7,000	£6,807	
		Saving	£193

Notes

(*a*) ICTA 1988, ss 287, 288 were repealed by *FA 1988, 14 Sch Part VIII* with effect for 1990/91 and subsequent years, husband and wife being taxed independently in any case. An election for 1989/90 may still be made (or withdrawn) by 5 April 1991.

(*b*) Under a wife's earnings election, the wife's earnings are to be charged to tax as if she were a single woman with no other income. The husband is still taxed on his wife's other income, e.g. state retirement pension not arising by virtue of her own contributions and her investment income. Wife's earnings for this purpose include unemployment benefit from 1987/88 and invalid care allowance from 1984/85. [*ICTA 1988, s 287(2)(3)*]. The personal reliefs are computed as if the husband and wife were not married which means that the husband is entitled only to the single personal allowance. [*ICTA 1988, s 287(4)*].

(c)   For 1988/89 and 1989/90, where a wife's earnings election was in force, husband and wife could jointly elect to allocate mortgage interest relief between them in whatever proportions they wished. [*ICTA 1988, s 356B(4)–(7); FA 1988, s 42*]. A similar election is available with effect from 1990/91 under independent taxation. [*ICTA 1988, s 356B; FA 1988, 3 Sch 14*]. Before 6 April 1988, mortgage interest payable by the wife had to be allocated against her own earned income even if she had investment income to cover it; this rule continued to apply for 1988/89 and 1989/90 as regards various other charges and reliefs paid by or due to the wife. [*ICTA 1988, s 287(7)*]. In the above example, there is no benefit in re-allocating the mortgage interest as both spouses pay tax at only basic rate after the wife's earnings election.

12   Mineral Royalties

[*ICTA 1988, s 122*]

12.1   Miss Quarry owns land containing valuable gravel pits. She receives a royalty from a construction company based on the tonnage removed. She has to bear part of the cost of the weighbridge and ancillary facilities.

In the year to 5 April 1991 she receives £15,700 of royalty and her share of the weighbridge expenses amounted to £1,000. This is her only source of income or gains for that year.

Her tax liabilities for 1990/91 are as follows

	£
Income Tax	
Royalty received £15,700	
Chargeable to income tax — one half	7,850
Management expenses £1,000	
Relief restricted to one half	500
	7,350
Deduct Personal allowance	3,005
	£4,345
Taxation thereon	
£4,345 at 25%	1,086.25
Income tax deducted (£15,700 at 25%)	3,925.00
Balance recoverable	£2,838.75
Capital Gains Tax	
Royalty received £15,700	
Chargeable to capital gains tax — one half	7,850
Deduct annual exemption	5,000
	£2,850
Taxation thereon at 25%	£712.50
Net tax recoverable (£2,838.75 − £712.50)	£2,126.25

13   Overseas Matters

13.1 **NON-RESIDENT ENTERTAINERS AND SPORTSMEN** [*ICTA 1988, ss 555–558; SI 1987/530*]

G, a professional golfer who is non-resident in the UK, visits the UK in July 1990 to play in a tournament from which he earns £40,000 in appearance and prize money. He directs that the money be paid to a non-resident company which he controls. During his visit, he receives £500 from a television company for a series of interviews and £1,500 from a national newspaper for a number of exclusive articles. He arranges for 20% of the latter sum to be paid direct to his agent, also non-resident and who pays tax on his income at a rate not exceeding 25%, who arranged the deal. He incurs allowable expenses of £12,000 in connection with the trip. He makes no other working visits to the UK during 1990/91, but in March 1991, during a private visit, he earns £400 from the same newspaper as before in respect of a further article; he does not however receive immediate payment, a cheque being sent to him abroad on 20.4.91. He has no other taxable income in the UK during 1990/91. He does not qualify for UK personal reliefs.

G's UK tax position for 1990/91 is as follows

		Taxable income £	Tax withheld at source £
Prize and appearance money	note (*b*)	40,000	10,000
Fee from television company	note (*c*)	500	—
Fee for newspaper articles	note (*d*)	1,500	375
		42,000	10,375
Deduct expenses		12,000	
		£30,000	

	£	
Tax payable		
£20,700 at 25%	5,175	
9,300 at 40%	3,720	
£30,000		8,895
Tax repayable		£1,480

Notes

(*a*)   G is considered to have carried on a trade in respect of the payments received, or deemed to have been received, by him in connection with his UK activities. The trade is distinct from any other trade carried on by him and is taxable on a current year basis. [*ICTA 1988, s 557*].

(*b*)   A payment to a company under the entertainer's (or sportsman's) control (defined in accordance with *ICTA 1988, s 416(1)–(6)*) is treated as a payment to him and withholding tax at the basic rate must be deducted at source. [*ICTA 1988, s 556(2)–(5); SI 1987/530, Reg 7*].

(*c*)   No withholding tax falls to be deducted from the television company fee as it does not exceed the de minimis limit of £1,000. [*SI 1987/530, Reg 4(3)*].

(*d*)   Although a percentage of the fee for newspaper articles was paid not to G but to his agent, it falls to be treated as G's income and is subject to withholding tax by virtue of his agent's being non-resident in the UK and liable to tax at a rate not exceeding 25% in his country of residence. [*SI 1987/530, Reg 7(2)(b)*].

(*e*)   Although G earns £400 in March 1991 (which would normally suffer withholding tax by virtue of his already having received payments exceeding £1,000 from the same source), payment is not received until 1991/92 and should not, on a liberal interpretation, be regarded as a payment received 'for 1990/91'. As it is not more than £1,000, it should not suffer tax by deduction at source.

(*f*)   It is assumed in the above example that G has not agreed, with the Inland Revenue, a reduced rate of withholding tax, which he could have attempted to do by making application in writing, under *Regulation 5*, not later than 30 days before any payment fell to be made.

13.2   **OFFSHORE FUNDS** [*ICTA 1988, ss 757–764, 27 and 28 Schs; FA 1989, s 140*]

R, who is resident, ordinarily resident and domiciled in the UK, invests in non-qualifying offshore funds as follows

		£
(i)	**ABC fund**	
30.11.82	1,000 shares purchased at £10 per share	10,000
1.1.84	Market value per share = £20	20,000
1.4.90	On amalgamation with XYZ fund (another non-qualifying offshore fund) the 1,000 original shares are exchanged for 2,000 new shares in XYZ which have a value of £15 per share	30,000
31.3.91	2,000 XYZ shares sold for £17.50 per share	35,000
(ii)	**DEF fund**	
1.8.83	500 units purchased at £25 per unit	12,500
1.1.84	Market value per unit = £20	10,000
1.2.90	500 units sold for £40 per unit	20,000
(iii)	**GHJ fund**	
1.4.88	1,000 units in sub-fund K purchased at £20 per unit	20,000
1.6.91	1,000 units in sub-fund K exchanged for 500 units in sub-fund L which have a market value of £50 per unit	25,000

R has offshore income gains and chargeable capital gains as follows

1989/90

Offshore income gains

Disposal on 1.2.90 of 500 DEF units	Post-1983 gain	Unindexed gain
	£	£
Disposal proceeds	20,000	20,000
Market value at 1.1.84	10,000	
Cost		12,500
	£10,000	£7,500

As the unindexed gain is less than the post-1983 gain, the offshore income gain chargeable under Schedule D, Case VI is £7,500.

Disposal on 1.4.90 of 1,000 ABC shares

Disposal consideration	30,000	30,000
Market value at 1.1.84	20,000	
Cost		10,000
	£10,000	£20,000

The offshore income gain chargeable under Schedule D, Case VI is the £10,000 post-1983 gain as this is less than the unindexed gain.

Chargeable capital gains
Disposal on 1.2.90 of 500 DEF units

	£
Disposal proceeds	20,000
Offshore income gain	7,500
	12,500
Cost	12,500
Unindexed gain	—
Indexation allowance (at 40.3%)	5,038
Allowable loss	£5,038

Disposal on 1.4.90 of 1,000 ABC shares
There is no capital gains tax liability as the share exchange is not treated as a disposal for capital gains tax purposes. [*CGTA 1979, s 85*].

1990/91

Offshore income gain
Disposal on 31.3.91 of 2,000 XYZ shares

	£
Disposal proceeds	35,000
Cost (market value at 1.4.90)	30,000
Offshore income gain	£5,000

Chargeable capital gain
Disposal on 31.3.91 of 2,000 XYZ shares

	£	£
Disposal proceeds		35,000
Offshore income gain		5,000
		30,000
Cost	10,000	
Deemed consideration for new holding in XYZ note (*b*)	10,000	
		20,000
Unindexed gain		10,000
Indexation allowance (say)		6,000
Chargeable gain		£4,000

1991/92

Offshore income gain
Disposal on 1.6.91 of 1,000 GHJ (sub-fund K) units   (see note (c))

	£
Disposal consideration	25,000
Cost (1.4.88)	20,000
Offshore income gain	£5,000

Chargeable capital gain

	£
Disposal consideration	25,000
Offshore income gain	5,000
	20,000
Cost	20,000
Unindexed gain	—
Indexation allowance (say)	6,000
Allowable loss	£6,000

Notes

(a)   Where a holding in a non-qualifying offshore fund was acquired before 1 January 1984, the offshore income gain on disposal is the lower of the unindexed gain (as calculated for capital gains tax) and the post-1983 gain (the gain accruing after 31 December 1983 on the assumption that the holding was sold and reacquired at market value on 1 January 1984). [*ICTA 1988, 28 Sch Part I*].

(b)   Where an offshore income gain arises on an exchange of shares within *CGTA 1979, s 85(3)*, the amount of that gain is treated as consideration for the new holding on a subsequent disposal. [*ICTA 1988, s 763(6)*].

(c)   An exchange after 13 March 1989 of rights in part of an 'umbrella fund' for rights in another part of that fund is a disposal for both capital gains tax and for the purposes of the offshore fund legislation, notwithstanding *CGTA 1979, ss 78, 82. [FA 1989, s 140]*.

14   Partnerships

14.1   CHANGES IN PARTNERS ETC. [*ICTA 1988, ss 61, 62, 113*]

P, Q and R carried on a trade in partnership for a number of years sharing profits in the ratio 2:2:1, preparing accounts to 5 July. On 5 June 1990, P left the partnership and Q and R thereafter shared the profits equally.

Results for all relevant years are as follows

Year ended	Partners' salaries			Adjusted Profit/(loss)
	P	Q	R	
	£	£	£	£
5.7.87	9,000	9,000	4,500	40,000
5.7.88	12,000	12,000	6,000	70,000
5.7.89	4,000	4,000	2,000	(10,000)
5.7.90	18,000	13,000	11,500	60,000
5.7.91	—	15,000	12,000	80,000
5.7.92	—	17,000	12,000	85,000
5.7.93	—	20,000	20,000	95,000
5.7.94	—	23,500	23,500	100,000
5.7.95	—	24,500	24,500	100,000
5.7.96	—	27,000	27,000	120,000

The assessments for the relevant years are as follows

(i) *ICTA 1988, s 113(2)* election made

		Basis period	£
Old partnership	1988/89	5.7.87	40,000
	1989/90	5.7.88	70,000
	1990/91	$\frac{2}{12}$ of 5.7.89	Nil
New partnership	1990/91	$\frac{10}{12}$ of 5.7.89	Nil
	1991/92	5.7.90	60,000
	1992/93	5.7.91	80,000
	1993/94	5.7.92	85,000
	1994/95	5.7.93	95,000
	1995/96	5.7.94	100,000
Loss claim 1989/90			(10,000)

(ii) *ICTA 1988, s 113(2)* election not made

Old Partnership

	Preceding year	Actual			
	£		£	£	£
1988/89	40,000	$\frac{3}{12}$ of 5.7.88	17,500		
		$\frac{9}{12}$ of 5.7.89	(7,500)	10,000	40,000
1989/90	70,000	$\frac{3}{12}$ of 5.7.89	(2,500)		
		$\frac{9}{12}$ of 5.7.90	45,000	42,500	70,000
Higher of	£110,000		and	£52,500	

1990/91		$\frac{2}{12}$ of 5.7.90			10,000	10,000

New Partnership

1990/91		$\frac{1}{12}$ of 5.7.90		5,000	
		$\frac{9}{12}$ of 5.7.91		60,000	65,000
1991/92		$\frac{3}{12}$ of 5.7.91		20,000	
		$\frac{9}{12}$ of 5.7.92		63,750	83,750
1992/93		$\frac{3}{12}$ of 5.7.92		21,250	
		$\frac{9}{12}$ of 5.7.93		71,250	92,500
1993/94		$\frac{3}{12}$ of 5.7.93		23,750	
		$\frac{9}{12}$ of 5.7.94		75,000	98,750

1994/95 and 1995/96

1994/95	95,000	$\frac{3}{12}$ of 5.7.94	25,000		95,000
		$\frac{9}{12}$ of 5.7.95	75,000	100,000	
1995/96	100,000	$\frac{3}{12}$ of 5.7.95	25,000		100,000
		$\frac{9}{12}$ of 5.7.96	90,000	115,000	
Lower of	£195,000		and	£215,000	

No claim will be made to adjust years 1994/95 and 1995/96 to actual.

(iii) The alternatives may be compared

		Election £	No election £
Old partnership	1988/89	40,000	40,000
	1989/90	70,000	70,000
	1990/91	Nil	10,000
New partnership	1990/91	Nil	65,000
	1991/92	60,000	83,750
	1992/93	80,000	92,500
	1993/94	85,000	98,750
	1994/95	95,000	95,000
	1995/96	100,000	100,000
Total assessable profits		530,000	655,000
Loss relief available	1989/90	10,000	10,000
Net assessable profits		£520,000	£645,000

The assessable profits, before taking account of any capital allowances are lower if an election under *ICTA 1988, s 113(2)* is made but the difference in tax payable will depend on the circumstances of the partners.

If it is assumed that an election is made, the assessments for four of the years will be allocated as follows:

	P £	Q £	R £	Total £
1988/89				
Salary $\frac{3}{12}$ of 5.7.88	3,000	3,000	1,500	7,500
$\frac{9}{12}$ of 5.7.89	3,000	3,000	1,500	7,500
Balance	10,000	10,000	5,000	25,000
	£16,000	£16,000	£8,000	£40,000

IT 14.1 Partnerships

1989/90

Salary $\frac{3}{12}$ of 5.7.89	1,000	1,000	500	2,500
$\frac{9}{12}$ of 5.7.90	13,500	9,750	8,625	31,875
Balance	14,250	14,250	7,125	35,625
	£28,750	£25,000	£16,250	£70,000

1990/91

Salary $\frac{3}{12}$ of 5.7.90	4,500	3,250	2,875	10,625
$\frac{9}{12}$ of 5.7.91	—	11,250	9,000	20,250
Balance to 5.6.90	(2,725)	(2,725)	(1,363)	(6,813
from 6.6.90	—	(17,031)	(17,031)	(34,062
	1,775	(5,256)	(6,519)	(10,000
Elimination of profit				
nil : £5,256 : £6,519	(1,775)	792	983	—
	—	£(4,464)	£(5,536)	£(10,000

1991/92

Salary $\frac{3}{12}$ of 5.7.91	—	3,750	3,000	6,750
$\frac{9}{12}$ of 5.7.92	—	12,750	9,000	21,750
Balance	—	15,750	15,750	31,500
	—	£32,250	£27,750	£60,000

Notes

(a) These commencement provisions apply to partnership changes after 19 March 1985 where no continuation election is made under *ICTA 1988, s 113(2)*. They do not apply where a new partnership is set up or where only one person is trading before, or remains trading after, the change. The charge to income tax in the first four years of assessment of the new partnership is made on the actual profits arising in those years. For subsequent years the charge is on the preceding year basis of assessment, with a right of election by the partnership for use of the 'actual basis' to be extended to the fifth and sixth years (but not to only one of these years). [*ICTA 1988, ss 61(4), 62(4)(5)*].

(b) It should be noted that the continuation election must be made within two years of the change. This is likely to be several years before the partnership can tell whether an election under *ICTA 1988, s 62(4)* will be beneficial.

14.2 **PARTNERSHIP LOSSES**

(A)   No change in profit-sharing ratios

A partnership of J, K and L have traded for some years and share profits equally. The results as adjusted for tax for the four years to 30.9.90 are as follows

		£
Year ended	30.9.87	2,000
	30.9.88	(12,000)
	30.9.89	3,000
	30.9.90	15,000

The three partners have different personal circumstances. J has considerable other income and wishes to obtain the benefit of the loss as soon as possible. K's wife inherited the residue of her mother's estate and interest from investments commenced in the year ended 5.4.90. L has no other income. To obtain the maximum benefit of the loss, the partners make loss claims under *ICTA 1988, ss 380(1), 380(2)* and *385(1)* respectively.

The effect on the partnership assessment of the above is as follows

1989/90 — Nil assessment

1990/91	J	K	L	Total
	£	£	£	£
Profit — year ended 30.9.89	1,000	1,000	1,000	3,000
Deduct loss claim				
L — *Sec 385(1)*			(1,000)	(1,000)
	£1,000	£1,000	Nil	£2,000
1991/92				
Profit — year ended 30.9.90	5,000	5,000	5,000	15,000
Deduct loss claim				
L — *Sec 385(1)*			(3,000)	(3,000)
	£5,000	£5,000	£2,000	£12,000

The loss available to the partners arising from the accounts for the year to 30.9.88 has been utilised as follows

	£	£	£	£
Share of loss	4,000	4,000	4,000	12,000
Sec 380(1) 1988/89	(4,000)			
Sec 380(2) 1989/90		(4,000)		
Sec 385(1) 1990/91			(1,000)	
	1991/92			(3,000)

Note

(a)   L would not make a claim under *ICTA 1988, s 380(1)* to set his share of the loss against the profits assessed in 1988/89 since he would thereby lose the benefit of personal allowances.

(B) Change in profit-sharing ratios
The facts and the loss relief claims made are as in (A) above, except that as from 1 October 1988, the partners share profits in the ratio 2:2:1.

The partnership assessments are now as follows

1989/90 — Nil assessment

1990/91

	J	K	L	Total
	£	£	£	£
Profit — year ended 30.9.89	1,200	1,200	600	3,000
Deduct loss claim				
L — Sec 385(1)			(600)	(600)
	£1,200	£1,200	Nil	£2,400

1991/92

Profit — year ended 30.9.90	6,000	6,000	3,000	15,000
Deduct loss claim				
L — Sec 385(1)			(3,000)	(3,000)
	£6,000	£6,000	Nil	£12,000

The loss available to the partners arising from the accounts for the year to 30.9.88 has been utilised as follows

	£	£	£	£
Share of loss for Sec 380				
£12,000 × $\frac{6}{12}$ × $\frac{1}{3}$ each	2,000	2,000		4,000
£12,000 × $\frac{6}{12}$ × $\frac{2}{5}$ each	2,400	2,400		4,800
Share of loss for Sec 385				
£12,000 × $\frac{1}{3}$			4,000	4,000
	4,400	4,400	4,000	12,800
Sec 380(1) 1988/89	(4,400)			
Sec 380(2) 1989/90		(4,400)		
Sec 385(1) 1990/91			(600)	
1991/92			(3,000)	
Sec 385(1) c/fwd			£400	

Note
(a) Although the loss amounted to £12,000, a total of £12,800 is available for relief. This is due to the fact that, for *section 380* purposes, the loss is apportioned according to sharing ratios for the year of assessment in which the accounting period of loss falls, whereas, for *section 385* purposes, it is apportioned in accordance with sharing ratios for the accounting period of loss.

14.3 LIMITED PARTNERSHIPS — LOSSES [*ICTA 1988, ss 117, 118*]

R, S and T Ltd, who have been trading in partnership for several years preparing accounts to 30 June, share profits and losses equally. S and T Ltd are limited partners.

For the year ended 30 June 1990, the partnership made a loss of £18,000. Other relevant details are as follows

	R £	S £	T Ltd £
Other income			
1990/91	10,000	8,000	
Year ended 30.6.90			20,000
Capital and accumulated profits			
At 5.4.91	4,000	5,000	
At 30.6.90			5,500

R and S may claim *Sec 380(1)* loss relief for 1990/91 as follows

	R £	S £
Other income	10,000	8,000
Share of partnership loss (restricted for S)	(6,000)	(5,000)
	£4,000	£3,000
Loss carried forward for set-off against future trading income	—	£1,000

T Ltd may claim *Sec 393(2)* loss relief for the year ended 30.6.90 as follows

	£
Other income	20,000
Share of partnership loss (restricted)	(5,500)
	£14,500
Loss carried forward for set-off against future trading profits	£500

Note

(*a*)   The amounts of partnership losses, interest, charges and allowances which a limited partner may set against non-trading income is restricted to the amount of his capital contribution and accumulated profits at the end of the year of assessment (accounting period if a company) of loss. No such restriction applies to unlimited partners. [*ICTA 1988, ss 117, 118*].

14.4 PARTNERSHIP WITH COMPANY

See the example in the Corporation Tax section at 116.1 PARTNERSHIPS and also 14.3 above.

15 Patents

Cross-reference. See 3.10 CAPITAL ALLOWANCES above for allowances for patent rights.

[*ICTA 1988, s 527*]

15.1 An inventor received £15,000 after deduction of tax at source (i.e. £20,000 gross) on 1 June 1990, for the use of his patent over a four-year period ending on that date. He is a single man and his only other income for the four years was a salary as set out below.

In the absence of spreading provisions, the assessments for the four years to 5 April 1991 are

Year of assessment	1987/88 £	1988/89 £	1989/90 £	1990/91 £
Earned income				
Salary	7,500	8,500	9,200	10,500
Patent rights				20,000
	7,500	8,500	9,200	30,500
Personal allowance	2,425	2,605	2,785	3,005
Taxable income	£5,075	£5,895	£6,415	£27,495
Tax thereon	1,370.25	1,473.75	1,603.75	7,893.00
Less tax deducted at source				5,000.00
	£1,370.25	£1,473.75	£1,603.75	£2,893.00
Total tax payable	£7,340.75			

The inventor may however claim under *ICTA 1988, s 527* for the assessment to be limited to the tax payable if the royalties had been spread over the four-year period to which they relate. The tax payable would then have been

Earned income				
Salary	7,500	8,500	9,200	10,500
Patent rights	5,000	5,000	5,000	5,000
	12,500	13,500	14,200	15,500
Personal allowance	2,425	2,605	2,785	3,005
Taxable income	£10,075	£10.895	£11,415	£12,495
Tax thereon	2,720.25	2,723.75	2,853.75	3,123.75
Less tax deducted at source	1,250.00	1,250.00	1,250.00	1,250.00
	£1,470.25	£1,473.75	£1,603.75	£1,873.75
Total tax payable	£6,421.50			

A claim would be beneficial in this case, saving tax of £919.25 over the four years.

16   Post-Cessation Etc. Receipts

[ICTA 1988, ss 103–110]

16.1   A trader retired and closed down his trade on 31 March 1990 and, in the year 1990/91, the following subsequent events occurred
   (i)   He paid a former customer £100 as compensation for defective work.
   (ii)   In the accounts at the date of closure a specific provision was made against a debt for £722 and in addition there was a general bad debt provision of £2,000. All debts were recovered in full.
   (iii)   Stock in trade considered valueless at the date of cessation was sold for £215.
   (iv)   He eventually sold a piece of machinery six months after cessation for £136. This had been valued at nil at cessation.
   (v)   At 31 March 1990, after obtaining maximum loss relief, there was a trading loss of £333 unrelieved.

The above will be subject to tax for 1990/91 as follows

Schedule D, Case VI	£	£
Sales		215
Bad debts recovered		722
		937
Deduct Compensation payment	100	
Balance of losses	197	
		297
		£640

Note
(*a*)   The proceeds of sale of the plant are taken into the final capital allowances computation *[CAA 1990, s 26(1)(e)]* and the loss forward of £333 has been reduced by the balancing charge to £197.

17 Retirement Annuities and Personal Pension Schemes

Cross-reference. See also 26.1(E) UNDERWRITERS below.

[*ICTA 1988, ss 618–629, 630–655; FA 1989, s 77, 7 Sch; SI 1990/679*]

17.1 RELIEF FOR CONTRIBUTIONS

(A) General

C is an employee whose date of birth is 30.4.38 and who does not participate in his employer's occupational pension scheme. His earnings, as computed for Schedule E purposes, for 1989/90 and 1990/91 are £70,000 and £75,000 respectively. C pays annual retirement annuity premiums of £6,000 under long-standing contracts. For all years up to and including 1988/89 he has paid additional retirement annuity premiums and personal pension scheme contributions so as to take maximum advantage of the relief available to him; he thus has no unused relief.

In August 1989, C makes a contribution of £8,250 to a personal pension scheme. In December 1989, his employer contributes £750 to this scheme.

In the year ended 5.4.91, C and his employer make contributions of £12,500 and £1,000 respectively to the scheme.

The maximum relief is calculated as follows

1989/90

	£	£
Maximum relief for personal pension contributions:		
25% of net relevant earnings of £60,000 — note (*c*)		15,000
Deduct retirement annuity relief claimed	6,000	
employer's contribution	750	6,750
Relief due		8,250
Amount paid		8,250
Unused relief		Nil
Maximum relief for retirement annuity premiums:		
17½% of net relevant earnings of £70,000		12,250
Amount paid		6,000
		6,250
Less relief claimed for personal pension contributions		8,250
Unused relief		Nil
Total relief due (£8,250 + £6,000)		£14,250

1990/91

	£	£
Maximum relief for personal pension contributions:		
30% of net relevant earnings of £64,800 — note (*c*)		19,440
Deduct retirement annuity relief claimed	6,000	
employer's contribution	1,000	7,000
Relief due		12,440
Amount paid (see note (*e*))		12,500
Unused relief		Nil

Maximum relief for retirement annuity premiums: £
20% of net relevant earnings of £75,000 15,000
Amount paid 6,000
———
9,000
Less relief claimed for personal pension contributions 12,440

Unused relief Nil

Total relief due (£12,440 + £6,000) £18,440

Notes

(*a*) Maximum relief is calculated by reference to a percentage of net relevant earnings, such percentage being dependent on C's age at the beginning of the tax year. In 1989/90, he was 50 at the beginning of the tax year. On 6.4.90, he was aged 51. Different percentages apply for personal pension scheme contributions and retirement annuity premiums. [*ICTA 1988, ss 626, 640; FA 1989, 7 Sch 3*].

(*b*) Contributions made by an employer and premiums paid under a retirement annuity contract approved under *ICTA 1988, s 620* must be taken into account in arriving at the maximum deduction available for personal pension scheme contributions. [*ICTA 1988, s 655 (1)(a)*].

(*c*) For 1990/91, any excess of net relevant earnings over £64,800 (£60,000 for 1989/90) is disregarded in computing maximum relief for personal pension contributions. [*ICTA 1988, s 640A; FA 1989, 7 Sch 4; SI 1990/679*].

(*d*) The employer's contribution is not assessable as a benefit-in-kind, providing that it is made to an approved scheme. [*ICTA 1988, s 643(1)*].

(*e*) For 1990/91, there are excess contributions of £60 which do not qualify for relief. These will be repaid to C as it is a condition for approval of a personal pension scheme that any such excess will be repaid. The refund is deemed to be primarily out of contributions made by the individual rather than by his employer. [*ICTA 1988, s 638(3)–(5)*].

(*f*) Although not illustrated in the above example, regulations permit the deduction of basic rate tax at source from contributions by employees, leaving higher rate relief to be given via the Notice of Coding or by deduction in a Schedule E assessment. [*SI 1988/1013*].

(B) Premiums related back

A is a partner in a firm of solicitors which prepares accounts to 5 April annually. His provisional share of profits for 1990/91 (based on the year ended 5 April 1990) is £25,000 but the final share will not be determined until the accounts to 5 April 1991 are complete (in order to have salary and interest adjusted). In November 1991, the share of profits is agreed at £23,800.

In December 1991, A's Schedule D woodlands loss for 1990/91 (allowable under the transitional provisions of *FA 1988, 6 Sch*) is agreed at £2,600. He also has a salary from a non-pensionable employment which for 1990/91 amounted to £4,800.

A pays an annual retirement annuity premium of £500 but no other premium had been paid in 1990/91. He was born on 25 February 1952.

IT 17.1 Retirement Annuities and Personal Pension Schemes

A's net relevant earnings for 1990/91 are

	£
Share of profits	23,800
Salary	4,800
	28,600
Deduct Woodlands losses	2,600
	£26,000
Limit of relief for qualifying premiums 20% of £26,000	£5,200

On 15 January 1992, A pays a single contribution of £5,000 to an approved personal pension scheme and elects, on 12 May 1992, under *ICTA 1988, s 641* to have £4,700 related back to 1990/91. This, together with the annual retirement annuity premium of £500, will maximise A's relief entitlement for 1990/91. The balance of £300 (£5,000 − £4,700) will be available for relief in 1991/92.

Note

(a) An election for a contribution, or part thereof, to be carried back to the preceding tax year must be made by 5 July in the year of assessment following that in which the contribution is actually paid. [*ICTA 1988, s 641(4)*].

(C) Unused relief

P, who was born in 1960, is in non-pensionable employment and his recent retirement annuity/personal pension scheme contribution record, assuming no unused relief before 6 April 1987, is as follows

Year	Net relevant earnings	Maximum relief due	Amount paid	Unused relief
	£	£	£	£
1987/88	15,000	2,625	2,425	200
1988/89	19,000	3,325	2,200	1,125
1989/90	22,000	3,850	3,375	475

In 1990/91, P pays an annual retirement annuity premium of £1,500 and a personal pension scheme contribution of £3,850. In October 1990, P acquires a farm and incurs a tax adjusted loss of £2,000 in the period to 5 April 1991. P makes a loss relief claim under *ICTA 1988, s 380(1)*.

His net relevant earnings for 1990/91 are

Salary	£28,000
Deduct Loss relief	2,000
	£26,000
Maximum retirement annuity relief (17½%)	£4,550
Premium paid	£1,500
Maximum personal pension scheme relief (17½%)	£4,550
Deduct retirement annuity relief	1,500
Revised maximum	3,050
Contributions made	3,850
Excess contributions	£800

Tax relief can be obtained in the following way

In 1989/90
£475 of the excess contributions for 1990/91 may be related back to 1989/90 and relief obtained in that year.

In 1990/91
The remainder of the excess contributions (£325) is matched on a first in, first out basis with the unused relief brought forward.

		£
Excess contributions as above		800
Deduct amount related back to 1989/90		475
		325
Unused relief 1987/88	£200	
Unused relief 1988/89	125	325

Thus, full relief is obtained for all amounts paid in 1990/91.

Notes
(*a*)   The balance of the 1988/89 unused relief amounting to £1,000 (£1,125 − £125) will have to be utilised by 5 April 1996 (i.e. 6 years plus 1 year carry-back).

(*b*)   As an alternative to carrying back £475 to 1989/90, P could utilise an additional £475 of his 1988/89 unused relief and obtain relief in 1990/91 for the whole of his contributions. The £475 unused relief for 1989/90 would then be carried forward. This might be beneficial if his marginal tax rate for 1990/91 is greater than for 1989/90, although by relating back to 1989/90 he may be able to obtain repayment supplement.

18   Schedule A — Property Income

[*ICTA 1988, ss 15, 21–43*]

18.1   RENTS ETC. AND EXPENSES DEDUCTIBLE

Mr Brown purchased a shop on 1 August which he lets to A Ltd for £20,000 p.a. payable quarterly in arrear. The following expenditure was incurred by Brown in the first (fiscal) year of letting: insurance £240, renewing roof of shop £6,000, general maintenance £400.

The Schedule A assessment for the first year of letting will be as follows

	£	£
Rent receivable (2 quarters)		10,000
Deduct Insurance	240	
General maintenance	400	
		640
		£9,360

Note

(*a*)   No allowance will be given for renewing the shop roof as the deterioration will have occurred before Brown purchased the shop and will, in theory, have reduced the purchase price.

18.2   EXPENSES AND DEFICIENCIES DEDUCTIBLE

Mr Grey lets out the following properties
Shop to B at full rent of £1,000 p.a., expenses £1,500 (landlord repairing lease)
Factory to C at full rent of £5,000 p.a., expenses £2,000 (landlord repairing lease)
Shop to D at full rent of £1,000 p.a., expenses £4,000 (tenant's repairing lease)
Shop to E at full rent of £6,000 p.a., expenses £500 (tenant's repairing lease)
House to F at less than full rent let at £200 p.a., expenses £500

The tax position will be as follows

	Landlord repairing leases		Tenant's repairing leases		Lease at less than full rent
	£	£	£	£	£
Rents	1,000	5,000	1,000	6,000	200
Deduct Expenses	1,500	2,000	4,000	500	500
Profit/(Loss)	(500)	3,000	(3,000)	5,500	(300)
Set-off	500	(500)	—	—	—
		2,500			
Set-off		(2,500)	2,500	—	—
Assessment		—	—	£5,500	—
Losses carried forward			£(500)	—	£(300)

102

18.3   **PREMIUMS ETC. ON LEASES OF UP TO 50 YEARS** [*ICTA 1988, ss 34–39, 87*]

Cross-reference. See also 212.3(C)(G)(H) LAND in the Capital Gains Tax section.

(A)
Mr Green grants a 30-year lease of premises in March 1991 for a premium of £35,000. Mr Green's other income for 1990/91 after deducting personal reliefs amounts to £8,000.

Mr Green's taxable income is calculated as follows

	£	£
Premium on 30 year lease	35,000	
Deduct (30 − 1) × 2% × £35,000	20,300	
		14,700
Other income		8,000
Taxable income		£22,700

Note
(*a*)   Before 6 April 1988, a form of top slicing relief was available. See the 1987/88 and earlier editions for details.

(B) Allowance to payer
Assuming the same figures as in (A) above
Premium paid *less* deduction   £14,700
Number of years of lease   30

The payer will obtain relief as follows

$$\frac{£14,700}{30} = £490 \text{ p.a. treated as a payment of additional rent for 30 years.}$$

19 Schedule D, Cases I and II

19.1 OPENING YEARS OF ASSESSMENT [*ICTA 1988, ss 60–62*]

A commenced business on 1 January 1989. His Schedule D, Case I adjusted profits were

	£
16 months to 30.4.90	16,000
Year to 30.4.91	36,000

His first five years' assessments will be

	Basis period			
1988/89	1.1.89 – 5.4.89	$\frac{3}{16} \times £16,000$		£3,000
Then, either				
1989/90	1.1.89 – 31.12.89	$\frac{12}{16} \times £16,000$		12,000
1990/91	1.1.89 – 31.12.89	$\frac{12}{16} \times £16,000$		12,000
				£24,000
Or				
1989/90	6.4.89 – 5.4.90	$\frac{12}{16} \times £16,000$		12,000
1990/91	6.4.90 – 30.4.90	$\frac{1}{16} \times £16,000$	1,000	
	1.5.90 – 5.4.91	$\frac{11}{12} \times £36,000$	33,000	
				34,000
				£46,000
1991/92	1.5.89 – 30.4.90	$\frac{12}{16} \times £16,000$		£12,000
1992/93	y/e 30.4.91			£36,000

Notes

(*a*) The taxpayer would choose to be assessed for 1989/90 on £12,000 and for 1990/91 on £12,000 as these assessments would, taken together, be less than the 'actual basis' under *ICTA 1988, s 62*. He *must* choose the same basis for both years.

(*b*) The assessment for 1990/91 on the normal basis would be the profits for the 12-month period ending in the previous fiscal year. As there is no such period, the Inland Revenue have power to decide which period of 12 months ending within 1989/90 will be taken. In practice the assessment would be based either on the 12 months to the date in the second tax year which will be the future accounts date or, if this is not possible (as in this example) the first 12 months. In 1991/92, the same problem applies, but this time the Revenue would choose the 12 months to 30.4.90 (although the assessment would be the same in either case).

(*c*) See 14.1 PARTNERSHIPS for basis of assessment where there is a deemed cessation and commencement under *ICTA 1988, s 113*.

19.2 **CHANGE OF ACCOUNTING DATE** [*ICTA 1988, s 60; Revenue pamphlet IR26*]

A UK resident trader who has been trading for some years has the following
Schedule D, Case I adjusted profits

	£
Year to 30.9.88	24,000
Year to 30.9.89	15,000
15 months to 31.12.90	32,000

The assessable profit for 1991/92 is to be determined under *Sec 60(4)* and that for
1990/91 is to be considered for revision under *Sec 60(5)*.

The assessments are calculated as follows
1991/92
Sec 60(4) determination
The 1991/92 assessment is based on 12 months to 31.12.90
i.e. $\frac{12}{15}$ of £32,000   £25,600

1990/91
The accounting periods to be considered are those entering in whole or in part into
the *Sec 60(4)* basis period(s) or the 'corresponding period' under *Sec 60(5)*; viz

		Year of assessment
12 months to 30.9.89	15,000	1990/91
15 months to 31.12.90	32,000	1991/92
27 months	£47,000	24 months

Sec 60(5) consideration

The following tests are undertaken to see if the 1990/91 assessment should be
amended

(i)   Aggregate Profit
      $\frac{24}{27}$ × £47,000   £41,777

(ii) Sum of assessments for relevant years without revision for 1990/91
      1990/91   £15,000
      1991/92   25,600
                                                                                      £40,600

(iii) Sum of assessments for relevant years with revision for 1990/91
      1990/91 (revised to year to 31.12.89)
      $\frac{9}{12}$ × £15,000   £11,250
      $\frac{3}{15}$ × £32,000   6,400
                                                                        17,650
      1991/92   25,600

      Sum of assessments   £43,250

As the figure at (i) £41,777 is intermediate between (ii) £40,600 and (iii) £43,250 the
revised assessment is
Figure at (i)   41,777
Assessed 1991/92   25,600

Revised assessment 1990/91   £16,177

IT 19.3 Schedule D, Cases I and II

Notes

(a) If the difference between the figures at (i) and (ii) above was less than 10% of the average of the 1991/92 assessment and the unrevised 1990/91 assessment (i.e. £25,600 and £15,000) and, in addition, the difference was under £1,000, the 1990/91 assessment would not have been amended i.e. it would remain at £15,000.

(b) If the figure at (i) was not intermediate between the figures at (ii) and (iii) above, the Inland Revenue would decide what revised assessments, if any, were necessary. This would also be the case if any year showed a loss.

19.3 CLOSING YEARS OF ASSESSMENT [*ICTA 1988, s 63*]

A ceased business on 30.6.90. His adjusted Schedule D, Case I profits were

	£
Year to 30.4.87	24,000
30.4.88	48,000
30.4.89	96,000
30.4.90	36,000
2 months to 30.6.90	5,000

His assessments will be

	Basis periods			
1990/91	6.4.90 – 30.4.90	$\frac{1}{12} \times 36,000$	3,000	
	1.5.90 – 30.6.90		5,000	
				£8,000

Then, either			
1989/90	Year to 30.4.88		48,000
1988/89	Year to 30.4.87		24,000
			£72,000

Or				
1989/90	6.4.89 – 30.4.89	$\frac{1}{12} \times 96,000$	8,000	
	1.5.89 – 5.4.90	$\frac{11}{12} \times 36,000$	33,000	
				41,000
1988/89	6.4.88 – 30.4.88	$\frac{1}{12} \times 48,000$	4,000	
	1.5.88–5.4.89	$\frac{11}{12} \times 96,000$	88,000	
				92,000
				£133,000

Note

(a) The Inland Revenue would assess A on profits of £41,000 for 1989/90 and on £92,000 for 1988/89 as these figures are greater in total than the profits originally assessed for these years.

19.4 PROFIT COMPUTATIONS

A UK trader commences trading on 1.10.89. His profit and loss account for the year to 30.9.90 is

	£	£
Sales		110,000
Deduct Purchases	75,000	
Less Stock and work in progress at 30.9.90	15,000	
		60,000
Gross profit		50,000
Deduct		
Salaries (all paid by 30.6.91)	15,600	
Rent and rates	2,400	
Telephone	500	
Heat and light	650	
Depreciation	1,000	
Motor expenses	2,700	
Entertainment	600	
Bank interest	900	
Hire-purchase interest	250	
Repairs and renewals	1,000	
Accountant's fee	500	
Bad debts	200	
Sundries	700	
		27,000
Net profit		23,000
Gain on sale of fixed asset		300
Rent received		500
Bank interest received (net)		150
Profit		£23,950

Further Information

(i) Rent and rates. £200 of the rates bill relates to the period from 1.6.89 to 30.9.89.

(ii) Telephone. Telephone bills for the trader's private telephone total £150. It is estimated that 40% of these calls are for business purposes.

(iii) Motor expenses. All the motor expenses are in respect of the proprietor's car. 40% of the annual mileage relates to private use and home to business use.

(iv) Entertainment		£
	Staff	100
	UK customers	450
	Overseas customers	50
		£600

(v) Hire-purchase interest. This is in respect of the owner's car.

(vi) Repairs and renewals. There is an improvement element of 20% included.

(vii) Bad debts. This is a specific write-off.

(viii) Sundries. Included is £250 being the cost of obtaining a bank loan to finance business expenditure and £200 for agent's fees in obtaining a patent for trading purposes.

(ix)   Other. The proprietor obtained goods for his own use from the business costing £400 (retail value £500) without payment.

Schedule D, Case I Computation Year to 30.9.90

	£	£
Profit per the accounts		23,950
Add		
Repairs — improvement element		200
Hire-purchase interest (40% private)		100
Entertainment note (*e*)		500
Motor expenses (40% private)		1,080
Depreciation		1,000
Telephone (60% × £150)		90
Rates (pre-trading expenditure) note (*d*)		200
Goods for own use		500
		27,620
Deduct		
Bank interest received — Taxed income	150	
Rent received — Schedule A	500	
Gain on sale of fixed asset	300	
		950
Schedule D, Case I adjusted profit		£26,670
Schedule D, Case I loss 1989/90 note (*d*)		£200

Notes

(*a*)   Costs of obtaining loan finance are specifically allowable. [*ICTA 1988, s 77*].

(*b*)   The trader would be entitled to capital allowances but these are not deductions in arriving at the adjusted Schedule D, Case I profit.

(*c*)   The adjusted profit of £26,670 would be subject to the commencement provisions for assessment purposes.

(*d*)   Pre-trading expenses are allowed as a separate loss of the year of assessment in which trade is commenced if they are incurred within five years of the commencement (three years where trade commenced before 1 April 1989) and would have been allowable if incurred after commencement. [*ICTA 1988, s 401; FA 1989, s 114*].

(*e*)   Expenditure incurred after 14 March 1988 on the entertaining of overseas customers is not an allowable deduction. Thus all entertainment expenses, other than staff entertaining, are non-deductible. [*FA 1988, s 72*].

(*f*)   See note (*a*) to 118.1 PROFIT COMPUTATIONS in the corporation tax section as regards deductibility of wages and salaries. This applies equally to individuals and partnerships as it does to companies. [*FA 1989, s 43*].

(*g*)   50% of the Class 4 national insurance contributions paid by a self-employed individual in respect of a year of assessment is allowed as a deduction from total income in that year. See example at 1.3 ALLOWANCES AND TAX RATES above.

19.5 FARMING AND MARKET GARDENING — AVERAGING [*ICTA 1988, s 96*]

A, who has been farming for several years, earns the following profits as adjusted for Schedule D, Case I (i.e. before capital allowances and stock relief)

Year ended	Schedule D, Case I Profit/(loss) £
30.9.87	20,000
30.9.88	14,000
30.9.89	(5,000)
30.9.90	12,000

Averaged profits for all years would be

		No averaging claims £	Averaging claims for all years £
1988/89	note (*a*)	20,000	17,000
1989/90 (after *ICTA 1988, s 380* loss claim)	note (*b*)	9,000	3,500
1990/91	note (*c*)	Nil	10,000
1991/92		12,000	10,500
		£41,000	£41,000

Notes

(*a*)

1988/89	20,000
1989/90	14,000
	£34,000 ÷ 2 = £17,000

As £14,000 does not exceed $\frac{7}{10}$ × £20,000, the straight average applies.

(*b*)

1989/90	17,000
1990/91	Nil
	£17,000 ÷ 2 = £8,500 (less loss relief of £5,000)

(*c*)

1990/91	8,500
1991/92	12,000
	£20,500

As £8,500 exceeds $\frac{7}{10}$ of £12,000 but does not exceed $\frac{3}{4}$, the adjustment is computed as follows

Difference £3,500 × 3	10,500	
Deduct $\frac{3}{4}$ × £12,000	9,000	
Adjustment	1,500	1,500
Existing 1990/91	8,500	
Existing 1991/92		12,000
	£10,000	£10,500

19.6   ASSESSABLE PROFITS, ALLOWABLE DEDUCTIONS

(A) Stock in trade and work in progress

CD is a long-established partnership engaged in manufacturing and makes up its accounts to 30 April. Its profit and loss account for the year ended 30 April 1990 can be summarised as follows

	£	£
Turnover		1,200,000
Opening stock and work in progress	300,000	
Allowable expenditure	1,000,000	
Non-allowable expenditure	100,000	
	1,400,000	
Closing stock and work in progress	400,000	
		1,000,000
Net profit		£200,000

CD is entitled to capital allowances of £30,000 for 1991/92.

During the year ended 30 April 1990, CD decided to change its basis of valuing stock and work in progress (by excluding certain overheads previously included). In the accounts, both opening and closing stock is valued on the new basis, but in the accounts to 30 April 1989, closing stock and work in progress (valued on the old basis) was included at a figure of £350,000. Both bases of valuation are accepted by the Inland Revenue as valid bases for tax purposes.

CD's Schedule D, Case I computation for 1991/92 is as follows

	£
Net profit per accounts	200,000
Add non-allowable expenditure	100,000
	300,000
Deduct difference between closing stock figure at 30.4.89 and opening stock figure at 1.5.89	50,000
Schedule D, Case I	250,000
Less capital allowances	30,000
Taxable profit	£220,000

Notes

(*a*)   When a change is made from one valid basis of valuation to another, the opening stock figure must for tax purposes be the same as the closing stock figure for the previous year. (Revenue Statement of Practice SP 3/90).

(*b*)   The above practice applies for periods of account ending after 9 January 1990, although the Revenue are prepared to apply it to open years based on accounts for periods ended before 10 January 1990 where, as in this example, the change in basis results in a lower opening valuation.

(B) Waste disposal — site preparation expenditure [*ICTA 1988, s 91B; FA 1990, s 78*]

B, who prepares accounts to 31 May, carries out waste disposal activities in the course of his trade. He holds a relevant licence as defined by *ICTA 1988, s 91A(6)* and for the years ended 31 May 1989 and 1990 makes a claim under *section 91B* for relief for site preparation expenditure incurred in respect of site A. None of the expenditure in question has previously qualified for tax relief, either as an allowable deduction or as capital expenditure qualifying for capital allowances. Relevant information is as follows

Expenditure
Pre 6.4.89	£80,000
6.4.89 – 31.5.89	£10,000
Y/e 31.5.90	Nil

Volume of waste (in cubic metres)
deposited on site
Pre 6.4.89	200,000
6.4.89 – 31.5.89	10,000
Y/e 31.5.90	79,000

Unused capacity of site (in cubic metres)
Immediately before 6.4.89	800,000
At 31.5.89	790,000
At 31.5.90	711,000

The amount allowable as a deduction against taxable profits is calculated as follows

Y/e 31.5.89
Total site preparation expenditure incurred before and during the period = £90,000. As part of this was incurred before 6.4.89, it is reduced by an amount calculated as follows

$$£80,000 \times \frac{200,000}{200,000 + 800,000} = \qquad £16,000$$

$$£90,000 - £16,000 = \qquad\qquad £74,000$$

Allowable amount

$$£74,000 \times \frac{10,000}{10,000 + 790,000} = \qquad \underline{£925}$$

Y/e 31.5.90
Total site preparation expenditure incurred before and during the period = £90,000, reduced as above to £74,000.

Allowable amount

$$(£74,000 - £925) \times \frac{79,000}{79,000 + 711,000} = \qquad \underline{£7,308}$$

Notes

(*a*)   The relief under *ICTA 1988, s 91B* applies for periods of account ending after 5 April 1989, but the formulae laid down by that section and used above effectively exclude pre-6 April 1989 expenditure to the extent that it relates to used capacity at that date.

(*b*)   Although not illustrated in this example, relief is also available for site restoration payments. [*ICTA 1988, s 91A; FA 1990, s 78*].

20   Schedule D, Case III

20.1   **BASIS OF ASSESSMENT** [*ICTA 1988, ss 18(2)–(4), 64, 66, 67, 479–482*]

A is credited with the following interest during the five years to 5 April 1991

Year to 5 April	1987	1988	1989	1990	1991
	£	£	£	£	£
Bank deposit account (net)	98	146	162	141	150
National Savings Bank (NSB)					
(ordinary account)	35	45	60	85	75
NSB investment account	—	50	110	90	85
£4,285 3½% War Loan	150	150	150	75	—
Deposit receipt interest					
(Scottish bank)	70	50	65	75	90
Loan interest received gross	75	80	80	95	95

The NSB investment account was opened in July 1987. All other sources had been in existence for many years. The NSB ordinary account was closed in November 1990 and the holding of War Loan was sold on 2 June 1989. The deposit receipt interest arose on a deposit made on 1 March 1984 treated as a qualifying time deposit.

A's Schedule D, Case III assessments for the four years 1987/88 to 1990/91 are

	1987/88	1988/89	1989/90	1990/91
	£	£	£	£
Bank deposit account	—	—	—	—
NSB ordinary account				
(less £70 exempt)	—	—	15 (CY)	5 (CY)
NSB investment account	50 (CY)	110 (CY)	90 (CY)	90 (PY)
£4,285 3½% War Loan	150 (PY)	150 (PY)	75 (CY)	—
Deposit receipt interest	50 (CY)	65 (CY)	75 (CY)	90 (CY)
Loan interest	75 (PY)	80 (PY)	80 (PY)	95 (PY)
	£325	£405	£335	£280

A will also be assessed to higher rate tax, if applicable, on bank deposit interest as follows

1987/88	1988/89	1989/90	1990/91
£200	£216	£188	£200

Notes

(a)   Under the composite rate scheme, the bank deposit interest is treated as income received net of basic rate tax. It is grossed up for higher rate assessment purposes.

(b)   Since the NSB ordinary account was closed in 1990/91, that year will be on the actual basis and the Revenue will also revise the penultimate year to actual since that figure is greater than the previous year's.

(c)   A will elect to have the NSB investment account interest for the year ended 5 April 1990, i.e. the third year in which income arose, assessed on an actual basis since that figure is lower than the previous year's.

(d) The deposit receipt interest is assessed on the actual basis as there is a new source each time such interest arises. As the interest arose from a deposit made before 6 July 1984 it is paid gross. [*ICTA 1988, s 482(9)*].

(e) The composite rate scheme will no longer apply after 5 April 1991. [*FA 1990, 5 Sch*].

20.2 **DEEP DISCOUNT SECURITIES** [*ICTA 1988, s 57, 4 Sch; FA 1989, s 93, 10 Sch; FA 1990, s 59, 10 Sch 26*]

(A)
Mr Knight subscribed for £10,000 of 3% loan stock 1996 issued by DDS plc on 1 July 1985 at a price of £55 for £100 stock. The interest is payable annually on 30 June until redemption on 30 June 1996. The securities are qualifying corporate bonds.

The yield to maturity of this stock is 9.9% and on each £100 loan stock certificate, the following figures appear as the income element for each income period.

Income period	Income element
	£
1.7.85 – 30.6.86	2.44
1.7.86 – 30.6.87	2.68
1.7.87 – 30.6.88	2.95
1.7.88 – 30.6.89	3.24
1.7.89 – 30.6.90	3.56
1.7.90 – 30.6.91	3.91
1.7.91 – 30.6.92	4.30
1.7.92 – 30.6.93	4.73
1.7.93 – 30.6.94	5.20
1.7.94 – 30.6.95	5.71
1.7.95 – 30.6.96	6.28
	£45.00

Mr Knight sold his holding on 19 December 1990 for £8,150.

His 1990/91 Schedule D, Case III assessment is as follows

	£	£
Interest received (£300 taxed at source)		—
Aggregate of income elements		
Complete income periods		
1.7.85 – 30.6.86	244	
1.7.86 – 30.6.87	268	
1.7.87 – 30.6.88	295	
1.7.88 – 30.6.89	324	
1.7.89 – 30.6.90	356	
	1,487	

Part income period (1.7.90 – 19.12.90)

	£	£
$\dfrac{172\ \text{days}}{365\ \text{days}} \times £391$	184	1,671
Schedule D, Case III assessment		£1,671

IT 20.2 Schedule D, Case III

Notes

(a) The disposal has no capital gains tax consequences as gains arising on disposals of qualifying corporate bonds after 1 July 1986 are exempt from capital gains tax. There will, however, be a Schedule D, Case VI charge under the accrued income scheme. See 22.3 SCHEDULE D, CASE VI below for method of calculation.

(b) The income element is calculated as follows

First income period
$$\frac{55 \text{ (issue price)} \times 9.9 \text{ (yield to maturity)}}{100} - 3 \text{ (actual interest)} = £2.44$$

Second income period
$$\frac{[55 + 2.44 \text{ (previous income elements)}] \times 9.9}{100} - 3 \qquad = £2.68$$

and so on.

(B)

Mrs Day purchased £15,000 of DDS plc loan stock (see (A) above) on 31 May 1989 for £8,550 ex div and sells her holding on 30 April 1990 for £8,600 cum div.

Her 1990/91 Schedule D, Case III assessment is as follows

	£	£
Interest received		—
Aggregate of income elements		
Part income period (31.5.89 – 30.6.89)		
$\dfrac{31 \text{ days}}{365 \text{ days}} \times £486$	41	
Part income period (1.7.89 – 30.4.90)		
$\dfrac{304 \text{ days}}{365 \text{ days}} \times £534$	445	486
Schedule D, Case III assessment		£486

Notes

(a) The income element for the period 1.7.88 to 30.6.89 is
$3.24 \times 150 = £486$
The income element for the period 1.7.89 to 30.6.90 is
$3.56 \times 150 = £534$

(b) There will also be Schedule D, Case VI consequences under the accrued income scheme. See 22.3 SCHEDULE D, CASE VI below for details.

20.3 **DEEP GAIN SECURITIES** [*FA 1989, s 94, 11 Sch; FA 1990, s 57, 10 Sch 27*]

Mr Noone subscribed for £10,000 of 7% loan stock 2006/2008 issued by DGS plc on 1 February 1989 at a price of £90 for £100 stock. Interest is payable annually on 31 January. The redemption price will be 100 and the redemption date will fall on 31 January in either 2007, 2008 or 2009, variable at the company's option. The security satisfies the first and second conditions prescribed by *FA 1989, 11 Sch 1*.

Mr Noone sold his holding on 30 June 1990 for £10,100 and incurs costs of sale amounting to £100.

The security is a deep gain security because

the discount, being not more than 15%, *may* nevertheless exceed $\frac{1}{2}$% per annum. If, for example, the redemption date is 31.1.2007, the excess will be 1% (10% − (18 × $\frac{1}{2}$%)). The amount payable on redemption *might* therefore constitute a deep gain, even though it would not if redemption were to be deferred until 2009. [*FA 1989, 11 Sch 1*].

Mr Noone's tax position for 1990/91 on the disposal is

	£	£
Transfer price		10,100
Less acquisition cost		9,000
		1,100
Deduct costs of transfer	100	
costs of acquisition	—	100
Schedule D, Case III assessment		£1,000

Notes

(a) The charge under Schedule D, Case III arises on transfers of deep gain securities after 13 March 1989, regardless of the date of acquisition. [*FA 1989, 11 Sch 5*].

(b) A deep gain security is also a qualifying corporate bond and thus no chargeable gain or allowable loss arises on disposal. [*FA 1984, s 64(3A)(5A); FA 1989, s 139(3)(4)*].

(c) The transfer of a deep gain security giving rise to a charge under *FA 1989, 11 Sch 5* is exempt from the accrued income scheme, thus preventing a double income tax charge on accrued income. [*FA 1989, 11 Sch 17*].

21   Schedule D, Cases IV and V

[*ICTA 1988, ss 18(2)–(4), 65–67*]

21.1   BASIS OF ASSESSMENT

(A)

In July 1985 S inherited shares in X (US) Inc., a company resident in the United States. S is resident, ordinarily resident and domiciled in the UK and pays income tax at the basic rate only. The dividends which arose and tax deducted therefrom were as follows (dividends arising on or after 1 October 1990 had UK tax deducted by a UK paying agent)

	Gross	Foreign tax at 15%	UK tax (at basic rate less foreign tax)
	£	£	£
1985/86	120	18.00	—
1986/87	180	27.00	—
1987/88	190	28.50	—
1988/89	175	26.25	—
1989/90	240	36.00	—
Period 6.4.90 – 30.9.90	135	20.25	—
		£156.00	
Period 1.10.90 – 5.4.91	145	21.75	14.50

S's assessments are as follows

	£	£
1985/86 (actual)	£120	
Tax thereon at 30%	36.00	
Deduct Tax credit relief	18.00	18.00
UK tax payable	£18.00	
1986/87 (actual)	£180	
Tax thereon at 29%	52.20	
Deduct Tax credit relief	27.00	27.00
UK tax payable	£25.20	
1987/88 (preceding year)	£180	
Tax thereon at 27%	48.60	
Deduct Tax credit relief	27.00	27.00
UK tax payable	£21.60	
1988/89 (preceding year)	£190	
Tax thereon at 25%	47.50	
Deduct Tax credit relief	28.50	28.50
UK tax payable	£19.00	
		c/f £100.50

	£	£
		b/f 100.50
1989/90 (actual)	£240	
Tax thereon at 25%	60.00	
Deduct Tax credit relief	36.00	36.00
UK tax payable	£24.00	
1990/91 (period 6.4.90 to 30.9.90)	£135	
Tax thereon at 25%	33.75	
Deduct Tax credit relief	20.25	20.25
UK tax payable	£13.50	
Total tax credit relief		£156.75

Notes

(*a*) S would choose to have the assessment for 1987/88 assessed under the preceding year basis since the income for 1986/87 is lower than that for 1987/88. [*ICTA 1988, s 66(1)(c)*].

(*b*) The effect of having UK tax deducted from 1.10.90 onwards is to have a cessation of the Case V source at 30.9.90. [*ICTA 1988, s 67(3)*]. The Inland Revenue would then invoke *section 67(1)(b)* to have the assessment for 1989/90 (the penultimate year) adjusted to an actual basis as the income for 1989/90 is higher than that for 1988/89. The assessment for the final period is on an actual basis.

(*c*) *ICTA 1988, s 804(5)* provides that, as a result of a cessation, the total tax credit relief given for all years cannot exceed the total foreign tax suffered. In this example, the excess is only £0.75 but where material amounts are involved the Inland Revenue will raise an assessment under Sch D, Case VI to recover the excess relief.

(*d*) The income of £145 for the period 1.10.90–5.4.91 would normally be assessed for 1990/91 as foreign dividends. However, no assessment need be raised as S is not liable to higher rate tax and the income has effectively suffered basic rate tax at source.

IT 21.1   Schedule D, Cases IV and V

(B) Remittance basis

F is resident and ordinarily resident in the UK but is domiciled in Ruritania. Investment income has arisen in Ruritania for several years and has been paid into a Ruritanian bank current account which also contains capital receipts. On 1.10.90, F drew a cheque for £1,000 on this account for the purpose of settling a debt incurred in the UK. The sterling equivalent balance of the account on that date was £3,000 comprising income receipts of £2,000 and others of £1,000.

The income arising in Ruritania in recent years has been

	£
1987/88	270
1988/89	310
1989/90	380
1990/91	360

F will be assessed as follows

1990/91 (CY basis)	£1,000

Notes

(a) As F is non-domiciled in the UK, he will be assessed on the remittance basis. [*ICTA 1988, ss 65(5), 66(6)*]. The income is assessed in 1990/91 as it is first remitted in that year and is therefore treated as a new source of income.

(b) By drawing a cheque for £1,000 to settle a UK debt, F will have made a 'constructive remittance' of income to the UK. The Ruritanian current account comprises income and capital and if F cannot clearly demonstrate that the £1,000 emanates from a capital source, the Inland Revenue will seek to treat the £1,000 wholly as income since the revenue balance on the account exceeds this sum. To avoid this, F could maintain separate accounts for revenue and capital so that remittances can be clearly identified. To the extent that capital remittances arise from foreign capital gains, these will be chargeable to UK capital gains tax under *CGTA 1979, s 14* but F will be entitled to the annual exemption if this is not fully covered by UK gains.

(c) Double taxation relief may be available under a treaty. If not, F could claim relief unilaterally to reduce the UK tax liability by the amount of any Ruritanian tax paid, but not so as to obtain a refund.

22   Schedule D, Case VI

Cross-reference. See also 13.2 OVERSEAS MATTERS for Schedule D, Case VI charge on gains on offshore funds.

22.1   FURNISHED LETTINGS [*ICTA 1988, ss 18(2)–(4), 69*]

Mrs A inherited a furnished cottage in a picturesque coastal village and she and her husband decided to spend their own holiday there during the month of July and to make the cottage available for letting to other holidaymakers during the remainder of the year. The rent charged was £400 per month from June to September inclusive and £250 per month for the remainder of the year. Mrs A has no other income. During 1990/91 the house was occupied from April until October, lay vacant during November, December and January and was let again for February and March.

Several lettings were for periods of more than 31 days.

Expenses were as follows

Standard community charge £480, Electricity £420 (£400 received from tenants through coin operated meters), Advertising £100, Cleaning between lettings £180, House contents insurance £72, Repairs £120.

Mrs A is not assessed under Case I as the letting does not constitute a trade. The cottage does not qualify for relief as 'furnished holiday accommodation' under *ICTA 1988, ss 503, 504* because of the length of the letting periods.

Case VI income	£	£
Rent received		2,450
Standard community charge $\frac{11}{12} \times 480$	440	
Electricity $(\frac{11}{12} \times 420) - 400$	(15)	
Advertising	100	
Cleaning $\frac{8}{9} \times 180$	160	
Insurance $\frac{11}{12} \times 72$	66	
Repairs $\frac{11}{12} \times 120$	110	
Depreciation 10% of £2,450 note (*a*)	245	
	—	1,106
		£1,344

Notes

(*a*)   Before the introduction of the community charge (on 1 April 1990 in England and Wales), general rates were deductible from rent received in arriving at the figure on which 10% depreciation is based. The Revenue have given no guidance on the subject but it is considered that this should not apply in the case of the standard community charge which is clearly the liability of the landlord and not the tenant.

(*b*)   As the rent is less than £10,000, it will be sufficient to submit to the Revenue only the following figures

	£
Rent received	2,450
Expenses	1,106
Net income	£1,344

The detailed accounts will still have to be prepared in order to arrive at the above summary.

(Revenue Press Release 7 November 1989).

22.2 **FURNISHED HOLIDAY ACCOMMODATION** [*ICTA 1988, ss 503, 504*]

Mr B owns and lets out furnished holiday cottages. None is ever let to the same person for more than 31 days. Three cottages have been owned for many years but Rose Cottage was acquired on 1 June 1990 (and first let on that day) while Ivy Cottage was sold on 30 June 1990 (and last let on that day).

In 1990/91 days available for letting and days let are as follows

	Days available	Days let
Honeysuckle Cottage	180	160
Primrose Cottage	130	100
Bluebell Cottage	150	60
Rose Cottage	150	60
Ivy Cottage	30	5

Additional information

Rose Cottage was let for 30 days between 6 April and 31 May 1991.
Ivy Cottage was let for 50 days in the period 1 July 1989 to 5 April 1990 but was available for letting for 110 days in that period.

Qualification as 'furnished holiday accommodation'

Honeysuckle Cottage qualifies as it meets both the 140-day availability test and the 70-day letting test.

Primrose Cottage does *not* qualify although it is let for more than 70 days as it fails to satisfy the 140-day test. Averaging (see below) is only possible where it is the 70-day test which is not satisfied.

Bluebell Cottage does not qualify by itself as it fails the 70-day test. However it may be included in an averaging claim.

Rose Cottage qualifies as furnished holiday accommodation. It was acquired on 1 June 1990 so qualification in 1990/91 is determined by reference to the period of twelve months beginning on the day it was first let, in which it was let for a total of 90 days.

Ivy Cottage was sold on 30 June 1990 so qualification is determined by reference to the period from 1 July 1989 to 30 June 1990 (the last day of letting). It does not qualify by itself as it was let for only 55 days in this period but it may be included in an averaging claim.

Averaging claim for 1990/91

	Days let
Honeysuckle Cottage	160
Bluebell Cottage	60
Rose Cottage	90
Ivy Cottage	55

$$\frac{160 + 60 + 60 + 5}{4} = 71.25 \text{ days} \quad \text{note } (b)$$

Notes

(*a*) Income from the commercial letting of furnished holiday accommodation is treated as trading income for most purposes. In addition, capital gains tax rollover relief, retirement relief and relief for gifts of business assets are also available. See 208 HOLD-OVER RELIEFS, 220 RETIREMENT RELIEF, 221 ROLLOVER RELIEF in the Capital Gains Tax section for these reliefs.

(*b*)   All four cottages included in the averaging claim qualify as furnished holiday accommodation as each is deemed to have been let for 71.25 days in the year 1990/91. If the average had been less than 70, any three of these cottages could have been included in an averaging claim leaving the other as non-qualifying. If this still did not produce the desired result, an average of any two could be tried. More than one averaging claim is possible for a year of assessment, but no cottage may be included in more than one claim.

(*c*)   Although Rose Cottage and Ivy Cottage can be included in the averaging claim, the number of days so included is restricted, on a strict interpretation of the legislation, to the days let during the year of assessment.

22.3   BONDWASHING — ACCRUED INCOME SCHEME [*ICTA 1988, ss 710–728*]

The following transactions take place during the year ended 5 April 1991

Settlement day	Sale by	Purchase by	Securities
15.6.90	X (cum div)	Y	£2,000 15% Exchequer 1997
31.12.90	X (ex div)	P	£3,000 12¾% Treasury Loan 1992
15.1.91	S (cum div)	Y	£1,000 9½% Conversion 2004

Interest payment days are as follows

15% Exchequer 1997	27 April, 27 October
12¾% Treasury Loan 1992	22 January, 22 July
9½% Conversion 2004	25 April, 25 October

Both X and Y owned chargeable securities with a nominal value in excess of £5,000 at some time in either 1989/90 or 1990/91, and both are resident and ordinarily resident in the UK. P is not resident and not ordinarily resident in the UK. The maximum value of securities held by S at any time in 1990/91 and 1991/92 is £4,000.

15.6.90 transaction
The transaction occurs in the interest period from 28.4.90 to 27.10.90 (inclusive)

Number of days in interest period	183
Number of days in interest period to 15.6.90	49
Interest payable on 27.10.90	£150

The accrued amount is

$$£150 \times \frac{49}{183} = £40$$

X is treated as receiving income (chargeable under Schedule D, Case VI) of £40 on 27.10.90.
Y is given credit for £40 against the interest of £150 he receives on 27.10.90. £110 remains taxable.

31.12.90 transaction

The transaction occurs in the interest period from 23.7.90 to 22.1.91 (inclusive)

Number of days in interest period	184
Number of days in interest period to 31.12.90	162
Interest payable on 22.1.91	£191

The rebate amount is

$$£191 \times \frac{184 - 162}{184} = \underline{£23}$$

X is given credit for £23 against the interest of £191 he receives on 22.1.91. £168 remains taxable.

P is not assessed on any notional income as he is neither resident nor ordinarily resident in the UK.

15.1.91 transaction

The transaction occurs in the interest period from 26.10.90 to 25.4.91 (inclusive)

Number of days in interest period	182
Number of days in interest period to 15.1.91	82
Interest payable on 25.4.91	£47

The accrued amount is

$$£47 \times \frac{82}{182} = \underline{£21}$$

S is not assessed on any notional income. He is not within the accrued income scheme provisions as his holdings do not exceed £5,000 at any time in 1990/91 or 1991/92.

Y is given credit for £21 against the interest of £47 he receives on 25.4.91. £26 remains taxable.

Note

(a)   An adjustment is made to the consideration in the transferor's capital gains tax computations to exclude the accrued amount or add the rebate amount. The sums allowed to the transferee on a future disposal are correspondingly adjusted. [*CGTA 1979, s 33A*].

23   Schedule E — Emoluments

23.1   **BASIC PRINCIPLES — ASSESSMENT** [*ICTA 1988, ss 19, 202A, 202B, 203; FA 1989, ss 36–42, 45*]

(A) Receipts basis after 5 April 1989

Smith has been a director of X Ltd for many years, receiving a salary and bonus assessable on the accounts year basis (see (B) below). The accounts for the four years to 30 September 1991 show the following

Year ended	Salary	Bonus	Total	Date bonus paid
	£	£	£	
30.9.88	20,000	8,000	28,000	March 1989
30.9.89	22,000	10,000	32,000	February 1990
30.9.90	26,000	12,000	38,000	May 1991
30.9.91	28,000	13,000	41,000	March 1992

Smith's monthly salary, paid at the end of the month, was always $\frac{1}{12}$ of his salary for the period of account concerned.

The assessments for 1988/89 to 1990/91 are as follows

1988/89

	£
Salary (year ended 30.9.88)	20,000
Bonus (year ended 30.9.88)	8,000
Schedule E assessment	£28,000

1989/90

	£
Salary (6.4.89 – 30.9.89)	11,000
Salary (1.10.89 – 5.4.90)	13,000
Bonus (received February 1990)	10,000
Schedule E assessment	£34,000

1990/91

	£
Salary (6.4.90 – 30.9.90)	13,000
Salary (1.10.90 – 5.4.91)	14,000
Schedule E assessment	£27,000

Notes

(*a*)   The receipts basis of assessment was introduced by *FA 1989, ss 36–45* with effect for 1989/90 and subsequent years. See (B), (C) below as regards transitional provisions preventing a double charge to tax in certain circumstances, and (D) below for further transitional provisions.

(*b*)   Note that Smith's salary of £11,000 received in the period 1.10.88 to 5.4.89 escapes assessment. It was received after the end of the period of account ended within 1988/89, so is not assessed on the accounts basis for 1988/89, and before 6.4.89, so escaping assessment on the receipts basis. There are no transitional provisions to correct this.

(c)   In 1991/92, Smith will be assessed on the bonuses paid in both May 1991 and March 1992 as he received both bonuses in that tax year.

(d)   See *ICTA 1988, s 202B* introduced by *FA 1989, s 37(1)* for rules determining the point at which emoluments are to be treated as received for the purpose of applying the receipts basis.

(B) Accounts year basis and earnings basis before 6 April 1989
Smith in (A) above received a salary of £18,000 in the year to 30 September 1987 and a bonus of £6,000 relating to that period of account and paid in late April 1988.

On the accounts basis, his assessments for 1987/88 and 1988/89 are as follows

1987/88

	£
Salary and bonus (year ended 30.9.87)	24,000
Schedule E assessment	£24,000

1988/89

	£
Schedule E assessment (as in (A) above)	£28,000

The 1989/90 assessment is as in (A) above, i.e. £34,000.

If Smith were assessed on the statutory earnings basis, his assessments would be as follows

1987/88

	£
Salary and bonus (6.4.87 – 30.9.87) (£24,000 × $\frac{6}{12}$)	12,000
Salary and bonus (1.10.87 – 5.4.88) (£28,000 × $\frac{6}{12}$)	14,000
Schedule E assessment	£26,000

1988/89

	£
Salary and bonus (6.4.88 – 30.9.88) (£28,000 × $\frac{6}{12}$)	14,000
Salary and bonus (1.10.88 – 5.4.89) (£32,000 × $\frac{6}{12}$)	16,000
	30,000
Deduct emoluments for 1988/89 unpaid at 5.4.89 note (a)	5,000
Schedule E assessment	£25,000

The 1989/90 assessment will again be as in (A) above, i.e. £34,000.

Notes
(a)   Transitional provisions operate to prevent emoluments being taxed more than once on the changeover to the receipts basis. See also (C) below. [*FA 1989, s 38*]. Smith's emoluments for 1988/89 include half the bonus of £10,000 for the year ended 30 September 1989 which was not paid until February 1990. The whole of that bonus is taxable in 1989/90 on the receipts basis and therefore, no part of it is taxed in an earlier year; thus, the £5,000 is removed

from the 1988/89 assessment. An adjustment might also have been required in respect of Smith's salary if it had not remained constant throughout the period of account straddling 6 April 1989. The relief is not given automatically, but requires a claim to be submitted by 5 April 1991.

(b)   Smith would not be able to claim the transitional relief if, having been assessable on the accounts year basis for 1987/88, he switched to the earnings basis for 1988/89. His unpaid remuneration at 5 April 1989 would then be calculated as if the accounts year basis was still in force and would be nil. [*FA 1989, s 38(7)–(9)*].

(C) Transitional provisions [*FA 1989, s 38*]
The facts are as in (A) above, except that the bonus of £8,000 for the year ended 30 September 1988 was paid in May 1989, i.e. after 5 April 1989.

The assessments for 1988/89 and 1989/90 would be as follows

(i)   No claim for transitional relief under *FA 1989, s 38*

1988/89

Schedule E assessment as in (A) above	£28,000

1989/90

	£
Salary (6.4.89 – 5.4.90)	24,000
Bonus (received May 1989)	8,000
Bonus (received February 1990)	10,000
Schedule E assessment	£42,000

(ii)   Claim for transitional relief under *FA 1989, s 38*

1988/89

	£
Salary and bonus (year ended 30.9.88)	28,000
Deduct unpaid at 5.4.89	8,000
Schedule E assessment	£20,000

1989/90

Schedule E assessment	£42,000

Notes
(a)   The total assessable emoluments for the two years are the same (£62,000) as in (A) above, assuming the claim for transitional relief is made. If he fails to make the claim by 5 April 1991, Smith is doubly assessed on £8,000.

(b)   See also (B) above.

IT 23.1 Schedule E — Emoluments

(D) Transitional provisions [*FA 1989, s 40*]
The facts are as in (A) above, except that £6,000 of the £10,000 bonus for the year ended 30 September 1989 is paid in March 1989, i.e. before 6 April 1989.

The assessment for 1988/89 and 1989/90 are as follows

1988/89

Schedule E assessment as in (A) above	£28,000

1989/90

	£
Salary (6.4.89 – 5.4.90)	24,000
Bonus (received February 1990)	4,000
Bonus (deemed to be received on 6.4.89 – note (*a*))	1,000
Schedule E assessment	£29,000

Note

(*a*)   Emoluments for 1989/90 (or any subsequent year) received before 6 April 1989 are treated as if they were received on 6 April 1989 and thus assessed for 1989/90 on the receipts basis. [*FA 1989, s 40*]. In Smith's case, £5,000 ($\frac{6}{12}$) of the £10,000 bonus for the year ended 30 September 1989 represents emoluments for 1989/90 and of that amount, £1,000 (£6,000 − £5,000) was received by Smith before 6 April 1989. £5,000 (£6,000 − £1,000) representing emoluments for 1988/89 will escape assessment.

23.2 EARNINGS FROM WORK DONE ABROAD

(A) Calculation of 365-day qualifying period [*ICTA 1988, s 193(1), 12 Sch*]

F is sales director of G (UK) Ltd, a UK resident company. He also holds an executive position with H (US) Inc, a wholly owned American subsidiary company. F is resident, ordinarily resident and domiciled in the UK and his passport reveals the following information regarding his travels

Departed UK	D1	30.9.89
Returned UK	R1	23.12.89
Departed UK	D2	3.1.90
Returned UK	R2	31.5.90
Departed UK	D3	30.6.90
Returned UK	R3	18.12.90
Departed UK	D4	16.1.91
Returned UK	R4	31.3.91

The following steps must be considered

(i)   The period D1-R1 consists of 84 consecutive days of absence and will therefore be a qualifying period.

(ii)   The period D1-R2 must next be considered to establish if the period R1-D2 exceeds 62 days or if that period exceeds $\frac{1}{6}$th of the number of days in the period D1-R2. Period R1-D2 comprises 11 days; it is therefore not more than 62 days and not more than $\frac{1}{6}$th of 243 days and so D1-R2 becomes a qualifying period.

(iii)   The period D1-R3 is then examined on the same basis as the previous period. Period R2-D3 comprises 30 days; it is therefore not more than 62 days and since R1-D2 (11 days) and R2-D3 (30 days), or 41 days in total, are not more than $\frac{1}{6}$th of D1-R3 (444 days), D1-R3 becomes a qualifying period.

(iv)   The final period D1-R4 (547 days) is then examined. Period R3-D4 comprises 29 days; it is therefore not more than 62 days and since the previous 41 days (see (iii) above) and the 29 days (70 days in total) are not more than $\frac{1}{6}$th of 547 days, D1-R4 becomes a qualifying period.

The position can be summarised as follows

Days out of UK	Days in UK	Cumulative Total	$\frac{1}{6}$th Total	Cumulative Days in UK
(D1-R1) 84		84		
	(R1-D2) 11	95		
(D2-R2) 148		243	41	11
	(R2-D3) 30	273		
(D3-R3) 171		444	74	41
	(R3-D4) 29	473		
(D4-R4) 74		547	91	70
477	70			

Note

(*a*)   In determining if a qualifying period has arisen, the day of departure from and day of return to the UK are qualifying and non-qualifying days respectively.

(B)   Emoluments eligible for relief [*ICTA 1988, 12 Sch 2*]

F in (A) above has emoluments of £40,000 for 1990/91, comprising £10,000 from G (UK) Ltd and £30,000 from H (US) Inc.

A fair measure of remuneration for full-time duties for the 359 days of the qualifying period falling within 1990/91 would have been £20,000 for G (UK) Ltd and £35,000 for H (US) Inc.

His duties with H (US) Inc are carried out wholly abroad as are some two-thirds of his duties with G (UK) Ltd. He divides his time equally between his respective employments.

F may claim exemption on

	£
UK company	
$£10,000 \times \frac{2}{3} \times 100\% \times \dfrac{359}{365}$	6,557
Overseas company	
$£30,000 \times 100\% \times \dfrac{359}{365}$	29,507
	£36,064

Inland Revenue may propose exemption on

UK company	
$£20,000 \text{ p.a.} \times \frac{2}{3} \times 100\% \div 2$	6,667
Overseas company	
$£35,000 \text{ p.a.} \div 2$	17,500
	£24,167

Notes

(a)   Only 359 days in 1990/91 (6 April 1990 to 30 March 1991 inclusive) fall within the qualifying period of 547 days established in (A) above, hence the restriction to $\frac{359}{365}$ of total emoluments for 1990/91.

(b)   The existence of separate contracts with different employers may help in justifying the higher proportion.

(c)   The actual emoluments qualifying for the 100% deduction would be subject to negotiation and probably lie somewhere between these alternatives.

(C)   Travelling expenses [*ICTA 1988, s 194*]

M, a married man resident and ordinarily resident in the UK, is employed by Bigbuild Ltd in Milnrow at a salary of £20,000 per annum and is involved in the management of the following construction projects.

29.8.90 – 30.11.90	Office block in Philippines
9.12.90 – 15.1.91	Factory in Germany
19.3.91 – 27.6.91	Housing development in Spain

Details of travel expenses incurred in 1990/91 are

	By M £	Reimbursed By Bigbuild £	By Bigbuild £
28. 8.90 Milnrow – Heathrow Airport (M)	40		
29. 8.90 Heathrow – Philippines (M)			400
20.10.90 Milnrow – Philippines (wife and children)			1,000
30.10.90 Philippines – Milnrow (wife and children)			1,000
30.11.90 Philippines – Milnrow (M)	500	500	
9.12.90 Milnrow – Manchester Airport (M)	10	10	
9.12.90 Manchester – Germany (M)			100
10.12.90 Milnrow – Germany (wife and children)			300
3. 1.91 Germany – Milnrow (wife and children)	300	300	
15. 1.91 Germany – Milnrow (M)			100
19. 3.91 Milnrow – Spain (M)	150	150	
31. 3.91 Milnrow – Spain (wife)	60		150
	£1,060	£960	£3,050

M will be assessed as follows

	£	£
Salary		20,000
Cost of expenses incurred by Bigbuild		3,050
Reimbursed travel expenses		960
		24,010
Deduct Allowable part of expenses incurred by Bigbuild	2,750	
Allowable expenses incurred by M	700	
Personal allowance	3,005	
Married couple's allowance	1,720	
		8,175
Taxable		£15,835
Income Tax @ 25%		£3,958.75

Note

(*a*)   A deduction is allowed for travelling expenses of the employee from any place in the UK to take up the overseas employment. In addition where the employee is out of the UK for 60 days or more continuously, an allowance is available for up to two outward and two return trips per fiscal year for the employee's wife and minor children provided the expense is borne or reimbursed by the employer. As M is away for less than 60 days in Germany, he cannot deduct the cost of his family's Christmas and New Year trip. The part of the cost of his wife's trip to Spain not reimbursed cannot be deducted.

IT 23.3 Schedule E — Emoluments

23.3 **PROFIT-RELATED PAY** [*ICTA 1988, ss 169–184, 8 Sch; FA 1989, s 61, 4 Sch*]
(A) Distributable pool – Method A
C Ltd operates an approved profit-related pay scheme (registered after 2 February 1989) with effect from its accounting year ending 31 March 1991. The scheme contains provisions for determining the distributable pool (i.e. the aggregate sum which may be paid to employees in respect of a profit period) using method A as defined by *ICTA 1988, 8 Sch 13* as amended by *FA 1989, 4 Sch 10, 11*.
The distributable pool is to be 15% of profits, but profits in excess of 160% of (for the first profit period) £500,000 are to be disregarded. The latter figure is the amount of profits for the year ended 31 March 1989 which is chosen as the base year under *ICTA 1988, 8 Sch 13(6)* as amended.

Profits, as computed for profit-related pay purposes, amount to £900,000 and £1 million for the years ended 31 March 1991 and 1992.

For the profit period 1.4.90 to 31.3.91, the distributable pool is

£800,000 (restricted to £500,000 @ 160%) × 15% =   £120,000

For the profit period 1.4.91 to 31.3.92, the distributable pool is

£1,000,000 (being less than £900,000 × 160%) × 15% =   £150,000

Notes
(a)   The rules for calculating the distributable pool were amended by *FA 1989, 4 Sch 10–13*. Schemes registered after 2 February 1989 fall within the new rules (Revenue Press Release 3 February 1989). See the 1988/89 edition for an illustration of the rules previously applying.

(b)   In the second and subsequent profit periods, the 160% restriction is by reference to profits for the preceding period rather than the base year. [*ICTA 1988, 8 Sch 13(4)*].

(c)   The base year can be any twelve-month period ending within two years prior to the start of the first profit period, but the base year so chosen must be specified when registering the scheme.

(B)   Distributable pool – Method B
D Ltd operates an approved profit-related pay scheme with effect from its accounting year ending 31 March 1990 (registered after 2 February 1989). The distributable pool is to be calculated using method B as defined by *ICTA 1988, 8 Sch 14* as amended by *FA 1989, 4 Sch 10, 12, 13*. The notional pool is specified as £300,000. The scheme provides that for every 3% increase (or decrease) in annual profits the distributable pool will increase (or decrease) by 2%. The scheme also provides that if annual profits fall below £500,000, no profit-related pay will be payable and that if profits exceed 160% of those for the preceding 12-month period, such excess will be disregarded.

Profits for the five years ending 31 March 1989, 1990, 1991, 1992 and 1993 are, respectively, £1,000,000, £1,060,000, £490,000, £769,000 and £1,300,000.

The distributable pool is calculated as follows

Year ending 31 March 1990

Increase in profits over previous year $\dfrac{1,060,000 - 1,000,000}{1,000,000} \times 100 = 6\%$

Increase in notional pool	£300,000 × 6% × $\frac{2}{3}$	£12,000
Distributable pool		£312,000

Year ending 31 March 1991
There will be no distribution of profit-related pay as profits are less than the specified minimum. However, the distributable pool must still be computed. See note (*a*).

Decrease in profits over previous year		54%
Decrease in distributable pool	£312,000 × 54% × $\frac{2}{3}$	£112,320
Distributable pool		£199,680

Year ending 31 March 1992

Increase in profits over previous year		57%
Increase in distributable pool	£199,680 × 57% × $\frac{2}{3}$	£75,878
Distributable pool		£275,558

Year ending 31 March 1993

Increase in profits over previous year	note (*b*)	60%
Increase in distributable pool	£275,558 × 60% × $\frac{2}{3}$	£110,223
Distributable pool		£385,781

Notes
(*a*)   Where, in respect of any year, there is no distributable pool, the distributable pool for the following year is calculated as if such a pool *had* existed, and had been computed in the normal way, in the previous year. [*ICTA 1988, 8 Sch 14(6)*].

(*b*)   Although profits have increased by 69% in the year to 31 March 1993, the increase is restricted to 60% for the purpose of calculating the distributable pool, the company having taken advantage of *ICTA 1988, 8 Sch 14(4)*.

(*c*)   See also note (*a*) to (A) above.

(C)   Relief from tax [*ICTA 1988, s 171; FA 1989, 4 Sch 2*]
E is employed by C Ltd, the company in (A) above and receives, on 1 May 1991, profit-related pay of £4,200 for the year to 31 March 1991. His earnings received in the year to 31 March 1991, excluding profit-related pay, amounted to £16,600 and he was also provided with a company car on which both car and fuel benefits arise.

The amount of profit-related pay to be included in E's taxable emoluments for 1991/92 is as follows

	£	£
Amount received		4,200
Deduct tax-free amount, being the *least* of		
(i) one half of amount received	2,100	
(ii) 10% of £20,800 note (*a*)	2,080	
(iii) note (*b*)	2,000	
		2,000
Taxable profit-related pay		£2,200

Notes

(*a*)   The calculation in (ii) above is 10% of the aggregate of the profit-related pay in respect of the profit period and the employee's other 'pay' received in the profit period. *Pay* excludes benefits-in-kind arising under *ICTA 1988, Part V, Chapter II. [ICTA 1988, s 169].*

(*b*)   To the extent that profit-related pay exceeds £4,000 (£3,000 for profit periods beginning before 1 April 1989), the excess is not eligible for the exemption. Thus, the maximum exempt amount can never exceed £2,000.

(*c*)   The taxable profit-related pay is taxed for the year of assessment *in* which it is received (under the normal receipts basis rules — see 23.1 above).

23.4   ASSESSABLE INCOME, ALLOWABLE DEDUCTIONS — EMPLOYEE USING OWN CAR

(A) Fixed Profit Car Scheme (FPCS) [*ICTA 1988, ss 197B–197F; FA 1990, 4 Sch; Revenue Press Release 21 June 1990*]

D is employed as a buyer by CB Ltd and uses his own 1,600 cc car for business. CB Ltd operates the FPCS and pays its employees a standard mileage allowance (regardless of engine capacity) of 35 pence per business mile for 1989/90 and 1990/91, increasing to 38 pence for 1991/92 purely to reflect increased motoring costs. D's business mileage is 10,000, 11,200 and 12,000 for the years 1989/90, 1990/91 and 1991/92 respectively.

The amounts to be included in D's taxable emoluments for the years 1989/90 to 1991/92 are as follows

1989/90

	£
Mileage allowances received 10,000 × 35p	3,500
Tax-free rate 10,000 × 30p	3,000
Taxable amount	£500

1990/91

	£	£
Mileage allowances received 11,200 × 35p		3,920
Tax-free rates:		
First 4,000 business miles at 32p	1,280	
Balance of 7,200 miles at 12.5p	900	
		2,180
Taxable amount subject to transitional relief		£1,740

Under transitional provisions, the taxable amount can be restricted to:

$$£500 \times \frac{11,200}{10,000} = \quad\quad £560$$

1991/92

	£	£
Mileage allowances received 12,000 × 38p		4,560
Tax-free rates:		
First 4,000 business miles at 32p	1,280	
Balance of 8,000 miles at 12.5p	1,000	
		2,280
Taxable amount before transitional relief		£2,280

Under transitional provisions, the taxable amount can be restricted to:

$$£500 \times \frac{12,000}{10,000} = £600 + £1,000 = \quad\quad £1,600$$

Notes

(a)   Tax-free rates changed with effect from 6 April 1990, with a lower rate applying after the first 4,000 business miles (see Revenue Press Release 20 June 1990). Transitional provisions ensure that there is no increase in taxable mileage allowances in 1990/91 other than that attributable to increased mileage, and that subsequent increases are restricted to £1,000 per year.

(b)   The transitional provisions do not apply where the amount of the mileage allowance increases over the 1989/90 figure other than by reference to certain allowable factors (one of which is an increase in motoring costs). [*ICTA 1988, s 197E*].

(B) Capital allowances [*CAA 1990, ss 24, 27, 79; FA 1990, s 87*]
H is employed by QP Ltd and uses his own car for business trips. The car is not considered to be 'necessarily provided for use in the performance of the duties of the employment' as required by *CAA 1990, s 27(2)(a)* and thus no capital allowances could have been claimed for years before 1990/91. H claims allowances for 1990/91 and 1991/92, but does not claim for 1992/93, for which year his employer operates the Fixed Profit Car Scheme (see (A) above). H sells the car on 1 June 1993 for £1,250 and claims a balancing allowance for 1993/94. The open market value of the car at 6 April 1990 was £4,000. In 1990/91, H's business mileage is 25% of his total mileage and in 1991/92, it is 20%.

IT 23.4   Schedule E — Emoluments

H's capital allowances are as follows

	Car £	Total Allowances £
1990/91		
Open market value 6.4.90	4,000	
WDA 25%	1,000	1,000
WDV at 5.4.91	£3,000	
Less 75% private use		750
Allowances claimed		£250
1991/92		
WDV b/fwd	3,000	
WDA 25%	750	750
WDV at 5.4.92	£2,250	
Less 80% private use		600
Allowances claimed		£150
1992/93 (No allowances claimed)		
1993/94		
WDV b/fwd	2,250	
Sale proceeds	1,250	
Balancing allowance before adjustment	£1,000	£1,000
Appropriate fraction (see note (*d*)) 3/4		750
Reduced by private use proportion: Say 1,350/1,750 × £750 note (*c*)		579
Balancing allowance claimed		£171

Notes

(*a*)   Capital allowances can be claimed from 1990/91 onwards in respect of a car provided by an employee for use in the performance of his duties. Previously, allowances could only be claimed if the car was 'necessarily' provided (and this still applies as regards other machinery and plant).

(*b*)   Where the car would have qualified for allowances at the end of 1989/90 had it not been for the condition mentioned in (*a*) above, the car is deemed to have been acquired at open market value on 6 April 1990. [*FA 1990, s 87 (3)*].

(*c*)   Allowances are reduced to the extent that the car is used other than for business. [*CAA 1990, s 79*]. It is reduced to 'such extent as may be just and reasonable'. For writing-down allowances, the restriction is normally calculated by reference to private usage in the year concerned. The balancing allowance in the above example has been computed by reference to the average private usage restriction for the two years for which writing-down allowances were claimed, which is considered to be one way of producing a just and reasonable result, although alternative methods might be used.

(*d*)   The balancing allowance is the 'appropriate fraction' of the excess of qualifying expenditure over sale proceeds. The fraction is equal to the number of years for which an allowance is claimed over the number of years for which it could have been claimed. [*CAA 1990, s 24(2A)*]. It is assumed that both the numerator and denominator must include the year for which the balancing allowance is claimed, and that the appropriate fraction must be computed *before* the private use restriction in (*c*) above. There is no provision for a balancing charge to be reduced (other than by reference to private use).

23.5   **BENEFITS — EMPLOYEES EARNING £8,500 PER ANNUM OR MORE AND DIRECTORS**
Cars and petrol [*ICTA 1988, ss 157, 158, 6 Sch; FA 1990, s 22*]
(A)
J is Managing Director of K Ltd and during the year ended 5 April 1991 the company provided two cars for his use. Car 1 was a two-year old Jaguar (over 2,000 cc with original market value less than £19,251) and it was used by J for both business and private purposes until 31 October 1990 when it was written off as a result of an accident. J was subsequently prosecuted for dangerous driving, banned for one year and incurred legal costs of £800 which were ultimately paid for by K Ltd. In the period to 31 October 1990 Car 1 had travelled 10,000 miles on business, while J had paid the company £20 per month as a contribution towards private petrol. J was then provided with the use of a new 2-litre Sierra (Car 2) and, since at first he had injuries which prevented him from driving and later lost his licence, a chauffeur. This replacement car was to be used for business purposes only.

J's benefits for 1990/91 relating to the cars are

	£
Car 1	
Car benefit	3,550
Car fuel benefit	900
	£4,450
Proportion for period 6.4.90–31.10.90 ($\frac{209}{365}$ × £4,450)	2,548
Legal costs	800
Car 2	
Annual scale charge	—
Provision of chauffeur	—
	£3,348

Notes
(*a*)   The car and car fuel scale charges for Car 1 are reduced because the car was not available for use for part of the year. [*ICTA 1988, s 158(5), 6 Sch 2*].

(*b*)   In determining if business use was at an annual rate of 18,000 miles or more, the reduction in (*a*) above is applied to 18,000 i.e. 18,000 × $\frac{209}{365}$ = 10,307. [*ICTA 1988, s 158(5), 6 Sch 3(2)*].

(*c*)   Since J makes a contribution for private petrol as distinct from private use (i.e. towards road tax, insurance etc.), a reduction in the car scale charge under *ICTA 1988, 6 Sch 4* will not be available. As J is not *required* to make good the *whole* of the expense incurred by K Ltd in providing fuel for private use, his contributions do not reduce the fuel benefit. [*ICTA 1988, s 158(6)*].

IT 23.5 Schedule E — Emoluments

(d) The legal costs will be assessable as a benefit following *Rendell v Went H/L 1964, 41 TC 641*.

(e) Since Car 2 is not available for private use, no scale benefit will arise [*ICTA 1988, s 157*] and while an emolument in respect of the chauffeur's wages will arise under *ICTA 1988, s 155(1)* a claim under *ICTA 1988, s 198* will eliminate the liability.

(B)

L is a single person employed by K Ltd who, at 5 April 1990 earned a salary of £20,000 p.a. From 6 April 1990, K Ltd offered to increase this to £24,000 p.a., or, if L wished, to £21,000 plus the use of a new 1.6 litre Sierra (original market value under £19,250). It was open for L to terminate the car arrangement and to revert to an annual salary of £24,000. L opted to take the reduced salary and car, the expenses of which were directly borne by the company with the exception of petrol bills for £400 which were paid by L who was then reimbursed by K Ltd. L estimates that three-quarters of the petrol in question was consumed on business use.

L's liability for 1990/91 is	£
Salary	21,000
Car benefit	2,200
Car fuel benefit	600
	23,800
Deduct	
Personal allowance	3,005
Taxable	£20,795
Tax thereon	£5,213.00

Notes

(a) Following the case of *Heaton v Bell H/L 1969, 46 TC 211*, the Inland Revenue could assess L on remuneration of £24,000. If so, L would not be assessed on the scale benefit of £2,200 since the use of the car (money's worth value) would already have been taxed under general Schedule E principles.

(b) The car fuel benefit will include all private petrol regardless of whether it was supplied from a company pump or from a garage. [*ICTA 1988, s 158*].

(C) Assets given and leased [*ICTA 1988, s 156*]
During 1990/91 K Ltd transferred to J a television set which it had previously leased to him for a nominal rent of £2 per month. The company also leased a suit to J under the same arrangements.

Television
First leased to J in May 1989 (when its market value was £350); transferred to J in March 1991 for £50, the market value at that time being £125.

J's benefits are	£	£
1989/90		
Cost of benefit 20% × £350		70
Deduct Rent paid by J (11 months)		22
Cash equivalent of benefit		£48
1990/91		
Cost of benefit 20% × £350		70
Deduct Rent paid by J (12 Months)		24
Cash equivalent of benefit		46
Greater of		
(i) Market value at transfer	125	
Deduct Price paid by J	50	
	£75	
and		
(ii) Original market value	350	
Deduct Cost of Benefits	140	
-	210	
Deduct Price paid by J	50	
	£160	
		160
Total		£206

Suit
First leased to J in November 1990 (when its market value was £200).

J's benefit for 1990/91 is	
Cost of benefit 20% × £200	40
Deduct Rent paid by J (5 months)	10
Cash equivalent of benefit	£30

Notes
(a)   Although each asset was either leased to J or transferred to him during a fiscal year, he will be assessed on the full cost of the benefit for that year (as reduced by any rent paid). There is no time apportionment as in the case of cars made available for private use.

(b)   On the transfer of the television set, the cost of the benefits to date, not the cash equivalent, is deducted from the original market value. [*ICTA 1988, s 156(4)*].

(D) Beneficial loans [*ICTA 1988, ss 160, 161, 7 Sch*]

D, who is an employee of A Ltd earning £15,000 per annum, obtained a loan of £6,000 from the company on 10 October 1989 for the purpose of buying a car. Interest at 7% p.a. is charged on the outstanding balance while the principal is being repaid by instalments of £500 on 31 December and 30 June commencing 31 December 1989. The interest paid by D in 1989/90 amounted to £195 and, in 1990/91 to £350. The official rates of interest were:

15.5% after 5 July 1989 and before 6 November 1989
16.5% after 5 November 1989

It is assumed purely for the purposes of the example that the rate is reduced to 16% from 6 October 1990 and that there are no further changes before 5 April 1991.

D will be assessed in 1989/90 as follows

Normal method (averaging)		£
Average balance for period $\dfrac{£6,000 + £5,500}{2}$		£5,750
$£5,750 \times \frac{5}{12}$		£2,396
$£2,396$ at 15.5% $\times \frac{27}{178}$		56
$£2,396$ at 16.5% $\times \frac{151}{178}$		335
		391
Deduct Interest paid in year		195
Cash equivalent of loan benefit		£196
Amount chargeable to tax		Nil

Alternative method

Period	Balance of loan in period £	Interest at official rate on balance	£
10.10.89 – 5.11.89	6,000	$£6,000 \times 15.5\% \times \frac{27}{365}$	69
6.11.89 – 31.12.89	6,000	$£6,000 \times 16.5\% \times \frac{56}{365}$	152
1.1.90 – 5.4.90	5,500	$£5,500 \times 16.5\% \times \frac{95}{365}$	236
			457
Deduct Interest paid in year			195
Cash equivalent of loan benefit			£262
Amount chargeable to tax			£262

D will be assessed in 1990/91 as follows

Normal method (averaging)   £

Average balance for year $\dfrac{£5,500 + £4,500}{2}$ £5,000

£5,000 at 16.5% $\times \frac{6}{12}$ 412
£5,000 at 16.0% $\times \frac{6}{12}$ 400
                                                                             ———
                                                                             812
Deduct Interest paid in year   350
                                                                             ———
Cash equivalent of loan benefit   £462
                                                                             ———

Alternative method

Period	Balance of loan in period	Interest at official rate on balance	
	£		£
6.4.90 – 30.6.90	5,500	£5,500 × 16.5% × $\frac{86}{365}$	214
1.7.90 – 5.10.90	5,000	£5,000 × 16.5% × $\frac{97}{365}$	219
6.10.90 – 31.12.90	5,000	£5,000 × 16.0% × $\frac{87}{365}$	190
1.1.91–5.4.91	4,500	£4,500 × 16.0% × $\frac{95}{365}$	187
			810
Deduct Interest paid in year			350
Case equivalent of loan benefit			£460

Notes
(a) The period 10 October 1989 to 5 April 1990 is, for the purpose of calculating the average balance, five complete months (months begin on the sixth day of each calendar month). However, for the purpose of applying the changing interest rates, the full number of days (178) during which the loan was outstanding is taken into account.

(b) There is no charge to tax in 1989/90 under the averaging method as the cash equivalent does not exceed £200. However, the inspector may require the alternative method to be applied, producing a taxable benefit of £262. The employee may elect for the alternative method where it is to his advantage, but must do so within certain time limits laid down by *ICTA 1988, 7 Sch 5* . In 1990/91, the two methods produce such similar results that it seems unlikely that either party would elect for the alternative method to apply.

(E) Beneficial loans — part interest eligible for relief [*ICTA 1988, s 160, 7 Sch*]
B, another employee of A Ltd, earns £20,000 per annum and obtained a loan from the company of £50,000 in January 1990 for house purchase (B's principal private residence). At 5 April 1990, no capital had been repaid but on 15 July 1990 B repays £7,500 of the loan and on 14 January 1991 he repays £3,000. The rate of interest on the loan is 5% per annum on the daily outstanding balance. The official rates of interest are as in (D) above (with the same assumption, for illustrative purposes only, as to a change of rate on 6 October 1990).

In 1990/91 B will pay interest which will be eligible for relief as follows

Interest paid		Interest eligible for relief	
6.4.90 – 15.7.90 (101 days)	£		£
£50,000 × 5% × $\frac{101}{365}$	692	$692 \times \dfrac{30,000}{50,000}$	415
16.7.90 – 14.1.91 (183 days)			
£42,500 × 5% × $\frac{183}{365}$	1,066	$1,066 \times \dfrac{30,000}{42,500}$	752
15.1.91 – 5.4.91 (81 days)			
£39,500 × 5% × $\frac{81}{365}$	438	$438 \times \dfrac{30,000}{39,500}$	332
	£2,196		£1,499

The interest not eligible for relief is £2,196 − £1,499 = £697

B will be assessed for 1990/91 as follows

Averaging method

Loan balance at		Proportionally reduced in ratio	
5.4.90	£50,000	$\dfrac{697}{2,196}$	£15,870
5.4.91	£39,500	$\dfrac{697}{2,196}$	12,537
			£28,407
∴ Average balance			£14,203

∴ Interest payable at official rate

£14,203 at 16.5% × $\frac{6}{12}$	1,172
£14,203 at 16.0% × $\frac{6}{12}$	1,136
	2,308
Deduct Interest paid not eligible for relief	697
Cash equivalent of loan benefit	£1,611

Note
(*a*)   The loan balances at 5 April 1990 and 1991 are both reduced by virtue of *ICTA 1988, 7 Sch 8(a)* in the proportion that interest paid not eligible for relief bears to the whole of interest paid.

Alternative method
Period 1 (6.4.90 – 15.7.90)   £
  (i)   Maximum amount outstanding up to 15 July 1990   £50,000

  (ii) Interest eligible for relief   £415
        Interest not eligible for relief   277
                                                                                   £692

  (iii) Maximum amount reduced to $50,000 \times \dfrac{277}{692}$ £20,014

  (iv) Sum of maximum amounts for period 6.4.90 – 15.7.90
        £20,014 × 101 days

  (v)   Interest at official rate for period
        $£20,014 \times \dfrac{101}{365}$ at 16.5%   914

Period 2 (16.7.90 – 14.1.91)

  (i)   £42,500

  (ii)   752
            314
         £1,066

  (iii) $£42,500 \times \dfrac{314}{1,066} = £12,519$

  (iv) £12,519 × 183 days

  (v) $£12,519 \times \dfrac{82}{365}$ at 16.5%   £464

        $£12,519 \times \dfrac{101}{365}$ at 16.0%   554   1,018

Period 3 (15.1.91–5.4.91)

  (i)   £39,500

  (ii)   332
            106
          £438

  (iii) $£39,500 \times \dfrac{106}{438} = £9,559$

  (iv) £9,559 × 81 days

		£
(v) $£9,559 \times \dfrac{81}{365}$ at 16.0%		339

	£
Total interest at official rate	2,271
Deduct Interest paid not eligible for relief (as in averaging method)	697
Cash equivalent of loan benefit	£1,574

Note
(*a*)   The maximum amount outstanding in each period is reduced by virtue of *ICTA 1988, 7 Sch 8(b)*.

(F) Beneficial loan partly allowable — no interest paid [*ICTA 1988, s 160, 7 Sch*]
C, who is a director of the CR Bank Ltd, was advanced £40,000, interest-free, in March 1990. Under the agreement, C was to repay £2,000 on 30 September annually, commencing in 1990. At 5 April 1991 the debt had therefore been reduced to £38,000. The loan was used to acquire his principal private residence. The official rates of interest are as in (D) above (with the same assumption, for illustrative purposes only, as to a change of rate on 6 October 1990).

C's assessable benefit for 1990/91 is

Averaging method note (*a*)
Amount that would have been payable for year at official rate

		£
Average balance for period $\dfrac{£40,000 + £38,000}{2}$		£39,000

	£
	£
$£39,000$ at $16.5\% \times \frac{6}{12}$	3,217
$£39,000$ at $16.0\% \times \frac{6}{12}$	3,120
	£6,337

Amount of interest that would not have been eligible for tax relief

		£
		£
$£40,000 \times \dfrac{10,000}{40,000}$	£10,000	
$£10,000 \times 16.5\% \times \frac{6}{12}$	£825	
$£10,000 \times 16.0\% \times \frac{6}{12}$	800	1,625
$£38,000 \times \dfrac{8,000}{38,000}$	£8,000	
$£8,000 \times 16.5\% \times \frac{6}{12}$	£660	
$£8,000 \times 16.0\% \times \frac{6}{12}$	640	1,300
		£2,925

	£
$\therefore$ Average non-eligible interest is $£2,925 \div 2$	£1,462

Loan balance at	Proportionally reduced by ratio	
£		
5.4.90 40,000	$\dfrac{1,462}{6,337}$	£9,228
5.4.91 38,000	$\dfrac{1,462}{6,337}$	£8,767

Average (reduced) balance $= \dfrac{£9,228 + £8,767}{2}$ £8,997

Interest at official rate	£
£8,997 at 16.5% $\times \frac{6}{12}$	742
£8,997 at 16.0% $\times \frac{6}{12}$	720
Cash equivalent of loan benefit	£1,462

Alternative method note (*b*)
Amount that would have been payable for the year at the official rate

(i)   £40,000 at 16.5% $\times \dfrac{178}{365}$ (6.4.90 – 30.9.90)   £3,218

(ii)   £38,000 at 16.5% $\times \dfrac{5}{365}$ (1.10.90 – 5.10.90)   86

(iii)   £38,000 at 16.0% $\times \dfrac{182}{365}$ (6.10.90 – 5.4.91)   3,031

Total   £6,335

Amount that would not have been eligible for relief

(i)   £3,218 $\times \dfrac{10,000}{40,000}$ 804

(ii)   £86 $\times \dfrac{8,000}{38,000}$ 18

(iii)   £3,031 $\times \dfrac{8,000}{38,000}$ 638

£1,460

Calculation of cash equivalent of loan benefit

(i)   6.4.90 – 30.9.90
Sum of maximum amounts outstanding on each day in period

£40,000 $\times$ 178

Reduced to £40,000 $\times$ 178 $\times \dfrac{804}{3,218}$ = £1,778,893

(ii)   1.10.90 – 5.10.90

Sum of maximum amounts outstanding on each day in period

£38,000 × 5

Reduced to $£38,000 \times 5 \times \dfrac{18}{86} = £39,767$

(iii)   6.10.90 – 5.4.91

Sum of maximum amounts outstanding on each day in period

£38,000 × 182

Reduced to $£38,000 \times 182 \times \dfrac{638}{3,031} = £1,455,760$

Cash equivalent of loan benefit

		£
$\dfrac{£1,778,893 + £39,767}{365}$ at 16.5%		822
$\dfrac{£1,455,760}{365}$ at 16.0%	638	£1,46(

Notes

(*a*)   The averaging method of calculation shown above follows that laid down ir *ICTA 1988, 7 Sch 9.*

(*b*)   The alternative method of calculation follows that laid down in *ICTA 1988, 7 Sch 9.* The same result can be achieved in this example as follows

$£10,000 \times \dfrac{178}{365}$ at 16.5%	£804
$£8,000 \times \dfrac{5}{365}$ at 16.5%	18
$£8,000 \times \dfrac{182}{365}$ at 16.0%	638 £1,46(

23.6 **BENEFITS — LIVING ACCOMMODATION** [*ICTA 1988, ss 145, 146, 163*]
   (A)
   N is employed as a caretaker/security officer by the G Property Co Ltd, earning
   £10,000 p.a. He occupies, rent-free, the basement flat of a block of flats for which
   he is caretaker/security officer. The annual value of the flat is determined at £250.
   In 1990/91 G Ltd incurred the following expenditure on the flat

	£
Heat and light	700
Decoration	330
Repairs	210
Cleaning	160
Conversion of large bedroom into two smaller bedrooms	2,000

In addition, the company pays N's personal community charge which amounts to
£500.

As the company does not have a pension scheme, N pays a personal pension
premium of £200 (net) on 31.10.90, but apart from his personal allowance, he has
no other reliefs.

N's taxable income for 1990/91 is	£
Salary	10,000
Annual value of flat	—
Heat and light, decoration, repairs, cleaning	
£1,400 restricted to	1,050
Community charge	500
	11,550
Deduct	
Personal allowance	3,005
Taxable	£8,545

Notes
(a)   N will not be assessed on the annual value of the flat if he can show that it is
      necessary for the proper performance of his duties for him to reside in the
      accommodation. [*ICTA 1988, s 145(4)(a)*]. He might equally well be able to
      claim under *ICTA 1988, s 145(4)(b)*.

(b)   The structural alterations costing £2,000 will not be regarded as a benefit.
      [*ICTA 1988, s 155(3)*].

(c)   The emoluments treated as having arisen in respect of the heat and light,
      decoration, repairs and cleaning costs will be restricted by *ICTA 1988, s 163*
      to the lesser of
      (i)   the expenses incurred   £1,400
      (ii) 10% × £10,500 (net emoluments)   £1,050

      The personal pension contribution is not deductible in arriving at net
      emoluments, although retirement annuity premiums and occupational pen-
      sion scheme contributions are so deductible. [*ICTA 1988, s 163 (4)*]. (The
      contribution is not shown above as a deduction from taxable income as basic
      rate relief has been given at source and higher rate relief is not applicable.)

(d)   Payment by the employer of the employee's personal community charge is a
      taxable benefit. The community charge is a personal liability and not a charge
      on the property. It will form part of the net emoluments in (c) above.

IT 23.6   Schedule E — Emoluments

(B)

S, the founder and Managing Director of S Ltd, a successful transport company, has for some years occupied a mansion house owned by S Ltd. The house was acquired by S Ltd in 1982 for £150,000 and, since acquisition, but before 6 April 1989, £80,000 has been spent by S Ltd on alterations and improvements to the house. The gross annual value of the house for rating purposes before 1 April 1990 (when the community charge replaced general rates) was £1,663. S pays annual rental of £2,000 to the company in respect of 1990/91 only. He pays all expenses relating to the property.

S will have an assessable benefit in respect of his occupation of the house as follows for 1989/90 and 1990/91

		£	£
1989/90			
Gross annual value			1,663
Additional charge			
Acquisition cost of house		150,000	
Cost of improvements		80,000	
		230,000	
Deduct		75,000	
Additional value		£155,000	
Additional value at 14.5%	note (*b*)		22,475
			£24,138
1990/91			
Gross annual value	note (*a*)		Nil
Additional charge			
Acquisition cost of house		150,000	
Cost of improvements		80,000	
		230,000	
Deduct		75,000	
Additional value		£155,000	
Additional value at 16.5%	note (*b*)		25,575
			25,575
Rental payable by S		2,000	
Deduct Gross annual value		1,663	
			337
			£25,238

Notes

(*a*)   No taxable gross annual value arises in 1990/91 because the rental of £2,000 payable by S exceeds the gross annual value of £1,663. The excess is deductible from the amount of the benefit arising under the additional charge.

(*b*)   The percentage to be used in determining the amount of the benefit is that used for the purposes of the beneficial loan arrangements (see 23.5(D)–(F) above) at the beginning of the year of assessment.

(c)   If S had moved into the house on, say, 6 April 1989 (more than six years after its acquisition by S Ltd), market value at that date would be substituted for cost plus improvements. If, however, original cost plus cost of improvements had not exceeded £75,000, the additional charge would not apply (regardless of market value at the date of first occupation by S) (Inland Revenue Press Release 18 August 1988).

[*ICTA 1988, s 146*].

23.7   **BENEFITS — MEDICAL INSURANCE AND VOUCHERS** [*ICTA 1988, ss 141, 143, 144, 153–155, 167; FA 1989, s 53*]

(A)

T earns £6,000 p.a. and during the year ended 5 April 1991 his employer provided him with, or paid on his behalf, the following

	£
BUPA contributions (self and family) of which 25% reimbursed by T	600
Special medical insurance for overseas business visit	250
Voucher exchangeable for rail season ticket	500
Gift token exchangeable for goods at local department store	75
Holiday pay scheme voucher, exchangeable for cash	350

The rail ticket voucher was purchased in March 1990 but was not handed to T until after 6 April 1990. The holiday pay voucher was received by T in June 1990 at which time PAYE was applied. The gift token was received in December 1990.

T's assessable emoluments for 1990/91 are	£
Salary	6,000
Rail ticket voucher	500
Gift token	75
Holiday pay scheme voucher	350
	£6,925

Notes

(a)   T is not a director or employee earning £8,500 a year or more and so the BUPA contributions are not an assessable benefit.

(b)   The rail ticket voucher will be assessable in 1990/91 being the later of the year of receipt by the employee and the year of expense incurred by the employer.

147

IT 23.7   Schedule E — Emoluments

(B)

Instead of earning £6,000 as in (A) above, T has a salary of £7,500 p.a.

T's assessable emoluments for 1990/91 are	£
Salary	7,500
BUPA contributions (£600 less 25%)	450
Rail ticket voucher	500
Gift token	75
Holiday pay scheme voucher	350
	£8,875

Notes

(*a*)   All chargeable benefits and expenses payments, before relief for business expenditure, are taken into account in determining whether or not the £8,500 limit has been reached.

(*b*)   The special medical insurance for the overseas business trip is exempted from charge by *ICTA 1988, s 155(6)*.

24   Settlements

24.1   ASSESSMENTS ON TRUST INCOME

A is sole life-tenant of a settlement which has income and expenses in the year 1990/91 of

	£
Untaxed interest	1,000
Taxed investment income (tax deducted at source £500)	2,000
	£3,000
Revenue expenses	£400

The tax assessable on the trustees will be £250 (£1,000 at 25%). The expenses are not deductible in arriving at the tax payable by the trustees.

Notes

(*a*)   By prior arrangement, the Inland Revenue may, where there is a sole life-tenant in a trust, allow the interest to be assessed directly on that beneficiary.

(*b*)   For treatment of the trust income in the hands of the beneficiary, see example 24.3(A) below.

24.2   ACCUMULATION TRUSTS [*ICTA 1988, ss 686, 832; FA 1988, s 24(4)*]

An accumulation and maintenance settlement set up by W for his grandchildren in 1973 now comprises quoted investments and an industrial property. The property is let to an engineering company who use the travelling cranes which form an integral part of the property. Charges for rates, electricity etc. are paid by the trust and recharged yearly in arrears to the tenant. As a result of the delay in recovering the service costs, the settlement incurs overdraft interest.

The relevant figures for the year ended 5 April 1991 are as follows

	£
Property rents (Schedule A)	30,000
Crane rents (Schedule D, Case VI)	10,000
UK dividends (including tax credits of £1,250)	5,000
	£45,000
Trust administration expenses — proportion chargeable to revenue	750
Overdraft interest	1,050
	£1,800

Tax is payable by the trustees of an accumulation and maintenance trust at a rate of 35% (i.e. basic rate plus the additional rate of 10%).

IT 24.3   Settlements

The tax liability of the trust for 1990/91 is as follows

	£	£
Schedule A £30,000 at 35%		10,500
Schedule D, Case VI £10,000 at 35%		3,500
Investment income	5,000	
Deduct Expenses (grossed) £1,800 × $\frac{100}{75}$	2,400	
	£2,600	
Tax at 10%	260	
Add Tax deducted at source	1,250	1,510
		£15,510

Notes

(*a*)   The grossed-up trust expenses and interest are allowed only against the additional 10% rate. They are not allowed against basic rate. The net revenue available for distribution to the beneficiaries, at the trustees' discretion, will be £27,690 (£45,000 – £15,510 – £1,800).

(*b*)   For treatment of the trust income in the hands of a beneficiary, see example 24.3(B) below.

24.3   INCOME OF BENEFICIARIES
(A) Life interest
A is sole life-tenant of the settlement at 24.1 above and as such is absolutely entitled to receive the whole settlement income.

A's income for 1990/91 will include

	£
Trust income (gross)	3,000
Deduct Basic rate tax (25%)	750
	2,250
Deduct Expenses	400
Net income entitlement	£1,850
Grossed-up amount (£1,850 × $\frac{100}{75}$)	£2,467

Note

(*a*)   This income falls to be included in A's return even if it is not actually paid to him as he is absolutely entitled to it. He will receive a tax certificate (Form R185E) from the trust agents showing gross income (£2,467), tax deducted (£617) and the net amount of trust income (£1,850).

(B) Accumulation trusts

M, the 17-year old grandson of W, is one of the five beneficiaries to whom the trustees can pay the settlement income in 24.2 above. The trustees make a payment of £3,000 to M on 31 January 1991. He has no other income in the year 1990/91 and is unmarried.

M's income from the trust is

	£
Net income	3,000.00
Tax at $\frac{35}{65}$	1,615.38
Gross income	£4,615.38

He can claim a tax repayment for 1990/91 of

	£
Total income	4,615
Deduct Personal allowance	3,005
	£1,610
Tax thereon at 25%	402.50
Tax accounted for by trustees	1,615.38
Repayment due	£1,212.88

Notes

(*a*)   If no income was actually paid to M from the settlement, nothing would fall to be included in his return.

(*b*)   For treatment of trust income where the beneficiary is an infant under a parent's settlement, see 24.4 below.

24.4   SETTLEMENT BY PARENT IN FAVOUR OF OWN CHILD [*ICTA 1988, ss 663–670*]

L set up an accumulation and maintenance trust for his two children, aged 6 and 4, in 1976. On 31 December 1978 and 31 December 1979, school fees of £500 were paid on behalf of each child. In January 1991 the trust was wound up and the assets transferred to the two beneficiaries, then aged 20 and 18, in equal shares. At that time there was £6,000 of undistributed income.

The income to be treated as the settlor's income will be as follows

1978/79	$£1,000 \times \dfrac{100}{52}$	£1,923.08
1979/80	$£1,000 \times \dfrac{100}{55}$	£1,818.18
1990/91	note (*b*)	Nil

Notes

(*a*)   The payments for 1978/79 and 1979/80 are grossed up in accordance with the basic and additional rates of tax for those years, i.e. for 1978/79 33% + 15% = 48%, for 1979/80 30% + 15% = 45%.

(*b*)   Income is not treated as that of the settlor if, at the time of payment, the children have either married or reached the age of eighteen.

24.5   LOANS AND REPAYMENT OF LOANS TO SETTLOR [*ICTA 1988, s 677*]

The trustees of a settlement with undistributed income of £1,375 at 5 April 1988 made a loan of £14,950 to B, the settlor, on 30 September 1988.

B repays the loan on 31 December 1990. Undistributed income of £3,500 arose in 1988/89, £6,500 in 1989/90 and £5,500 in 1990/91. B has taxable income of £50,000 in each year.

B will be treated as receiving the following income

	£
1988/89 $£4,875 \times \dfrac{100}{65}$	7,500
1989/90 $£6,500 \times \dfrac{100}{65}$	10,000
1990/91 $£3,575 \times \dfrac{100}{65}$ note (*b*)	5,500

B will pay additional tax of

	£
1988/89 £7,500 at 5% (40% – 35%)	375
1989/90 £10,000 at 5% (40% – 35%)	500
1990/91 £5,500 at 5% (40% – 35%)	275
	£1,150

Notes

(*a*)   The amount to be included as part of B's income for each year is limited to the amount of undistributed income, grossed up at the basic and additional rates, available within the settlement at the end of the tax year, but excluding any such income which has already been 'matched' under these provisions.

(*b*)   The amount treated as income in 1990/91 is limited to the amount of the loan less amounts previously treated as income (£14,950 – (£4,875 + £6,500)).

(*c*)   Different rules applied to loans made before 6 April 1981 but any part of such a loan which had not been 'matched' with undistributed income at that date is treated as having been made on that date, so that the current rules apply.

24.6 **SETTLEMENTS OF INCOME ONLY** [*ICTA 1988, ss 674A, 683; FA 1989, s 109*]

A married man makes payments under deeds of covenant. In the year ended 5 April 1991, he has income and makes payments as follows

		£	£
Earnings			31,350
Investment income			10,000
			41,350
Building Society mortgage interest paid (under MIRAS)	gross	4,000	
Deeds of covenant — to parents	gross	4,000	
to children over 18	gross	3,500	
to charities	gross	1,000	
			12,500
			£28,850

All deeds of covenant to parents and children were made before 15 March 1988.

On 2 January 1991, he makes a settlement of £10,000 on his parents which produced income of £375 (received gross) in 1990/91. The capital is to revert to him on the death of the last surviving parent.

On 31 March 1991, he makes a single gift to charity of £750 under the Gift Aid rules in *FA 1990, s 25*.

The income tax liability for the year 1990/91 is

	£	£
Tax at basic rate		
Income note (*d*)	41,725	
Deduct Personal allowance	(3,005)	
Married couple's allowance	(1,720)	
	£37,000	
Tax at 25% payable by assessment		9,250.00
Deduct Tax retained at basic rate on mortgage interest and covenants £13,500 at 25% note (*e*)		(3,375.00)
		5,875.00

Tax at higher rates	£	
Basic rate tax band	20,700	
Extension re charitable covenants note (*e*)	2,000	
Extension re building society interest	4,000	
	26,700	
£26,700 at Nil (25% – 25%)	—	
10,300 at 15% (40% – 25%)	1,545.00	
£37,000		1,545.00
Total tax liability		£7,420.00

Notes

(*a*) Payments under settlements are treated as income of the settlor for the purposes of higher tax unless specifically excluded (e.g. from 1986/87 all covenanted payments to charity are so excluded). [*ICTA 1988, s 683 (3)–(5)*].

(*b*) In this example, £10,795.00 will be payable by assessment and tax relief of £3,375.00 has already been obtained by deduction of tax at source from payments made. Thus, £7,420.00 is the net liability.

(*c*) All non-charitable covenants made after 14 March 1988 do not attract tax relief and payments are made gross. [*FA 1988, s 36*].

(*d*) Income arising from certain settlements of income only, made after 13 March 1989, is treated as income of the settlor for both basic and higher rate taxes. Thus, £375 is added to income. [*ICTA 1988, s 674A; FA 1989, s 109*].

(*e*) The single donation to charity is treated as if it were a covenanted payment equal to the grossed-up amount. [*FA 1990, s 25(6)*].

25   Share Incentives and Options

25.1   SHARE OPTIONS — CHARGE TO TAX [*ICTA 1988, ss 135–137, 140*]

An employee is granted an option exercisable within 5 years to buy 1,000 shares at £5 each. The option costs 50p per share. He exercises the option in 1990/91 when the shares are worth £7.50.

He is chargeable to income tax under Schedule E in 1990/91 as follows

	£	£
Open market value of shares 1,000 × £7.50		7,500
Price paid 1,000 × £5 — shares	5,000	
1,000 × 50p — option	500	
		5,500
Assessable		£2,000

Notes

(*a*)   The result would be the same if instead of exercising the option the employee, for example, transferred his option to a third party for £2,500.

(*b*)   The capital gains tax base cost of the shares will be £7,500. [*CGTA 1979, s 32A(3); ICTA 1988, 29 Sch 18*].

25.2   UNAPPROVED EMPLOYEE SHARE SCHEMES — CHARGES TO TAX [*ICTA 1988, ss 138–140; FA 1988, ss 77–89*]

(A) Charge where restrictions removed, etc.

E, an employee of Perks Ltd, exercised, on 1 June 1983, an option, conferred on him by reason of his employment, to acquire 3,000 shares in that company, their open market value at that time being £10,000. He was duly charged to tax under Schedule E under the rules in 25.1 above. The shares were subject to one of the restrictions in *ICTA 1988, s 138(6)*. Market value per share at 26 October 1987 and at 1 June 1990 was £4.50 and £4.75 respectively. On 1 November 1990, a chargeable event under *FA 1988, s 78(2)* occurs by virtue of the restriction being removed. Removal of the restriction increases the value per share from £5.00 to £7.50. E has remained in the company's employment throughout the period and at no time has the company been a 'dependent subsidiary' as defined by *FA 1988, s 86*.

E will be charged to income tax under Schedule E in 1990/91 as follows

		£	£
(i) *Charge under ICTA 1988, s 138(1)(a)*			
Market value at 26.10.87	note (*a*)	13,500	
Less market value at 1.6.83		10,000	
			3,500
(ii) *Charge under FA 1988, s 78(3)*			
Increase in market value resulting from chargeable event (3,000 × £2.50)	note (*b*)		7,500
Schedule E assessment for 1990/91 will, in addition to salary and benefits, include			£11,000

Notes

(a)   A charge arises on the seventh anniversary of acquisition (1 June 1990), but under the transitional provisions of *FA 1988, s 88(2)* it is calculated by reference to market value at 26 October 1987, the date from which the *Finance Act 1988* provisions apply, as this is less than market value at 1 June 1990.

(b)   The charge under *FA 1988, s 78(3)* is on the increase in value as a result of the chargeable event. Note that the increase between 26 October 1987 and 31 October 1990 escapes any charge to income tax. If the value had decreased, no relief would have been available for the decrease.

(c)   On a sale of the shares, the capital gains tax base cost would be £21,000, i.e. £10,000 + £11,000, the amounts chargeable under (i) and (ii) above being regarded as consideration given for the acquisition of the shares, under *CGTA 1979, s 32A(4)* and *FA 1988, s 84* respectively. It is not clear exactly *when* such consideration is deemed to have been given, which could be important as regards both indexation and the re-basing rules in *Finance Act 1988*, but the logical interpretation of the exact wording used in these *sections* is that it is deemed to have been given at the date of acquisition, so that in this example, expenditure of £11,000 would be deemed to have been incurred on 1 June 1983.

(B) Charge for shares in dependent subsidiaries
On 1 February 1990, P acquires 1,000 shares with an open market value of £4,000 in a company of which he is a director. The shares are acquired under an unapproved share option scheme open only to the directors. The company is a 'dependent subsidiary' as defined by *FA 1988, s 86*. On 1 August 1990, P gifts his shares to his daughter, Q. On 31 March 1991, Q sells the shares at their then market value of £5,000.

P will be charged to tax under Schedule E in 1990/91 as follows

		£
Open market value at 31 March 1991	note (a)	5,000
Less open market value at 1 February 1990		4,000
Schedule E assessment on P		£1,000

Notes

(a)   A charge arises under *FA 1988, s 79* by virtue of P's ceasing to have a beneficial interest in the shares on 31 March 1991. His gift to Q is disregarded in determining who has the beneficial interest, this being a disposal other than by way of an arm's length bargain with an unconnected person. [*FA 1988, s 83(2)*].

(b)   If P had retained the beneficial interest until 1 February 1997, the seventh anniversary of acquisition, a charge under *Sec 79* would arise at that time, i.e. in 1996/97.

(c)   The gift to Q is a disposal for capital gains tax purposes. As in (A) above, the amount of the Schedule E charge is deemed to have been expended by P on the acquisition of the shares, thus increasing their base cost for capital gains tax. Q will be regarded for capital gains tax purposes as having acquired the shares on 1 August 1990 at their market value at that date.

25.3 APPROVED SHARE OPTION SCHEMES [*ICTA 1988, ss 185, 187, 9 Sch*]

The employee in 25.1 above is instead granted his option under a non-savings-related share option scheme approved under *ICTA 1988, 9 Sch*.

Provided that the option is exercised not less than three nor more than ten years after being granted, there is no charge under *ICTA 1988, s 135* (see 25.1 above) when the option is exercised and no charge under the *Finance Act 1988* provisions (see 25.2 above) on any growth in value of the shares. The capital gains tax base cost of the shares (subject to indexation) will then be £5.50 per share. [*ICTA 1988, s 185(1)–(3)(5)*].

If, however, the market value of the shares at the date the option is granted was, say, £6.00 per share, there would still be no charge under the above mentioned provisions, but there would be an income tax charge under Schedule E for the year in which the option is granted, as follows

	£	£
Market value 1,000 × £6.00		6,000
Price payable 1,000 × £5.00 — shares	5,000	
1,000 × 50p — option	500	
		5,500
Schedule E assessment		£500

The capital gains tax base cost, subject to indexation, will then be £6.00 per share. [*ICTA 1988, s 185(6)(7)*].

25.4 PROFIT SHARING SCHEMES [*ICTA 1988, ss 186, 187, 9 and 10 Schs; FA 1989, s 63*]

(A) Charge to tax

In 1990/91, an employee has appropriated to him, under his company's approved profit sharing scheme, 1,000 ordinary shares valued at £1 each.

No tax charge arises at that time.

He sells the shares in 1994 on the fourth anniversary of acquisition for £1,200.

He is liable at that time for the tax under Schedule E on

75% of the 'locked-in value' (i.e. 75% of £1,000)	£750
or	
75% of the value of the shares at that time	£900
whichever is the less, i.e.	£750

Notes

(a) The tax is withheld under PAYE.

(b) If the employee retained the shares for 5 years (before 25 July 1985, 7 years), no income tax liability would arise.

(c) If the employee had disposed of the shares before the fourth anniversary of the acquisition, the charge would have been on 100% of the 'locked-in value'.

(d) 'Locked-in value' is the initial market value when appropriated as reduced by certain capital receipts charged to income tax.

(B) Limit on initial market value of shares appropriated

In 1989/90 and 1990/91 an employee's salary (excluding benefits) subjected to tax under the PAYE system is £62,000 and £50,000 respectively. The maximum initial market value of shares which may be appropriated to him within the limit for 1990/91 is calculated as follows

Overall limit	£6,000
Year of appropriation 10% of PAYE salary	£5,000
Preceding year 10% of PAYE salary	£6,200

The maximum initial market value is restricted to £6,000. The relevant salary figure, which is the greater of 10% of the PAYE salary for the year of appropriation (£5,000) or the preceding year (£6,200), is subject to the overall limit of £6,000.

Note
(a)   The annual limit was increased from £5,000 to £6,000 with effect for 1989/90 and subsequent years. There is also a minimum limit of £2,000 (£1,250 before 1989/90).

25.5 EMPLOYEE SHARE OWNERSHIP TRUSTS [*FA 1989, ss 67–74, 5 Sch*]

YME plc makes payments of £20,000 and £30,000 on 1 September 1989 and 1990 respectively to a qualifying employee share ownership (ESOP) trust. The company claims and receives corporation tax relief for these payments under *FA 1989, s 67*. The trustees purchase shares in the company as follows

	No of shares	Cost of shares £	Costs of acquisition £
1.10.89	24,500	19,600	400
10.9.90	23,500	28,200	600
	48,000	£47,800	£1,000

On 1 June 1991, the trustees, having previously transferred 30,000 shares to beneficiaries, make a transfer of 15,000 shares to beneficiaries on terms which are not qualifying terms under *FA 1989, s 69(4)*. The market value of the shares on the date of transfer was £1.50 per share.

The trustees of the ESOP trust will realise a chargeable gain (subject to indexation) on 1.6.91 as follows

	£
Consideration (15,000 × £1.50)	22,500
Deduct cost $\dfrac{15,000}{48,000} \times (£47,800 + £1,000)$	15,250
Unindexed gain	£7,250

The trustees will also be chargeable to income tax under Schedule D, Case VI for 1991/92 as follows

	£	£
Chargeable amount under *FA 1989, s 70(2)*		15,250
Previous chargeable amounts		—
		15,250
Deductible amount under *FA 1989, s 72(4)*	50,000	
Excess of chargeable amounts over deductible amount		—
Schedule D, Case VI assessment		£15,250
Tax payable by trustees at 35%		£5,337.50

Notes

(a)   Tax is payable under Schedule D, Case VI at a rate equal to the sum of the basic rate and additional rate. It is assumed that these rates are the same for 1991/92 as for 1990/91, i.e 25% and 10%.

(b)   Although the tax, and any interest thereon, is payable by the trustees of the ESOP trust, the Revenue have a right of recourse to the company in the event of non-payment.

(c)   The chargeable amount in this case is the amount deductible for capital gains tax purposes under *CGTA 1979, s 32(1)(a)(b)* on the transfer giving rise to the chargeable event. This does not include indexation allowance. The aggregate of past and present chargeable amounts cannot exceed the total amount for which a corporation tax deduction has been claimed.

(d)   Regardless of whether or not a chargeable event occurs, each beneficiary will be chargeable to income tax under Schedule E on the market value of shares received less any amount paid by him as consideration. In practice, an ESOP trust is likely to be used in conjunction with an approved profit sharing scheme such that beneficiaries incur no tax liability when shares are appropriated to them.

26   Underwriters

[ICTA 1988, ss 450–457, 19A Sch; FA 1988, ss 58–61, 5 Sch; SI 1974, No 896; SI 1990/627]

26.1   SCHEDULE D ASSESSMENTS ON UNDERWRITING PROFITS

Throughout examples (A)–(D), reference to 'Profit' is to profit arising from underwriting business, and excludes syndicate investment income. For the 1986 and subsequent underwriting accounts, syndicate investment income is also taxed as part of the Schedule D, Case I profit.

(A)

J commenced underwriting on 1 January 1986 and ceased on 31 December 1990. His results were

Account	Profit
	£
1986	1,250
1987	3,500
1988	1,600
1989	820
1990	1,460

The taxable profits are as follows

	£
1985/86	Nil
1986/87	1,250
1987/88	3,500
1988/89	1,600
1989/90	820
1990/91	1,460

Note

(a)   Since J commenced underwriting after 1 January 1971, there are no commencement or cessation adjustments.

(B)

M, who has been an underwriter since the 1960s, retired on 31 December 1987. In August 1990 M was advised of the results of the 1987 account. The results from the 1984 account onwards were

Account	Profit
	£
1984	4,500
1985	2,700
1986	3,400
1987	1,850

The 1972 profit came to £1,100

The taxable profits are as follows

	£
1984/85	4,500
1985/86	2,700

		£	£
1986/87	1986 Account	3,400	
	Deduct 1972 profit	1,100	
			2,300
1987/88	Period 6.4.87 – 31.12.87		
	(Say) $\frac{3}{4}$ × £1,850		1,388

Note

(a) Since M commenced on or before 1 January 1971, the profits of his first underwriting year would have been assessed $2\frac{1}{4}$ times under the old system. Since no profits fall out of assessment on a cessation under the new system, the cessation of a pre-1971 underwriter is treated as above. [*SI 1974/896, Reg 21(1)–(3)*].

(C)

S, who commenced underwriting in 1968, died on 31 October 1987, having shared in 10 months of the 1987 account results. By September 1990 the 1987 result was available and the results for years 1985 onwards were

Account	Profit
	£
1985	2,400
1986	1,200
1987	1,800 (10 months)

The 1972 profit came to £1,100

The taxable profits are as follows

		£	£
1985/86			2,400
1986/87	1986 Account	1,200	
	Deduct 1972 profit	1,100	
			100
1987/88	Period 6.4.87 – 31.10.87		
	(Say) $\frac{7}{10}$ × £1,800		1,260

Notes

(a) The final year of assessment will always be that during which the underwriter dies and his taxable profit for that year will depend on his involvement in the account during which he dies.

(b) If S had died on 31 January 1988 having shared in one month of the 1988 account, the final year of assessment would also have been 1987/88 and assuming a share of profits for the full 1987 account of £2,160 his taxable profit would be as follows

	£
Period 6.4.87 – 31.12.87	
$\frac{9}{12}$ × £2,160	1,620
Period 1.1.88 – 31.1.88 say	500
	£2,120

IT 26.1 Underwriters

(D)

T, who began underwriting in 1973, died on 31 March 1988 having shared in three months of the 1988 account. The results from the 1985 account onwards were

Account	Profit £
1985	10,000
1986	9,200
1987	5,600
1988	7,200 (3 months)

The taxable profits are as follows

		£
1985/86		10,000
1986/87		9,200
1987/88	1987 Account	5,600
	Period 1.1.88 – 31.3.88	7,200
		12,800

Note

(a) If T had died on 30 September 1988, his final year of charge would have been 1988/89 which would have been based on his share of the 1988 results.

(E) Personal pension contributions and non-underwriting losses

A is a working name at Lloyd's. His wife B shares in the profits and losses of a farming partnership with their son C (who is over 18 years of age). The income of A and B for 1987/88, as known at 5.4.90, is as follows

	£
A	
Lloyd's	Not yet known
Investment income	6,500
B	
Share of farm loss	(4,250)
Investment income	1,700

B, by virtue of *ICTA 1970, s 168(1)* (now *ICTA 1988, s 380(1)*), could have made a loss claim for 1987/88 by 5.4.90 but, due to the absence of Lloyd's information, withholds a decision until 5.4.92 at the latest. (The two year extension for underwriting loss claims applies also to non-underwriting losses.)

In late 1990, A learns that his Lloyd's results for the 1987 account (assessable 1987/88) are

	£
Profits from underwriting business	7,400
Syndicate investment income	2,750
Schedule D, Case I profit	£10,150

In February 1991, A (who is 45 years of age) pays a personal pension contribution of £1,500 and elects to have part of this premium carried back to 1987/88 under *ICTA 1988, s 641(2)*. B also makes a loss claim for 1987/88 under *ICTA 1970, s 168(1)*.

A's assessable income for 1987/88 is as follows

	£	£
Investment income (wife)	1,700	
Deduct Farm loss (part)	1,700	—
Schedule D, Case I (Lloyd's)	10,150	
Deduct Balance of wife's farm loss		
(£4,250 – £1,700)	2,550	
	7,600	
Investment income (self)	6,500	
		14,100
		14,100
Deduct		
Personal pension contribution	1,330	
Personal allowance — married	3,795	
		5,125
Taxable income		£8,975

Notes

(a) Relief for the personal pension contribution is restricted to £1,330, being $17\frac{1}{2}$% of £7,600. A would therefore elect to have £1,330 of the premium carried back to 1987/88, the balance of £170 (£1,500 − £1,330) being available for relief in the normal way. A personal pension contribution carried back to a year prior to 1988/89 is treated as if it were a retirement annuity premium. [*ICTA 1988, s 655(2); FA 1988, s 54(2)(b)(i)*].

Prior to 1986/87, syndicate investment income did not form part of the Case I profit and thus did not constitute relevant earnings for pension contributions or retirement annuity relief.

(b) B's losses would be taken into account in calculating net relevant earnings by virtue of *ICTA 1970, s 227(5)(b)*(now *ICTA 1988, s 623(6)(c)*).

26.2 LOSSES

(A)

J, who commenced underwriting on 1 January 1986 and is not a working name, had the following underwriting results

	Underwriting Loss	Syndicate Investment Income	Net Sch D, Case I Loss
	£	£	£
Account 1986	2,600	1,800	800
Account 1987	8,900	2,300	6,600

His other income and allowances, for relevant years, comprise

	Schedule D, Case I	Schedule D Woodlands Losses	Dividends (gross)	Retirement Annuity Premiums	Personal Allowance
	£	£	£	£	£
1984/85	12,600	(2,400)	3,350	1,785	3,155
1986/87	8,400	(2,250)	2,900	923	3,655
1987/88	4,800	(1,750)	3,100	457	3,795

IT 26.2   Underwriters

J had already claimed relief under *ICTA 1970, s 168(1)* (now *ICTA 1988, s 380(1)*) in respect of the woodlands losses and the 1986 underwriting loss.

His options regarding the 1987 loss are

(i)   Carry the loss forward to be set off against future underwriting profits. [*ICTA 1970, s 171(1); ICTA 1988, s 385(1)*].

(ii)   Relieve the loss under *ICTA 1970, s 168(1); ICTA 1988, s 380(1)* against other income for 1987/88.

(iii)   Relieve the loss under *FA 1978, s 30; ICTA 1988, s 381* against other income for 1984/85.

Option (ii) (1987/88)	£	£
Dividends (gross)		3,100
Deduct Underwriting losses (1986 account)	6,600	
Restricted to	3,100	3,100
Balance	£3,500	—
Profits		4,800
Deduct Woodlands losses	1,750	
Underwriting losses to cover balance	3,050	4,800
		Nil

Notes

(*a*)   There is no tax liability and £450 of underwriting losses (£3,500 – £3,050) are available either to carry forward or carry back to the immediately preceding tax year.

(*b*)   Prior to the 1986 Account, there was no requirement for underwriting losses to be set firstly against syndicate investment income. With effect for the 1986 Account and subsequent Accounts, syndicate investment income is aggregated with profits or losses from underwriting business to arrive at a net Schedule D, Case I profit or loss. [*FA 1973, 16 Sch 2A; ICTA 1988, s 450(2); FA 1988, s 58*].

(*c*)   Since J is a non-working name, the 1987 net underwriting losses will be relieved against investment income in priority to earned income.

(*d*)   J does not obtain relief for either his personal allowance or the retirement annuity premium of £457.

Option (iii) 1984/85	£	£
Dividends (gross)		3,350
Deduct Underwriting losses (1986 account)	6,600	
Restricted to	3,350	3,350
	£3,250	—
Profits		12,600
Deduct Woodlands losses	2,400	
Balance of underwriting losses	3,250	5,650
		c/f 6,950

		£
		b/f 6,950

Deduct
Retirement annuity relief

$17\frac{1}{2}\% \times (£12,600 - £2,400)$	1,785	
Personal allowance — married	3,155	4,940
Taxable		£2,010

Notes

(*a*)   The retirement annuity relief is not restricted on account of the underwriting losses since any underwriting profits would not constitute relevant earnings (due to J's being a non-working name).

(*b*)   The facility to carry back losses under *FA 1978, s 30; ICTA 1988, s 381* is available to non-working names as well as working names.

(*c*)   The normal time limits for claiming loss relief under either of options (ii) and (iii) is extended by two years. [*SI 1990/627, Reg 3(2)*].

(B)

M has been a member of Lloyd's since 1973 and in the year to 31 December 1987 he incurred a Schedule D, Case I underwriting loss of £5,150. For the same year, there was a withdrawal from the special reserve fund of £2,960 (gross). M is a full-time director of an underwriting agency company and hence is a working name. He is a single man and his other income for 1987/88 comprises

	£	£
Salary		24,000
Commission		100
Dividends (gross)		7,800
Schedule A rents		350

M's tax position for 1987/88 becomes

Salary		24,000
Commission		100
		24,100
Deduct Underwriting loss	note (*a*)	2,190
		21,910
Dividends	7,800	
Schedule A	350	
		8,150
		30,060
Deduct Personal allowance		2,425
Taxable		£27,635

Note

(*a*)   The loss of £5,150 must first be set against the withdrawal from the special reserve fund amounting to £2,960, the tax deducted from which of £799.20 (£2,960 at 27%) is repaid. The balance of £2,190 (£5,150 – £2,960) must then be set off firstly against earned income since M is a working name.

IT 26.3 Underwriters

26.3 **SPECIAL RESERVE FUND** [*ICTA 1988, s 452*]

(A) Payment into special reserve fund

F wishes to make a transfer in respect of the year ended 31 December 1987, the results for which are

	£
Schedule D, Case I underwriting profit	4,621
Foreign tax	502

The income in 1987/88 from the personal reserve, Lloyd's deposit and special reserve fund assets totalled £1,230 (all taxed investment income).

The maximum transfer to the fund is calculated as follows

	£
Schedule D, Case I underwriting profit	4,621
Foreign tax	502
Personal reserve etc.	1,230
	£6,353

	Gross	Tax (at 27%)	Net
	£	£	£
35% transfer	2,223.55	600.36	1,623.19
15% transfer	952.95	257.29	695.66
	£3,176.50	£857.65	£2,318.85

Notes

(*a*) The gross transfer is £3,176.50 since that figure is less than the overriding maximum of £7,000. The basic 35 per cent. transfer cannot exceed £5,000 gross. The additional 15 per cent. transfer may exceed £2,000 providing the total transfer does not exceed £7,000.

(*b*) The tax deducted will vary in line with the basic rate for the year concerned.

(*c*) The cash outlay by F will amount to £2,318.85 (assuming he makes the maximum transfer); in turn, the gross equivalent will be deductible for the purposes of higher rate tax.

(*d*) Notification of the transfer must be made to the Inspector by 31 December 1990. The payment into the fund must be made by 30 January 1991 or, if later, within thirty days of the Inspector's agreement to the amount of the transfer. [*ICTA 1988, s 452(6)*]. The Revenue *may* announce extensions to these time limits in years where many Underwriting results are themselves delayed until after 31 December.

(B)

F in (A) above is a married man whose non-Lloyd's income in 1987/88 is taxed investment income of £28,625. Prior to obtaining the Lloyd's results he received a 1987/88 higher rate assessment on taxed income in October 1988. He paid the tax on the due date, 1 December 1988.

1987/88 non-Lloyd's taxed income assessment

	£
Non-Lloyd's investment income	28,625
Personal reserve etc.	1,230
	29,855
Deduct Personal allowance — married	3,795
	£26,060

Tax payable

	£
£17,900 at 27%	4,833.00
2,500 at 40%	1,000.00
5,000 at 45%	2,250.00
660 at 50%	330.00
£26,060	8,413.00

Deduct Tax credits	
£29,855 at 27%	8,060.85
Tax payable	£352.15

In November 1990 F makes the special reserve fund transfer of £3,176.

F will receive a higher and additional rate assessment on the Schedule D, Case I underwriting profits as shown below. The tax is payable on 1 July 1991 or thirty days after the issue of the notice of assessment if later.

1987/88 Lloyd's assessment

	£
Schedule D, Case I	4,621
Foreign tax	502
	5,123
Deduct Special Reserve Fund transfer	3,176
	£1,947

Tax payable

		£
£1,947 at 50%		973.50
Deduct		
Basic rate tax already paid by syndicates		
£1,947 at 27%	note (*a*)	525.69
Tax payable		£447.81

Note

(*a*)   The syndicates will have received relief for the foreign tax of £502 against the basic rate tax accounted for to the Collector of Taxes on 1 January 1991.

IT 26.3 Underwriters

(C) Payments out of the special reserve fund

In the year to 31 December 1987, G had the following results

	£
Underwriting loss	(10,240)
Foreign tax	176
Accountancy fees	500
Syndicate investment income	5,024
Personal reserve etc. income (1987/88)	1,938

The amount withdrawn would be	£
Underwriting loss	(10,240)
Add Accountancy fees	(500)
	(10,740)
Syndicate investment income	5,024
Schedule D, Case I loss	£5,716
Personal reserve etc. income	1,938
Total loss	£(3,778)
Gross withdrawal	3,778.00
Tax at 27%	1,020.06
Net withdrawal	£2,757.94

Notes

(a) The withdrawal will come primarily from that part of the fund comprising transfers made at 35%. Any balance will then come from the 15% fund. Should the total loss exceed the balance in the special reserve fund, then the whole fund must be withdrawn.

(b) Relief for the Case I loss must be obtained firstly against the gross withdrawal, resulting in repayment of the basic rate tax deducted therefrom.

Corporation Tax

101 Accounting Periods

101.1 **EFFECT OF AN ACCOUNTING PERIOD OVERLAPPING TWO FINANCIAL YEARS HAVING DIFFERENT RATES OF CORPORATION TAX** [*ICTA 1988, ss 8(3), 834(4)*]

For the year ended 30.6.86, the following information is relevant to A Ltd

	£
Schedule D, Case I	610,600
Schedule A	5,000
Schedule D, Case III	10,000 — received in two equal amounts on 1.1.86 and 30.6.86
Charges paid (gross)	1,000 — on 31.7.85
	9,000 — on 31.3.86

The rate of corporation tax for the financial year 1985 is 40% and the rate for the financial year 1986 is 35%.

The corporation tax computation of A Ltd for the 12-month accounting period ended on 30.6.86 will be

	£	
Schedule D, Case I	610,600	
Schedule A	5,000	
Schedule D, Case III	10,000	
	625,600	
Charges	10,000	
	£615,600	

Total profits apportioned		
1.7.85 — 31.3.86	$\frac{9}{12} \times$ £615,600	£461,700
1.4.86 — 30.6.86	$\frac{3}{12} \times$ £615,600	£153,900

Tax chargeable	
40% × £461,700	184,680
35% × £153,900	53,865
Total tax charge	£238,545

101.2 **PERIODS OF ACCOUNT EXCEEDING 12 MONTHS** [*ICTA 1988, ss 12(3), 72, 834(4)*]

B Ltd has prepared accounts for 16 months ending on 31.3.91. The following information is relevant

	£
Profit for 16 months	800,000
Schedule D, Case III income received on 1 March and	
1 September each year	50,000
Charges paid on 1 January each year (gross)	70,000
Capital gain (after indexation)	
arising on 1.6.90	100,000
Tax written down value of plant pool at 1.12.89	40,000
Plant purchased 1.2.90	200,000
Plant purchased 1.2.91	246,000
Proceeds of plant sold 31.12.90 (less than cost)	6,000

B Ltd will be assessed to corporation tax as follows

		Accounting period 12 months to 30.11.90 £	Accounting period 4 months to 31.3.91 £
Adjusted profits (apportioned 12:4)		600,000	200,000
Capital allowances	note (a)	(60,000)	(35,000)
Schedule D, Case I		540,000	165,000
Schedule D, Case III	note (b)	100,000	50,000
Chargeable gain	note (c)	100,000	—
		740,000	215,000
Charges on income	note (d)	(70,000)	(70,000)
Chargeable profits		£670,000	£145,000

Notes

(a)   Capital allowances

	Pool £	Allowances £
12 months to 30.11.90		
WDV brought forward	40,000	—
Additions	200,000	
	240,000	
Writing-down allowance (25%)	(60,000)	60,000
WDV carried forward	£180,000	
Total allowances		£60,000

CT 101.2 Accounting Periods

4 months to 31.3.91

WDV brought forward	180,000	
Additions	246,000	
Disposal proceeds	(6,000)	
	420,000	
Writing-down allowance (25% × $\frac{4}{12}$)	(35,000)	35,000
WDV carried forward	£385,000	
Total allowances		£35,000

Writing-down allowances are a proportionately reduced percentage of 25% if the accounting period is only part of a year. [*CAA 1990, s 24(2)*].

(*b*) Schedule D, Case III £

12 months to 30.11.90

	1.3.90 receipt	50,000
	1.9.90 receipt	50,000
		£100,000

4 months to 31.3.91

	1.3.91 receipt	£50,000

The total amount received is not apportioned on a time basis. [*ICTA 1988, s 9(1)*].

(*c*) The capital gain is not apportioned on a time basis, but is included for the period in which it arises. [*ICTA 1988, s 345(1)*].

(*d*) The charges are not apportioned on a time basis, but are included for the period in which they are paid. [*ICTA 1988, s 338(1)*].

102 Advance Corporation Tax

102.1 REDUCTION IN AMOUNT OF ACT PAYABLE BY REFERENCE TO FRANKED INVESTMENT INCOME (FII) RECEIVED [*ICTA 1988, s 241, 13 Sch*]

(A) No change in rate of ACT

C Ltd prepares accounts to 31 March each year. During the two years ended 31.3.91, it paid and received the following dividends

		£
20.6.89	Paid	7,500
3.3.90	Received	10,500
25.6.90	Paid	7,500
30.11.90	Received	5,250
25.3.91	Paid	4,500

The ACT movements are summarised by the following table

Return period		Franked payment £	FII £	Cumulative franked payments less FII £	ACT paid/ (repaid) £
Year ended 31.3.90					
30.6.89		10,000		10,000	2,500
30.9.89	No return			10,000	
31.12.89	No return			10,000	
31.3.90	note (a)		14,000	(4,000)	(2,500)
Surplus FII carried forward note (b)				£(4,000)	
Year ended 31.3.91					
Surplus FII brought forward				(4,000)	
30.6.90		10,000		6,000	1,500
30.9.90	No return			6,000	
31.12.90	note (a)		7,000	(1,000)	(1,500)
31.3.91		6,000		5,000	1,250
Net ACT paid in year note (c)					£1,250

Notes

(a) The ACT repayment is restricted to the ACT paid in the accounting period. [*ICTA 1988, 13 Sch 4*].

(b) Surplus FII is carried forward to the next accounting period. [*ICTA 1988, s 241 (3)*].

(c) Net ACT paid is available for set-off against the CT liability of the year ended 31.3.91 (subject to normal set-off limits). [*ICTA 1988, s 239 (1)(2)*].

(B) Change in rate of ACT

D Ltd prepares accounts to 31 July each year. During the year ended 31 July 1988, it paid and received the following dividends.

		£
25.9.87	Paid	7,300
25.3.88	Received	5,110
5.7.88	Received	5,250

The rates of ACT were $\frac{27}{73}$ for the year ended 31 March 1988 and $\frac{25}{75}$ for the year ended 31 March 1989.

The ACT movements are summarised by the following table

Return period		Franked payment £	FII £	Cumulative franked payments less FII £	ACT paid/ (repaid) £
30.9.87		10,000		10,000	2,700
31.12.87	No return			10,000	
31.3.88			7,000	3,000	(1,890)
30.6.88	To 5.4.88 note (a)			3,000	
				—	
	To 30.6.88			—	
31.7.88	note (b)		7,000	(7,000)	
Surplus FII carried forward				£(7,000)	
Net ACT paid in year note (c)					£810

Notes

(a) Because the rate of ACT changed on 6 April 1988, the return period is deemed to consist of two separate periods, ending on 5 April and 30 June, although only one return is required. In this example, no return need be made for the quarter to 30.6.88. [*ICTA 1988, s 246(6)(b)*].

(b) Because of the change of rate of ACT, this FII cannot be used to frank dividends paid before the change. It is carried forward to the next accounting period as surplus FII. [*ICTA 1988, s 246(6)(b)*].

(c) The net ACT paid is available for set-off against the CT liability of the relevant year (subject to normal set-off limits). [*ICTA 1988, s 239(1)(2)*].

(d) A change of rate of ACT when surplus FII exists has no practical effect, the surplus FII at 5 April being available against future franked payments in the normal way.

102.2 SET-OFF OF ACT AGAINST CORPORATION TAX

(A) No change in rate of ACT

E Ltd, a company with no associated companies, has the following profits for the year ending 31.3.91

	£
Schedule D, Case I	1,100,400
Schedule A	6,000
Schedule D, Case III	15,000
Chargeable gains	3,600

Annual charges of £75,000 are paid

During the year, E Ltd pays a final dividend of £600,000 in respect of the year ended 31.3.90, and an interim dividend of £337,500 in respect of the year ending 31.3.91. ACT on dividends amounts to £200,000 and £112,500 respectively. The dividends were paid on 30.6.90 and 1.1.91.

The CT liability will be

	£	£
Schedule D, Case I		1,100,400
Schedule A		6,000
Schedule D, Case III		15,000
		1,121,400
Chargeable gains		3,600
		1,125,000
Annual charges		(75,000)
Chargeable profits		£1,050,000
CT at 35%		367,500
Deduct lesser of		
ACT paid	312,500	
Maximum set-off 25% × £1,050,000	262,500	262,500
Surplus ACT	£50,000	
'Mainstream' CT liability		£105,000

Notes

(a) The ACT available for set-off is that relating to distributions paid in the year ending 31.3.91. [*ICTA 1988, s 239(1)*].

(b) The ACT set-off is restricted to 25% of the chargeable profits. [*ICTA 1988, s 239(2)*]. Before 17.3.87, ACT could only be offset against income and it was necessary to deduct annual charges from income rather than from gains.

(c) If profits were £200,000 or less and thus chargeable at the small companies rate of 25%, the maximum 25% ACT set-off (assuming it did not exceed the ACT actually paid) would extinguish taxable profits.

(d) Surplus ACT may be treated in one of the following ways.
  (i) Carried back against the liabilities of accounting periods beginning in the six preceding years and applied against a more recent period before a more remote one. [*ICTA 1988, s 239(3)*].
  (ii) Carried forward and set off against corporation tax liabilities on future chargeable profits. [*ICTA 1988, s 239(4)*].

(B) Change in rate of ACT [*ICTA 1988, ss 239(2), 246(5)*]
F Ltd has adjusted trading profits of £630,000 for the year ended 31.12.88. It paid a dividend on 30.4.88 of £600,000. ACT on the dividend was £200,000.

The CT liability is

	£	£
35% × £630,000		220,500
Deduct lesser of		
ACT paid	200,000	
Maximum set-off note (*a*)	160,650	160,650
Surplus ACT	£39,350	
'Mainstream' CT liability		£59,850

Note
(*a*)   Maximum ACT set-off is

$\frac{3}{12}$ × £630,000	157,500 × 27%	42,525
$\frac{9}{12}$ × £630,000	472,500 × 25%	118,125
	£630,000	£160,650

(C) Effect of losses
G Ltd commenced trading on 1.4.88 and had the following adjusted trading profits

		£
Year ended 31.3.89		540,000
Year ended 31.3.90		800,000
Year ended 31.3.91	loss	(690,000)

The company paid on 1.11.89 a final dividend of £300,000 for the year ended 31.3.89 and on 1.3.90 an interim dividend of £375,000 for the year ended 31.3.90. It accounted for the ACT of £100,000 and £125,000 respectively.

Prior to the claim for loss relief for the year ended 31.3.91, the CT position was as follows

Year ended	31.3.89	31.3.90	31.3.91
	£	£	£
Profit	540,000	800,000	—
Corporation tax	189,000	280,000	—
ACT set-off note (*a*)	25,000	200,000	—
'Mainstream' liability	£164,000	£80,000	—

As a result of the loss, a claim under *ICTA 1988, s 393(2)* **will result in the following amended figures**

Year ended	31.3.89	31.3.90	31.3.91
Profit (loss)	£540,000	£800,000	£(690,000)
Sec 393(2) claim	—	(690,000)	690,000
Revised Profits	£540,000	£110,000	
Corporation tax	189,000	27,500	note (c)
ACT set-off notes (a) & (b)	135,000	27,500	
'Mainstream' liability	£54,000	Nil	
Surplus ACT carried forward		£62,500	

Notes

(a)   The ACT is available for set-off first against the liability of the accounting period in which the dividends are paid and then against the liabilities of accounting periods beginning in the six preceding years assuming the relevant claim is made. It must be applied for a more recent period before a more remote one. [*ICTA 1988, s 239(3)*].

(b)   The ACT set-off in the years ended 31.3.89 and 31.3.90 is restricted to 25% of the taxable profit.

(c)   As profits are reduced to less than £150,000 for the year to 31 March 1990, small companies rate at 25% applies.

102.3 SURPLUS ACT — HOW IT CAN BE USED [*ICTA 1988, s 239*]

H Ltd is a trading company which has no connection with any other company. The following tables summarise the company's Schedule D, Case I profits and its distributions.

	Year ended 30.9.84	Year ended 30.9.85	6 months to 31.3.86	Year ended 31.3.87
	£	£	£	£
Schedule D, Case I profits	40,000	33,000	4,000	7,000
Dividends paid	—	—	—	42,600
ACT on dividends	—	—	—	17,400

The appropriate rates of ACT and CT are

ACT	$\frac{3}{7}$	$\frac{3}{7}$	$\frac{3}{7}$	$\frac{29}{71}$
CT	30%	30%	30%	29%

The following table shows how the ACT can be used

	£	£	£	£
CT liability	12,000	9,900	1,200	2,030
ACT set-off				
1987 dividend	(4,270)	(9,900)	(1,200)	(2,030)
1990 dividend (see below)	(7,730)	—	—	—
'Mainstream' liability	—	—	—	—

CT 102.4   Advance Corporation Tax

	Year ended 31.3.88 £	Year ended 31.3.89 £	Year ended 31.3.90 £	Year ended 31.3.91 £
Schedule D, Case I profits	30,000	30,000	1,000	24,000
Dividends paid	—	—	78,000	7,500
ACT on dividends	—	—	26,000	2,500

The appropriate rates of ACT and CT are

ACT	$\frac{27}{73}$	$\frac{25}{75}$	$\frac{25}{75}$	$\frac{25}{75}$
CT	27%	25%	25%	25%

The following table shows how the ACT can be used

	£	£	£	£
CT liability	8,100	7,500	250	6,000
ACT set-off				
1990 dividend	(8,100)	(7,500)	(250)	(2,420)
1991 dividend	—	—	—	(2,500)
'Mainstream' liability	—	—	—	£1,080
Surplus ACT carried forward at period end	—	—	£2,420	—

Notes

(*a*)   The ACT set-off is restricted in effect to basic rate income tax on the taxable income. With the exception of the year ended 31.3.91, the ACT set-off is the maximum possible.

(*b*)   The 1987 ACT is used firstly against the liability for that year and then carried back against liabilities of accounting periods beginning in the six preceding years, taking later periods first.

(*c*)   The 1990 ACT is similarly offset firstly against 1990 corporation tax and the balance then carried back. The earliest period in which it may be used is the year to 30.9.84 as the year to 30.9.83 (not illustrated in this example) would have begun more than six years prior to the beginning of the year to 31.3.90. Surplus ACT of £2,420 (£26,000 − (£250 + £7,500 + £8,100 + £7,730)) can be carried forward to the year ended 31.3.91 and can be fully used in that year as the maximum set-off of £6,000 is not thereby breached.

102.4 GROUPS OF COMPANIES

For examples on surrender of ACT within groups of companies, see 109.1 and 109.2 GROUPS OF COMPANIES.

103   Capital Allowances

Capital allowances are dealt with in detail in the Income Tax section at 3 CAPITAL ALLOWANCES.

103.1 TRANSFER OF TRADE WITHIN GROUP: PERIOD OF ACCOUNT EXCEEDING 12 MONTHS [*ICTA 1988, s 343; CAA 1990, ss 3, 24*]

A Ltd owns 80% of the ordinary share capital of both B Ltd and C Ltd, the latter companies carrying on similar trades.

A Ltd and C Ltd prepare accounts annually to 30 April. B Ltd which previously prepared accounts to 31 January each year has prepared accounts for 15 months ending on 30 April 1991.

On 30 September 1990, C Ltd transferred the whole of its trade to B Ltd under circumstances covered by *ICTA 1988, s 343*.

The following information is relevant to B Ltd

		£
Trading profit for 15 months to 30.4.91		200,000
1.2.90	Tax written-down value of machinery and plant pool	5,800
11.3.90	Plant purchased	3,000
3.7.90	Plant purchased	2,000
4.8.90	Plant sold (original cost £9,000)	6,800
10.2.91	Plant sold (original cost £40,000)	24,488
15.3.91	Plant purchased	30,000
1.5.90	Tax written-down value of machinery and plant pool owned by C Ltd	9,216

	£
Original cost of 10-year old building, owned by C Ltd, a building qualifying for industrial buildings allowances	300,000

B Ltd will have Schedule D, Case I assessments as follows

	Accounting period 12 months to 31.1.91	Accounting period 3 months to 30.4.91
	£	£
Trading profits	160,000	40,000
Capital allowances on machinery and plant	(1,768)	(1,000)
Industrial buildings allowance	(4,000)	(3,000)
Schedule D, Case I assessment	£154,232	£36,000

CT 103.1 Capital Allowances

Capital allowances

Machinery and plant

	Pool £	Allowances £
12 months to 31.1.91		
WDV at 1.2.90	5,800	
Additions	5,000	
Transfer from C Ltd note (a)	8,256	
	19,056	
Disposals	(6,800)	
	12,256	

WDA on assets transferred from C Ltd £9,216 × 25% × $\frac{4}{12}$		
note (a)	(768)	768
WDA on balance of expenditure (£12,256 − £8,256) = £4,000 × 25%	(1,000)	1,000
WDV at 31.1.91	£10,488	

Total allowances £1,768

	Pool £	Allowances £
3 months to 30.4.91		
WDV at 1.2.91	10,488	
Additions	30,000	
	40,488	
Disposals	(24,488)	
	16,000	
WDA (25% × $\frac{3}{12}$) note (c)	1,000	£1,000
WDV at 30.4.91	£15,000	

Industrial building	Allowances
12 months to 31.1.91	
£300,000 × 4% × $\frac{4}{12}$	£4,000
3 months to 30.4.91	
£300,000 × 4% × $\frac{3}{12}$	£3,000

Notes

(a) Where a trade is transferred part way through an accounting period the Inland Revenue take the view that writing-down allowances are calculated on the pool of expenditure held by the transferee at the end of its accounting period and those allowances are apportioned to the companies on a time basis for the period in which each company carried on the trade. (CCAB Guidance Note TR 500, 10 March 1983.)

	£
The transfer value of machinery and plant obtained from C Ltd is	
Tax written-down value at 1.5.90	9,216
WDA due to C Ltd (£9,216 × 25% × $\frac{5}{12}$)	960
	8,256
WDA due to B Ltd (£9,216 × 25% × $\frac{4}{12}$)	768
	£7,488

(*b*)   The 'successor' company (B Ltd) is entitled to the capital allowances which the 'predecessor' company (C Ltd) would have been able to claim if it had continued to trade. [*ICTA 1988, s 343(1)(2)*].

(*c*)   Writing-down allowances are reduced proportionately where the accounting period is less than one year. [*CAA 1990, s 24(2)*].

103.2 **DISCLAIMER OF WRITING-DOWN ALLOWANCES** [*CAA 1990, s 24(4)*]

D Ltd is a company with one wholly-owned subsidiary, E Ltd, and no other associated companies. Both companies prepare accounts to 31 March. For the year ended 31 March 1991, D Ltd has trading profits of £100,000 before capital allowances, whilst E Ltd incurs a trading loss of £100,000. E Ltd also has trading losses brought forward such that it is unlikely to have any taxable profits in the foreseeable future. In the year to 31 March 1991, D Ltd spent £100,000 on machinery and plant. There was a written-down value of £20,000 on the machinery and plant pool at 1 April 1990 and there were no disposals during the year.

Assuming a group relief claim is made under *ICTA 1988, s 402*, D Ltd's Schedule D, Case I computation for the year to 31 March 1991 will be as follows

	£
Trading profit	100,000
Less capital allowances (see below)	30,000
	70,000
Less loss surrendered by E Ltd	70,000
Taxable profit	Nil

E Ltd has unrelieved losses carried forward of £30,000 which will not be relieved in the foreseeable future.

D Ltd's capital allowances computation is as follows

	Machinery & plant pool £	Total allowances £
WDV at 1.4.90	20,000	
Additions	100,000	
	120,000	
WDA (25%)	30,000	£30,000
WDA at 31.3.91	£90,000	

D Ltd then disclaims its capital allowances

	£
Trading profit	100,000
Less loss surrendered by E Ltd	100,000
Taxable profit	Nil

CT 103.2   Capital Allowances

Capital allowances computation

	Machinery & plant pool £	Total allowances £
WDV at 1.4.90	20,000	
Additions	100,000	
	120,000	
WDA — disclaimed	—	Nil
WDV at 31.3.91	£120,000	

Notes

(a)   D Ltd may disclaim its writing-down allowances by giving notice in writing to the Inspector of Taxes by 31.3.93, i.e. within two years of the end of the accounting period. Instead of disclaiming the whole allowance, it could have claimed a reduced allowance if circumstances had so warranted.

(b)   As a result of the disclaimer, all of E Ltd's current year losses have been relieved, and D Ltd has a higher written-down value to carry forward on its machinery and plant pool.

(c)   It was held in *Elliss v BP Oil Northern Ireland Refinery Ltd* and *Elliss v BP Tyne Tanker Co Ltd C/A 1986, 59 TC 474* that a company may claim capital allowances or not, as it chooses. It was previously considered that the making of writing-down allowances was mandatory, subject only to a disclaimer as in (a) above.

(d)   See 109.3 – 109.7 GROUPS OF COMPANIES for group relief generally.

104   Capital Gains

Note: Unless otherwise stated all gains and losses referred to in this chapter are after any indexation allowance. See the capital gains tax section generally for computations of gains.

104.1 **CAPITAL LOSSES** [*FA 1972, s 93(2); F(No 2) A 1987, 5 Sch; ICTA 1988, s 345(1)*]

P Ltd has the following capital gains/(losses)

Year ended		£
31.7.87	Gains arising before 17.3.87	17,000
	Gains arising after 16.3.87	2,000
	Losses (all arising after 16.3.87)	(5,000)
31.7.88	Gains	20,000
31.7.89	Losses	(20,000)
31.7.90	Gains	40,000
	Losses	(30,000)

The gains and losses would be dealt with as follows in the CT computations of P Ltd

		£	Gain assessable £
31.7.87			
1.8.86 to 16.3.87			
Chargeable gains		17,000	
Deduct unrelieved losses	note (*c*)	3,000	
		14,000	
Reduced by $\frac{1}{7}$		2,000	12,000
17.3.87 to 31.7.87			
Chargeable gains (net)			Nil
Gains assessable to CT			£12,000
31.7.88			
Gains assessable to CT			£20,000
31.7.89			
Unrelieved losses carried forward		£(20,000)	Nil
31.7.90			
Chargeable gains (net)		10,000	
Deduct unrelieved losses brought forward		20,000	
Unrelieved losses carried forward		£(10,000)	Nil

Notes

(*a*)   Unrelieved losses cannot be set off against future trading profits, but are available to relieve future gains.

(*b*)   Gains assessable to CT may be covered by trading losses for the same or the succeeding accounting period [*ICTA 1988, s 393(2)*]. See 115 LOSSES below.

(c)   The year ended 31 July 1987 is divided into two component periods. Losses arising in one such period must first be offset against gains arising in that period, but any excess losses are offset against gains arising in the other component period. [*F(No 2)A 1987, 5 Sch 2(4)*].

104.2 **CLOSE COMPANY TRANSFERRING ASSET AT UNDERVALUE** [*CGTA 1979, s 75*]

(A)

G Ltd (a close company) sold a building in 1988 to an associated company Q Ltd which is not a member of the same group as G Ltd, at a price below market value at the time. Relevant values relating to the asset were

	£
Cost 1984	45,000
Market value at date of disposal	95,000
Sale proceeds received	75,000

The issued share capital of G Ltd was held as follows

	£1 ordinary shares	Value prior to sale of asset £
C	25,000	50,000
D	30,000	60,000
E	20,000	40,000
F	25,000	50,000
	100,000	£200,000

Sale proceeds on subsequent sale (at market value) in June 1990 of C's total share holding (originally purchased at par after 31 March 1982) in G Ltd were £47,000.

G Ltd's chargeable gain on the sale of the building is

		£
Market value	note (*d*)	95,000
Cost		45,000
Unindexed gain		50,000
Indexation allowance at say 20% on £45,000		9,000
Chargeable gain		£41,000

C's gain on the disposal of the shares will be

		£	£
Sale proceeds			47,000
Deduct Allowable cost			
Purchase price		25,000	
Less Apportioned undervalue	note (*a*)	5,000	20,000
Unindexed gain			£27,000

184

Notes

(*a*)   The apportionment of undervalue on disposal is

	£
Market value at time of sale	95,000
Deduct Sale proceeds	75,000
	£20,000

Proportion of shareholding		Value apportioned £
C	$\frac{25}{100} \times £20,000$	5,000
D	$\frac{30}{100} \times £20,000$	6,000
E	$\frac{20}{100} \times £20,000$	4,000
F	$\frac{25}{100} \times £20,000$	5,000
		£20,000

(*b*)   Indexation allowance is computed by reference to the allowable cost as reduced by the apportioned undervalue. [*FA 1982, s 86(3)*].

(*c*)   Transfers of assets on or before 31 March 1982 are disregarded in respect of disposals after 5 April 1988 to which re-basing applies. [*FA 1988, 8 Sch 7*].

(*d*)   In the computation of the company's gain, market value is substituted for proceeds under *CGTA 1979, s 29A*.

(B)

Assume the same facts as in (A) above except that the building had a market value of £195,000 at the date of disposal and C subsequently sold his shares for their market value of £22,000. Assume now also that C purchased his shares at par before 31 March 1982 and that their value on that date was £35,000.

G Ltd's chargeable gain will be computed under the same principles as in (A) above

C's unindexed gain on the disposal of the shares will be as follows

(i) By reference to cost

	£	£
Sale proceeds		22,000
Deduct Allowable cost	25,000	
Purchase price		
Less Apportioned undervalue note (*a*)	30,000	—
Unindexed gain		22,000
Indexation allowance (see below)		3,000
Gain after indexation		£19,000

CT 104.2   Capital Gains

(ii) By reference to 31.3.82 value

	£	£
Sale proceeds		22,000
Deduct Allowable cost		
31 March 1982 value	35,000	
Less Apportioned undervalue note (*a*)	30,000	
		5,000
Unindexed gain		17,000
Indexation at say 60% on £5,000		3,000
Gain after indexation		£14,000
Chargeable gain		£14,000

Notes

(*a*) The apportionment of undervalue on disposal is

	£
Market value at time of sale	195,000
Deduct Sale proceeds	75,000
	£120,000

	Proportion of shareholding	Value apportioned £
C	$\frac{25}{100} \times £120,000$	30,000
D	$\frac{30}{100} \times £120,000$	36,000
E	$\frac{20}{100} \times £120,000$	24,000
F	$\frac{25}{100} \times £120,000$	30,000
		£120,000

(*b*) See also notes (*b*) and (*c*) to (A) above.

104.3 GROUPS OF COMPANIES

(A) Intra-group transfers of assets which are trading stock of one company but not of the other — transfer from a 'capital asset' company to a 'trading stock' company [*ICTA 1970, s 274(1); CGTA 1979, s 122*]

X Ltd transfers an item classed as a fixed asset to another group company Y Ltd, which treats it as trading stock.

The following information is relevant

	Case (i) £	Case (ii) £
Original cost (after 31.3.82)	100,000	100,000
Market value at date of transfer	120,000	40,000
Eventual sale proceeds	140,000	140,000
Indexation allowance due on original cost at date of transfer	17,000	17,000

The position of Y Ltd will be as follows if there is no election under *CGTA 1979, s 122(3)*

Chargeable gain/(allowable loss) on appropriation		
Market value	120,000	40,000
Deemed cost of asset note (*a*)	117,000	117,000
Chargeable gain/(allowable loss)	£3,000	£(77,000)

Trading profit at date of sale		
Sale proceeds	140,000	140,000
Deemed cost of asset	120,000	40,000
Trading profit	£20,000	£100,000

With an election under *CGTA 1979, s 122(3)*

No chargeable gain or allowable loss arises on appropriation

Trading profit at date of sale				
Sale proceeds		140,000		140,000
Market value at appropriation	£120,000		£40,000	
Adjustment for (gain)/loss otherwise (chargeable)/allowable	(3,000)	117,000	77,000	117,000
Trading profit		£23,000		£23,000

Note

(*a*) The intra-group transfer by X Ltd to Y Ltd is treated as a disposal on which neither a gain nor a loss accrues after taking account of any indexation allowance due. X Ltd has no liability on the transfer and Y Ltd has a deemed acquisition cost of £117,000. [*ICTA 1970, s 273(1); FA 1982, 13 Sch 2*].

(B) Intra-group transfers of assets which are trading stock of one company but not of the other — transfer from a 'trading stock' company to a 'capital asset' company [*ICTA 1970, s 274(2)*]

P Ltd acquires from another group company Q Ltd as a fixed asset an item previously treated as trading stock.

	£
Cost to Q Ltd (after 31.3.82)	100,000
Market value at date of transfer	150,000
Eventual sale proceeds	200,000
Indexation allowance due on transfer value at date of sale	10,000

The group will have the following trading profits and chargeable gains

	£	£
Q Ltd trading profit [*CGTA 1979, s 122(2)*]		
Deemed sale proceeds		150,000
Cost to Q Ltd		100,000
Trading profit		£50,000
P Ltd chargeable gain [*ICTA 1970, s 273(1)*]		
Sale proceeds		200,000
Cost of asset	150,000	
Indexation allowance	10,000	
		160,000
Chargeable gain		£40,000

(C) Rollover relief on the replacement of business assets [*ICTA 1970, s 276; CGTA 1979, ss 115, 116, 118*]

M Ltd and N Ltd are 75% subsidiaries of H Ltd. On 1.2.91 M Ltd sold a showroom for £200,000, realising a chargeable gain of £110,000. N Ltd purchased a factory for £150,000 within three years after the date of sale of the showroom.

Rollover relief could be claimed as follows

	£	£
Gain otherwise chargeable to corporation tax		110,000
Deduct Unrelieved gain		
Sale proceeds	200,000	
Less Amount reinvested	150,000	
Chargeable gain	£50,000	50,000
Rollover relief		£60,000

New base cost of factory

Purchase price	150,000
Deduct Rollover relief	60,000
	£90,000

Notes

(*a*)   To qualify for relief, the two companies concerned need not be members of the same group throughout the period between the transactions but each must be a member at the time of its own particular transaction.

(*b*)   N Ltd will be entitled to an indexation allowance based on the deemed cost of £90,000 on a subsequent sale.

(*c*)   See also the capital gains tax section under 221 ROLLOVER RELIEF and also under 204.2 ASSETS HELD AT 31 MARCH 1982.

CT 104.3 Capital Gains

(D) A company ceasing to be a member of a group [*ICTA 1970, ss 273(1), 278(1)(3)*]
A Ltd had the following transactions

1.3.79   Purchased a freehold property £10,000.
31.3.82   Market value £30,000
1.5.87   Sold the freehold to B Ltd (a wholly-owned subsidiary) for £20,000 (market value £50,000).
31.7.90   Sold its interest in B Ltd.

Both companies prepare accounts to 31 March.

Relevant values of the RPI are: March 1982 79.4, May 1987 101.9.

The taxation consequences are
(i) There will be no chargeable gain on A Ltd's disposal of the property to B Ltd as the disposal is one on which, after taking account of the indexation allowance neither gain nor loss arises. [*ICTA 1970, s 273(1); FA 1982, 13 Sch 2*].

Indexation factor
$$\frac{101.9 - 79.4}{79.4} = 0.283$$

	£
Cost to A Ltd	10,000
Indexation allowance $0.283 \times £30,000$ note (*a*)	8,490
Deemed cost to B Ltd	£18,490

(ii) Following the sale of the shares in B Ltd on 31.7.90, B Ltd will have a corporation tax liability as follows for the year ended 31.3.88.

	£
Deemed disposal on 1.5.87	
Market value	50,000
Deemed cost	18,490
	31,510
Reduced by $\frac{1}{2}$ note (*b*)	(15,755)
Chargeable gain subject to CT	£15,755
B Ltd's new base cost for future gains	£50,000

Notes
(*a*)   The indexation allowance is calculated by reference to the market value at 31 March 1982 as this is higher than the original cost. For disposals before 6 April 1988, a claim had to be made for the 31 March 1982 value to be so used. [*FA 1985, s 68*].

(*b*)   Where a gain accrues under *ICTA 1970, s 278(3)* by reason of an event occurring after 5 April 1988 (i.e. a company leaving the group), then, if the asset was acquired by that company before 6 April 1988 and the gain is at least partly attributable to a disposal before 6 April 1988 by a person who held the asset at 31 March 1982, the gain is halved if the taxpayer so claims. [*FA 1988, s 97, 9 Sch 1,3,8*]. See also the capital gains tax section under 204.2 ASSETS HELD AT 31 MARCH 1982.

(*c*)   Note that the gain is treated as accruing to the transferee company on 1 May 1987 and not on 31 July 1990.

105   Close Companies

Note

See the 1988/89 and earlier editions for examples relating to apportionment of close company income under ICTA 1988, ss 423 – 430. These provisions were repealed by *FA 1989, s 103, 17 Sch Part V* for accounting periods beginning after 31 March 1989.

105.1   **CLOSE COMPANY — DEFINITION** [*ICTA 1988, ss 414 – 417*]

    (A)

A plc is a quoted company whose ordinary share capital is owned as follows

		%
B	a director	10
C	wife of B	5
D	father of B	4
E		17
F	business partner of E	2
G	a director	10
H		8
I Ltd	a non-close company	30
J		7
100	other shareholders	7
		100

It can be shown that A plc is a close company by considering the following three steps

(i) Is A plc controlled by five or fewer participators or by its directors?

		%	%
I Ltd			30
B	own shares	10	
	C's shares	5	
	D's shares	4	
			19
E	own shares	17	
	F's shares	2	
			19
			68

As A plc is controlled by three participators, the initial conclusion is that the company is close. [*ICTA 1988, ss 414(1), 416(2)*].

(ii) Is A plc a quoted company, with at least 35% of the share capital owned by the public?

		%
I Ltd		30
J		7
100	other shareholders	7
		44

As at least 35% of the share capital is owned by the public it appears that A plc is exempt from close company status, subject to step (iii). [*ICTA 1988, s 415(1)*].

(iii) Is more than 85% of the share capital of A plc owned by its principal members?

	%
I Ltd	30
B	19
E	19
G	10
H	8
	86

Because the principal members own more than 85% of the share capital A plc is a close company. [*ICTA 1988, s 415(2)(6)(7)*].

Note

(*a*)   Although J owns more than 5% of the share capital, he is not a principal member because five other persons each hold more than 7% and so themselves constitute the principal members. [*ICTA 1988, s 415(6)*].

(B)

The ordinary share capital of A Ltd (an unquoted company) is owned as follows

		%
B	a director	9
C	son of B	9
D	works manager	5
E	wife of D	15
F	a director	9
G	a director	1
H	a director	1
J	a director	1
K	a director	1
49	other shareholders with 1% each	49
		100

A Ltd is a close company because it is controlled by its directors, thus

		%	%
B	own shares	9	
	C's shares	9	
			18
D	own shares	5	
	E's shares	15	
			20
F	own shares		9
G			1
H			1
J			1
K			1
			51

Note

(*a*)   A manager is deemed to be a director if he and his associates own 20% or more of the ordinary share capital. [*ICTA 1988, s 417(5)*].

(C)
The ordinary share capital of A Ltd (an unquoted company) is owned as follows

		%
B	a director (unmarried)	15
C	a director	10
D	brother-in-law of B	5
E and F	trustees of G, deceased Will trust	5
H	a director	6
J		6
K		4
49	other shareholders with 1% each	49
		100

The shares held by E and F are held entirely in their capacity as trustees. The shares were settled by G, deceased, who was the father of B. B and D are joint life tenants of the settlement.

Before 6 April 1986, A Ltd would have been a close company by reason of its being in the control of five participators, as follows

		%	%
B	own shares	15	
	shares held by trustees note (a)	5	
	D's shares note (b)	5	
			25
C	own shares		10
H			6
J			6
K			4
			51

After 5 April 1986, A Ltd is no longer a close company as it is no longer necessary to aggregate D's shares with those of B and thus the company is no longer controlled by five or fewer participators   note (c)

Notes

(a)   The trustee's shares are aggregated with those of B as the settlor was a relative of his. [*ICTA 1988, s 417(3)(b)*].

(b)   Before 6 April 1986, D's shares are aggregated with those of B as they are co-beneficiaries of a trust and have an interest in shares of the company which are subject to that trust. [*ICTA 1970, s 303(3)(c)* as originally enacted].

(c)   After 5 April 1986, D ceases to be an associate of B, although B's shares must still be aggregated with those of the trustees and D's shares must now be separately aggregated with those of the trustees. [*ICTA 1988, s 417(3)(c)*].

(D)

The ordinary share capital of A Ltd is owned as follows

		%
B	a director	9
C	a director	9
D	a director	9
E		9
F		9
G Ltd	a close company	8
47	other shareholders with 1% each	47
		100

The ordinary share capital of G Ltd is owned as follows

		%
B	a director	50
C	a director	50
		100

A Ltd is not a close company under the control test because it is not under the control of five or fewer participators. The five largest shareholdings comprise only 45% of the share capital. [*ICTA 1988, ss 414(1), 416(2)*].

A Ltd is a close company under the distribution of assets test because B and C would each become entitled to one-half of G Ltd's share of the assets of A Ltd. [*ICTA 1988, s 414(2)–(2D); FA 1989, s 104*]. The shares of assets attributable to the five largest shareholdings become

		%	%
B	own share	9	
	50% of G Ltd's share	4	
			13
C	own share	9	
	50% of G Ltd's share	4	
			13
D			9
E			9
F			9
			53

194

(E)
A Ltd is an unquoted company with the following capital structure, owned as
shown

	£1 ordinary shares	£1 non-participating preference shares (no votes attached)
B	6,000	—
C	15,000	25,000
D	6,000	19,000
E	5,000	10,000
F	1,600	13,000
G	2,000	—
Other shareholders owning less than 1,000 shares each	64,400	33,000
	100,000	100,000

The company is close by reference to share capital as follows

	Control by votes	Control of issued capital
B	6,000	6,000
C	15,000	40,000
D	6,000	25,000
E	5,000	15,000
F	—	14,600
G	2,000	—
	34,000	100,600

Note
(a)   Control of the company includes control of more than one-half of
   (i)   voting power; or
   (ii)   issued share capital.
[*ICTA 1988, s 416(2)*].

105.2 **LOANS TO PARTICIPATORS** [*ICTA 1988, ss 419(1)(3)(4), 421(1)*]
P is a participator in Q Ltd, a close company. Q Ltd loaned P £73,000 on 29 August
1987. On 24 February 1990 P repaid £36,500 and on 30 June 1990 Q Ltd agreed to
waive the balance of the loan.

The effect of these transactions on Q Ltd and P is as follows

Q Ltd

On 29.8.87	The company becomes liable to pay, within 14 days of it being assessed, 'notional ACT' of £73,000 × $\frac{27}{73}$	£27,000
On 24.2.90	The company is entitled to repayment of 'notional ACT' to the extent of £36,500 × $\frac{27}{73}$	£13,500
On 30.6.90	No more 'notional ACT' can be recovered	

P

On 30.6.90 P's 1990/91 unearned income is increased by
$(£73,000 - £36,500) \times \frac{100}{75}$ £48,667

and
he is credited with basic rate income tax paid of
£48,667 at 25%   £12,166.75

Notes

(a) The repayment of 'notional ACT' is at the same rate as that paid on the advance, regardless of any change in the rate of ACT in the meantime.

(b) The income tax credit on the waived loan is based on the current rate at the time of the waiver, irrespective of the rate at the time the loan was made.

(c) Prior to 19 March 1986, no charge to 'notional ACT' could be made in respect of a loan to a participator which had been repaid before an assessment had been made, and thus close companies could avoid this charge by making successive loans and repayments. For loans made after 18 March 1986, tax can be assessed even if the loan has been repaid.

105.3 BENEFITS IN KIND FOR PARTICIPATORS [*ICTA 1988, s 418*]

R is a participator in S Ltd, a close company, but he is neither a director nor an employee earning £8,500 a year or more. For the whole of 1990/91, S Ltd provides R with a new 1,250cc car, for which the scale benefit is £1,700 and in which R makes no journeys on the company's business. R is required to pay S Ltd £300 a year for the use of the car. The cost of providing the car, charged in S Ltd's accounts for its year ending 31 March 1991, is £2,200.

Deemed distribution

If the benefit of the car were assessable under Schedule E, it would be:

	£
Scale benefit £1,700 × 1.5 (no business use)	2,550
Less contribution	300
	£2,250

S Ltd is treated as making a distribution of £2,250 to R.

ACT payable £2,250 × $\frac{25}{75}$ £750

Income of R for 1990/91 £2,250 × $\frac{100}{75}$ £3,000

Tax credit for R for 1990/91 £3,000 × 25%   £750

S Ltd's taxable profits

In computing S Ltd's profits chargeable to corporation tax, the actual expenditure charged (£2,200) must be added back.

106   Controlled Foreign Companies

106.1 IDENTIFICATION AS CONTROLLED FOREIGN COMPANY

(A) Basic identification rules [*ICTA 1988, ss 747, 750, 24 Sch*]

CC Co, an unquoted company, is incorporated and resident in Blueland and carries on business there as a wholesaler. It obtains the majority of its goods from associated companies although 10% is obtained from local suppliers. The goods are exported to UK customers — the major one of which is ADE Co Ltd. CC Co has a share capital of 1,000 ordinary shares which are owned as follows:

SS Co Ltd (UK incorporated but non-resident company)	50
ADE Co Ltd (UK incorporated and resident company)	150
John James (UK domiciled and resident individual)	300
Mrs James (wife of John James)	300
Caroline James (daughter of Mr & Mrs James) living in France	200
	1,000

The shareholders of SS Co are all non-UK residents. The shareholders of ADE Co Ltd are Mr & Mrs Andrew James (parents of John James).

The following figures (converted into sterling) have been obtained for CC Co for the year to 30 June 1990.

	£
Profit before tax	7,000,000
Depreciation	1,000,000
Dividend proposed for year	500,000
Blueland tax paid on profits of year	808,000
Market value of plant and machinery at 1.7.89	2,500,000
Additions to plant and machinery in year	1,800,000
Original cost of industrial buildings (acquired prior to 1.7.89)	1,500,000

There were no disposals of fixed assets during the year.

CC is a controlled foreign company because

  (i) it is resident outside the UK

 (ii) it is controlled by persons resident in the UK, as follows

	UK residents Ordinary shares	Non-UK residents Ordinary shares
ADE Co Ltd	150	
John James	300	
Mrs James	300	
SS Co Ltd		50
Caroline James		200
	750	250
Percentage holding	75%	25%

197

(iii) it is subject to a lower level of taxation in the country where it is resident

Notional UK chargeable profits

Year ended 30 June 1990

	£
Profit before tax	7,000,000
Add Depreciation	1,000,000
	8,000,000
Capital allowances note (*b*)	1,135,000
	£6,865,000

Tax thereon	
£6,865,000 × 35%	£2,402,750
50% thereof	£1,201,375
Overseas tax paid	£808,000

The overseas tax paid (£808,000) is less than half the 'corresponding UK tax' (£1,201,375) so the company is regarded as being subject to a lower level of taxation. [*ICTA 1988, s 750*].

Notes

(*a*)   To be a controlled foreign company a company must be
   (i)   resident outside the UK
   (ii)   controlled by persons resident in the UK
   (iii)   subject to a 'lower level of taxation' in the territory in which it is resident.
   [*ICTA 1988, s 747*].

(*b*)   **Capital allowances**

Plant and machinery	WDA pool	Allowances
	£	£
Market value of plant and machinery at 1.7.89	2,500,000	
Additions	1,800,000	
	4,300,000	
WDA (25%)	1,075,000	1,075,000
WDV at 30.6.90	£3,225,000	

Industrial buildings allowance
Original cost of building = £1,500,000

WDA £1,500,000 at 4%		60,000
Total allowances		£1,135,000

[*ICTA 1988, 24 Sch 10*].

(*c*)   It is assumed that SS Co Ltd comes within *FA 1988, 7 Sch 3* and thus continues to be non-resident in the UK, despite being incorporated there, for up to five years from 15 March 1988, notwithstanding *FA 1988, s 66*.

(B) Effect of operation in second overseas territory [*ICTA 1988, ss 416, 747, 749, 750, 756, 24 Sch*]

FC Co is an unquoted company incorporated and resident in Redland where tax is levied at 16.5% and carries on business there as an importer/exporter. The majority of goods are exported to UK customers.

FC Co also has a presence in Whiteland where the tax rate is 35%. There is no double tax treaty in existence between Whiteland and Redland and the Whiteland authorities have ruled that the presence in Whiteland constitutes a permanent establishment. Redland gives unilateral double taxation relief in the same way as the UK. The following figures (converted into sterling) have been obtained for FC Co for the year to 31 December 1990

	Whiteland £	Redland £	Total £
Profit before tax	40,000,000	50,000,000	90,000,000
Depreciation	—	6,000,000	6,000,000
Local tax paid on profits for year	14,000,000	8,250,000	22,250,000
Market value of plant and machinery at 1.1.90			24,000,000
Additions to fixed assets — plant and machinery			8,000,000

There were no disposals of fixed assets during the year.

FC Co has a share capital of £1,000 ordinary shares (registered) and 1,000 bearer shares which are owned as follows

	Ordinary shares	Bearer shares
TT Co Ltd (UK incorporated but non-resident company)	50	
BDE Co Ltd (UK incorporated and resident company)	250	
XY Co (Blackland subsidiary of OY Co)	50	
Roger Brown (UK domiciled and resident individual)	300	
TS Discretionary Trust		300
OY Co (incorporated and resident in Purpleland)	100	200
Will Rodgers (resident in Yellowland)		500
ACD Co (Orangeland incorporated and resident company)	250	
	1,000	1,000

The bearer shares have rights only to dividends (i.e. no voting rights).

The shares of BDE Co Ltd are owned by ACD Co. The shareholders of ACD Co are Orangeland residents.

The TS Discretionary Trust was established by Roger Brown's grandfather in 1970 and is resident in Purpleland. The beneficiaries who benefited from distributions by the Trust in 1989 and 1990 were UK residents.

OY Co purchased the shares in FC Co on 1 September 1990 from XZ Co Ltd — a UK incorporated and resident company — which had held the shares in FC Co for the previous three years. XZ Co Ltd is owned by UK residents.

CT 106.1 Controlled Foreign Companies

FC is a controlled foreign company because

(i) it is resident outside the UK

(ii) it is controlled by UK residents. The Revenue may ignore the bearer shares as they have no voting rights. The ordinary shares are held as follows

	UK residents Ordinary shares	Non-UK residents Ordinary shares
TT Co Ltd		50
BDE Co Ltd	250	
XY Co		50
Roger Brown	300	
OY Co		100
ACD Co		250
	550	450
Percentage holding	55%	45%

(iii) it is subject to a lower level of taxation in the country where it is resident

Notional UK chargeable profits

Year ended 31 December 1990

	£
Profit before tax	90,000,000
Add Depreciation	6,000,000
	96,000,000
Capital allowances note (*a*)	8,000,000
	£88,000,000
Tax thereon	
£88,000,000 × 35%	30,800,000
Less Double tax relief (Whiteland tax)	14,000,000
	£16,800,000
50% thereof	£8,400,000
Overseas tax paid note (*b*)	£8,250,000

£8,250,000 is less than £8,400,000 so the company is regarded as being subject to a lower level of taxation. [*ICTA 1988, s 750*].

Notes

(*a*)   **Capital allowances**

	WDA pool £	Allowances £
Market value of plant and machinery at 1.1.90	24,000,000	
Additions	8,000,000	
	32,000,000	
WDA (25%)	8,000,000	8,000,000
WDV at 31.12.90	£24,000,000	
Total allowances		£8,000,000

(*b*)   **Overseas tax paid**
Whiteland
Profit before tax   £40,000,000

Whiteland tax at 35%   £14,000,000

Redland	Whiteland	Redland	Total
Profit before tax	£40,000,000	£50,000,000	£90,000,000
Redland tax at 16.5%	6,600,000	8,250,000	14,850,000
Less credit for Whiteland tax			
(restricted to 16.5%)	(6,600,000)		(6,600,000)
Tax in Redland	—	£8,250,000	£8,250,000

The overseas tax brought into the CFC calculation is that paid in the country of residence. Therefore even though the total tax paid during the year was £22,250,000 only the £8,250,000 paid in Redland is taken into account.

106.2 **APPORTIONMENT OF PROFITS** [*ICTA 1988, s 752*]

(A)
In 106.1(A) above CC Co's notional UK chargeable profits and creditable tax are apportioned among the persons who had an interest in the company during its accounting period.

Shareholder	% shareholding	Attributable profits £	Creditable tax £
SS Co Ltd	5	343,250	40,400
ADE Co Ltd	15	1,029,750	121,200
John James	30	2,059,500	242,400
Mrs James	30	2,059,500	242,400
Caroline James	20	1,373,000	161,600
	100%	£6,865,000	£808,000

ADE Co Ltd is the only UK resident company to which chargeable profits and creditable tax are apportioned. ADE Co Ltd is chargeable to corporation tax on a sum equal to the profits of CC Co which are apportioned to it, and this corporation tax charge is then reduced by the apportioned amount of creditable tax. The corporation tax rate applicable is the rate (or average rate) applicable to ADE Co Ltd's own profits for the accounting period in which CC Co's accounting period ends. ADE Co Ltd has a 31 March year end.

CT 106.2   Controlled Foreign Companies

ADE Co Ltd

Tax computations — before apportionment

Year to 31 March	1991
	£
Schedule D, Case I	8,000,000
Losses brought forward	—
	8,000,000
Schedule D, Case III	50,000
Schedule D, Case V	1,250,000
Chargeable gains	250,000
	£9,550,000
UK tax	3,342,500
DTR on Schedule D, Case V income	(437,500)
ACT	—
Mainstream CT liability	£2,905,000

Tax computations — after apportionment

Schedule D, Case I	8,000,000
Losses brought forward	—
	8,000,000
Schedule D, Case III	50,000
Schedule D, Case V	1,250,000
Chargeable gains	250,000
CFC apportionment	1,029,750
	£10,579,750
UK tax	3,702,912
DTR on Schedule D, Case V income	(437,500)
ACT	—
CFC creditable tax	(121,200)
Mainstream CT liability	£3,144,212
Additional tax	£239,212

(B)

In 106.1(B) above both BDE Co Ltd and XZ Co Ltd will be chargeable to corporation tax on the profits of FC Co apportioned to them. XZ Co Ltd is liable because it owned shares in FC Co at some time during the year to 31 December 1990 (even though it had disposed of its shareholding before that date). It is likely that the Revenue will apportion a proportion of the profits attributable to the period to 31 August 1990 to XZ Co Ltd.

106.3 **ACCEPTABLE DISTRIBUTION POLICY** [*ICTA 1988, s 748, 25 Sch Pt 1*]

DEF Co Ltd, a UK incorporated and resident company with one associated company, holds 15% of the shares of LNB Co, an unquoted trading controlled foreign company resident in Pinkland, where tax is levied at only 10%.
LNB Co has a net profit after tax for the year ended 31 March 1990 of £450,000 and an anticipated profit for the year ended 31 March 1991 of £650,000. No withholding tax is applicable in Pinkland.
The following information is available in respect of DEF.

Year to 31 March	1990	1991
	£	£
Schedule D, Case I profit	600,000	780,000
Schedule D, Case III income	10,000	10,000
Chargeable gains	90,000	—
Schedule D, Case V income (gross) (tax suffered £30,000)	100,000	—
ACT paid	155,000	157,500

LNB Co

Calculation of profits apportioned to DEF Co Ltd and dividend required to avoid apportionment

Profit for the year ended 31 March 1990	£450,000
Amount of distribution required to avoid apportionment $\frac{1}{2} \times$ £450,000	£225,000

	Apportionment of profit	Dividend
DEF share	£	£
15% × £450,000: 15% × £225,000	67,500	33,750
Underlying tax (10%)	7,500	3,750
	£75,000	£37,500

DEF Co Ltd

With apportionment

Year to 31 March	1990	1991
	£	£
Schedule D, Case I	600,000	780,000
Schedule D, Case III	10,000	10,000
Chargeable gains	90,000	
Schedule D, Case V income	100,000	
CFC apportionment	75,000	
	£875,000	£790,000
UK tax thereon at 35%	306,250	276,500

Less

DTR on Case V income	(30,000)		
CFC creditable tax	(7,500)		
		(37,500)	
ACT		(155,000)	(157,500)
Mainstream tax payable		£113,750	£119,000

CT 106.3 Controlled Foreign Companies

DEF Co Ltd

If dividend paid

Year to 31 March	1990	1991
	£	£
Schedule D, Case I	600,000	780,000
Schedule D, Case III	10,000	10,000
Chargeable gains	90,000	—
Schedule D, Case V income	100,000	37,500
	£800,000	£827,500
UK tax thereon at 35%	280,000	289,625
Less		
DTR	(30,000)	(3,750)
ACT	(155,000)	(157,500)
Mainstream tax payable	£95,000	£128,375
Tax saving (cost)	£18,750	£(9,375)

DEF Co Ltd will make a net tax saving of £9,375 in tax if LBN Co pays a dividend for the year ended 31 March 1990 by 30 September 1991 (or such later time as the Revenue may allow).

Note

(*a*) If a controlled foreign company pursues an acceptable distribution policy in respect of an accounting period no apportionment is made.

106.4 SUBSEQUENT DIVIDEND [*ICTA 1988, s 754(5), 26 Sch 4*]

JF Co has been the subject of a direction in respect of the year ended 31 March 1989. In consequence an apportionment of its profit for that year (£900,000) has been made and KLM Ltd, a UK incorporated and resident company with a $\frac{1}{3}$ interest in JF Co, has been apportioned chargeable profits of £300,000 (gross). Creditable tax attributed to KLM is £30,000.

On 1 November 1990 following the direction notice JF Co paid a dividend of £528,000 in respect of the year ended 31 March 1989. There is no withholding tax and the underlying tax rate is 12%.

The corporation tax computations for KLM Ltd show that in the three years ended 31 March 1991 its Schedule D, Case I profits were £100,000, £300,000 and £450,000 respectively. Schedule D, Case III income for the three years was £10,000 per annum. For the year ended 31 March 1990 there were chargeable gains of £16,000 and charges on income of £8,000. Small companies rate does not apply, because there are several associated companies.

KLM Ltd has paid annual dividends of £165,000.

KLM Ltd

Tax computations

Year to 31 March	1989	1990	1991
	£	£	£
Schedule D, Case I profits	100,000	300,000	450,000
Schedule D, Case III income	10,000	10,000	10,000
Chargeable gains	—	16,000	—
CFC apportionment	300,000	—	—
Schedule D, Case V income (gross)	—	—	200,000
	410,000	326,000	660,000
Charges on income		(8,000)	
	£410,000	£318,000	£660,000
Tax at 35%	143,500	111,300	231,000
CFC creditable tax	(30,000)		
DTR on dividend (£200,000 at 12%)			(24,000)
Credit for UK tax on			
apportionment note (*a*)			(50,000)
ACT	(55,000)	(55,000)	(55,000)
	£58,500	£56,300	£102,000

		£
Note		
(*a*)	Tax on CFC apportionment — £300,000 × 35%	105,000
	CFC creditable tax	(30,000)
	Net tax suffered	£75,000
	Actual dividend (gross) — £200,000	
	Credit for UK tax on apportionment $\frac{2}{3}$ × £75,000	£50,000

107   Double Tax Relief

107.1 MEASURE OF RELIEF

(A) Relief for withholding tax [*ICTA 1988, ss 790(4)–(6), 795, 796, 797(1)(4)*]

A Ltd owns 5% of the share capital of B Ltd, a company resident in an overseas country which has no double taxation agreement with the UK. The following facts relate to A Ltd's accounting period for the year ended 31 March 1991

	£
Trading profits	1,000,000
Dividend from B Ltd (i.e. £20,000 less withholding tax)	15,000
Dividend paid by A Ltd 28.2.91	300,000
ACT on above dividend	100,000
Surplus ACT brought forward	190,000

A Ltd's tax liability is

	Schedule D Case I £	Schedule D Case V £	Total £
Profits	1,000,000	20,000	1,020,000
CT at 35%	350,000	7,000	357,000
Relief for foreign tax note (*a*)	—	(5,000)	(5,000)
	350,000	2,000	352,000
ACT set-off note (*b*)	(250,000)	(2,000)	(252,000)
	£100,000	—	£100,000

Notes

(*a*)   Because the shareholding in B Ltd is less than 10%, no credit is available for the underlying foreign tax on B Ltd's profits. Credit is available for withholding tax.

(*b*)   ACT set off against foreign income is restricted to the lower of 25% of income and the CT liability after relief for foreign tax. Surplus ACT carried forward is £38,000.

	£
ACT on dividend	100,000
ACT brought forward	190,000
	290,000
ACT set-off	252,000
	£38,000

(B) Relief for underlying tax [*ICTA 1988, ss 790(6), 795–797, 799*]
H Ltd, a UK resident company, which prepares accounts to 31 March each year, owns 40% of the share capital and voting power of S Ltd, a company resident abroad. On 3.2.91 H Ltd received a dividend of £70,000 from S Ltd which had suffered withholding tax at 30%. The dividend was paid out of the profits for the year ended 30.6.90. The following is an extract from the profit and loss account of S Ltd for that year

	£	£
Profit before tax		900,000
Tax on profits	270,000	
Deferred tax	130,000	400,000
Profit after tax		£500,000

Foreign tax actually paid was £250,000.

H Ltd may obtain relief as follows

	£	£
Dividend received		70,000
Add Withholding tax		30,000
		100,000
Add Underlying tax at $33\frac{1}{3}$% note (*a*)		50,000
		£150,000
UK Corporation tax at 35%		52,500
Overseas tax suffered		
Withholding tax	30,000	
Underlying tax	50,000	
	80,000	
Limited to UK tax	52,500	(52,500)
Overseas taxation unrelieved	£27,500	

Note

(*a*)   Rate of underlying tax $= \dfrac{\text{actual tax paid} \times 100}{\text{actual tax paid} + \text{relevant profit}}$

$= \dfrac{250,000 \times 100}{250,000 + 500,000}$

$= 33\frac{1}{3}$%

107.2 **ALLOCATION OF CHARGES ETC.** [*ICTA 1988, ss 790(6), 795–797, 799*]
The following information about A Ltd (which owns 20% of the voting power of B
Ltd, a non-resident company) for the year ended 31 March 1991 is relevant

	£
UK income	800,000
UK chargeable gains	66,000
Overseas income (tax rate 40%) from B Ltd (gross)	280,000
Charges paid (gross)	140,000
ACT paid	285,000

**A Ltd may allocate charges and ACT as it wishes in order to obtain maximum double
tax relief. The following calculation shows how this is best done**

	UK income and gains £	Overseas income £	Total £
Income and gains	866,000	280,000	1,146,000
Deduct Charges note (*c*)	140,000	—	140,000
	£726,000	£280,000	£1,006,000
CT at 35%	254,100	98,000	352,100
Deduct Double tax relief note (*d*)	—	(98,000)	(98,000)
	254,100	—	254,100
Deduct ACT	(181,500)	—	(181,500)
'Mainstream' liability	£72,600	—	£72,600

Notes

(*a*)   Surplus ACT carried forward is £103,500 (£285,000 − £181,500).

(*b*)   Relief for foreign tax is given before ACT set-off. [*ICTA 1988, s 797(4)(a)*].

(*c*)   To obtain the best advantage, charges should be set off firstly against UK
income and gains and then against overseas income subject to a lower rather
than a higher rate of overseas tax. (See note (*e*) below). (Where chargeable
gains arose before 17 March 1987, charges should be set against such gains
prior to income, as ACT cannot be offset against such gains.)

(*d*)   Double tax relief is the lower of
  (i)   Overseas tax suffered, 40% × £280,000   £112,000

  and
  (ii) CT liability on overseas income   £98,000

  Therefore, double tax relief   £98,000

(*e*)   If charges were set off against overseas income first, the following tax would be payable

	UK income and gains £	Overseas income £	Total £
Income and gains	866,000	280,000	1,146,000
Deduct Charges	—	140,000	140,000
	£866,000	£140,000	£1,006,000
CT at 35%	303,100	49,000	352,100
Deduct Double tax relief	—	(49,000)	(49,000)
Deduct ACT	(216,500)	—	(216,500)
'Mainstream' liability	£86,600	—	£86,600

This gives a maximum double tax relief of £49,000. Compared with the recommended allocation, £49,000 of double tax relief (£98,000 − £49,000) is lost, with an increase in the mainstream liability of £14,000 (£86,600 − £72,600) and a decrease of £35,000 (£103,500 − £68,500) in the surplus ACT carried forward.

108   Franked Investment Income

108.1 SURPLUS FII

Relief for trading losses and later year adjustments [*ICTA 1988, ss 242(4)(5)(9), 244(2)*]

The following information regarding A Ltd, a company with four associated companies, is relevant

	12 months ended 30.9.87 £	12 months ended 30.9.88 £	6 months ended 31.3.89 £	12 months ended 31.3.90 £	12 months ended 31.3.91 £
Trading profit/(loss)		100,000	(400,000)	450,000	700,000
Schedule A income		100,000	100,000	100,000	100,000
Franked investment income	100,000	500,000	500,000	—	100,000
Franked payments		100,000	350,000	500,000	700,000

Relief for the loss sustained in the six months ended 31.3.89 may be obtained under *ICTA 1988, s 242* by treating surplus FII as profits. The following calculations show how this is done and also how the loss is reinstated in later years. When relief is given under *section 242*, the tax credit relating to the FII used is repaid to A Ltd.

'Mainstream' corporation tax liability

		12 months ended 30.9.88 £	6 months ended 31.3.89 £	12 months ended 31.3.90 £	12 months ended 31.3.91 £
Schedule D, Case I		100,000	—	450,000	700,000
Sec 393(1) relief	note (*a*)	—	—	(50,000)	(150,000)
		100,000	—	400,000	550,000
Schedule A		100,000	100,000	100,000	100,000
		200,000	100,000	500,000	650,000
Sec 393(2) relief	note (*a*)	(100,000)	(100,000)	—	—
Assessable profits		£100,000	—	£500,000	£650,000
Corporation tax		£35,000	—	175,000	227,500
Deduct ACT paid	note (*h*)			12,500	150,000
Less Not available for set-off	note (*j*)			(12,500)	(37,500)
				—	112,500
'Mainstream' liability				£175,000	£115,000

Notes

(a)   Relief for trading loss of 6 months ended 31.3.89

		£
Loss incurred		400,000
Sec 393(2) relief in 6 months ended 31.3.89	note (b)	(100,000)
Sec 393(2) relief in 12 months ended 30.9.88	note (b)	(100,000)
Sec 242 relief in 6 months ended 31.3.89	note (d)	(150,000)
Sec 242 relief in 12 months ended 30.9.88	note (e)	(50,000)
Loss carried forward		—
Loss reinstated in 12 months ended 31.3.90	note (f)	50,000
Sec 393 (1) relief in 12 months ended 31.3.90		(50,000)
Loss carried forward		—
Loss reinstated in 12 months ended 31.3.91	note (g)	150,000
Sec 393(1) relief in 12 months ended 31.3.91		(150,000)
Loss carried forward		—

(b)   Profits must be relieved under *ICTA 1988, s 393(2)* before relief can be claimed under *Sec 242*. For the 12 months ended 30.9.88, relief is restricted to a period equal in length to the loss-making period, i.e. 6 months. Thus the set-off against profits of the preceding year is

	£
$\frac{1}{2} \times$ trading profit (£100,000)	50,000
$\frac{1}{2} \times$ Schedule A income (£100,000)	50,000
	£100,000

(c)   Summary of franked payments and receipts

	12 months ended 30.9.87	12 months ended 30.9.88	6 months ended 31.3.89	12 months ended 31.3.90	12 months ended 31.3.91
	£	£	£	£	£
Surplus FII b/f	—	100,000	450,000	450,000	—
FII	100,000	500,000	500,000	—	100,000
Franked payments	—	(100,000)	(350,000)	(500,000)	(700,000)
Sec 242 relief: notes (d)(e)	—	(50,000)	(150,000)	—	—
Surplus FII c/f	£100,000	£450,000	£450,000	—	—
Surplus franked payments				£(50,000)	£(600,000)

(d)   Relief under *ICTA 1988, s 242* in 6 months ended 31.3.89 is the lower of

(i) Surplus FII in period	£150,000
and	
(ii) Loss not relieved by *Sec 393(2)*	£200,000
Therefore, *Sec 242* relief	£150,000

211

CT 108.1   Franked Investment Income

(e)   Relief under *ICTA 1988, s 242* in 12 months ended 30.9.88 is the lower of

(i)   Surplus FII in period restricted to 50%
because the period of loss was 6 months
50% × £400,000   £200,000
and
(ii)   Loss not yet relieved   £50,000

Therefore, *Sec 242* relief   £50,000

(f)   Amount of loss reinstated in 12 months ended 31.3.90 is the lower of

(i)   Surplus franked payments   £50,000
and
(ii)   *Sec 242* relief given   £200,000

Therefore, reinstated loss   £50,000

(g)   Amount of loss reinstated in 12 months ended 31.3.91 is the lower of

(i)   Surplus franked payments   £600,000
and
(ii)   *Sec 242* relief not yet reinstated   £150,000

Therefore, reinstated loss   £150,000

(h)   ACT paid

(i)   12 months ended 31.3.90
= 25% × surplus franked payments
= 25% × £50,000   £12,500

(ii)   12 months ended 31.3.91
= 25% × surplus franked payments
= 25% × £600,000   £150,000

(j)   Set-off of ACT is restricted to ACT which has not been paid to reinstate the
loss
Tax credit repaid under *Sec 242*
= 25% × £200,000 (assuming all received under
a $\frac{25}{75}$ ACT rate)   £50,000
ACT paid in 12 months ended 31.3.90
not available for set-off (£50,000 loss re-instated)   12,500

ACT not available for set-off in 12 months ended 31.3.91   £37,500
(£150,000 loss re-instated)

109   Groups of Companies

109.1 **SURRENDER OF ACT** [*ICTA 1988, ss 239(1)-(4), 240(1)(4)*]

A Ltd owns 51% of the share capital of B Ltd which owns 51% of the share capital of C Ltd. An election under *ICTA 1988, s 247* is in force between A Ltd and B Ltd, and between B Ltd and C Ltd. All three companies prepare accounts to 31 March each year.

The following information is relevant

	Year ended		
	31.3.89	31.3.90	31.3.91
	£	£	£
A Ltd			
ACT surrendered to B Ltd	1,500	—	—
B Ltd			
Income	4,000	10,000	5,000
Dividends paid other than to A Ltd	2,475	3,750	4,605
ACT thereon	825	1,250	1,535

B Ltd may surrender ACT for the year ended 31.3.90 to C Ltd as follows

Year ended 31.3.89

		£	£
CT on income at 25%			1,000
Deduct ACT paid			
Surrendered by A Ltd		1,500	
Paid by B Ltd		825	
		2,325	
Deduct Set-off (restricted)	note (*a*)	1,000	1,000
Surplus carried forward		£1,325	
'Mainstream' corporation tax liability			—

Year ended 31.3.90

		£	£
CT on income at 25%			2,500
Deduct ACT paid			
During the year		1,250	
Brought forward from previous period	note (*a*)	1,325	
Carried back from succeeding period	note (*b*)	285	
		2,860	
Deduct Surrendered to C Ltd	note (*c*)	2,075	785
'Mainstream' corporation tax liability			£1,715

Year ended 31.3.91

		£	£
CT on income at 25%			1,250
Deduct ACT paid		1,535	
Carried back to previous period	note (*b*)	285	1,250
'Mainstream' corporation tax liability			—

213

Notes
(a) Maximum set-off of ACT for the year ended 31.3.89 is
£4,000 × 25%   =   £1,000

This leaves £1,325 (£2,325 − £1,000) to carry forward to future periods. (It is assumed that there is no possibility of B Ltd either carrying back any of its own ACT (i.e. £825) to previous periods or of surrendering all or part of that sum to C Ltd.) Because ACT surrendered to B Ltd is relieved in priority to B's own ACT, the ACT carried forward will be made up as follows

	£
ACT surrendered by A Ltd	500
Own ACT	825
	£1,325

(b) Maximum set-off of ACT for the year ended 31.3.91 is
£5,000 × 25%   =   £1,250

Therefore, surplus ACT is £285 (£1,535 − £1,250) which may be carried back to the previous period.

(c) Normally one would expect B Ltd to use its own ACT against its own CT liability, but it is not obliged to do so. For the year ended 31.3.90 B Ltd may surrender ACT to C Ltd as follows

		£
ACT paid by B Ltd during year ended 31.3.90		1,250
Surplus ACT brought forward from previous period which was paid by B Ltd	note (a)	825
		£2,075

The following ACT may not be surrendered to C Ltd		
ACT previously surrendered by A Ltd	note (a)	500
ACT which has been carried back from a succeeding period	note (b)	285
		£785

109.2 **SURRENDER OF ACT: EFFECT ON SUBSIDIARY** [*ICTA 1988, ss 239(4), 240(1)-(5), 245A; FA 1989, ss 97, 98*]

A Ltd owns 51% of the share capital of B Ltd and also a small shareholding in C Ltd. On 1.2.90, A Ltd acquires the entire share capital of D Ltd (another trading company) which prepares accounts to 31 December each year. The following dividend payments have been made

A Ltd   paid interim dividend of £3,750 on 5.2.90
           paid final dividend of £7,500 on 30.11.90
           received dividend of £2,250 on 4.12.90 from C Ltd
B Ltd   paid dividends of £5,250 on 2.2.91

A Ltd prepares accounts to 31 December each year and B Ltd prepares accounts to 31 March each year. B Ltd had taxable profits of £20,000 for the year ended 31.3.90 and £7,500 for the year ended 31.3.91. A Ltd decides to surrender the ACT arising on its 1990 dividends.

B Ltd may use ACT surrendered by A Ltd as follows

			Year ended 31.3.90
		£	£
CT on profit of £20,000 at 25%			5,000
Deduct ACT paid			
Surrendered by A Ltd	note (*a*)	1,000	
Carried back from the year			
ended 31.3.91	note (*b*)	1,750	2,750
'Mainstream' corporation tax liability			£2,250

			Year ended 31.3.91
		£	£
CT on profit of £7,500 at 25%			1,875
Deduct ACT paid			
Surrendered by A Ltd	note (*a*)	2,000	
Paid by B Ltd (£5,250 × $\frac{25}{75}$)		1,750	
		3,750	
Deduct Carried back to previous year	note (*b*)	(1,750)	
Carried forward to future years	note (*c*)	(125)	1,875
'Mainstream' corporation tax liability			Nil

Notes

(*a*)   ACT surrendered by A Ltd

Date	Dividend paid/(received)by A Ltd	ACT paid
	£	£
5.2.90	3,750 × $\frac{25}{75}$	1,250
30.11.90	7,500 × $\frac{25}{75}$	2,500
4.12.90	(2,250) × $\frac{25}{75}$	(750)
ACT surrendered		£3,000

This ACT is apportioned as follows

(i)   Applicable to dividend paid on 5.2.90

$$\frac{\text{Dividend paid on 5.2.90}}{\text{Total dividend for the year}} \times £3,000$$

$$= \frac{3,750}{3,750 + 7,500} \times £3,000 = £1,000$$

Therefore, B Ltd is treated as having paid ACT of £1,000 on 5.2.90, i.e. during the year ended 31.3.90

(ii)   Applicable to dividend paid on 30.11.90
Total ACT surrendered less applicable to 5.2.90
= £3,000 − £1,000   = £2,000

Therefore, B Ltd is treated as having paid ACT of £2,000 on 30.11.90, i.e. during the year ended 31.3.91.

(b) ACT surrendered by A Ltd must be used before ACT paid by B Ltd. As surrendered ACT exceeds the maximum set-off allowed for the year ended 31 March 1991 (25% × profit = 25% × £7,500 = £1,875), ACT paid by B Ltd may be carried back in accordance with the usual rules.

(c) ACT surrendered by A Ltd exceeds the maximum set-off allowed (see note (b)) by £125. This may not be carried back to previous periods but may be carried forward to future periods. However, if B Ltd was to leave the group, any such surplus ACT could not be used during the period in which it left the group or afterwards. Further anti-avoidance rules were introduced by *FA 1989, s 98* preventing the use of surrendered ACT following a change of ownership occurring after 13 March 1989 where it is preceded or followed by a major change in the nature of the surrendering company's trade.

(d) A Ltd cannot surrender any of its 1990 ACT to D Ltd, because the latter was not a subsidiary throughout the year ended 31.12.90.

109.3 GROUP RELIEF [*ICTA 1988, ss 402(1)(2), 403, 413(3)*]

A Ltd has a subsidiary company B Ltd in which it owns 75% of the ordinary share capital. Relevant information for the year ended 31.3.91 is as follows

		£
A Ltd	Trading profit	30,000
	Property income	10,000
	Capital gains	15,000
	Charges paid	2,000
B Ltd	Trading loss	10,000
	Capital allowances	38,000
	Charges paid	2,000

In addition, B Ltd has trading losses brought forward of £25,000.

Group relief is available as follows

	£	£
A Ltd		
Trading profit		30,000
Property income		10,000
Capital gains		15,000
		55,000
Deduct Charges paid		2,000
Profits		53,000
Deduct Loss surrendered by B Ltd		50,000
Assessable profits		£3,000
B Ltd		
Losses brought forward		25,000
Trading loss for the year	10,000	
Capital allowances	38,000	
Charges paid	2,000	
	50,000	
Deduct Loss surrendered to A Ltd	50,000	—
Losses carried forward		£25,000

109.4 **KINDS OF GROUP RELIEF** [*ICTA 1988, ss 393(9), 403(3)(4)(7)(8)*]

A Ltd is an investment company which has three trading subsidiaries B Ltd, C Ltd and D Ltd in which it owns 100% of the share capital. The companies have the following results for the two years ending 31 December 1990

		Year ended 31.12.89 £	Year ended 31.12.90 £
A Ltd	Profits	10,000	20,000
	Management expenses	(20,000)	(50,000)
B Ltd	Trading loss	(10,000)	(20,000)
	Schedule D, Case III income		30,000
C Ltd	Trading profit/(loss)	(10,000)	30,000
	Schedule A income		1,000
	Capital allowances — trading assets		(5,000)
	— Schedule A assets (given by discharge or repayment		(2,000)
	Charges paid		(40,000)
D Ltd	Profits		70,000

Group relief may be claimed for trading losses, management expenses, capital allowances and charges on income, as follows

		Year ended 31.12.89 £	Year ended 31.12.90 £
A Ltd			
Profits		10,000	20,000
Management expenses		(20,000)	(50,000)
Excess management expenses		(10,000)	(30,000)
Deduct Surrendered to D Ltd		—	30,000
Management expenses not available for group relief	note (*a*)	£(10,000)	—
B Ltd			
Trading loss brought forward		—	(10,000)
Trading loss		(10,000)	(20,000)
Trading loss carried forward		£(10,000)	—
			(30,000)
Deduct Surrendered to D Ltd	note (*b*)		20,000
Trading loss carried forward (not available for group relief or set-off against non-trading income)			£(10,000)
Profits chargeable to corporation tax			£30,000

C Ltd	£	£
Trading loss brought forward	—	(10,000)
Trading loss	(10,000)	
Trading loss carried forward	£(10,000)	
Trading profit (£30,000) *less* trade		
capital allowances (£5,000)		25,000
		15,000
Schedule A income (£1,000) less		
Schedule A capital allowances (£1,000) note (*c*)		—
		15,000
Charges paid (£40,000) less surrendered		
to D Ltd (£15,000) note (*d*)		(25,000)
Trading loss (i.e. excess charges) carried forward		£(10,000)

D Ltd		
Profits		70,000
Deduct Surrendered by A Ltd	30,000	
Surrendered by B Ltd	20,000	
Surrendered by C Ltd		
capital allowances	1,000	
charges	15,000	66,000
Profits chargeable to corporation tax		£4,000

Notes

(*a*)   It is not possible in 1990 to deduct the excess management expenses brough forward from 1989 before deducting 1990 management expenses to arrive a the amount available for group relief. The excess management expenses c £10,000 arising in 1989 are carried forward to 1990 but may not be surren dered and are, therefore, again carried forward.

(*b*)   Although a company might normally relieve a trading loss against othe income of the year before surrendering the loss, it is not obliged to do so.

(*c*) Total capital allowances on Schedule A assets	£
(given by way of discharge or repayment)	2,000
Deduct Relieved against Schedule A income	1,000
Available for surrender to D Ltd	£1,000

(*d*)   Group relief for excess charges is restricted to

Charges paid	40,000
Deduct Profits before *Sec 393(1)* relief	25,000
	£15,000

C Ltd's charges have been relieved as follows

Charges paid	40,000
Deduct Charges relieved against income	(15,000)
Surrendered to D Ltd	(15,000)
Excess charges carried forward	£10,000

218

109.5 **GROUP RELIEF 'CORRESPONDING ACCOUNTING PERIOD'**
(**A**) [*ICTA 1988, ss 402, 403(1), 408*]
A Ltd has a subsidiary B Ltd in which it owns 85% of the ordinary shares. A Ltd
prepares accounts to 31 December each year. B Ltd prepares accounts to 31 March
each year and had profits of £60,000 for the year to 31 March 1990 and £20,000 for
the year to 31 March 1991. During the year to 31 December 1990, A Ltd had a loss
of £40,000.

Group relief is available as follows

			Losses
A Ltd		£	£
Loss for the year ended 31.12.90			40,000
Deduct Loss surrendered to B Ltd			
For the year ended 31.3.90	note (*b*)	10,000	
For the year ended 31.3.91	note (*b*)	15,000	25,000
Loss not available for group relief			£15,000

		Year ended 31.3.90	Year ended 31.3.91
B Ltd		£	£
Profits		60,000	20,000
Deduct Loss surrendered by A Ltd	note (*b*)	10,000	15,000
Assessable profits		£50,000	£5,000

Notes

(*a*) Corresponding periods

	1989			1990				1991
	31.3	30.6	30.9	31.12	31.3	30.6	30.9	31.12	31.3

A Ltd   ├───£40,000 loss───┤
B Ltd   ├───£60,000 profit───┤ ├───£20,000 profit───┤
Common period   ├──3m──┤ ├────9m────┤

(*b*) Calculation of loss relieved
  (i) Against profits of the year ended 31.3.90
       Lower of loss in corresponding period $\frac{3}{12} \times £40,000 = £10,000$
                 and
       profits in corresponding period $\frac{3}{12} \times £60,000 = £15,000$

       Therefore, the loss relieved   £10,000

  (ii) Against profits of the year ended 31.3.91
       Lower of loss in corresponding period $\frac{9}{12} \times £40,000 = £30,000$
                 and
       profits in corresponding period $\frac{9}{12} \times £20,000 = £15,000$

       Therefore, the loss relieved   £15,000

(B) [*ICTA 1988, ss 408, 409, 411(3)*]
A Ltd has several wholly owned subsidiaries, including B Ltd and C Ltd. A Lt
prepares accounts to 31 December, the other two companies to 31 March.
Their results were as follows

			£
A Ltd	year ended 31.12.90	loss	(150,000)
B Ltd	year ended 31.3.91	profit	100,000
C Ltd	year ended 31.3.91	profit	100,000

The common period is the nine months to 31.12.90 and A Ltd could surrender losse
as follows

		9 months to 31.12.90	Surrender	
		£	£	
A Ltd's loss	$\frac{9}{12}$	(112,500)	(75,000)	to B Lt
B Ltd's profit	$\frac{9}{12}$	75,000		
A Ltd's loss	$\frac{9}{12}$	(112,500)	(75,000)	to C Lt
C Ltd's profit	$\frac{9}{12}$	75,000		
			£(150,000)	

Note
(*a*)   The surrender by A Ltd is not limited overall to $\frac{9}{12}$ of its loss for the yea
ended 31.12.90.
However, if B Ltd and C Ltd were themselves members of a group and ha
become subsidiaries of A Ltd on 1.4.90 the maximum surrender by A Lt
would have been restricted to that which could have been claimed by on
company joining the group on 1.4.90 i.e. to $\frac{9}{12}$ of A Ltd's loss. The surrende
in this case would be restricted to £112,500 in total, but the amount could b
allocated at will between B Ltd and C Ltd so long as neither compan
received relief of more than £75,000.

109.6 GROUP RELIEF: COMPANIES JOINING OR LEAVING THE GROUP [*ICT*
1988, ss 402, 403, 408–410]
On 1 April 1990 B Ltd was held as to 90% by A Ltd and 10% by a non-resident.
On 1 September 1990 C Ltd became a 75% subsidiary of A Ltd.
On 31 December 1990 A Ltd sold 30% of the shares in B Ltd (retaining 60%). A
Ltd, B Ltd and C Ltd all prepare accounts to 31 March each year. During the yea
ended 31 March 1991 the results of the companies are as follows

		£
A Ltd	Profit	60,000
B Ltd	Loss	(240,000)
C Ltd	Profit	30,000

Group relief for the loss sustained by B Ltd in the year ended 31.3.91 is available a
follows
Corresponding periods

Loss making period	1.4.90	30.6.90	1.9.90	31.12.90	31.3.9

Period for which B Ltd was a
'75% subsidiary' of A Ltd |—————— 9 months ——————|

Period for which B Ltd and C Ltd
were '75% subsidiaries' of A Ltd |—4 months —|

Calculation of loss relieved
Against profits of A Ltd

Lower of loss in corresponding period	$\frac{9}{12} \times$ £240,000 =	£180,000
and		
profits in corresponding period	$\frac{9}{12} \times$ £60,000 =	£45,000
Therefore, loss relieved		£45,000

Against profits of C Ltd

Lower of loss in corresponding period	$\frac{4}{12} \times$ £240,000 =	£80,000
and		
profits in corresponding period	$\frac{4}{12} \times$ £30,000 =	£10,000
Therefore, loss relieved		£10,000

Summary

	A Ltd	B Ltd	C Ltd
	£	£	£
Profit/(loss)	60,000	(240,000)	30,000
Group relief (claim)/surrender	(45,000)	55,000	(10,000)
Chargeable profit/(loss carried forward)	£15,000	£(185,000)	£20,000

Notes

(a)   If A Ltd had sold 40% or more of the shares in B Ltd, B Ltd would have been treated for group relief purposes as not being in the same group as A Ltd and C Ltd for any accounting period during which 'arrangements' for such a sale were in existence. [*ICTA 1988, s 410*].

(b)   When a company joins or leaves a group, the profit or loss is apportioned on a time basis unless this method would work unreasonably or unjustly. In the latter event a just and reasonable method of apportionment shall be used. [*ICTA 1988, s 409(2)*].

109.7 **GROUP RELIEF: RELATIONSHIP TO OTHER RELIEFS** [*ICTA 1988, ss 338(1), 393, 402, 403, 407*]

B Ltd is a subsidiary of A Ltd. Both companies prepare accounts to 31 March each year. The results for the three years ended 31 March 1991 were as follows

				£
A Ltd year ended 31 March	1989	Loss		(4,000)
	1990	Loss		(3,000)
	1991	Loss		(5,000)
B Ltd year ended 31 March	1989	Loss		(5,000)
	1990	Profit		10,000
	1991	Loss		(20,000)
	1989	Schedule A income		1,000
	1990	Schedule A income		1,000
	1991	Schedule A income		1,000
	1989	Business charges paid		(1,000)
	1990	Business charges paid		(1,000)
	1991	Business charges paid		(1,000)
	1991	Chargeable gains		5,000

The losses can be used as follows

	Year ended 31.3.89 £	Year ended 31.3.90 £	Year ended 31.3.91 £
B Ltd			
Trading profit/(loss)	(5,000)	10,000	(20,000)
Schedule D, Case I	—	10,000	—
Sec 393(1) loss relief	—	(5,000)	—
Schedule A	1,000	1,000	1,000
Income	1,000	6,000	1,000
Chargeable gains	—	—	5,000
Sec 393(2) loss relief current year	(1,000)	—	(6,000)
	—	6,000	—
Charges paid note (b)	—	(1,000)	—
Profit subject to group relief	—	5,000	—
Loss surrendered by A Ltd	—	(3,000)	—
Sec 393(2) loss relief from subsequent period	—	(3,000)	—
Charges becoming unrelieved	—	1,000	—
Assessable profits	—	—	—
Losses brought forward	—	(5,000)	(1,000)
Loss of the period	(5,000)	—	(20,000)
Used Sec 393(1) relief	—	5,000	—
Sec 393(2) relief current year	1,000	—	6,000
preceding year	—	—	3,000
Unrelieved business charges note (b)	(1,000)	(1,000)	(1,000)
Losses carried forward	£(5,000)	£(1,000)	£(13,000)

	Year ended 31.3.89 £	Year ended 31.3.90 £	Year ended 31.3.91 £
A Ltd			
Trading loss	4,000	3,000	5,000
Deduct Surrendered to B Ltd	—	(3,000)	—
	4,000	—	5,000
Loss brought forward	—	4,000	4,000
Loss (not available for group relief) carried forward	£4,000	£4,000	£9,000

Notes

(a)   Losses brought forward from previous periods must be used before claiming group relief.

(b)   Relief for charges paid in a period must be obtained before group relief is claimed but after any other relief from tax. In the year ended 31.3.90, charges cannot be relieved because a loss is carried back from the next year and this must be relieved before charges. The charges are initially relieved before group relief but are then displaced by the Sec 393(2) claim.

(c)   If group relief is claimed for the year ended 31.3.90 this restricts the amount which may be carried back from the succeeding period under *Sec 393(2)*.

(d)   No group relief is available for the year ended 31.3.91 even if the company does not claim *Sec 393(2)* relief for losses in the same period.

109.8 CONSORTIUM RELIEF

(A) Loss by company owned by consortium [*ICTA 1988, ss 402(3)(a), 403(1)(9)*]
On 1 April 1990 the share capital of E Ltd was owned as follows:

	%
A Ltd	40
B Ltd	40
C Ltd	20
	100

All the companies were UK resident for tax purposes.

During the year ended 31.3.91 the following events took place

On 1.7.90   D Ltd bought   20% from A Ltd
On 1.10.90   C Ltd bought   10% from B Ltd

The companies had the following results for the year ended 31.3.91

		£
A Ltd	Profit	40,000
B Ltd	Profit	33,000
C Ltd	Profit	10,000
D Ltd	Profit	70,000
E Ltd	Loss	(100,000)

Consortium relief for the loss sustained by E Ltd would be available as follows

	A Ltd £	B Ltd £	C Ltd £	D Ltd £
Profits for the year ended 31.3.90	40,000	33,000	10,000	70,000
Deduct Loss surrendered by				
E Ltd note (*b*)	(25,000)	(33,000)	(10,000)	(15,000)
Assessable profits	£15,000	—	—	£55,000

		£	Losses £
E Ltd			
Loss for the year ended 31.3.90			100,000
Deduct Loss surrendered to A Ltd		(25,000)	
B Ltd		(33,000)	
C Ltd		(10,000)	
D Ltd		(15,000)	(83,000)
Not available for consortium relief			£17,000

Notes
(a)   Loss relief for each member of the consortium is the lower of its share of the loss and its own profit for the year. Since D Ltd was a member of the consortium for only nine months, its claim would be limited to $\frac{9}{12} \times$ £70,000 = £52,500 if its share of losses exceeded this figure.

(b)   The share of losses of E Ltd appropriate to each member is

		%	£
A Ltd	$40\% \times \frac{3}{12} + 20\% \times \frac{9}{12}$	25	25,000
B Ltd	$40\% \times \frac{6}{12} + 30\% \times \frac{6}{12}$	35	35,000
C Ltd	$20\% \times \frac{6}{12} + 30\% \times \frac{6}{12}$	25	25,000
D Ltd	$20\% \times \frac{9}{12}$	15	15,000
		100	£100,000

(B) Loss by company owned by consortium: claim by member of consortium company's group [*ICTA 1988, ss 405(1)–(3), 406(1)–(4), 413(2)*]
A Ltd owns 100% of the share capital of B Ltd
B Ltd owns 40% of the share capital of D Ltd
C Ltd owns 60% of the share capital of D Ltd
D Ltd owns 100% of the share capital of E Ltd
D Ltd owns 100% of the share capital of F Ltd

This can be shown as follows

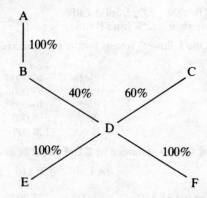

There are two groups, A and B, and D, E and F, and D is owned by a consortium of B and C. This relationship has existed for a number of years with all companies having the same accounting periods. None of the companies has any losses brought forward.

The companies have the following results for year ended 31 July 1990

A Ltd	£100,000 profit
B Ltd	£(30,000) loss
C Ltd	£Nil
D Ltd	£(20,000) loss
E Ltd	£10,000 profit
F Ltd	£(3,000) loss

E Ltd claims group relief as follows

	£	£
Profit		10,000
Deduct group relief: loss surrendered by F Ltd note (*b*)	3,000	
group relief: loss surrendered by D Ltd note (*b*)	7,000	(10,000)
		—

A Ltd can claim group relief and consortium relief as follows

		£	£
Profit			100,000
Deduct group relief: loss surrendered by B Ltd	note (*c*)	30,000	
consortium relief: loss surrendered by D Ltd	note (*d*)	5,200	(35,200)
Chargeable profit			£64,800

Notes

(*a*)　Where a company owned by a consortium is also a member of a group, its losses may be surrendered partly as group relief and partly as consortium relief.

(*b*)　Where a loss of a company owned by a consortium or of a company within its group may be used both as group relief and consortium relief, group relief claims take priority. In determining the consortium relief available, it is assumed that the maximum possible group relief is claimed after taking account of any other actual group relief claims within the consortium owned company's group. [*ICTA 1988, s 405(1)–(3)*]. As F Ltd has surrendered losses of £3,000 to E Ltd, D Ltd can only surrender £7,000 to E Ltd. Consortium relief is restricted to the balance of D Ltd's loss, i.e. £13,000. If E Ltd had not claimed £3,000 group relief for F Ltd's loss, D Ltd could have surrendered £10,000 to E Ltd by way of group relief and this would have reduced B Ltd's loss for consortium relief purposes to £10,000.

(*c*)　Group relief available to A Ltd is the lower of £100,000 and £30,000.

(*d*)　Consortium relief available to A Ltd is the lower of £70,000 (its profit as reduced by group relief) and £5,200 (40% of £13,000, see note (*b*) above). The relief available to A Ltd is the same as that which B Ltd could have claimed if it had had sufficient profits. A Ltd could also have claimed consortium relief in respect of F Ltd's loss if that had exceeded the £10,000 necessary to cover E Ltd's profit. [*ICTA 1988, s 406(1)–(4)*].

(C) Loss by subsidiary of company owned by consortium [*ICTA 1988, ss 402(3)(b), 403(1)(9), 411(9), 413(7)–(10)*]
Throughout 1990 the share capital of E Ltd was owned as follows

	%
A Ltd	35
B Ltd	30
C Ltd	25
D Ltd	10
	100

E Ltd owned 90% of the share capital of F Ltd, a trading company. The companies had the following results for the year ended 31.12.90

		£
A Ltd	Profit	100,000
B Ltd	Loss	(40,000)
C Ltd	Profit	30,000
D Ltd	Profit	80,000
E Ltd	Profit	40,000
F Ltd	Loss	(240,000)

All the above companies were UK resident for tax purposes.

Group relief of £40,000 of the loss sustained by F Ltd is claimed by E Ltd   note (c)

Consortium relief for the loss sustained by F Ltd would be available as follows

	A Ltd £	B Ltd £	C Ltd £	D Ltd £
Profits for the year ended 31.12.90	100,000	—	30,000	80,000
Deduct Loss surrendered by				
F Ltd note (a)	(70,000)	—	(30,000)	(20,000)
	£30,000	—	—	£60,000

		Losses £
F Ltd		
Loss for the year ended 31.12.90		240,000
Deduct Loss surrendered to E Ltd		(40,000)
		200,000
Deduct Loss surrendered to A Ltd	(70,000)	
C Ltd	(30,000)	
D Ltd	(20,000)	(120,000)
Not available for consortium relief		£80,000

Notes

(a) Loss relief for each consortium member is the lower of its share of the loss and its own profit for the year.

(b) The share of the balance of losses (after group relief) of F Ltd appropriate to each member is

	%	£
A Ltd	35	70,000
B Ltd	30	60,000
C Ltd	25	50,000
D Ltd	10	20,000
	100	£200,000

(c) Group relief claims take priority over claims for consortium relief and reduce the losses available for consortium relief. See also notes (a) and (b) to (B) above.

(D) Loss by consortium member [*ICTA 1988, ss 402(3), 403(9), 408(2)*]
A Ltd, B Ltd, C Ltd and D Ltd have for many years held 40%, 30%, 20% and 10% respectively of the ordinary share capital of E Ltd. All five companies are UK resident and have always previously had taxable profits. However, for the year ended 30.6.90 D Ltd had a tax loss of £100,000, followed by taxable profits of £40,000 for the subsequent year. E Ltd's taxable profits were £80,000 and £140,000 for the two years ended 31.12.89 and 31.12.90 respectively.

With the consent of A Ltd, B Ltd and C Ltd, D Ltd can (if it wishes) surrender the following part of its loss of £100,000 to E Ltd

Common period 1.7.89 to 31.12.89

		£
E Ltd's profit	$\frac{6}{12} \times £80,000 \times \frac{1}{10}$	4,000
D Ltd's loss	$\frac{6}{12} \times £100,000$	(50,000)

Common period 1.1.90 to 30.6.90

E Ltd's profit	$\frac{6}{12} \times £140,000 \times \frac{1}{10}$	7,000
D Ltd's loss	$\frac{6}{12} \times £100,000$	(50,000)

The lower common figures for the two periods are £4,000 and £7,000.

Therefore, E Ltd can claim £4,000 of D Ltd's loss against its own profits for the year ended 31.12.89 and £7,000 against its profits for the year ended 31.12.90.

Note
(*a*)   The share of E Ltd's profit against which D Ltd's losses may be relieved is restricted to D Ltd's share in E Ltd i.e. $\frac{1}{10}$th.

110 Income Tax in relation to a Company

110.1 **ACCOUNTING FOR INCOME TAX ON RECEIPTS AND PAYMENTS** [*ICTA 1988, s 7(2), 16 Sch*]

S Ltd prepares accounts each year to 30 April. During the two years ended 30 April 1990 it has made several annual payments from which income tax has been deducted and has received several sums under deduction of income tax.

The following items are shown net

	Receipts £	Payments £
25.6.88		7,500
4.7.88	3,750	
9.2.89	7,500	
24.4.89	11,250	
21.9.89		7,500
14.2.90		7,500

The adjusted profits (i.e. after allowing for the gross equivalents of the above amounts) were

	£
Year ended 30.4.89	600,000
Year ended 30.4.90	820,000

S Ltd will use the following figures in connection with the CT61 returns rendered to the Collector of Taxes and will also be able to set off against its corporation tax liability the income tax suffered as shown

Return period		Payments £	Receipts £	Cumulative payments less receipts £	Income tax paid/ (repaid) with return £
Year ended 30.4.89					
1.5.88 to 30.6.88		7,500		7,500	2,500
1.7.88 to 30.9.88			3,750	3,750	(1,250)
1.10.88 to 31.12.88	(No return)			3,750	
1.1.89 to 31.3.89			7,500	(3,750)	(1,250)
1.4.89 to 30.4.89			11,250	(15,000)	
					—
Year ended 30.4.90					
1.5.89 to 30.6.89	(No return)				
1.7.89 to 30.9.89		7,500		7,500	2,500
1.10.89 to 31.12.89	(No return)			7,500	
1.1.90 to 31.3.90		7,500		15,000	2,500
1.4.90 to 30.4.90	(No return)			15,000	
					£5,000

228

Tax payable

		Year ended 30.4.89	Year ended 30.4.90
		£	£
CT on profits	note (a)	210,000	287,000
Deduct Income tax suffered	note (b)	5,000	
Net liability		£205,000	£287,000

Notes

(a)   Corporation tax

Year ended 30.4.89
£600,000 × 35%   £210,000

Year ended 30.4.90
£820,000 × 35%   £287,000

(b)   This represents tax suffered on receipts, less that which has been offset against tax deducted from payments.

	£
Tax on total receipts £(3,750 + 7,500 + 11,250) × $\frac{25}{75}$ =	7,500
Tax deducted from payments and recovered from the	
Revenue £7,500 × $\frac{25}{75}$ =	2,500
	£5,000

(c)   Any change in the basic rate of income tax during an accounting period would not affect the duration of any return period or the right to set off tax borne against tax payable. This is in contrast to the position on changes in the rate of ACT — see 102.1(B) ADVANCE CORPORATION TAX ABOVE.

111   Interest on Overpaid Tax

[*ICTA 1988, s 825*]

111.1 The earliest due date for payment of corporation tax by X Ltd is 9 months after the end of each accounting period. An estimated assessment showing tax payable of £15,000 in respect of the accounting period for the year ended 31 December 1987 is raised on 1 June 1988. Tax of £15,000 is paid on 1 October 1988. An appeal is made against the estimated assessment.

The appeal is not determined until 1 June 1990 and an amended assessment is issued on 15 June increasing the total tax charged to £18,935. Further tax of £3,935 is paid on 15 July 1990.

Relief is subsequently claimed under *ICTA 1988, s 393(2)* for the carry back of losses from the following accounting period and the tax payable on the reduced assessment is £13,946, a reduction of £4,989. The repayment is made on 1 July 1991.

Repayment supplement is calculated as follows

(i)

On tax of £3,935, interest runs from the beginning of the income tax month following the first anniversary of the material date after the date of payment i.e.

Date of payment	15 July 1990
Anniversary of material date	1 October 1990
Interest runs from	6 October 1990

Interest runs to 5 July 1991, a total of 9 months

See also note (*a*) below.

(ii)

The balance of the repayment (£1,054) is attributable to the tax paid on 1 October 1988.

Interest runs from the beginning of the income tax month following 1 October 1989, i.e. from 6 October 1989.

Interest runs to 5 July 1991, a total of 21 months.

Note

(*a*)   Interest on overdue tax will be payable initially on additional tax of £3,935 charged by the amended assessment from the reckonable date to the date of payment, as follows

Reckonable date	1 April 1989
Date of payment	15 July 1990

This interest will eventually be repaid to X Ltd.
[*TMA 1970, ss 86, 91; FA 1989, s 156(1)*].

112   Interest on Unpaid Tax

[*TMA 1970, s 86; FA 1989, s 156(1)*]

112.1 A CT assessment is issued to X Ltd for its accounting year ended 31 October 1989. The relevant facts are as follows

Corporation tax charged	£75,000	
Assessment issued		15.8.90
Company appealed and claimed to postpone £30,000 of the tax charged		2.9.90
Commissioners determined that only £25,000 of all the tax charged could be postponed		17.10.90
Appeal determined, total tax payable £85,000		28.2.91
Amended assessment raised by Inspector		3.3.91
Normal due date		1.8.90
Table date		1.2.91
Tax payments made £45,000		20.12.90
£40,000		25.3.91

Interest on unpaid tax will be calculated over the following periods

£45,000	16.11.90 to 20.12.90	note (*a*)
£5,000	16.11.90 to 25.3.91	note (*a*)
£25,000	1.2.91 to 25.3.91	note (*b*)
£10,000	1.2.91 to 25.3.91	note (*c*)

Notes

(*a*)   16.11.90 is 30 days after the Commissioners' determination of the amount that could be postponed.

(*b*)   The reckonable date here is the later of
   (i)   what would have been the due date had there been no appeal, i.e. 14.9.90; and
   (ii)   the table date 6 months after the normal due date, i.e. 1.2.91.

(*c*)   Interest is chargeable on the £10,000 tax due over and above the original assessment as if it had been included in the assessment issued on 15.8.90.

113 Investment Companies

113.1 MANAGEMENT EXPENSES [*ICTA 1988, ss 75, 130*]

XYZ Ltd, an investment company, makes up accounts to 31 March.
The following details are relevant.

	31.3.90 £	31.3.91 £
Rents received	38,000	107,000
Interest received gross	10,000	5,000
Chargeable gains	18,000	48,000
Management expenses		
attributable to property	20,000	25,000
attributable to management	50,000	40,000
Capital allowances		
attributable to property	1,000	500
attributable to management	2,000	1,000
Business charges on income	30,000	30,000
Charitable charges on income	5,000	5,000

The corporation tax computations are as follows

Year ended 31.3.90

	£	£
Schedule A		
Rents		38,000
Deduct Capital allowances	1,000	
Management expenses	20,000	(21,000)
		17,000
Schedule D, Case III		10,000
Chargeable gains		18,000
		45,000
Deduct Management expenses	50,000	
Capital allowances	2,000	(52,000)
		(7,000)
Deduct Business charges	30,000	
Charitable charges	5,000	(35,000)
Unrelieved balance carried forward		£(42,000)

Year ended 31.3.91

	£	£
Schedule A		
Rents		107,000
Deduct Capital allowances	500	
Management expenses	25,000	(25,500)
		81,500
Schedule D, Case III		5,000
Chargeable gains		48,000
		c/f 134,500

	£	£
		b/f 134,500
Deduct Management expenses	40,000	
Capital allowances	1,000	
Unrelieved balance from		
previous accounting period	42,000	(83,000)
		51,500
Deduct Business charges	30,000	
Charitable charges	5,000	(35,000)
Profit chargeable to CT		£16,500

Notes

(*a*) Because of the restricted use of Schedule A losses, it is necessary to distinguish expenses of a general management nature from those pertaining to properties etc.

(*b*) The excess management expenses (including capital allowances) in the accounting period ended 31.3.90 are carried forward to the accounting period ended 31.3.91 and are set against total profits of that period. If profits in the year ended 31.3.91 had been insufficient the excess management expenses could have been carried forward to subsequent periods until fully used. See also note (*d*) below.

(*c*) Non-business charges would be disallowed only where, after set-off, the amount to be carried forward exceeds the total management expenses and total business charges.

(*d*) Management expenses brought forward from earlier accounting periods cannot be included in a group relief claim but may be set against franked investment income under *ICTA 1988, s 242*.

114 Liquidation

114.1 **ACCOUNTING PERIODS IN A LIQUIDATION** [*ICTA 1988, ss 12(7), 342*]
On 31 August 1987 a resolution was passed to wind up X Ltd. The company's normal period of account ends on 31 December.
It was later agreed between the liquidator and the Inspector that 31 January 1989 would be the assumed date of completion of winding-up. The actual date of completion was 30 June 1990.

The last accounting period of the company before liquidation is
1.1.87 to 31.8.87 — 8 months

The accounting periods during the liquidation are as follows
1.9.87 to 31.8.88 — 12 months
1.9.88 to 31.1.89 — 5 months
1.2.89 to 31.1.90 — 12 months
1.2.90 to 30.6.90 — 5 months

Notes
(*a*)   The final and penultimate financial years for the above accounting periods are 1990 and 1989 respectively. Assuming the small companies rate of CT is applicable for all financial years concerned, the rate of 25% applies to the income of financial year 1989. As the rate for the financial year 1990 was proposed by Budget resolution before completion of the winding-up, that rate will apply to the income of that year.

(*b*)   If the company is a close company, it may be unable, following the commencement of winding-up, to comply with *ICTA 1988, s 13A(2)*. It would then be a close investment-holding company and liable to the full rate of corporation tax whatever the level of profits. This applies to accounting periods beginning after 31 March 1989 but does not apply to the accounting period beginning on commencement of the winding-up. [*ICTA 1988, ss 13(1)(b), 13A; FA 1989, s 105*].

115   Losses

115.1 **SET-OFF OF TRADING LOSSES** [*ICTA 1988, s 393(2)*]

The results of X Ltd for the year ended 31.3.91 show

	£
Trading loss	(10,000)
Schedule A	3,000
Schedule D, Case III	4,000
Chargeable gains	7,200
Business charges on income	2,000

The loss may be relieved as follows

	£
Schedule A	3,000
Schedule D, Case III	4,000
Chargeable gains	7,200
	14,200
Deduct Trading loss	(10,000)
	4,200
Deduct Business charges on income	(2,000)
Profits chargeable to CT	£2,200
CT payable at 25%	£550

Note

(*a*)   See the 1987/88 edition for note of the position regarding small companies rate and any ACT set-off where chargeable gains arose before 17.3.87.

115.2 **CARRY-FORWARD OF TRADING LOSSES** [*ICTA 1988, ss 338(1), 393(1)(2)(9)*]

X Ltd has carried on the same trade for many years. The results for the years ended 30 September 1988, 1989 and 1990 are shown below

	1988	1989	1990
	£	£	£
Trading profit/(loss)	(20,000)	10,000	5,000
Schedule A	3,000	1,000	2,000
Schedule D, Case III	2,000	2,000	3,000
Chargeable gains	5,625	4,725	3,000
Business charges on income	(3,000)	(9,000)	(5,000)

235

CT 115.2 Losses

X Ltd has the option to elect to set off the 1988 loss against other profits of the period.
Assuming the election is made, the loss will be set off as follows

Year ended 30 September 1988

	£	Loss memorandum £
Trading loss		(20,000)
Schedule A	3,000	
Schedule D, Case III	2,000	
Chargeable gains	5,625	
	10,625	
Deduct Trading loss	(10,625)	10,625
	—	(9,375)
Business charges on income	—	(3,000)
Profits chargeable to CT	—	
		(12,375)

Year ended 30 September 1989

	£	£
Schedule D, Case I	10,000	
Deduct Loss brought forward	(10,000)	10,000
	—	(2,375)
Schedule A	1,000	
Schedule D, Case III	2,000	
Chargeable gains	4,725	
	7,725	
Deduct Business charges on income (restricted)	(7,725)	
Balance of business charges carried forward		(1,275)
Profits chargeable to CT	—	
		(3,650)

Year ended 30 September 1990

	£	£
Schedule D, Case I	5,000	
Deduct Loss brought forward	(3,650)	3,650
	1,350	—
Schedule A	2,000	
Schedule D, Case III	3,000	
Chargeable gains	3,000	
	9,350	
Deduct Business charges on income	(5,000)	
Profits chargeable to CT	£4,350	

115.3 CARRY-BACK OF TRADING LOSSES
(A) General [*ICTA 1988, s 393(2)(3)(9)*]
X Ltd has the following results for the years ending 31 December 1989 and 1990

	1989	1990
	£	£
Trading profit/(loss)	4,500	(20,000)
Schedule A	1,000	3,000
Schedule D, Case III	500	4,000
Chargeable gains	1,500	2,250
Business charges on income	4,000	2,000

The loss can be relieved as follows

			Loss memorandum
	£	£	£
Year ended 31 December 1990			
Trading loss			(20,000)
Schedule A		3,000	
Schedule D, Case III		4,000	
Chargeable gains		2,250	
		9,250	
Deduct Trading loss		(9,250)	9,250
Profits chargeable to CT		—	
			(10,750)
Unrelieved business charges carried forward	(2,000)		
Year ended 31 December 1989			
Schedule D, Case I		4,500	
Schedule A		1,000	
Schedule D, Case III		500	
Chargeable gains		1,500	
		7,500	
Deduct Loss carried back		(7,500)	7,500
Profits chargeable to CT		—	
Unrelieved business charges carried forward	(4,000)		
Losses to carry forward	£(6,000)		£(3,250)

Note

(*a*) The loss to be carried forward to set off against future years' trading profits is therefore

	£
1990 trading loss not relieved	3,250
1989 unrelieved business charges	4,000
1990 unrelieved business charges	2,000
	£9,250

CT 115.3   Losses

(B) Accounting periods of different lengths [*ICTA 1988, s 393(2)(3)(9)*]
X Ltd, which previously made up accounts to 31 March, changed its accounting
date to 31 December. Its results for the three accounting periods up to 31
December 1990 were as follows

	12 months 31.3.89 £	9 months 31.12.89 £	12 months 31.12.90 £	Loss memorandum £
Trading profit/ (loss)	14,000	12,000	(28,000)	
Schedule A	2,000	1,000	1,000	
Chargeable gains	—	2,000	1,000	
Business charges	—	3,000	3,000	

The computations are summarised as follows

	12 months 31.3.89	9 months 31.12.89	12 months 31.12.90	Loss memorandum
Schedule D, Case I/(trading loss)	14,000	12,000	(28,000)	28,000
Schedule A	2,000	1,000	1,000	
Chargeable gains	—	2,000	1,000	
	16,000	15,000	2,000	
Loss relief				
Sec 393(2)			(2,000)	(2,000)
Sec 393(2)(3)	(4,000)	(15,000)		(19,000)
Profits chargeable to CT	£12,000	—	—	
Unrelieved charges to carry forward Sec 393(9)		£3,000	£3,000	
Unrelieved losses to carry forward Sec 393(1)				£(7,000)

Note
(*a*)   The loss for the year to 31.12.90 can, to the extent that it cannot be relieved
against 1990 profits, be set against profits of accounting periods ending within
the preceding twelve months (the period to 31.12.90 being itself a twelve-
month accounting period). The accounting period to 31.3.89 ends within that
preceding twelve months but falls partly outside it. Loss relief against profits
of that period is restricted to $\frac{3}{12} \times £16,000 = £4,000$, profits being assumed to
accrue evenly throughout the accounting period.

115.4 **CARRY-BACK OF TERMINAL LOSSES** [*ICTA 1988, ss 338(1), 393(9), 394*]

X Ltd which had been trading continuously for many years ceased to trade on 30.9.90. The company's recent results, as adjusted for tax, are as follows

	Year ended 31 December				Period to 30 September
	1986	1987	1988	1989	1990
	£	£	£	£	£
Trading income/(loss)	4,000	12,000	8,000	(4,000)	(13,000)
Business charges paid	2,000	2,000	2,000	2,000	1,000

The loss of the year ended 31.12.89 will first be used as follows

	£	£	£
Income of year to 31.12.88			8,000
Loss carried back from year to 31.12.89			(4,000)
Adjusted trading income of year to 31.12.88			£4,000

The terminal loss is
9 months to 30.9.90

Trading loss	13,000		
Charges	1,000		
		14,000	
12 months to 31.12.89			
Charges £2,000 × $\frac{3}{12}$		500	£14,500

The terminal loss is relieved as follows

Year ended	Trading income £	Charges £	Available for relief £	Claim £
31 December 1989	Nil	1,500	Nil	Nil
31 December 1988	4,000	2,000	2,000	2,000
31 December 1987	12,000	2,000	10,000	10,000
31 December 1986 ($\frac{3}{12}$)	1,000	Nil	1,000	1,000
				£13,000

Notes

(*a*) The terminal loss relief of £14,500 is used only to the extent of £13,000.

(*b*) The trading income of the year to 31.12.88 is after taking into account the loss of the year to 31.12.89.

(*c*) The charges paid in 1986 are relieved entirely against the $\frac{9}{12}$ of the trading income of the year which is not eligible for terminal loss relief.

(*d*) Trade charges wholly and exclusively for the purposes of the trade must be deducted before terminal loss relief.

115.5 **LOSSES ON UNQUOTED SHARES** [*FA 1985, s 68; ICTA 1988, ss 573, 575, 576*]
Z Ltd has been an investment company since its incorporation in 1970. It is not part of a trading group and has no associated companies. It makes up accounts to 31 December. On 6.3.90, Z Ltd disposed of part of its holding of shares in T Ltd for full market value. Z Ltd makes no election under *FA 1988, s 96(5)*.

Details of disposal

Contract date	6.3.90
Shares sold	2,000 Ord
Proceeds (after expenses)	£4,500
Indexation factors (March 1982 to March 1990)	0.528
(April 1984 to March 1990)	0.370

Z acquired its shares in T as follows

				£
6.4.70 subscribed for	1,000 shares	cost (with expenses)		5,000
6.4.84 acquired	1,500 shares	cost (with expenses)		3,000
	2,500			£8,000

T shares were valued at £2.50 per share at 31.3.82. T has been a UK resident trading company since 1970. Its shares are not quoted on a recognised stock exchange.

Z may claim that part of the loss incurred be set off against its income as follows

Identification on last in, first out basis
 (i) Shares acquired 6.4.84 (not subscribed for)

	£
Proceeds of 1,500 shares	
$\dfrac{1,500}{2,000} \times £4,500$	3,375
Cost of 1,500 shares	(3,000)
Unindexed gain	375
Indexation allowance £3,000 × 0.370	(1,110)
Capital loss not available for set-off against income	£(735)

(ii) Shares acquired 6.4.70 (subscribed for)	Cost basis £	31.3.82 value basis £
Proceeds of 500 shares		
$\dfrac{500}{2,000} \times £4,500$	1,125	1,125
Cost of 500 shares	(2,500)	
31.3.82 value		(1,250)
Unindexed loss	(1,375)	(125)
Indexation allowance £2,500 × 0.528	(1,320)	(1,320)
	£(2,695)	£(1,445)
Capital loss available for set-off against income		£(1,445)

Notes

(*a*)   A claim under *ICTA 1988, s 573* is restricted to the loss in respect of the shares *subscribed* for.

(*b*)   The claim must be submitted within two years of the end of the accounting period in which the loss was incurred.

(*c*)   If an election under *FA 1988, s 96(5)* were in force, indexation allowance in (ii) above would be based on 31 March 1982 value. [*FA 1985, s 68(4)(5); FA 1988, 8 Sch 11*].

(*d*)   See also 10.5 LOSSES and 213.3 LOSSES in the income tax and capital gains tax sections respectively for further examples on this topic.

115.6 RESTRICTION OF TRADING LOSSES ON RECONSTRUCTION [*ICTA 1988, ss 343, 344*]

(A) Transfer of trade

A Ltd and B Ltd are two wholly owned subsidiaries of X Ltd. All are within the charge to corporation tax although A Ltd has accumulated trading losses brought forward and unrelieved of £200,000 and has not paid tax for several years. As part of a group reorganisation A Ltd's trade is transferred to B Ltd on 31 October 1990.

A Ltd's balance sheet immediately before the transfer is as follows

	£		£
Share capital	100,000	Property	90,000
Debenture secured		Plant	20,000
on property	50,000	Stock	130,000
Group loan	10,000	Trade debtors	120,000
Trade creditors	300,000		
Bank overdraft	60,000		
	520,000		
Deficit on			
reserves	(160,000)		
	£360,000		£360,000

Book values represent the approximate open market values of assets. B Ltd takes over the stock and plant to continue the trade, paying £150,000 to A Ltd and taking over £15,000 of trade creditors relating to stock. A Ltd is to collect outstanding debts and pay remaining creditors.

A Ltd's 'relevant assets' are

	£
Freehold property (£90,000 − £50,000)	40,000
Trade debtors	120,000
Consideration from B Ltd	150,000
	£310,000

CT 115.6 Losses

A Ltd's 'relevant liabilities' are

	£
Bank overdraft	60,000
Group loan	10,000
Trade creditors	285,000
	£355,000

Tax losses transferable with trade

£200,000 − £(355,000 − 310,000) = £155,000

Notes

(a)   Assets taken over by the successor to the trade are not included in relevant assets. Loan stock is not a relevant liability, but where the loan is secured on an asset which is not transferred, the value of the asset is reduced by the amount secured.

(b)   The assumption by B Ltd of liability for £15,000 of trade creditors does not constitute the giving of consideration and is not, therefore, a relevant asset of A Ltd. A Ltd's relevant liabilities are, however, reduced by the amount taken over.

(B) Transfer of part of a trade

D Ltd and E Ltd are wholly owned subsidiaries of X Ltd. On 1 November 1990 D Ltd transfers the manufacturing part of what has been an integrated trade to E Ltd. D Ltd has accumulated trading losses brought forward and unrelieved of £150,000, of which £50,000 are attributable to the manufacturing operations.

Immediately before the transfer D Ltd's balance sheet is as follows .

	£		£
Share capital	100,000	Property — shops	110,000
Share premium	18,000	factory	70,000
Loan stock	50,000	Plant	45,000
Trade creditors	290,000	Vehicles	20,000
Bank overdraft	42,000	Stock	30,000
	500,000	Trade debtors	65,000
Deficit on			
reserves	(160,000)		
	£340,000		£340,000

Book values represent the approximate open market value of assets. E Ltd takes over the manufacturing business together with the factory, plant and £18,000 of stock for a total consideration of £134,000.

Approximately 60% of D Ltd's turnover relates to manufacturing, and it is agreed that trade debtors and creditors are proportional to turnover.

242

D Ltd's 'relevant assets' apportioned to the trade transferred are

	£
Trade debtors (60%)	39,000
Consideration received from E Ltd	134,000
	£173,000

'Relevant liabilities' apportioned to the trade are

	£
Trade creditors (60%)	174,000
Overdraft (33%) note (a)	14,000
	£188,000

Tax losses transferable are restricted to
£50,000 − £(188,000 − 173,000) = £35,000

Notes

(a)   On the transfer of part of a trade, such apportionments of receipts, expenses, assets or liabilities shall be made as may be just. It is assumed that it is reasonable to apportion trade debtors and creditors in proportion to turnover and the overdraft in proportion to losses.

(b)   Loan stock, share premium and share capital are not relevant liabilities unless they have arisen in replacing relevant liabilities within the preceding year.

(c)   If the trade were transferred as a whole for market value of the assets, no restriction would apply to the losses transferable.

116 Partnerships

For examples on partnerships between individuals, see 14 PARTNERSHIPS in the income tax section.

116.1 ASSESSMENTS [*ICTA 1988, ss 114, 115*]

X Ltd and Mr Brown have been in partnership for many years and share profits in the ratio 2:1. The partnership's trading results for the years ended 30 September 1989 and 1990 are as follows

	Trading profits £	Capital allowances £
1989	27,000	15,000
1990	33,000	9,000

X Ltd's corporation tax assessments in respect of the partnership are

Year ended 30.9.89

	£
Trading profits	18,000
Deduct Capital allowances	10,000
Schedule D, Case I	£8,000

Year ended 30.9.90

	£
Trading profits	22,000
Deduct Capital allowances	6,000
Schedule D, Case I	£16,000

Mr Brown will have the following assessments and allowances

		Basis of assessment	Profit £	Capital allowances £
1988/89	Capital allowances (part)	actual		
	$\frac{6}{12} \times £5,000$			2,500
1989/90	Capital allowances	actual		
	$\frac{6}{12} \times £5,000 + \frac{6}{12} \times £3,000$			4,000
1990/91	Profits	y/e 30.9.89	9,000	
	Capital allowances (part)	actual		
	$\frac{6}{12} \times £3,000$			1,500
1991/92	Profits	y/e 30.9.90	11,000	

Note

(*a*) Profits apportioned to the individual partner are assessed to income tax on the normal preceding year basis. However, capital allowances are given for the actual year of assessment of the accounting period with apportionment between years where necessary. [*ICTA 1988, s 114(3)*].

117   Payment of Tax

117.1 **COMPANIES TRADING BEFORE 1 APRIL 1965** [*ICTA 1970, s 244; ICTA 1988, s 10(1)(b), 30 Sch 1*]

(A)
X Ltd, a trading company, was within the charge to income tax prior to 1 April 1965 and has since continued to be within the charge to corporation tax in respect of the same trade. The company prepares its accounts to 31 August each year.

The dates on which Corporation tax is due for payment for the years ending 31 August 1987 to 1990 are as follows

		Due date
Year ended 31 August 1987	note (*a*)	1 January 1989
Year ended 31 August 1988	note (*b*)	21 Ocober 1989
Year ended 31 August 1989	note (*b*)	11 August 1990
Year ended 31 August 1990	note (*c*)	1 June 1991

Notes

(*a*)   The accounts for the year ended 31 August 1964 would have formed the basis period for the year of assessment 1965/66, with payment of tax being due on 1 January 1966, an interval of 16 months. Thereafter the interval between the end of the accounting period and the payment date remains at 16 months. [*ICTA 1970, s 244*].

(*b*)   The 16-month interval is reduced to a 9-month interval in 3 equal stages, starting with the first accounting period beginning after 16 March 1987. [*ICTA 1988, 30 Sch 1*]. Thus for the year ended 31 August 1988, the interval is reduced by 71 days being one third, ignoring fractions of days, of the difference. The succeeding period is further reduced by 71 days.

(*c*)   Following the two transitional years, the payment interval becomes fixed at nine months thus bringing the company into line with those companies which were not trading before 1 April 1965 and which are governed by *ICTA 1988, s 10(1)(b)*.

(*d*)   *In any case* corporation tax is not payable earlier than thirty days after the date of the notice of assessment. [*ICTA 1970, s 244(1); ICTA 1988, s 10(1)(b)*].

(B)

The facts are as in (A) above except that in 1988, X Ltd decided to change its accounting date, preparing accounts to 30 June 1988 and thereafter to 30 June each year.

The dates on which Corporation tax is due for payment for the periods ending 31 August 1987 and 30 June 1988 to 1990 are as follows

		Due date
Year ended 31 August 1987		1 January 1989
10 months ended 30 June 1988	note (a)	2 September 1989
Year ended 30 June 1989	note (a)	23 June 1990
Year ended 30 June 1990		1 April 1991

Note

(a) Where either the first accounting period beginning after 16 March 1987 or the following accounting period is less than twelve months, the period of reduction (71 days in the previous example) is proportionately reduced. In this case the 16-month interval from 30 June 1988 is reduced by 59 days (71 days $\times \frac{10}{12}$, ignoring fractions). The payment interval for the year ended 30 June 1989 is reduced by a further 71 days.

118 Profit Computations

118.1 COMPUTATIONS

Y Ltd's accounts for the 12 months to 31.12.90 showed the following

	£		£
Wages and salaries	80,500	Gross trading profit	205,000
Rent, rates and insurance	5,000	Net rents	1,510
Motor expenses	8,000	Building society interest (gross)	
Legal expenses	2,000	(received 31.12.90)	1,500
Directors' remuneration	25,000	Dividend from UK company	
Audit and accountancy	2,500	(received 30.9.90)	4,500
Miscellaneous expenses	2,600	Profit on sale of investment	5,500
Debenture interest (gross)	3,375		
Ordinary dividend paid	15,000		
Depreciation	6,125		
Premium on lease written off	14,000		
Net profit	53,910		
	£218,010		£218,010

Analysis of various items gave the following additional information

(i) Legal expenses	£
Re staff service agreements	250
Re debt collecting	600
Re new issue of debentures	1,150
	£2,000

(ii) Miscellaneous expenses are	£
Staff outing	300
Subscriptions: Chamber of Commerce	250
Political party	50
Interest on unpaid tax	200
Contribution (on 1.11.90) to training and enterprise council	300
Charitable donation to trade benevolent fund	150
Single charitable donation (gross)	800
Other charitable donation (gross)	550
	£2,600

All charitable donations other than that to the trade benevolent fund were paid after deduction of basic rate income tax. The 'single donation' was made on 1 December 1990. Y Ltd is not a close company.

(iii) On 1.7.90, Y Ltd was granted a lease on office accommodation for a period of 7 years from that date for which it paid a premium of £14,000.

(iv) Profit on sale of investment is the unindexed gain arising from the sale of quoted securities on 28.2.90. The chargeable gain after indexation is £2,070.

(v) Capital allowances for the year to 31.12.90 are £10,000.

(vi) The new debentures are deep discount securities [*ICTA 1988, s 57, 4 Sch*]. They were issued on 1 April 1990 at 65 (for redemption at 100) with a yield to maturity of 5% per six-monthly interest period. Total nominal value is £180,000. Interest of $2\frac{1}{2}$% a year is payable half yearly, the first payment being made on 30.9.90. The charge in the accounts for debenture interest includes £1,125 accrued for the period 1.10.90 to 31.12.90.

(vii) All wages and salaries were paid during the period of account apart from directors' bonuses of £20,000, accrued in the accounts, voted at the AGM on 1.11.91 and not previously paid or credited to directors' accounts with the company.

The corporation tax computation is

	£	£
Net profit		53,910
Add		
Depreciation	6,125	
Directors' remuneration note (*a*)	20,000	
Subscription to political party	50	
Charitable donations notes (*d*) and (*e*)	1,350	
Interest on unpaid tax	200	
Debenture interest	3,375	
Dividend paid	15,000	
Premium on lease written off	14,000	60,100
		114,010
Deduct		
Net rents	1,510	
Building society interest	1,500	
Dividend received	4,500	
Profit on sale of investment	5,500	
		13,010
		101,000
Deduct		
Capital allowances	10,000	
Allowance for lease premium		
$\frac{1}{7} \times (£14,000 - \left(\frac{7-1}{50} \times £14,000\right)) \times \frac{6}{12}$	880	
		10,880
Schedule D, Case I trading profit		90,120
Schedule A		1,510
Building society interest		1,500
Chargeable gains		2,070
		95,200
Deduct Charges paid — debenture interest	2,250	
— income element of deep		
discount security	3,600	
— charitable donations		
note (*e*)	1,350	
		7,200
Profits chargeable to corporation tax		£88,000

Notes

(a)   Director's remuneration of £20,000 is disallowed as it remained unpaid 9 months after the end of the period of account. It will, however, be allowable in the tax computation for the year to 31 December 1991, i.e. the period of account in which it is paid. For periods of account beginning before 6 April 1989 and ending before 6 April 1990, these provisions applied by reference to a period of 18 months rather than 9 months. [*FA 1989, s 43*]. See *ICTA 1988, s 202B* as applied by *FA 1989, s 43(12)* as to the time when emoluments are treated as paid.

(b)   Legal expenses re the new issue of debentures are allowable under *ICTA 1988, s 77*.

(c)   The contribution to a training and enterprise council is allowable under *ICTA 1988, s 79A; FA 1990, s 76*.

(d)   The charitable donation to trade benevolent fund is allowable under *ICTA 1988, s 577(9)*.

(e)   The single charitable donation of £600 (net), equivalent to £800 (gross), is allowable, as an annual charge, under the Gift Aid provisions introduced by *Finance Act 1990* for payments made after 30 September 1990. The other donation of £412.50 (net), equivalent to £550 (gross) is also allowable. For accounting periods ending before 1 October 1990, the allowable amount was restricted to 3% of ordinary dividends paid in the accounting period. If Y Ltd had been a close company, the donation would not have been allowable as a qualifying donation as it is less than £600 (net). [*ICTA 1988, ss 338, 339, 339A; FA 1990, ss 26, 27*].

(f)   The proportion of the lease premium allowable is calculated under *ICTA 1988, ss 34(1), 87*.

(g)   The income element of deep discount securities is treated as a charge on income.

$$\frac{(£180,000 \times 0.65) \times 5}{100} - 2,250 = £3,600$$

[*ICTA 1988, 4 Sch 4, 5*].

118.2 **ALLOWANCE FOR CHARGES ON INCOME** [*ICTA 1988, ss 338, 393(9)*]
X Ltd, a UK resident company made a Schedule D, Case I profit of £5,000 in the
year to 31.10.90 and had unfranked investment income of £7,000.
It paid the following charges

	Situation (i)	Situation (ii)
	£	£
For business purposes (e.g. loan interest)	10,000	1,000
For non-business purposes (e.g. charitable deed of covenant)	4,000	13,000

The corporation tax position is

	£	£
Schedule D, Case I	5,000	5,000
Unfranked investment income	7,000	7,000
	12,000	12,000
Charges on income £14,000, restricted to	12,000	12,000
	Nil	Nil
Excess charges carried forward	£2,000	£1,000

Note
(*a*)   The amount available for carry forward is always the lower of
  (i)   the excess charges; or
  (ii) charges incurred wholly and exclusively for the purposes of the trade.

119   Small Companies Rate

119.1 **MARGINAL RELIEF** [*ICTA 1988, s 13; FA 1990, s 20*]

(A)

In its accounting period 1 April 1990 to 31 March 1991, X Ltd, a trading company, has chargeable profits of £200,000 including capital gains of £20,000, and also has franked investment income of £50,000. X Ltd has no associated companies.

Corporation tax payable is calculated as follows

	£
Corporation tax at full rate of 35% on £200,000	70,000
$\frac{1}{40} \times £(1,000,000 - 250,000) \times \dfrac{200,000}{250,000}$	15,000
Corporation tax payable	£55,000

(B)

In its accounting period 1 April 1990 to 31 March 1991, Y Ltd, a trading company has chargeable profits of £250,000 including capital gains of £20,000, but has no franked investment income. Y Ltd has no associated companies.

Corporation tax payable is calculated as follows

	£
Corporation tax at full rate of 35% on £250,000	87,500
$\frac{1}{40} \times £(1,000,000 - 250,000)$	18,750
Corporation tax payable	£68,750

Note

(*a*)   An alternative method, where there is no franked investment income, is to apply small companies rate up to the small companies rate limit and marginal rate ($37\frac{1}{2}$% for FY 1990) to the balance of profits. Thus

	£
£200,000 at 25%	50,000
50,000 at $37\frac{1}{2}$%	18,750
£250,000	£68,750

CT 119.1   Small Companies Rate

(C) [*ICTA 1988, s 13(3)(6); FA 1990, s 20(3)*]
In its accounting period 1 January 1990 to 31 December 1990, Z Ltd has chargeable profits of £360,000 and franked investment income of £40,000. Z Ltd has no associated companies.

Corporation tax payable is calculated as follows

Part of the accounting period falling in financial year 1989

		£	£

Profits $\frac{3}{12} \times$ £400,000 = £100,000
Basic profits $\frac{3}{12} \times$ £360,000 =   £90,000
Lower relevant maximum   =   £37,500   note (*b*)

Corporation tax at full rate
£90,000 at 35%   31,500.00

Less marginal relief

$\frac{1}{40} \times$ £(187,500 − 100,000) $\times \dfrac{90,000}{100,000}$ 1,968.75   29,531.25

Part of the accounting period falling in financial year 1990

Profits $\frac{9}{12} \times$ £400,000 = £300,000
Basic profits $\frac{9}{12} \times$ £360,000 = £270,000
Lower relevant maximum   = £150,000   note (*b*)

Corporation tax at full rate
£270,000 at 35%   94,500.00
Less marginal relief

$\frac{1}{40} \times$ £(750,000 − 300,000) $\times \dfrac{270,000}{300,000}$ 10,125.00   84,375.00

Corporation tax payable   £113,906.25

Notes

(*a*)   An accounting period which overlaps the end of a financial year is treated when calculating relief as if the part before and the part after were separate accounting periods.

(*b*)   The relevant maximum and minimum amounts are proportionately reduced for an accounting period of less than twelve months.

Upper relevant maximum amount
Financial year 1989 $\frac{3}{12} \times$ £750,000 = £187,500
Financial year 1990 $\frac{9}{12} \times$ £1,000,000 = £750,000

Lower relevant maximum amount
Financial year 1989 $\frac{3}{12} \times$ £150,000 =   £37,500
Financial year 1990 $\frac{9}{12} \times$ £200,000 = £150,000

119.2 **A COMPANY WITH AN ASSOCIATED COMPANY OR COMPANIES** [*ICTA 1988, s 13(3)-(6); FA 1990, s 20*]

Y Ltd has chargeable profits of £120,000 for the 12-month accounting period ended 30 September 1990 and has no franked investment income. It had no associated company until 1 August 1990 when all of its share capital was acquired by a company with four wholly-owned subsidiaries, of which one was dormant throughout the 12-month period and another was resident overseas.

Corporation tax payable is calculated as follows

Part of the accounting period falling in financial year 1989

			£	£
Profits $\frac{6}{12} \times$ £120,000	= £60,000			
Lower relevant maximum	= £15,000	note (b)		
Upper relevant maximum	= £75,000	note (b)		
Corporation tax at full rate £60,000 at 35%			21,000	
Less marginal relief				
$\frac{1}{40} \times$ £(75,000 − 60,000)			375	20,625

Part of the accounting period falling in financial year 1990

			£	£
Profits $\frac{6}{12} \times$ £120,000	= £60,000			
Lower relevant maximum	= £20,000	note (b)		
Upper relevant maximum	= £100,000	note (b)		
Corporation tax at full rate £60,000 at 35%			21,000	
Less marginal relief				
$\frac{1}{40} \times$ £(100,000 − 60,000)			1,000	20,000
Corporation tax payable				£40,625

Notes

(a)   An accounting period which overlaps the end of a financial year is treated as if the part before and the part after were separate accounting periods.

(b)   The relevant maximum and minimum amounts are proportionately reduced for an accounting period of less than twelve months and also where the company has associated companies (other than dormant ones) at any time during the year.

Upper relevant maximum amount
Financial year 1989 $\frac{6}{12} \times \frac{1}{5} \times$ £750,000 =   £75,000
Financial year 1990 $\frac{6}{12} \times \frac{1}{5} \times$ £1,000,000 = £100,000

Lower relevant maximum amount
Financial year 1989 $\frac{6}{12} \times \frac{1}{5} \times$ £150,000 =   £15,000
Financial year 1990 $\frac{6}{12} \times \frac{1}{5} \times$ £200,000 =   £20,000

Capital Gains Tax

Retail Price Index

	1982	1983	1984	1985	1986
January	—	82.6	86.8	91.2	96.2
February	—	83.0	87.2	91.9	96.6
March	79.4	83.1	87.5	92.8	96.7
April	81.0	84.3	88.6	94.8	97.7
May	81.6	84.6	89.0	95.2	97.8
June	81.9	84.8	89.2	95.4	97.8
July	81.9	85.3	89.1	95.2	97.5
August	81.9	85.7	89.9	95.5	97.8
September	81.9	86.1	90.1	95.4	98.3
October	82.3	86.4	90.7	95.6	98.5
November	82.7	86.7	91.0	95.9	99.3
December	82.5	86.9	90.9	96.0	99.6

	1987	1988	1989	1990	1991
January	100.0	103.3	111.0	119.5	(134.2)
February	100.4	103.7	111.8	120.2	(135.3)
March	100.6	104.1	112.3	121.4	(136.5)
April	101.8	105.8	114.3	125.1	(137.6)
May	101.9	106.2	115.0	126.2	(138.7)
June	101.9	106.6	115.4	126.7	(139.9)
July	101.8	106.7	115.5	(127.7)	(141.1)
August	102.1	107.9	115.8	(128.8)	(142.2)
September	102.4	108.4	116.6	(129.9)	(143.4)
October	102.9	109.5	117.5	(130.9)	(144.6)
November	103.4	110.0	118.5	(132.0)	(145.8)
December	103.3	110.3	118.8	(133.1)	(147.0)

Notes

(a) Figures in brackets from July 1990 onwards are assumed figures.

(b) The index was re-referenced in January 1987 from 394.5 to 100. The figures above which relate to months before January 1987 have been worked back from the new base and are not, therefore, those produced at the time by the Department of Employment.

(c) See 209.1(A) below for an example of how to use the above table in calculating the indexation factor for capital gains tax purposes.

(d) The following pages give details of indexation factors for disposals between April 1989 and June 1990 inclusive, which have been used in this section of the book where appropriate. As regards disposals before April 1989 and after June 1990, each relevant example quotes the indexation factor used, which in the case of post-June 1990 disposals will be an assumed figure.

Indexation factors for disposals in 1989/90

RI Month	1989									1990		
	April	May	June	July	Aug.	Sept.	Oct.	Nov.	Dec.	Jan.	Feb.	Mar.
March 1982	0.439	0.448	0.453	0.454	0.458	0.468	0.479	0.492	0.495	0.504	0.513	0.528
April	0.410	0.419	0.424	0.425	0.429	0.439	0.450	0.462	0.466	0.475	0.483	0.498
May	0.400	0.409	0.414	0.415	0.419	0.429	0.440	0.452	0.455	0.464	0.473	0.487
June	0.396	0.405	0.410	0.411	0.415	0.425	0.436	0.448	0.451	0.460	0.469	0.483
July	0.396	0.405	0.409	0.411	0.414	0.424	0.435	0.447	0.451	0.460	0.468	0.483
August	0.396	0.404	0.409	0.410	0.414	0.424	0.435	0.447	0.451	0.459	0.468	0.482
September	0.396	0.405	0.410	0.411	0.415	0.425	0.436	0.448	0.451	0.460	0.469	0.483
October	0.390	0.398	0.403	0.404	0.408	0.418	0.428	0.441	0.444	0.453	0.461	0.476
November	0.383	0.391	0.396	0.397	0.401	0.411	0.421	0.434	0.437	0.446	0.454	0.469
December	0.385	0.394	0.399	0.400	0.403	0.413	0.424	0.436	0.440	0.448	0.457	0.471
January 1983	0.384	0.392	0.397	0.398	0.402	0.411	0.422	0.434	0.438	0.447	0.455	0.470
February	0.378	0.386	0.391	0.392	0.396	0.405	0.416	0.428	0.432	0.440	0.449	0.463
March	0.375	0.384	0.388	0.390	0.393	0.403	0.414	0.426	0.429	0.438	0.446	0.461
April	0.356	0.364	0.369	0.370	0.374	0.383	0.394	0.406	0.410	0.418	0.426	0.440
May	0.350	0.359	0.363	0.365	0.368	0.378	0.388	0.400	0.404	0.412	0.420	0.434
June	0.347	0.355	0.360	0.361	0.365	0.374	0.385	0.397	0.400	0.409	0.417	0.431
July	0.340	0.348	0.353	0.354	0.358	0.367	0.378	0.389	0.393	0.401	0.409	0.423
August	0.334	0.342	0.347	0.348	0.352	0.361	0.371	0.383	0.387	0.395	0.403	0.417
September	0.328	0.336	0.341	0.342	0.346	0.355	0.365	0.377	0.380	0.389	0.397	0.411
October	0.323	0.332	0.336	0.337	0.341	0.350	0.361	0.372	0.376	0.384	0.392	0.406
November	0.319	0.327	0.332	0.333	0.336	0.345	0.356	0.367	0.371	0.379	0.387	0.401
December	0.315	0.323	0.328	0.329	0.333	0.342	0.352	0.364	0.367	0.375	0.383	0.397
January 1984	0.316	0.324	0.329	0.330	0.333	0.343	0.353	0.365	0.368	0.376	0.384	0.398
February	0.311	0.319	0.323	0.325	0.328	0.337	0.347	0.359	0.362	0.370	0.378	0.392
March	0.307	0.315	0.319	0.320	0.324	0.333	0.343	0.355	0.358	0.366	0.374	0.388
April	0.289	0.297	0.302	0.303	0.306	0.315	0.326	0.337	0.340	0.348	0.356	0.370
May	0.285	0.293	0.297	0.298	0.302	0.311	0.321	0.332	0.335	0.343	0.351	0.364
June	0.281	0.289	0.294	0.295	0.298	0.307	0.317	0.328	0.332	0.340	0.348	0.361
July	0.283	0.291	0.295	0.296	0.300	0.309	0.319	0.330	0.333	0.341	0.349	0.363
August	0.271	0.279	0.283	0.284	0.288	0.296	0.306	0.318	0.321	0.329	0.336	0.350
September	0.268	0.276	0.281	0.282	0.285	0.294	0.304	0.315	0.318	0.326	0.334	0.347
October	0.261	0.268	0.273	0.274	0.277	0.286	0.296	0.307	0.310	0.318	0.326	0.339
November	0.257	0.264	0.269	0.270	0.273	0.282	0.292	0.303	0.306	0.314	0.322	0.335
December	0.258	0.265	0.270	0.271	0.274	0.283	0.293	0.304	0.307	0.315	0.323	0.336
January 1985	0.253	0.261	0.265	0.266	0.270	0.278	0.288	0.299	0.303	0.310	0.318	0.331
February	0.243	0.251	0.255	0.256	0.260	0.268	0.278	0.289	0.292	0.300	0.307	0.320
March	0.232	0.239	0.244	0.245	0.248	0.256	0.266	0.277	0.280	0.288	0.295	0.308
April	0.206	0.213	0.218	0.219	0.222	0.230	0.240	0.250	0.253	0.261	0.268	0.281
May	0.201	0.208	0.212	0.213	0.216	0.225	0.234	0.245	0.248	0.255	0.262	0.275
June	0.198	0.205	0.209	0.211	0.214	0.222	0.232	0.242	0.245	0.252	0.260	0.272
July	0.200	0.208	0.212	0.213	0.216	0.224	0.234	0.244	0.247	0.255	0.262	0.275
August	0.197	0.204	0.209	0.210	0.213	0.221	0.231	0.241	0.244	0.251	0.259	0.271
September	0.198	0.205	0.209	0.210	0.213	0.222	0.231	0.242	0.245	0.252	0.259	0.272
October	0.196	0.203	0.207	0.208	0.211	0.220	0.229	0.240	0.243	0.250	0.257	0.270
November	0.192	0.199	0.203	0.204	0.207	0.216	0.225	0.235	0.239	0.246	0.253	0.266
December	0.190	0.197	0.202	0.203	0.206	0.214	0.223	0.234	0.237	0.244	0.251	0.264

Indexation factors

Indexation factors for disposals in 1989/90 (continued)

RI Month	1989 April	May	June	July	Aug.	Sept.	Oct.	Nov.	Dec.	1990 Jan.	Feb.	Mar.
January 1986	0.188	0.195	0.199	0.200	0.203	0.211	0.221	0.231	0.234	0.242	0.249	0.261
February	0.183	0.190	0.195	0.196	0.199	0.207	0.216	0.227	0.230	0.237	0.244	0.257
March	0.182	0.189	0.193	0.194	0.197	0.205	0.215	0.225	0.228	0.235	0.243	0.255
April	0.170	0.177	0.182	0.183	0.186	0.194	0.203	0.213	0.216	0.224	0.231	0.243
May	0.168	0.175	0.179	0.180	0.184	0.192	0.201	0.211	0.214	0.221	0.228	0.241
June	0.169	0.176	0.180	0.181	0.184	0.192	0.201	0.212	0.215	0.222	0.229	0.241
July	0.172	0.179	0.183	0.184	0.187	0.196	0.205	0.215	0.218	0.225	0.233	0.245
August	0.168	0.176	0.180	0.181	0.184	0.192	0.201	0.211	0.214	0.222	0.229	0.241
September	0.163	0.170	0.174	0.175	0.178	0.186	0.195	0.205	0.209	0.216	0.223	0.235
October	0.161	0.168	0.172	0.173	0.176	0.184	0.193	0.204	0.207	0.214	0.221	0.233
November	0.151	0.158	0.162	0.163	0.166	0.174	0.183	0.193	0.196	0.204	0.211	0.223
December	0.147	0.154	0.158	0.159	0.162	0.170	0.179	0.190	0.193	0.200	0.207	0.219
January 1987	0.143	0.150	0.154	0.155	0.158	0.166	0.175	0.185	0.188	0.195	0.202	0.214
February	0.138	0.145	0.149	0.150	0.153	0.161	0.170	0.180	0.183	0.190	0.197	0.209
March	0.136	0.143	0.147	0.148	0.151	0.159	0.168	0.178	0.181	0.188	0.195	0.207
April	0.123	0.130	0.134	0.135	0.138	0.145	0.154	0.164	0.167	0.174	0.181	0.193
May	0.122	0.129	0.132	0.133	0.136	0.144	0.153	0.163	0.166	0.173	0.180	0.191
June	0.122	0.129	0.132	0.133	0.136	0.144	0.153	0.163	0.166	0.173	0.180	0.191
July	0.123	0.130	0.134	0.135	0.138	0.145	0.154	0.164	0.167	0.174	0.181	0.193
August	0.119	0.126	0.130	0.131	0.134	0.142	0.151	0.161	0.164	0.170	0.177	0.189
September	0.116	0.123	0.127	0.128	0.131	0.139	0.147	0.157	0.160	0.167	0.174	0.186
October	0.111	0.118	0.121	0.122	0.125	0.133	0.142	0.152	0.155	0.161	0.168	0.180
November	0.105	0.112	0.116	0.117	0.120	0.128	0.136	0.146	0.149	0.156	0.162	0.174
December	0.106	0.113	0.117	0.118	0.121	0.129	0.137	0.147	0.150	0.157	0.164	0.175
January 1988	0.106	0.113	0.117	0.118	0.121	0.129	0.137	0.147	0.150	0.157	0.164	0.175
February	0.102	0.109	0.113	0.114	0.117	0.124	0.133	0.143	0.146	0.152	0.159	0.171
March	0.098	0.105	0.109	0.110	0.112	0.120	0.129	0.138	0.141	0.148	0.155	0.166
April	0.080	0.087	0.091	0.092	0.095	0.102	0.111	0.120	0.123	0.129	0.136	0.147
May	0.076	0.083	0.087	0.088	0.090	0.098	0.106	0.116	0.119	0.125	0.132	0.143
June	0.072	0.079	0.083	0.083	0.086	0.094	0.102	0.112	0.114	0.121	0.128	0.139
July	0.071	0.078	0.082	0.082	0.085	0.093	0.101	0.111	0.113	0.120	0.127	0.138
August	0.059	0.066	0.070	0.070	0.073	0.081	0.089	0.098	0.101	0.108	0.114	0.125
September	0.054	0.061	0.065	0.065	0.068	0.076	0.084	0.093	0.096	0.102	0.109	0.120
October	0.044	0.050	0.054	0.055	0.058	0.065	0.073	0.082	0.085	0.091	0.098	0.109
November	0.039	0.045	0.049	0.050	0.053	0.060	0.068	0.077	0.080	0.086	0.093	0.104
December	0.036	0.043	0.046	0.047	0.050	0.057	0.065	0.074	0.077	0.083	0.090	0.101
January 1989	0.030	0.036	0.040	0.041	0.043	0.050	0.059	0.068	0.070	0.077	0.083	0.094
February	0.022	0.029	0.032	0.033	0.036	0.043	0.051	0.060	0.063	0.069	0.075	0.086
March	0.018	0.024	0.028	0.028	0.031	0.038	0.046	0.055	0.058	0.064	0.070	0.081
April		0.006	0.010	0.010	0.013	0.020	0.028	0.037	0.039	0.045	0.052	0.062
May			0.003	0.004	0.007	0.014	0.022	0.030	0.033	0.039	0.045	0.056
June				0.001	0.003	0.010	0.018	0.027	0.029	0.036	0.042	0.052
July					0.003	0.010	0.017	0.026	0.029	0.035	0.041	0.051
August						0.007	0.015	0.023	0.026	0.032	0.038	0.048
September							0.008	0.016	0.019	0.025	0.031	0.041
October								0.009	0.011	0.017	0.023	0.033
November									0.003	0.008	0.014	0.024
December										0.006	0.012	0.022
January 1990											0.006	0.016
February												0.010

Indexation factors for disposals in April to June 1990

	1990		
RI Month	April	May	June
March **1982**	0.575	0.589	0.595
April	0.544	0.557	0.563
May	0.533	0.546	0.552
June	0.528	0.542	0.548
July	0.528	0.541	0.547
August	0.527	0.541	0.547
September	0.528	0.542	0.548
October	0.521	0.534	0.540
November	0.513	0.527	0.533
December	0.516	0.530	0.536
January **1983**	0.514	0.528	0.534
February	0.508	0.521	0.527
March	0.505	0.518	0.524
April	0.484	0.497	0.503
May	0.478	0.491	0.497
June	0.475	0.487	0.493
July	0.467	0.480	0.485
August	0.460	0.473	0.479
September	0.454	0.466	0.472
October	0.449	0.461	0.467
November	0.443	0.456	0.462
December	0.440	0.452	0.458
January **1984**	0.441	0.453	0.459
February	0.435	0.447	0.453
March	0.430	0.443	0.448
April	0.411	0.424	0.429
May	0.406	0.418	0.424
June	0.402	0.415	0.420
July	0.404	0.416	0.422
August	0.391	0.403	0.409
September	0.388	0.400	0.406
October	0.380	0.392	0.397
November	0.375	0.388	0.393
December	0.377	0.389	0.394
January **1985**	0.372	0.384	0.389
February	0.361	0.373	0.378
March	0.348	0.360	0.365
April	0.320	0.332	0.337
May	0.314	0.326	0.331
June	0.311	0.323	0.328
July	0.314	0.325	0.330
August	0.310	0.322	0.327
September	0.311	0.322	0.328
October	0.309	0.320	0.325
November	0.304	0.316	0.321
December	0.303	0.314	0.319

Indexation factors for disposals in April to June 1990 (continued)

RI Month	1990 April	May	June
January 1986	0.300	0.311	0.316
February	0.295	0.306	0.312
March	0.293	0.305	0.310
April	0.281	0.292	0.297
May	0.279	0.290	0.295
June	0.279	0.290	0.296
July	0.283	0.294	0.299
August	0.279	0.290	0.295
September	0.273	0.284	0.289
October	0.271	0.282	0.287
November	0.260	0.271	0.276
December	0.256	0.267	0.272
January 1987	0.251	0.262	0.267
February	0.246	0.257	0.262
March	0.244	0.254	0.259
April	0.229	0.240	0.245
May	0.228	0.238	0.243
June	0.228	0.238	0.243
July	0.229	0.240	0.245
August	0.225	0.236	0.241
September	0.222	0.232	0.237
October	0.216	0.226	0.231
November	0.210	0.221	0.225
December	0.211	0.222	0.227
January 1988	0.211	0.222	0.227
February	0.206	0.217	0.222
March	0.202	0.212	0.217
April	0.182	0.193	0.198
May	0.178	0.188	0.193
June	0.174	0.184	0.189
July	0.172	0.183	0.187
August	0.159	0.170	0.174
September	0.154	0.164	0.169
October	0.142	0.153	0.157
November	0.137	0.147	0.152
December	0.134	0.144	0.149

Indexation factors for disposals in April to June 1990 (continued)

RI Month	1990 April	May	June
January **1989**	0.127	0.137	0.141
February	0.119	0.129	0.133
March	0.114	0.124	0.128
April	0.094	0.104	0.108
May	0.088	0.097	0.102
June	0.084	0.094	0.098
July	0.083	0.093	0.097
August	0.080	0.090	0.094
September	0.073	0.082	0.087
October	0.065	0.074	0.078
November	0.056	0.065	0.069
December	0.053	0.062	0.066
January **1990**	0.047	0.056	0.060
February	0.041	0.050	0.054
March	0.030	0.040	0.044
April		0.009	0.013
May			0.004

201   Annual Rates and Exemptions

Cross-reference. See also 214.1 MARRIED PERSONS

201.1 **GAINS CHARGEABLE AT INCOME TAX RATES** [*FA 1988, s 98*]

M, a single person and sole trader, had trading income of £13,000 for the year ended 30 April 1989 (assessable for 1990/91), but made a trading loss of £11,000 for the year ended 30 April 1990. He had no other source of income, but realised a capital gain of £30,000 in 1990/91 from the sale of a country cottage. He claims relief for the trading loss under *ICTA 1988, s 380* against his income for 1990/91.

M's income tax position for 1990/91 is as follows

	£
Schedule D, Case I	13,000
Less: Loss relief	11,000
	2,000
Less: Personal allowance (maximum £3,005)	2,000
Taxable income	Nil

His capital gains tax computation is as follows

	£
Gain	30,000
Annual exemption	5,000
Gain chargeable to tax	£25,000

Capital gains tax payable	£
£20,700 at 25%	5,175.00
4,300 at 40%	1,720.00
£25,000	£6,895.00

Note

(*a*)   After 5 April 1988, capital gains are charged at income tax rates as if they formed the top slice of taxable income. The unused personal allowance of £1,005 is not available to reduce the chargeable gain. If M's trading losses had exceeded his total income, then, similarly, the unused losses could not have been used to reduce the gain.

202   Anti-Avoidance

202.1   VALUE SHIFTING [*CGTA 1979, s 25*]

J owns the whole of the ordinary share capital of K Ltd. (One share is held by a nominee for him). The shares were acquired on subscription in 1967 for £1,000 and had a value of £99,000 on 31 March 1982. In December 1990, the trustees of J's family settlement subscribed at par for 3,000 £1 ordinary shares in K Ltd, thereby acquiring 75% of the voting power in the company. It is agreed that the price an unconnected party would have paid for 75% of the equity in a transaction at arm's length is £150,000. J's remaining 25% holding is valued at £15,000.

	£
Proceeds of deemed disposal	150,000
Allowable cost $\dfrac{150,000}{150,000 + 15,000} \times £99,000$	90,000
Unindexed gain	£60,000

202.2   VALUE-SHIFTING TO GIVE TAX-FREE BENEFIT [*CGTA 1979, s 26, 6 Sch 11*]

M owns the whole of the issued share capital in C Ltd, an unquoted company. (One share is held by a nominee for him). He is also a director of the company. M receives an offer of £100,000 from a public company for his shares. Prior to sale, C Ltd pays M £30,000 for loss of his office as director.

On the sale of M's shares, the Inland Revenue may seek to adjust the consideration in computing M's chargeable gain on the grounds that M has received a tax-free benefit and the value of his shares has been materially reduced.

202.3   VALUE SHIFTING: DISTRIBUTION WITHIN A GROUP FOLLOWED BY A DISPOSAL OF SHARES [*CGTA 1979, ss 26, 26A; FA 1989, ss 135, 136*]

Topco Ltd owns 100% of A Ltd, which owns 100% of B Ltd. (At each level, one share is held by a nominee). Both A and B were acquired for negligible amounts. A bought some land in 1983 for a relatively small sum. It is now worth £100,000. In an attempt to realise the proceeds of the land at a tax saving, Topco arranges for B to borrow £100,000. In June 1990, A sells the land to B for this amount, and A, which previously had no undistributed reserves, then pays a dividend of £100,000 to Topco. No ACT is payable as there is a group election under *ICTA 1988, s 247* in force. Topco then sells all of its shares in A Ltd to an unconnected person at their market value which is now a nominal sum.

On the sale of the A Ltd shares, the Revenue may seek to apply *CGTA 1979, ss 26, 26A* to increase the consideration to £100,000.

202.4 **ASSETS DISPOSED OF IN A SERIES OF TRANSACTIONS** [*FA 1985, s 71, 21 Sch*]

L purchased a set of 6 antique chairs in 1969 at a cost of £3,600. He gave 2 chairs to his daughter in February 1988, another pair to his son in November 1989, and sold the final pair to his brother for their market value in August 1990.

The market value of the chairs at the relevant dates were

	2 chairs	4 chairs	6 chairs
	£	£	£
February 1988	3,000	7,000	12,000
November 1989	3,500	10,000	16,200
August 1990	4,000	12,000	21,000

The market value of the set of 6 chairs at 31 March 1982 was £9,000. L has elected under *FA 1988, s 96(5)* for all his assets held at 31 March 1982 to be regarded as having been disposed of and re-acquired at market value on that date.

Indexation factors are

March 1982 – February 1988	0.305
March 1982 – November 1989	0.492
March 1982 – August 1990 (assumed)	0.622

The capital gains tax computations are as follows

February 1988
Disposal to daughter

Deemed consideration	£3,000

As the consideration does not exceed £3,000, the disposal is covered by the chattel exemption of *CGTA 1979, s 128*. See note (*a*).

November 1989
(i)   *1987/88 disposal to daughter recomputed*

Original market value (deemed disposal consideration at February 1988)	£3,000
Reasonable proportion of aggregate market value as at February 1988 of all assets disposed of to date £7,000 × $\frac{2}{4}$	£3,500

	£
Deemed consideration (greater of £3,500 and £3,000)	3,500
Allowable cost $\dfrac{3,000}{3,000 + 7,000} \times £3,600$	1,080
Unindexed gain	2,420
Indexation allowance $\dfrac{3,000}{3,000 + 7,000} \times £9,000 = £2,700$	
£2,700 × 0.305	824
Chargeable gain 1987/88	£1,596

(ii) *1989/90 disposal to son*

Original market value (deemed disposal consideration)	£3,500

Reasonable proportion of aggregate market value as at
November 1989 of all assets disposed of to date
£10,000 × $\frac{2}{4}$ £5,000

	£
Deemed consideration (greater of £5,000 and £3,500)	5,000

31.3.82 value $\dfrac{3,500}{3,500 + 3,500} \times \left(£9,000 \times \dfrac{2,520}{3,600}\right)$ 3,150

Unindexed gain	1,850
Indexation allowance £3,150 × 0.492	1,550
Chargeable gain 1989/90	£300

August 1990
(i) *Gain on 1987/88 disposal to daughter recomputed*

Original market value (deemed consideration in recomputation at November 1989)	£3,500

Reasonable proportion of aggregate market value as at
February 1988 of all assets disposed of to date
£12,000 × $\frac{2}{6}$ £4,000

	£
Deemed consideration (greater of £4,000 and £3,500)	4,000
Allowable cost (as before)	1,080
Unindexed gain	2,920
Indexation allowance (as before)	824
Revised chargeable gain 1987/88	£2,096

(ii) *Gain on 1989/90 disposal to son recomputed*

Original market value (deemed consideration in computation at November 1989)	£5,000

Reasonable proportion of aggregate market value as at
November 1989 of all assets disposed of to date
£16,200 × $\frac{2}{6}$ £5,400

	£
Deemed consideration (greater of £5,000 and £5,400)	5,400
31.3.82 value (as before)	3,150
Unindexed gain	2,250
Indexation allowance (as before)	1,550
Revised chargeable gain 1989/90	£700

(iii)   *Gain on 1990/91 disposal to brother*

Original market value (actual consideration)	£4,000
Reasonable proportion of aggregate market value as at August 1990 of all assets disposed of to date £21,000 × $\frac{2}{6}$	£7,000

	£
Deemed consideration (greater of £4,000 and £7,000)	7,000
31.3.82 value £9,000 × $\dfrac{1,260}{3,600}$	3,150
	3,850
Indexation allowance £3,150 × 0.622	1,959
Chargeable gain 1990/91	£1,891

Notes

(a)   The disposal in February 1988 is at first covered by the chattel exemption in *CGTA 1979, s 128*. As the second disposal in November 1989 is to a person connected with the recipient of the first disposal, the two must then be looked at together for *Sec 128* purposes, and neither the chattel exemption nor the marginal relief is available. For disposals after 5 April 1989, the chattel exemption limit is £6,000. [*FA 1989, s 123*]. See also 207.1(C) EXEMPTIONS AND RELIEFS.

(b)   The three disposals are linked transactions within *FA 1985, s 71, 21 Sch* as they are made after 19 March 1985 by the same transferor to persons with whom he is connected.

(c)   It is assumed in the above example that it is 'reasonable' to apportion the aggregate market value in proportion to the number of items. In other instances a different basis may be needed to give the 'reasonable' apportionment required by *FA 1985, 21 Sch 3*.

(d)   Where a series of disposals would all have been within the old provisions of *CGTA 1979, s 151* if they had taken place before 20 March 1985 and would all have been within the current provisions if on or after that date, disposals before that date are linked with subsequent disposals under the current rules if they occur within the two years before the first of the later disposals. [*FA 1985, s 71(8)*].

(e)   The proportion of 31 March 1982 value allocated to disposals after 5 April 1988 is equivalent in each case to the proportion of original cost not previously relieved.

202.5 DEPRECIATORY TRANSACTIONS: GROUPS OF COMPANIES [*ICTA 1970, s 280*]

G Ltd owns 100% of the share capital of Q Ltd, which it acquired in June 1982 for £75,000. Q Ltd owns land which it purchased in 1978 for £50,000. In 1987, the land, then with a market value of £120,000, was transferred to G Ltd for £50,000. In April 1990, Q Ltd was put into liquidation, and G Ltd received liquidation distributions totalling £30,000.

The loss on the Q Ltd shares is £45,000 (£75,000 − £30,000) increased to £84,600 by indexation allowance of £39,600 i.e. £75,000 × 0.528. The Inland Revenue will be likely to disallow the whole or part of the allowable loss on the shares because it resulted from the depreciatory transaction involving the transfer of land at less than market value.

Note

(*a*) For disposals after 5 April 1988 on which the gain or loss is computed by reference to 31 March 1982 value, depreciatory transactions before 31 March 1982 are not taken into account. [*FA 1988, 8 Sch 6*].

203   Assets held on 6 April 1965

203.1 **QUOTED SHARES AND SECURITIES** [*CGTA 1979, 5 Sch 1–6; FA 1982, ss 86–88, 13 Sch 8–11; FA 1985, s 68, 19 Sch*]
(A) Basic computation of gain/loss
H acquired 3,000 U plc ordinary shares in 1962 for £15,000. Their market value was £10 per share on 6 April 1965 and £12 per share on 31 March 1982. In September 1990, H sells 2,000 of the shares for £8 per share. The indexation factor for March 1982 to September 1990 is assumed to be 0.636.

	£	£	£
Sale proceeds	16,000	16,000	16,000
Cost	10,000		
6 April 1965 value		20,000	
31 March 1982 value			24,000
Unindexed gain/(loss)	6,000	(4,000)	(8,000)
Indexation allowance			
£24,000 × 0.636	15,264	15,264	15,264
Loss after indexation	£(9,264)	£(19,264)	£(23,264)
Allowable loss	£9,264		

Notes
(a)   The comparison is firstly between the loss arrived at by deducting cost and that arrived at by deducting 6 April 1965 value. The smaller of the two losses is taken. If, however, an election had been made under either *CGTA 1979, 5 Sch 4* or *FA 1985, 19 Sch 6(3)* for 6 April 1965 value to be used in computing all gains and losses on quoted shares held at that date, this comparison need not be made and the allowable loss, subject to (b) below, would be £19,264.

(b)   The second comparison is between the figure arrived at in (a) above and the loss using 31 March 1982 value. As the latter is greater, the figure in (a) above is used, as by virtue of *FA 1988, s 96(3)(b)*, re-basing to 1982 cannot increase a loss. If, however, an irrevocable election is made under *FA 1988, s 96(5)*, 31 March 1982 value is used and the allowable loss would thus be £23,264. The election must extend to all assets held at 31 March 1982.

(c)   Indexation is based on 31 March 1982 value in all three calculations. [*FA 1985, s 68(4)(5); FA 1988, 8 Sch 11*].

(d)   All comparisons are between gains and losses *after* indexation.

(B) Basic computation—no gain/no loss disposals
The facts are as in (A) above except that in 1965, the company had suffered a temporary slump and the market value of the shares at 6 April 1965 was only £0.25 per share.

	£	£
Sale proceeds	16,000	16,000
Cost	10,000	
6 April 1965 value		500
Unindexed gain	6,000	15,500
Indexation allowance		
£24,000 × 0.636	15,264	15,264
(Loss)/gain after indexation	£(9,264)	£236
Chargeable gain/allowable loss		Nil

Notes

(a)   As one computation shows a loss and the other a gain, the disposal is treated as producing no gain and no loss. There is no need to prepare a third computation based on 31 March 1982 value as re-basing cannot disturb a no gain/no loss position. [*FA 1988, s 96(3)(c)*].

(b)   If an election to use 6 April 1965 value had been made, there would be a chargeable gain of £236. This would then need to be compared with the result using 31 March 1982 value, a loss of £23,264 as in (A) above. As the effect of re-basing would be to turn a gain into a loss, the disposal is again treated, by virtue of *FA 1988, s 96(4)*, as producing no gain and no loss. If, however, an election to use 31 March 1982 value had been made under *FA 1988, s 96 (5)*, an allowable loss of £23,264 would arise. Once such an election is made, events prior to 31 March 1982 cease to be relevant and there is no need to consider cost or 6 April 1965 value.

(C) Position after *FA 1985* — parts of holding acquired at different times
L has the following transactions in shares of A plc, a quoted company

Date	Number of shares bought/(sold)	Cost/ (proceeds) £
9.1.55	1,500	1,050
10.11.62	750	600
15.7.69	1,200	3,000
12.10.80	1,400	7,000
16.12.83	850	5,950
17.3.84	1,150	9,200
19.4.90	(6,000)	(51,000)

Market value of A shares at 6 April 1965 was £1.60.
Market value of A shares at 31 March 1982 was £5.00.

Indexation factors	March 1982 to April 1990	0.575
	December 1983 to April 1985	0.091
	March 1984 to April 1985	0.083
	April 1985 to April 1990	0.320

CGT 203.1 Assets held on 6 April 1965

(i) No election made to substitute 1965 market value

Identify 6,000 shares sold on a LIFO basis as follows
Post 5.4.82 pool

	Shares	Qualifying Expenditure £	Indexed Pool £
16.12.83 acquisition	850	5,950	5,950
£5,950 × 0.091			541
17.3.84 acquisition	1,150	9,200	9,200
£9,200 × 0.083			764
6.4.85 pool	2,000	15,150	16,455
Indexed rise: April 1985 to April 1990			
£16,455 × 0.320			5,266
			21,721
19.4.90 disposal	(2,000)	(15,150)	(21,721)
Balance of pool	—	—	—

	£
Sale proceeds (2,000 × £8.50)	17,000
Cost (as above)	15,150
Unindexed gain	1,850
Indexation allowance (£21,721 − £15,150)	6,571
Allowable loss	£4,721

1982 pool	£	£
Sale proceeds (1,200 + 1,400) × £8.50	22,100	22,100
Cost (£3,000 + £7,000)	10,000	
Market value 31.3.82 (2,600 × £5)		13,000
Unindexed gain	12,100	9,100
Indexation allowance £13,000 × 0.575	7,475	7,475
Gain after indexation	£4,625	£1,625
Chargeable gain		£1,625

10.11.62 acquisition	£	£	£
Sale proceeds (750 × £8.50)	6,375	6,375	6,375
Cost	600		
Market value 6.4.65 (750 × £1.60)		1,200	
Market value 31.3.82 (750 × £5)			3,750
Unindexed gain	5,775	5,175	2,625
Indexation allowance £3,750 × 0.575	2,156	2,156	2,156
Gain after indexation	£3,619	£3,019	£469
Chargeable gain			£469

9.1.55 acquisition (part)

	£	£	£
Sale proceeds (650 × £8.50)	5,525	5,525	5,525
Cost (650 × £0.70)	455		
Market value 6.4.65 (650 × £1.60)		1,040	
Market value 31.3.82 (650 × £5)			3,250
Unindexed gain	5,070	4,485	2,275
Indexation allowance £3,250 × 0.575	1,869	1,869	1,869
Gain after indexation	£3,201	£2,616	£406
Chargeable gain			£406

Summary of chargeable gains (allowable losses)	Number of shares	Chargeable gain/(loss) £
Post 5.4.82 pool	2,000	(4,721)
1982 pool	2,600	1,625
10.11.62 acquisition	750	469
9.1.55 acquisition (part)	650	406
	6,000	£(2,221)

Remaining shares
850 acquired on 9.1.55 for £595

(ii) Election made to substitute 1965 market value

Identify 6,000 shares on a LIFO basis as follows

Post 5.4.82 pool Allowable loss on 2,000 shares as in (i) above   £(4,721)

1982 pool	Shares		Pool cost £
9.1.55	1,500 × £1.60		2,400
10.11.62	750 × £1.60		1,200
15.7.69	1,200		3,000
12.10.80	1,400		7,000
	4,850		13,600
19.4.90 Disposal	4,000	4,000/4,850 × £13,600	11,216
Remaining shares	850		£2,384

	£	£
Sale proceeds (4,000 × £8.50)	34,000	34,000
Cost (as above)	11,216	
Market value 31.3.82 (4,000 × £5)		20,000
Unindexed gain	22,784	14,000
Indexation allowance £20,000 × 0.575	11,500	11,500
Gain after indexation	£11,284	£2,500
Chargeable gain		£2,500

Summary of chargeable gains/allowable losses	Number of shares	Chargeable gain/(loss) £
Post 5.4.82 pool	2,000	(4,721)
1982 pool	4,000	2,500
	6,000	£(2,221)

Notes

(a)   Because re-basing to 31 March 1982 applies in this case, the result is the same whether or not the election to substitute 6 April 1965 value has been made, but with a lower 31 March 1982 value the computations could produce differing overall gains/losses.

(b)   Note that indexation is based on 31 March 1982 value whenever this gives the greater allowance, and that comparisons are between gains *after* indexation.

(c)   See the 1986/87 edition at 202.1(B) and (C) for examples of the position before *FA 1982*, and after *FA 1982* but before *FA 1985*.

203.2 **LAND REFLECTING DEVELOPMENT VALUE** [*CGTA 1979, 5 Sch 9; FA 1982, ss 86, 87; FA 1985, s 68, 19 Sch 1, 2*]

K sells a building plot, on which planning permission has just been obtained, in November 1990 for £200,000. He acquired the plot by gift from his father in 1953 when its value was £2,000. The market value was £5,000 at 6 April 1965 and £8,500 at 31 March 1982, and the current use value in November 1990 is £10,000. The indexation factor for March 1982 to November 1990 is assumed to be 0.662.

	£	£	£
Sale proceeds	200,000	200,000	200,000
Cost	2,000		
Market value 6.4.65		5,000	
Market value 31.3.82			8,500
Unindexed gain	198,000	195,000	191,500
Indexation allowance £8,500 × 0.662	5,627	5,627	5,627
Gain after indexation	£192,373	£189,373	£185,873
Chargeable gain			£185,873

Notes

(a)   Time apportionment would have substantially reduced the gain of £192,373, using cost, such that re-basing to 31 March 1982 would have given a greater gain than that based on cost and would not therefore have applied. However, as the plot has been sold for a price in excess of its current use value, no time apportionment can be claimed.

(b)   Gains are compared after applying the indexation allowance, which is itself based on 31 March 1982 value being greater than either cost or 6 April 1965 value.

203.3 **OTHER ASSETS** [*CGTA 1979, 5 Sch 11, 12; FA 1982, ss 86, 87; FA 1985, s 68*]
(A) Businesses
L who is 55 acquired a retail business, for which he paid £20,000, on 6 August 1962.
On 1 April 1990, he sold the business as a going concern for £100,000. The purchase
cost and sale proceeds are apportioned as follows

	Cost £	Proceeds £
Freehold shop	12,000	70,000
Goodwill	6,000	20,000
Fixtures and fittings	2,000	10,000

The market value of the freehold shop and goodwill at 31.3.82 was £75,000.

The computation (using time apportionment) is

Period of ownership	27 years 8 months
Period of ownership after 6 April 1965	25 years
Gain on freehold shop (£70,000 – £12,000)	£58,000
Gain on goodwill (£20,000 – £6,000)	£14,000

	£
Unindexed gain	72,000
Indexation allowance £75,000 × 0.575	43,125
Gain after indexation	£28,875

Time apportionment

Chargeable gain £28,875 × $\dfrac{25y}{27y\ 8m}$	£26,092

The computation (with re-basing to 1982) is

	£
Sale proceeds	90,000
Market value 31.3.82	75,000
Unindexed gain	15,000
Indexation allowance £75,000 × 0.575	43,125
Loss after indexation	£(28,125)

The overall result is that, as one calculation produces a gain and the other a loss, no
chargeable gain or allowable loss arises. [*FA 1988, s 96(4)*].

Notes
(a)   Provided no individual item of fixtures and fittings was sold for more than
£6,000, no liability arises on disposal. [*CGTA 1979, s 128; FA 1989, s 123*].

(b)   An election under *FA 1988, s 96(5)* for all assets to be treated as disposed of
and immediately re-acquired at 31 March 1982 would create an allowable loss
of £28,125.

(c)   Note that when comparing a gain subject to time apportionment with a gain
using re-basing rules, it is the time apportioned gain that is taken into account
rather than the full gain before time apportionment. [*FA 1988, 8 Sch 10*].

(d) An election for 6.4.65 value could not be beneficial, as, whether it resulted in a gain or a loss, the end result would be the same.

(e) If L sold the business and retired on ill-health grounds, and assuming the figures were such as to produce a chargeable gain, he might be entitled to retirement relief. See 220 RETIREMENT RELIEF below.

(f) The High Court ruled in July 1990, overturning a decision of the Special Commissioners, that time apportionment should be applied to the gain *after* indexation (*Smith v Schofield C/D,* [*1990*] *STC 602*). The position is thus restored, pending any appeal by the taxpayer in the above-mentioned case, to that set out in Revenue Statement of Practice SP 3/82.

(B) Chattels

M inherited a painting on the death of his mother in 1933, when it was valued for probate at £5,000. On 5 October 1990 he sold the painting for £220,000 net. The painting's value was £130,000 at 6 April 1965, but only £125,000 at 31 March 1982. The indexation factor for March 1982 to October 1990 is assumed to be 0.649.

(i) Time apportionment

Period of ownership since 6 April 1945	45 years 6 months
Period of ownership since 6 April 1965	25 years 6 months

	£
Unindexed gain (£220,000 − £5,000)	215,000
Indexation allowance £125,000 × 0.649	81,125
	£133,875

$$\text{Gain after indexation } £133,875 \times \frac{25\text{y } 6\text{m}}{45\text{y } 6\text{m}} \qquad £75,029$$

(ii) Election for 6.4.65 value

	£
Sale proceeds	220,000
Market value 6.4.65	130,000
Unindexed gain	90,000
Indexation allowance £130,000 × 0.649	84,370
Gain after indexation	£5,630

Election for 6.4.65 value is beneficial subject to re-basing.

(iii) Re-basing to 1982

	£
Sale proceeds	220,000
Market value 31.3.82	125,000
Unindexed gain	95,000
Indexation allowance £130,000 × 0.649	84,370
Gain after indexation	£10,630

Re-basing cannot increase a gain. [*FA 1988, s 96(3)(a)*]. **Therefore, the gain of £5,630 stands and the election remains beneficial.**

Notes

(*a*)   Under time apportionment, the period of ownership is limited to that after 5 April 1945.

(*b*)   In (i) above, indexation is based on 31.3.82 value, being greater than cost — it cannot be based on 6 April 1965 value as this does not enter into the calculation. In (ii), indexation is on the higher of 31.3.82 value and 6.4.65 value. This is also the case in (iii) as one is comparing the position using 6.4.65 value and 31.3.82 value. See *FA 1985, s 68(4)(5); FA 1988, 8 Sch 11*.

(*c*)   The High Court ruled in July 1990, overturning a decision of the Special Commissioners, that time apportionment should be applied to the gain *after* indexation (*Smith v Schofield C/D, [1990] STC 602*). The position is thus restored, pending any appeal by the taxpayer in the above-mentioned case, to that set out in Revenue Statement of Practice SP 3/82.

(C) Land and buildings

X acquired land on 5 June 1959 as a specie distribution on liquidation of his company. The value of the land was then £8,000. He acquired access land adjoining the property for £500 on 1 January 1960 and, having obtained planning consent, on 30 July 1962 incurred expenditure of £15,000 in building houses on the land, which were let. On 6 September 1990, X sells the houses with vacant possession for £300,000, net of expenses. The value of the houses and land is £20,000 at 6 April 1965 and £210,000 at 31 March 1982.

The indexation factor for March 1982 to September 1990 is assumed to be 0.636.

The gain using time apportionment is

	£	£
Net proceeds of sale		300,000
Deduct Cost of land	8,000	
Cost of addition	500	
Cost of building	15,000	23,500
Unindexed gain		276,500
Indexation allowance £210,000 × 0.636		133,560
Gain after indexation		£142,940

Apportion to allowable expenditure	£	£
(i) Land $\dfrac{8,000}{23,500} \times £142,940$	48,661	
Time apportion £48,661 × $\dfrac{25y\ 5m}{31y\ 3m}$		39,578
(ii) Addition $\dfrac{500}{23,500} \times £142,940$	3,041	
Time apportion £3,041 × $\dfrac{25y\ 5m}{30y\ 8m}$		2,520
		c/f £42,098

	£	£
		b/f 42,098
(iii) Building $\dfrac{15,000}{23,500} \times £142,940$	91,238	
Time apportion £91,238 $\times \dfrac{25y\ 5m}{28y\ 1m}$		82,574
Gain after indexation and time apportionment		£124,672

The gain using re-basing to 1982 is

	£
Net proceeds of sale	300,000
Market value at 31.3.82	210,000
Unindexed gain	90,000
Indexation allowance £210,000 × 0.636	133,560
Loss after indexation	£43,560

The chargeable gain/allowable loss is   Nil

Notes

(a)   An election for 6 April 1965 valuation could not be favourable, even were it not for the effect of re-basing, as the value is less than historic costs.

(b)   The High Court ruled in July 1990, overturning a decision of the Special Commissioners, that time apportionment should be applied to the gain *after* indexation (*Smith v Schofield C/D*, *[1990] STC 602*). The position is thus restored, pending any appeal by the taxpayer in the above-mentioned case, to that set out in Revenue Statement of Practice SP 3/82.

(c)   As one calculation produces a gain and the other a loss, neither a gain nor a loss arises. Whilst it makes no difference in this example, note that it is always the gain/loss *after* time apportionment that is compared with the gain/loss produced by re-basing. [*FA 1988, s 96(2)–(4), 8 Sch 10*].

(D) Unquoted shares — share exchange before 6 April 1965 [*CGTA 1979, 5 Sch 14*]
N purchased 5,000 £1 ordinary shares in R Ltd, an unquoted company, on 1
January 1961. The purchase price was £3 per share, a total of £15,000. On 1
December 1964, R Ltd was acquired by the D group of companies, whose shares
are not listed on The Stock Exchange, as a result of which N received 10,000 8%
convertible preference shares in D Ltd in exchange for his holding of R shares. In
November 1990, N sold the D shares for £3.25 per share. The market value of the D
shares was £2.03 per share at 6 April 1965 but only £1.50 per share at 31 March
1982. The indexation factor for March 1982 to November 1990 is assumed to be
0.662.

The loss, disregarding re-basing, is

		£
Disposal consideration	10,000 at £3.25	32,500
Allowable cost	10,000 at £2.03	20,300
Unindexed gain		12,200
Indexation allowance £20,300 × 0.662		13,439
Loss after indexation		£1,239

The gain using re-basing to 1982 is

	£
Disposal consideration (as above)	32,500
Market value 31.3.82 10,000 at £1.50	15,000
Unindexed gain	17,500
Indexation allowance £20,300 × 0.662	13,439
Gain after indexation	£4,061

The overall result is

Chargeable gain/allowable loss	Nil

Notes

(*a*)   Subject to re-basing, allowable cost must be taken as 6.4.65 value [*CGTA
1979, 5 Sch 14(1)*].

(*b*)   Indexation is based on the greater of 31.3.82 value and 6.4.65 value. [*FA
1985, s 68(4)(5); FA 1988, 8 Sch 11*].

(*c*)   Where the effect of re-basing would be to substitute a gain for a loss or vice
versa, the disposal is treated as producing neither a chargeable gain nor an
allowable loss. [*FA 1988, s 96(3)(a)(b)(4)*].

(E) Unquoted shares — share exchange after 5 April 1965 [*CGTA 1979, 5 Sch 14*]
S purchased 10,000 £1 ordinary shares in L Ltd for £5,000 on 31 May 1959. The shares are not quoted, and their value at 6 April 1965 was £6,000. On 1 September 1983, the shares are acquired by R plc, in exchange for its own ordinary shares on the basis of 1 for 2. The offer valued L ordinary shares at £2.23 per share. In February 1991, S sells the R shares for £8.20 per share. The agreed value of the L Ltd shares at 31 March 1982 was £2.10 per share.

Indexation factors (actual) March 1982 to September 1983		0.083
(assumed) March 1982 to February 1991		0.704

The gain without re-basing to 1982 is

	£	£
Disposal consideration 5,000 at £8.20		41,000
Allowable cost		5,000
Unindexed gain		36,000
Indexation allowance 10,000 × £2.10 × 0.704		14,784
		21,216
Less gain subject to time apportionment		
Market value at 1.9.83	22,300	
Allowable cost	5,000	
	17,300	
Indexation allowance to 1.9.83 £5,000 × 0.083	415	
	£16,885	16,885
		4,331

Add chargeable part of time apportioned gain

Chargeable part of gain $\dfrac{18\text{y } 5\text{m}}{24\text{y } 3\text{m}} \times £16,885$		12,823
Gain		£17,154

If S elected for 6.4.65 value to apply, the computation would be

	£
Disposal consideration	41,000
Allowable cost	6,000
Unindexed gain	35,000
Indexation allowance 10,000 × £2.10 × 0.704	14,784
Gain	£20,216

The election should not therefore be made.

The gain using re-basing to 1982 is

	£
Disposal consideration	41,000
Market value 31.3.82 10,000 × £2.10	21,000
Unindexed gain	20,000
Indexation allowance 10,000 × £2.10 × 0.704	14,784
Gain after indexation	£5,216

The overall result is

Chargeable gain   £5,216

Re-basing applies as it produces neither a larger gain than that using time apportionment nor a loss.

Notes

(*a*)   31.3.82 value cannot be used for indexation purposes in the calculation of the gain to 1.9.83 as a deemed disposal occurs on that date and must, it would seem, be computed by reference to legislation extant on that date.

(*b*)   The above example illustrates the interaction of the time apportionment rules and the indexation rules as a practical approach to legislation which is not entirely clear.

(*c*)   If an election is made for 6.4.65 value, no valuation is required at 1.9.83.

(*d*)   The deemed disposal on 1.9.83 is *only* for the purposes of *CGTA 1979, 5 Sch 11* (time apportionment). In the re-basing calculation, the shares disposed of in 1991 are regarded as standing in the place of those held at 31.3.82.

(F) Part disposals after 5 April 1965 [*CGTA 1979, 5 Sch 11(8)*]

H bought land for £15,000 on 31 October 1962. Its value at 6 April 1965 is £17,200. On 1 February 1987, H sells part of the land for £50,000, the balance being then worth £200,000. In May 1990, H gives the remaining land to his daughter. Its value is then £240,000. The agreed value of the total estate at 31 March 1982 was £180,000 and H makes a claim on the February 1987 disposal for that value to be used for indexation purposes.

Indexation factors March 1982 to February 1987   0.264
                    March 1982 to May 1990   0.589

1987 disposal

	£
Proceeds of part disposal	50,000
Deduct allowable cost $\dfrac{50,000}{50,000 + 200,000} \times £15,000$	3,000
Unindexed gain	47,000

Indexation allowance £180,000 $\times \dfrac{50,000}{50,000 + 200,000} = £36,000$

£36,000 × 0.264	9,504
Gain after indexation	£37,496

Time apportionment

Chargeable gain $\dfrac{21\text{y } 10\text{m}}{24\text{y } 3\text{m}} \times £37,496$ £33,759

If an election were made to substitute 6 April 1965 valuation, the computation would be

	£
Proceeds of part disposal	50,000
Deduct allowable cost $\dfrac{50,000}{50,000 + 200,000} \times £17,200$	3,440
Unindexed gain	46,560

Indexation allowance $£180,000 \times \dfrac{50,000}{50,000 + 200,000} = £36,000$

£36,000 × 0.264	9,504
Chargeable gain	£37,056

An election would not therefore be beneficial.

1990 disposal

The gain without re-basing to 1982 is

	£	£
Disposal proceeds		240,000
Allowable cost (£15,000 − £3,000)		12,000
Unindexed gain		228,000
Indexation allowance £180,000 − £36,000 = £144,000 × 0.589		84,816
		143,184
Less gain subject to time apportionment		
Market value at 1.2.87	200,000	
Allowable cost	12,000	
	188,000	
Indexation allowance to 1.2.87 £144,000 × 0.264	38,016	
	£149,984	149,984
		(6,800)
Add chargeable part of time apportioned gain		
Chargeable part of gain $\dfrac{21y\ 10m}{24y\ 3m} \times £149,984$		135,037
Gain after indexation		£128,237

The gain using re-basing to 1982 is

	£
Disposal proceeds	240,000
Market value 31.3.82 £180,000 × $\dfrac{12,000}{15,000}$ note (*c*)	144,000
Unindexed gain	96,000
Indexation allowance £144,000 × 0.589	84,816
Gain after indexation	£11,184

The overall result is

Chargeable gain   £11,184

Re-basing applies as it produces neither a larger gain nor a loss.

Notes

(*a*)   The above example illustrates the interaction of the time apportionment rules and the indexation rules as a practical approach to legislation which is not entirely clear.

(*b*)   The deemed disposal on 1 February 1987 is *only* for the purposes of *CGTA 1979, 5 Sch 11(3)–(5)* (time apportionment). For re-basing purposes, it would appear that the asset is still regarded as having been held at 31 March 1982.

(*c*)   Where there has been a part disposal after 31 March 1982 and before 6 April 1988 of an asset held at 31 March 1982, the proportion of 31 March 1982 value to be brought into account in the re-basing calculation is that which the cost previously unallowed bears to the total cost, giving the same effect as if re-basing had applied to the part disposal. [*FA 1988, 8 Sch 4*].

(*d*)   The Revenue will also accept an alternative basis of calculation on the part disposal of land. Under this method, the part disposed of is treated as a separate asset and any fair and reasonable method of apportioning part of the total cost to it will be accepted e.g. a reasonable valuation of that part at the acquisition date. (Revenue Statement of Practice SP D1).

(*e*)   The High Court ruled in July 1990, overturning a decision of the Special Commissioners, that time apportionment should be applied to the gain *after* indexation (*Smith v Schofield C/D, [1990]* STC 602). The position is thus restored, pending any appeal by the taxpayer in the above-mentioned case, to that set out in Revenue Statement of Practice SP 3/82.

204 Assets held on 31 March 1982

204.1 GENERAL COMPUTATION OF GAINS/LOSSES [*FA 1988, s 96, 8 Sch*].

(A)

Rodney purchased a painting on 1 October 1979 for £60,000 (including costs of acquisition) and sold it at auction for £150,000 (net of selling expenses) on 15 August 1990. Its value at 31 March 1982 was £80,000 and the indexation factor for the period March 1982 to August 1990 is assumed to be 0.622.

	£	£
Net sale proceeds	150,000	150,000
Cost	60,000	
Market value 31.3.82		80,000
Unindexed gain	90,000	70,000
Indexation allowance £80,000 × 0.622	49,760	49,760
Gain after indexation	£40,240	£20,240
Chargeable gain		£20,240

Notes

(a) The asset, having been held at 31 March 1982 and disposed of after 5 April 1988, is deemed to have been sold and immediately re-acquired at its market value at 31 March 1982. [*FA 1988, s 96(1)(2)*]. This is known as re-basing to 1982.

(b) Re-basing does not apply if it would produce a larger gain or larger loss than would otherwise be the case, nor if it would turn a gain into a loss or vice versa, nor if the disposal would otherwise be a no gain/no loss disposal. [*FA 1988, s 96(3)(4)*].

(c) An *irrevocable* election may be made to treat, broadly speaking, *all* assets held on 31 March 1982 as having been sold and re-acquired at their market value on that date, in which case the restrictions in (b) above will not apply [*FA 1988, s 96(5)*]. If the election had been made in this example, the gain would still be £20,240, but there would have been no need to compute the gain by reference to cost and make a comparison with that using re-basing.

There are some minor exclusions from the rule that the election must extend to all assets. [*FA 1988, 8 Sch 12*]. There are also special rules for groups of companies. [*FA 1988, 8 Sch 13, 14*].

(d) Indexation is automatically based on 31 March 1982 value, without the need to claim such treatment, but if a greater allowance would be produced by reference to cost, that takes precedence for indexation purposes. [*FA 1985, s 68(4)(5); FA 1988, 8 Sch 11*].

(e) See also 203 ASSETS HELD ON 6 APRIL 1965 for the general application of the re-basing provisions to such assets.

(B)
The facts are as in (A) above, except that net sale proceeds amount to £85,000.

	£	£
Net sale proceeds	85,000	85,000
Cost	60,000	
Market value 31.3.82		80,000
Unindexed gain	25,000	5,000
Indexation allowance (as in (A))	49,760	49,760
Loss after indexation	£24,760	£44,760
Allowable loss	£24,760	

Note

(a)   An election under *FA 1988, s 96(5)* would have the effect of creating an allowable loss of £44,760, an increase of £20,000, but as the election must extend to, broadly speaking, *all* assets, it should only be made if likely to prove beneficial overall.

(C)
The facts are as in (A) above, except that net sale proceeds amount to £110,000.

	£	£
Net sale proceeds	110,000	110,000
Cost	60,000	
Market value 31.3.82		80,000
Unindexed gain	50,000	30,000
Indexation allowance (as in (A))	49,760	49,760
Gain/(loss) after indexation	£240	£(19,760)
Chargeable gain/(allowable loss)		Nil

Notes

(a)   Where the effect of re-basing would be to substitute a loss for a gain (or vice versa), re-basing doesn't apply and the transaction is treated as giving rise to no chargeable gain and no allowable loss. [*FA 1988, s 96(3)(4)*].

(b)   The effect of an election under *FA 1988, s 96(5)* would be to create an allowable loss of £19,760 instead of a nil gain/nil loss position, but as the election must extend to, broadly speaking, *all* assets held at 31 March 1982, it should only be made if likely to be beneficial overall.

204.2 **DEFERRED CHARGES ON GAINS BEFORE 31 MARCH 1982** [*FA 1988, s 97, 9 Sch*]
(A) Gains rolled over or held-over
Kirk purchased 3,000 unquoted ordinary shares in W Limited for £9,000 on 1 January 1980 and later gave them to his son, Michael, claiming hold-over relief under *FA 1980, s 79*. Michael sells the shares for £20,000 (net) on 10 April 1990. The shares had a value of £11,000 at 31 March 1982.

CGT 204.2   Assets held on 31 March 1982

Assuming the gift to have taken place on

(i)   1 February 1982 (market value of shares £10,500),
(ii)   30 April 1988 (market value £19,500), and
(iii)   1 June 1985 (market value £15,000),

the capital gains position is as set out below. The relevant indexation factors are

March 1982 to June 1985	0.202
March 1982 to April 1988	0.332
March 1982 to April 1990	0.575
June 1985 to April 1990	0.311
April 1988 to April 1990	0.182

(i) Gift on 1 February 1982

Kirk's chargeable gain (deferred) (£10,500 − £9,000)	£1,500
Michael's acquisition cost (£10,500 − £1,500)	£9,000

Michael's chargeable gain is

	£	£
Proceeds 10.4.90	20,000	20,000
Cost (as above)	9,000	
Market value 31.3.82		11,000
Unindexed gain	11,000	9,000
Indexation allowance		
£11,000 × 0.575	6,325	6,325
Gain after indexation	£4,675	£2,675
Chargeable gain		£2,675

The deferred gain of £1,500 effectively falls out of charge as Michael held the shares at 31.3.82 and thus receives the benefit of re-basing to 1982.

(ii) Gift on 30 April 1988

Kirk's chargeable gain is

	£	£
Disposal value	19,500	19,500
Cost	9,000	
Market value 31.3.82		11,000
Unindexed gain	10,500	8,500
Indexation allowance		
£11,000 × 0.332	3,652	3,652
Gain after indexation	£6,848	£4,848
Chargeable gain (deferred)		£4,848

Michael's chargeable gain is

	£	£
Proceeds 10.4.90		20,000
Cost	19,500	
Deduct deferred gain	4,848	
	14,652	
Indexation allowance £14,652 × 0.182	2,667	17,319
Chargeable gain		£2,681

Michael cannot re-base to 1982 as he did not hold the shares at 31.3.82. However, as the deferred gain was itself computed by reference to the 31.3.82 value, he has effectively received full relief for the uplift in value between 1.1.80 and 31.3.82. The small difference between his gain of £2,681 and that of £2,675 in (i) above is entirely due to the rounding of indexation factors to three decimal places.

(iii) Gift on 1 June 1985

Kirk's chargeable gain is

	£	£
Disposal value		15,000
Cost	9,000	
Indexation allowance £11,000 × 0.202	2,222	11,222
Chargeable gain (deferred)		£3,778

It is assumed that a claim would have been made to base indexation on the 31.3.82 value, this being greater than cost.

Michael's chargeable gain is

	£	£
Proceeds 10.4.90		20,000
Cost	15,000	
Deduct one-half of deferred gain		
£3,778 × ½	1,889	
	13,111	
Indexation allowance £13,111 × 0.311	4,077	17,188
Chargeable gain		£2,812

Michael cannot benefit from re-basing to 1982 as he did not hold the shares at 31.3.82, nor is the deferred gain itself calculated by reference to the re-basing rules as the disposal (i.e. the gift) took place before 6.4.88. Under *FA 1988, s 97, 9 Sch*, the deduction in respect of a deferred gain is halved where the deferral took place after 31.3.82 and before 6.4.88 and was, wholly or partly, in respect of a chargeable gain accruing on an asset held at 31.3.82, thus giving some relief, albeit on an arbitrary basis.

Notes
(a) A claim must be made, within two years of the end of the year of assessment in which the ultimate disposal takes place, for the deduction to be halved. [*FA 1988, 9 Sch 8*].

(b)   The provisions of *FA 1988, s 97, 9 Sch* apply not only to hold-over relief on gifts, under *FA 1980, s 79*, but to a number of situations in which gains are held-over or rolled over, as listed in *FA 1988, 9 Sch 2(3)*, of which the most common is rollover relief, on replacement of business assets, under *CGTA 1979, s 115*. [*FA 1988, 9 Sch 1, 2*].

(c)   There are special rules where the disposal giving rise to the deferral is preceded by a no gain/no loss disposal (as defined by *FA 1988, 8 Sch 1*) and where the ultimate disposal is preceded by a no gain/no loss disposal. [*FA 1988, 9 Sch 4, 5*].

(d)   An Inland Revenue press release of 8 July 1988 explains the provisions.

(e)   See also 208 HOLD-OVER RELIEFS and 221 ROLLOVER RELIEF for the general application of these reliefs.

(f)   Hold-over relief under *FA 1980, s 79* is not available for gifts after 13 March 1989.

(B) Postponed charges

Dennis buys a sculpture for £15,000 on 15 March 1981 and gives it to his wife on 1 September 1982. She gives it to her daughter, Sharon, on 25 December 1984 when its market value was £22,175. The chargeable gain on the latter gift is £5,000 and a claim is made for this to be deferred under *FA 1980, s 79*. On 8 April 1990, Sharon, who still owns the sculpture, goes to live abroad in circumstances such that a charge arises under *FA 1981, s 79* by virtue of her becoming non-resident in the UK.

The gain chargeable in April 1990 is

$£5,000 \times \frac{1}{2} =$ £2,500

Notes

(a)   Subject to a claim to that effect, the postponed gain is halved, the gain being attributable to a disposal before 6 April 1988 of an asset acquired before 31 March 1982 by the person making the disposal, with the event triggering the charge taking place after 5 April 1988. [*FA 1988, 9 Sch 3*].

(b)   The asset is deemed to have been acquired before 31 March 1982 by Sharon's mother as she acquired it by means of a no gain/no loss disposal from her husband, who *did* acquire the asset before that date. [*FA 1988, 9 Sch 4*].

(c)   The provisions extend to a number of circumstances under which a gain can be postponed, as listed in *FA 1988, 9 Sch 3(2)*.

(d)   Note that the 31 March 1982 value of the asset is irrelevant. Even if the asset had fallen in value between date of acquisition and 31 March 1982, the deferred gain is still halved. If the gift to the daughter had taken place after 5 April 1988, the deferred gain would itself be calculated by reference to the re-basing rules of *Finance Act 1988* and there would be no reduction in the postponed charge.

(e)   Hold-over relief under *FA 1980, s 79* is not available for gifts after 13 March 1989.

205 Companies

Cross-references. See also 216.4 OVERSEAS MATTERS for transfer of assets to non-resident company and 104 CAPITAL GAINS in the Corporation Tax section.

205.1 CAPITAL LOSSES

P Ltd, which makes up accounts to 30 June annually, changes its accounting date to 31 December. It makes up 18-month accounts to 31 December 1990, and its chargeable gains and allowable losses are as follows

	Gains/(losses) £
31.7.89	4,600
19.10.89	11,500
1.12.89	3,500
28.3.90	(8,300)
21.7.90	8,500
1.9.90	(25,000)
20.12.90	7,000

The period of account is split into two accounting periods

1.7.89 – 30.6.90
Net chargeable gain   £11,300
1.7.90 – 31.12.90
Net allowable loss   £9,500

Notes

(*a*) The loss must be carried forward and cannot be set off against the £11,300 net gain.

(*b*) For a further example, which illustrates the position as regards accounting periods straddling 17 March 1987, see under Corporation Tax at 104.1 CAPITAL GAINS.

205.2 SHARES — ACQUISITIONS AND DISPOSALS WITHIN SHORT PERIOD
[*F(No 2)A 1975, s 58*]

S Ltd has the following transactions in shares in Q plc, a quoted company with share capital of £1m divided into 25p ordinary shares.

	Date	Number of shares	Price £
Purchase	1.6.83	100,000	62,000
Purchase	1.8.90	50,000	49,000
Sale	15.8.90	80,000	60,000
Purchase	31.8.90	50,000	35,000

The position is as follows

The shares sold on 15.8.90 are identified with the two purchases on 1.8.90 and 31.8.90.

£

(i) Purchase on 1.8.90

Proceeds $\dfrac{50,000}{80,000} \times £60,000$ 37,500

Cost   49,000

Allowable loss   £11,500

(No indexation allowance is due.)

(ii) Purchase on 31.8.90

Proceeds $\dfrac{30,000}{80,000} \times £60,000$ 22,500

Cost $\dfrac{30,000}{50,000} \times £35,000$ 21,000

Chargeable gain   £1,500

(No indexation allowance is due.)

Allowable loss on transaction   £10,000

Notes

(*a*) Where a company disposes of shares (including securities other than gilt-edged securities) and acquires similar shares within one month before or after the disposal through a stock exchange or ARIEL or within six months in other circumstances, the shares acquired and disposed of are matched. For these rules to apply, the number of shares held at some time in the one month (or six months) before the disposal must be not less than 2% of the number issued. Shares acquired within one month (or six months) before or after the disposal are called 'available shares'.

(*b*) Subject to *CGTA 1979, s 66* (matching of same day acquisitions and disposals), disposals are identified first from 'available shares' taking acquisitions before the disposal (latest first) before acquisitions after the disposal (earliest first). Once all 'available shares' have been matched with the disposal, the identification of any remaining shares disposed of follows the ordinary rules.

(*c*) Indexation allowance is not available as the disposal is in the same month as the acquisitions. [*FA 1982, s 87; FA 1985, 19 Sch 2*].

206 Disposal

206.1 ALLOWABLE AND NON-ALLOWABLE EXPENDITURE

(A) Allowable expenditure [*CGTA 1979, ss 32, 33*]

In 1990/91 T sold a house which he had owned since 1983 and which was let throughout. The house cost £34,000, with legal costs of £900. T spent £800 on initial repairs and refurbishment, which was disallowed for income tax in computing the rental income. In 1985, he added an extension at a cost of £5,000 for which he received a local authority grant of £2,000. Legal costs of £500 were incurred on obtaining vacant possession at the end of the final tenancy, and £600 was spent on making good damage by the outgoing tenant. The sale proceeds were £70,000 before legal costs of £1,200.

	£	£	£
Sale proceeds		70,000	
Deduct costs of sale		1,200	
			68,800
Cost of house		34,000	
Add incidental costs of purchase		900	
		34,900	
Improvement costs			
initial repairs	800		
extension, less grant	3,000		
		3,800	
Cost of obtaining vacant possession			
(enhancement cost)		500	
			39,200
Unindexed gain			£29,600

Note

(*a*)   The costs of making good dilapidations at the end of the final tenancy are disallowed by virtue of *CGTA 1979, s 33*, being a deduction against income.

(B) Non-allowable expenditure — capital allowances [*CGTA 1979, s 34*]

S Ltd acquired land in March 1983 for £50,000 on which it constructed a factory for use in its manufacturing trade. The cost of construction was £25,000 incurred in June 1983. In April 1990, the company sold the freehold factory for £60,000, of which £45,000 related to the land and £15,000 to the building. Industrial buildings allowances of £24,750 had been given and there was a balancing charge of £14,750.

	Land	Building	
	£	£	£
Disposal consideration	45,000		15,000
Allowable cost	50,000	25,000	
Deduct net allowances given		10,000	15,000
Unindexed gain/(loss)	(5,000)		—
Indexation allowance £50,000 × 0.505	25,250		
£15,000 × 0.475			7,125
Allowable loss	£30,250		£7,125

289

206.2 **PART DISPOSALS** [*CGTA 1979, s 35*]

Note. See also 212.1 LAND below for small part disposals of land.

(A)

T purchased a 300 acre estate in 1971 for £1m plus legal and other costs of £50,000. In 1975 he spent £100,000 on improvements to the main house on the estate (not his main residence), which he sells in September 1990 for £600,000. The costs of sale are £40,000. The value of the remaining land is £2.2m. The market value of the whole estate at 31 March 1982 was £1.4m and the indexation factor from March 1982 to September 1990 is assumed to be 0.636.

Gain without re-basing to 1982

	£	£
Sale proceeds		600,000
Deduct incidental costs		40,000
		560,000
Cost £1,050,000 × $\dfrac{600,000}{600,000 + 2,200,000}$	225,000	
Improvement costs	100,000	
		325,000
Unindexed gain		235,000
Indexation allowance £325,000 × 0.636		206,700
Gain after indexation		£28,300

Gain with re-basing to 1982

	£
Net proceeds as above	560,000
Market value 31.3.82	
£1,400,000 × $\dfrac{600,000}{600,000 + 2,200,000}$	300,000
Unindexed gain	260,000
Indexation allowance £325,000 × 0.636	206,700
Gain after indexation	£53,300
Chargeable gain	£28,300

Notes

(*a*)   Re-basing does not apply as its effect would be to increase a gain. Indexation is based on allowable cost in both calculations as this gives a greater allowance than by using market value of £300,000. [*FA 1988, s 96(3), 8 Sch 11*].

(*b*)   The improvements expenditure is not apportioned in the first calculation as it relates entirely to the part of the estate being sold. [*CGTA 1979, s 35(4)*]. In the second calculation, this fact would appear to be irrelevant as the whole estate is deemed to have been sold and re-acquired on 31 March 1982. If this expenditure had been incurred after 31 March 1982, then, for re-basing purposes, the 31 March 1982 value of the estate would be apportioned, but the improvements expenditure would be deductible in full from the proceeds of the part disposal.

(B)
U inherited some land at a probate value of £500,000 in November 1981. Its market value at 31 March 1982 was £540,000. In November 1986, he sold part of the land for £240,000, the remaining land then being worth £480,000. He sells the remaining land in April 1990 for £600,000 and elects under *FA 1988, s 96(5)* for all his assets held at 31 March 1982 to be treated as sold and re-acquired by him at their market value on that date.

The gain, subject to indexation, on the part disposal in November 1986 is

	£
Proceeds	240,000
Cost £500,000 × $\dfrac{240,000}{240,000 + 480,000}$	166,667
Unindexed gain	£73,333

The gain, subject to indexation, on the disposal in April 1990 is

	£
Proceeds	600,000
Market value 31.3.82	
£540,000 × $\dfrac{480,000}{240,000 + 480,000}$	360,000
Unindexed gain	£240,000

Note
(a) Where re-basing applies, whether or not the election under *FA 1988, s 96(5)* is made, and there has been a part disposal after 31 March 1982 and before 6 April 1988, the proportion of 31 March 1982 value to be brought into account on the ultimate disposal is the same as the proportion of cost unallowed on the part disposal, as if the re-basing provisions had applied to the part disposal. [*FA 1988, 8 Sch 4*].

(C)
V bought the film rights of a novel for £50,000 in May 1983. A one-third share of the rights was sold to W Ltd in March 1984 for £20,000, when the rights retained had a value of £45,000. In December 1990, V's rights were sold to a film company for £100,000 plus a right to royalties, such right being estimated to be worth £150,000. The indexation factor for the period May 1983 to December 1990 is assumed to be 0.573.

March 1984	£
Sale proceeds	20,000
Cost £50,000 × $\dfrac{20,000}{20,000 + 45,000}$	15,385
Chargeable gain	£4,615

December 1990

Sale proceeds (£100,000 + £150,000)	250,000
Cost (£50,000 − £15,385)	34,615
Unindexed gain	215,385
Indexation allowance £34,615 × 0.573	19,834
Chargeable gain	£195,551

Notes

(a) The right to royalties is itself an asset and so could be the subject of a future disposal. See 206.3(B) below and, if applicable, 225 WASTING ASSETS below.

(b) No indexation allowance is available on the March 1984 disposal as the rights sold had not been held for the 12-month qualifying period then in force.

(D)

C inherited land valued at £110,000 in May 1982. He granted rights of way over the land to a neighbouring landowner in March 1983, in consideration for a parcel of land adjacent to his, valued at £12,000. The value of the land subject to the right of way was then £120,000. In April 1990, C sold the whole of the land for £180,000.

Part disposal in March 1983

	£
Disposal consideration	12,000
Allowable expenditure	
$\dfrac{12,000}{12,000 + 120,000} \times £110,000$	10,000
Chargeable gain	£2,000

Disposal in April 1990

Disposal consideration		180,000
Deduct Original land £(110,000 − 10,000)	100,000	
Addition	12,000	112,000
Unindexed gain		68,000
Indexation allowance		
(a) Original land		
£100,000 × 0.533	53,300	
(b) Addition		
£12,000 × 0.505	6,060	59,360
Chargeable gain		£8,640

Notes

(a) It is assumed that the additional land is merged with the existing land to give a single asset.

(b) On disposals before 6 April 1986, a part disposal of land exceeding 5% of the total was not a small part disposal under *CGTA 1979, s 107*.

(c) No indexation allowance is available on the March 1983 disposal as the asset had not been held for the 12-month qualifying period which was then in force.

206.3 CAPITAL SUMS DERIVED FROM ASSETS [*CGTA 1979, s 20(1)*]

(A) General

A Ltd holds the remainder of a 99-year lease of land, under which it has mineral rights. The lease, which commenced in 1974, was acquired in April 1982 by assignment for £80,000. Following a proposal to extract minerals, the freeholder pays A Ltd £100,000 in June 1990 in consideration of relinquishing the mineral rights, in order to prevent such development. The value of the lease after the alteration is £150,000.

	£
Disposal proceeds	100,000
Allowable cost $\dfrac{100,000}{100,000 + 150,000} \times £80,000$	32,000
Unindexed gain	£68,000

(B) Deferred consideration

Z owns 2,000 £1 ordinary shares in B Ltd, for which he subscribed at par in August 1983. On 31 March 1986, he and the other shareholders in B Ltd sell their shares to another company for £10 per share plus a further unquantified amount calculated by means of a formula relating to the future profits of B Ltd. The value in March 1986 of the deferred consideration is estimated at £2 per share. On 30 April 1990, Z receives a further £4.20 per share under the sale agreement. The indexation factor for the period August 1983 to March 1986 is 0.128.

1985/86

	£	£
Disposal proceeds 2,000 at £10	20,000	
Value of rights 2,000 at £2	4,000	24,000
Cost of acquisition		2,000
Unindexed gain		22,000
Indexation allowance £2,000 × 0.128		256
Chargeable gain		£21,744

1990/91

	£
Disposal of rights to deferred consideration	
Proceeds 2,000 × £4.20	8,400
Deemed cost of acquiring rights	4,000
Unindexed gain	4,400
Indexation allowance £4,000 × 0.293	1,172
Chargeable gain	£3,228

Notes

(*a*)   A right to unquantified and contingent future consideration on the disposal of an asset is itself an asset, and the future consideration when received is a capital sum derived from that asset (*Marren v Ingles H/L 1980, 54 TC 76* and *Marson v Marriage C/D 1979, 54 TC 59*).

(b)   See 223.4(E) SHARES AND SECURITIES below for concession applicable where deferred consideration is to be satisfied in shares and/or debentures in the acquiring company.

(C)

Suppose that in the previous example, the deferred consideration was valued at £4.20 per share in March 1986, but only £2 per share was received on 30 April 1990.

1985/86

	£	£
Disposal proceeds	20,000	
Value of rights	8,400	28,400
Cost of acquisition		2,000
Unindexed gain		26,400
Indexation allowance £2,000 × 0.128		256
Chargeable gain		£26,144

1990/91

	£
Disposal of rights	4,000
Deemed acquisition cost	8,400
Unindexed loss	4,400
Indexation allowance £8,400 × 0.293	2,461
Allowable loss	£6,861

Note
(a)   There is no provision for reopening the 1985/86 assessment or setting off the 1990/91 loss against the 1985/86 gain.

206.4 **RECEIPT OF COMPENSATION** [*CGTA 1979, ss 20, 21*]
(A)

C owns a freehold warehouse which is badly damaged by fire as a result of inflammable goods having been inadequately packaged. The value of the warehouse after the fire is £90,000, and it cost £120,000 in 1983. The owner of the goods is held liable for the damage and pays C £60,000 compensation in October 1990.

	£
Disposal proceeds	60,000
Allowable cost $\dfrac{60,000}{60,000 + 90,000} \times £120,000$	48,000
Unindexed gain	£12,000

(B) Restoration using insurance moneys
A diamond necklace owned by D cost £100,000 in 1985. D is involved in a motor accident in which the necklace is damaged. Its value is reduced to £80,000. D receives £30,000 under an insurance policy in May 1990 and spends £35,000 on having the necklace restored.

(i) No claim under *CGTA 1979, s 21*

	£
Disposal proceeds	30,000
Allowable cost $\dfrac{30,000}{30,000 + 80,000} \times £100,000$	27,273
Unindexed gain	£2,727
Allowable cost in relation to subsequent disposal £100,000 − £27,273 + £35,000	£107,727

(ii) Claim under *CGTA 1979, s 21*
No chargeable gain arises

Allowable cost originally	100,000
Deduct amount received on claim	30,000
	70,000
Add expenditure on restoration	35,000
Allowable cost in relation to subsequent disposal	£105,000

(C) Part application of capital sum received
E is the owner of a large estate consisting mainly of parkland which he acquired for £150,000 in August 1982. He grants a one-year licence in August 1990 to an exploration company to prospect for minerals, in consideration for a capital sum of £50,000. The exploration proves unsuccessful and on expiry of the licence E spends £20,000 on restoration of the drilling sites to their former state. The market value of the estate both after granting the licence and immediately before restoration is £350,000 and it is £400,000 after restoration.

(i) No claim under *CGTA 1979, s 21*

	£
Disposal proceeds	50,000
Deduct allowable cost $\dfrac{50,000}{50,000 + 350,000} \times £150,000$	18,750
Unindexed gain	£31,250
Allowable expenditure remaining £150,000 − £18,750 + £20,000	£151,250

(ii) Claim made under *CGTA 1979, s 21*

Deemed disposal proceeds (£50,000 − £20,000)	30,000

Deduct

Allowable cost $\dfrac{30,000}{30,000 + 400,000} \times £(150,000 + 20,000)$	11,860
Unindexed gain	£18,140

Allowable expenditure remaining
£150,000 − £20,000 − £11,860 + £20,000   £138,140

(D) Capital sum exceeding allowable expenditure

F inherited a painting in 1980 when it was valued at £2,000. Its value at 31 March 1982 was £3,000. In March 1987, by which time its value had increased considerably, the painting suffered damage whilst on loan to an art gallery and F received £10,000 compensation. The value of the painting was then £30,000. It then cost F £9,800 to have the painting restored. In June 1990, he sells the painting for £50,000.

(i) No election under *CGTA 1979, s 21(2)*

	£
Disposal proceeds March 1987	10,000
Allowable cost $\dfrac{10,000}{10,000 + 30,000} \times £2,000$	500
Unindexed gain 1986/87	£9,500

Allowable cost in relation to subsequent
disposal
£2,000 − £500 + £9,800   £11,300

	£	£
Disposal proceeds June 1990	50,000	50,000
Allowable cost without re-basing	11,300	
Allowable cost with re-basing		
$£3,000 \times \dfrac{30,000}{10,000 + 30,000} = £2,250 + £9,800$		12,050
Unindexed gain 1990/91	£38,700	£37,950

It is clear that re-basing will apply and the chargeable gain will be £37,950 less indexation allowance.

(ii) Election under *CGTA 1979, s 21(2)*

	£
Disposal proceeds March 1987	10,000
Less allowable expenditure	2,000
Unindexed gain 1986/87	£8,000

Allowable cost in relation to subsequent
disposal
£2,000 − £2,000 + £9,800   £9,800

	£	£
Disposal proceeds June 1990	50,000	50,000
Allowable cost without re-basing	9,800	
Allowable cost with re-basing		
£3,000 − £2,000 + £9,800		10,800
Unindexed gain 1990/91	£40,200	£39,200

Again, re-basing will clearly apply and the chargeable gain will be £39,200 less indexation allowance.

Notes

(a)   Although not illustrated in this example, indexation allowance must be deducted before comparing the positions with and without re-basing in order to ascertain whether or not re-basing applies.

(b)   Where there is a disposal after 5 April 1989 to which re-basing applies and, if re-basing had not applied, the allowable expenditure would have fallen to be reduced under *CGTA 1979, s 21(2)* by reference to a capital sum received after 31 March 1982 but before 6 April 1988, the 31 March 1982 value is reduced by the amount previously allowed against the capital sum. [*FA 1989, 15 Sch 3*].

(E) Indexation allowance [*FA 1982, ss 86–88, 13 Sch; FA 1985, s 68, 19 Sch Part I*]
A Ltd owns a freehold factory which cost £100,000 in June 1982. Because of mining operations nearby, part of the factory is severely damaged by subsidence and has to be demolished and rebuilt. The value of the factory after the damage is £160,000. The risk is not covered under A's insurance policy but the mining company agrees to pay compensation of £50,000 in full settlement, received in April 1990. The cost of demolition and rebuilding is £60,000 incurred in February 1990. The factory is sold in December 1991 for £400,000.

Indexation factors	June 1982 to April 1990	0.528
	June 1982 to December 1991 (assumed)	0.795
	February 1990 to December 1991 (assumed)	0.223
	April 1990 to December 1991 (assumed)	0.175

CGT 206.4 Disposal

(i) No claim under *CGTA 1979, s 21(1)*

			£
(*a*)	Part disposal April 1990		
	Disposal proceeds		50,000
	Deduct allowable cost $\dfrac{50,000}{50,000 + 160,000} \times £100,000$		23,810
	Unindexed gain		26,190
	Indexation allowance £23,810 × 0.528		12,572
	Chargeable gain		£13,618

			£
(*b*)	Disposal December 1991		
	Disposal proceeds		400,000
	Deduct allowable cost		
	£(100,000 − 23,810) + £60,000		136,190
	Unindexed gain		263,810
	Indexation allowance		
	Original cost £(100,000 − 23,810) × 0.795	60,571	
	Rebuilding cost £60,000 × 0.223	13,380	73,951
	Chargeable gain		£189,859

(ii) Claim under *CGTA 1979, s 21(1)*

			£
(*a*)	No chargeable gain in April 1990		
	Allowable cost		100,000
	Rebuilding cost		60,000
			160,000
	Deduct receipt rolled over		50,000
	Revised allowable cost		£110,000

			£
(*b*)	Disposal December 1991		
	Disposal proceeds		400,000
	Deduct allowable cost		110,000
	Unindexed gain		290,000
	Indexation allowance		
	Original cost £100,000 × 0.795	79,500	
	Rebuilding cost £60,000 × 0.223	13,380	
		92,880	
	Deduct		
	Receipt rolled over £50,000 × 0.175	(8,750)	84,130
	Chargeable gain		£205,870

206.5 **OPTIONS** [*CGTA 1979, ss 37, 38, 137*]

(A)

On 1 February 1988 F granted an option to G for £10,000 to acquire freehold land bought by F for £50,000 in September 1985. The option is for a period of 5 years, and the option price is £100,000 plus 1% for each month since the option was granted. On 1 February 1990, G sold the option to H for £20,000. On 30 June 1991, H exercised the option and paid F £141,000 for the land. Neither G nor H intended to use the land for the purposes of a trade.

Indexation factors September 1985 to June 1991 (assumed)   0.466
                    February 1988 to February 1990   0.159

1988 Grant of option by F

	£
Disposal proceeds	10,000
Allowable cost	—
Chargeable gain	£10,000

1990 Disposal of option by G

	£
Disposal proceeds	20,000
Allowable cost $\dfrac{5-2}{5} \times £10,000$	6,000
Unindexed gain	14,000
Indexation allowance £6,000 × 0.159	954
Chargeable gain	£13,046

1991 Exercise of option

(i)   Earlier assessment on F vacated

	£
(ii) Aggregate disposal proceeds (£10,000 + £141,000)	151,000
Allowable cost of land	50,000
Unindexed gain	101,000
Indexation allowance £50,000 × 0.466	23,300
Chargeable gain (on F)	£77,700

H's allowable expenditure is

	£	£
Cost of option	20,000	
Deduct wasted up to date exercised $\left(\dfrac{1\text{y } 5\text{m}}{3\text{y}}\right)$	9,444	
		10,556
Cost of land		141,000
		£151,556

299

(B)

In February 1988, P granted T Ltd an option to purchase 100,000 £1 ordinary shares (unquoted) in R Ltd at £2 per share. The option price was £15,000, and P acquired the shares at par on 31 March 1982. The option was to be exercised within 24 months of the date it was granted. In May 1989, T Ltd exercised the option. In July 1991, T Ltd sold the shares to another company for £280,000, their then market value.

Indexation factors	March 1982 to May 1989	0.448
	February 1988 to July 1991 (assumed)	0.361
	May 1989 to July 1991 (assumed)	0.227

P

		£
(*a*)	*Disposal of option*	
	Disposal consideration	15,000
	(No allowable cost)	—
	Chargeable gain (1987/88)	£15,000
(*b*)	*Disposal of shares*	
	Earlier assessment is vacated	
	Aggregate disposal proceeds	
	(£15,000 + £200,000)	215,000
	Allowable cost	100,000
	Unindexed gain	115,000
	Indexation allowance £100,000 × 0.448	44,800
	Chargeable gain (1989/90)	£70,200

T Ltd
Disposal of shares

Disposal consideration			280,000
Allowable cost			
Shares		200,000	
Option	15,000		
Wasted $\frac{15}{24}$ × £15,000	9,375	5,625	205,625
Unindexed gain			74,375
Indexation allowance			
Shares £200,000 × 0.227		45,400	
Option £5,625 × 0.361		2,031	
			47,431
Chargeable gain (1991/92)			£26,944

207 Exemptions and Reliefs

Cross-references. See also 218 PRIVATE RESIDENCES and 219 QUALIFYING CORPORATE BONDS.

207.1 **CHATTELS** [*CGTA 1979, s 128; FA 1989, s 123*]

(A) Marginal relief

On 1 April 1982, Y acquired by inheritance a painting valued for probate at £800. He sold it for £7,200 on 30 October 1990, incurring costs of £150. The indexation factor for the period April 1982 to October 1990 is assumed to be 0.616.

	£	£
Disposal proceeds	7,200	
Incidental costs	150	7,050
Acquisition cost		800
Unindexed gain		6,250
Indexation allowance 0.616 × £800		493
Chargeable gain		£5,757
Marginal relief		
Chargeable gain limited to $\frac{5}{3}$ × (£7,200 – £6,000)		£2,000

Note

(*a*) If the asset had been held on 31 March 1982, and if re-basing applied, the gain using re-basing would be compared with that using marginal relief and the lower of the two taken to be the chargeable gain.

(B) Loss relief

Z bought a piece of antique jewellery for £7,000 in February 1983. In January 1991, he is forced to sell it but at auction it realises only £1,500 and Z incurs costs of £100. The indexation factor for the period February 1983 to January 1991 is assumed to be 0.617.

	£	£
Deemed disposal consideration		6,000
Cost of disposal	100	
Cost of acquisition	7,000	7,100
Unindexed loss		1,100
Indexation allowance 0.617 × £7,000		4,319
Allowable loss		£5,419

(C) Partial disposal of assets forming sets

AB purchased a set of six 18th century dining chairs in 1976 for £3,000. After incurring restoration costs of £1,000 in 1980, he sold two of them in May 1984 to an unconnected person for £2,000. In October 1990, he sold the other four to the same buyer for £8,200. It is agreed that the chairs are worth more as a set of six than in two separate sets of two and four and that the value of the complete set at 31 March 1982 was £5,000.

Indexation factors	March 1982 to May 1984 (actual)	0.120
	March 1982 to October 1990 (assumed)	0.649

The two disposals are treated as one for the purposes of marginal relief, the consideration for which is £10,200. Marginal relief on this basis would give a total chargeable gain of £7,000 ([£10,200 − £6,000] × $\frac{5}{3}$) which is to be compared with the following

	£	£
May 1984		
Disposal proceeds		2,000
Acquisition cost	3,000	
Enhancement cost	1,000	
	£4,000	
Proportion of cost in respect of disposal $\frac{2}{6}$ × £4,000		1,333
Gross gain		667
Indexation allowance 0.120 × £1,333		160
Chargeable gain		£507

	£	£
October 1990		
Disposal proceeds	8,200	8,200
Allowable cost (£4,000 − £1,333)	2,667	
Market value 31.3.82 £5,000 × $\frac{4}{6}$		3,333
Unindexed gain	5,533	4,867
Indexation allowance £5,000 × $\frac{4}{6}$ × 0.649	2,163	2,163
Gain after indexation	£3,370	£2,704
Chargeable gain		£2,704
Total chargeable gains (£507 + £2,704)		£3,211

Marginal relief is therefore ineffective.

208   Hold-Over Reliefs

208.1 **RELIEF FOR GIFTS** [*CGTA 1979, s 147A; FA 1989, 14 Sch 4*]
(A)
B owns a house which he has not occupied as a private residence. He purchased the house for £2,200 inclusive of costs in 1972 and in January 1991 he gives it to a discretionary trust of which he is the settlor. The market value of the house is agreed to be £40,000 at the date of transfer, and B incurs transfer costs of £500. The indexation factor for March 1982 to January 1991 is assumed to be 0.690. The house had a value of £21,000 at 31 March 1982.

	£	£
Disposal consideration	40,000	40,000
Deduct costs of disposal	500	500
	39,500	39,500
Cost	2,200	
Market value 31.3.82		21,000
Unindexed gain	37,300	18,500
Indexation allowance £21,000 × 0.690	14,490	14,490
Gain after indexation	£22,810	£4,010
Chargeable gain		£4,010

If B elects under *CGTA 1979, s 147A*, his chargeable gain is reduced to nil, and the trustees' acquisition cost of the house is treated as £35,990 (£40,000 − £4,010).

Notes
(*a*)   Relief under *CGTA 1979, s 147A* is restricted, generally, to transfers which are, or would but for annual exemptions be, chargeable lifetime transfers for inheritance tax purposes. It is not available for potentially exempt transfers. A more general relief for gifts, computed in an identical fashion, was available for transfers before 14 March 1989 [*FA 1980, s 79; FA 1981, s 78; FA 1982, s 82*; all repealed by *FA 1989, 17 Sch Part VII*]. If, under this former relief, the house had been given to an individual, who had used it as his main residence, such that, in the event of his selling it, the private residence exemption would apply in full (see 218 PRIVATE RESIDENCES), the deferred gain would never become chargeable.

(*b*)   If the gift had taken place before 31 March 1982, the house was sold by the donee after 5 April 1988 and re-basing applied on the sale, the deferred gain would fall out of charge. There are special rules where deferral took place after 31 March 1982 but before 6 April 1988, for which see 204.2 ASSETS HELD AT 31 MARCH 1982. No special rules apply where, as in this example, deferral takes place after 5 April 1988.

(B)

The facts are as in (A) above except that B sells the house to the trustees for £24,000.

	£	£
Chargeable gain (as above) note (*a*)		4,010
Deduct		
Actual consideration passing	24,000	
B's allowable costs	(21,000)	
		3,000
Held-over gain		£1,010

(i)	B's chargeable gain is reduced to £4,010 − £1,010	£3,000
(ii)	The trustees' allowable cost is reduced to £40,000 − £1,010	£38,990

Notes

(*a*) The disposal consideration is taken as the open market value of the house at the date of disposal because B and the trustees are connected persons.

(*b*) The adjustment for consideration paid takes no account of any indexation allowance due to B as the indexation allowance is not a sum allowable under *CGTA 1979, s 32*.

(C)

The facts are as in (A) above. Before transferring the house, B had made substantial chargeable transfers, and he dies in 1991. Inheritance tax of £16,000 in total is payable on the transfer. The trustees sell the house in July 1992 for £70,000. The indexation factor for January 1990 to July 1992 is assumed to be 0.270.

	£	£
Disposal proceeds		70,000
Acquisition cost	40,000	
Deduct held-over gain	4,010	
		35,990
Unindexed gain		34,010
Indexation allowance £35,990 × 0.270		9,717
		24,293
IHT on earlier transfer		16,000
Chargeable gain		£8,293

Notes

(*a*) The IHT deduction is not indexed as it is not relevant allowable expenditure under *FA 1982, s 86*.

(*b*) The IHT deduction is limited to the amount of the gain and cannot create or increase a loss.

208.2 **RELIEF FOR GIFT OF BUSINESS ASSETS** [*CGTA 1979, s 126; FA 1989, 14 Sch 1*]

S has carried on his antique dealing business for 10 years. The assets of the business are valued as follows

	£
Freehold shop and office	235,000
Goodwill	70,000
Stocks	50,000
Debtors	9,500
Cash	4,500

Before the business began, S let the shop premises for one year. In October 1990, S transfers the business as a going concern to a company which he has formed with share capital of £1,000, held wholly by him. The transfer consideration is £1. At the time of the transfer S is 63. The gain arising in respect of the freehold is £200,000 and on goodwill it is £63,000 (both after deducting indexation allowance).

	£	£
Gains eligible for retirement relief		
(£200,000 + £63,000)		263,000
Relief £125,000 × 100%	125,000	
£138,000 × 50%	69,000	194,000
Chargeable gain		£69,000

If S and the company elect jointly under *CGTA 1979, s 126*, part of the chargeable gain may be rolled over, as follows

	Freehold	Goodwill
	£	£
Total gain	200,000	63,000
Reduction for non-trade use [*CGTA 1979, 4 Sch 5*] ($\frac{1}{11}$)	18,182	
	£181,818	£63,000
Held-over gain before adjustment	244,818	
Retirement relief [*CGTA 1979, 4 Sch 8*]	194,000	
Held-over gain	£50,818	

Notes

(*a*) The chargeable gain neither relieved nor held over is therefore £18,182 (£263,000 − £194,000 − £50,818).

(*b*) There is no statutory formula for apportioning retirement relief between different assets for the purpose of calculating hold-over under *Sec 126*. The following is therefore one possible method of computing the revised base costs in the hands of the company.

Freehold

Gain held over $\frac{181,818}{244,818} \times £50,818$	£37,741
Revised base cost (£235,000 − £37,741)	£197,259

305

Goodwill

Gain held over $\dfrac{63,000}{244,818} \times £50,818$ £13,077

Revised base cost (£70,000 − £13,077)   £56,923

(c)   If S had transferred the business to the company in consideration for the issue of shares, *CGTA 1979, s 123* would have applied but business assets relief would not. Retirement relief would still have applied in priority so that the chargeable gain would have been £69,000. This gain would then have been rolled over against the base cost of the shares acquired by S.

(d)   See 204.2 ASSETS HELD AT 31 MARCH 1982 for the relief given under *FA 1988, 9 Sch* where gains are held over after 31 March 1982 and before 6 April 1988 and a disposal occurs after 5 April 1988. This relief applies, inter alia, to gains held over under *CGTA 1979, s 126*.

208.3 TRANSFER OF BUSINESS TO A COMPANY [*CGTA 1979, s 123*]

W carries on an antiquarian bookselling business. He decides to form a company, P Ltd, to carry on the business. He then transfers, in August 1990, the whole of the business undertaking, assets and liabilities to P Ltd, in consideration for the issue of shares, plus an amount left outstanding on interest-free loan. The business assets and liabilities transferred are valued as follows

	£	£	Chargeable gain £
Freehold shop premises		80,000	55,000
Goodwill		36,000	26,000
Fixtures and fittings		4,000	—
Trading stock		52,000	—
Debtors		28,000	—
		200,000	
Mortgage on shop	50,000		
Trade creditors	20,000	70,000	—
		£130,000	£81,000

The company issues 100,000 £1 ordinary shares, valued at par, to W, and the amount left outstanding is £30,000. Later, W sells 20,000 of his shares for £40,000 to X. W's remaining shareholding is then worth £140,000.

(i) Amount of chargeable gain rolled over on transfer of the business

$\dfrac{100,000}{130,000} \times £81,000$ £62,308

Of the chargeable gain £18,692 (£81,000 − £62,308) remains taxable.

The allowable cost of W's shares is £37,692 (£100,000 − £62,308).

(ii) On the sale of shares to X, W realises a chargeable gain

	£
Disposal consideration	40,000
Allowable cost £37,692 × $\dfrac{40,000}{40,000 + 140,000}$	8,376
Unindexed gain	£31,624

Notes

(*a*)   Indexation allowance on the disposal is given from the date of transfer to the date of disposal. It is calculated by deducting the indexed rise in the chargeable gain held over (£62,308) from the indexed rise in the cost of the shares (£100,000).

(*b*)   See 204.2 ASSETS HELD AT 31 MARCH 1982 for the relief given under *FA 1988, 9 Sch* where gains are held over after 31 March 1982 and before 6 April 1988 and a disposal occurs after 5 April 1988. This relief applies, inter alia, to gains held over under *CGTA 1979, s 123*.

209 Indexation

209.1 **INDEXATION ALLOWANCE — GENERAL RULES** [*FA 1982, ss 86, 87; FA 1985, s 68, 19 Sch Part I; FA 1988, 8 Sch 11*]
(A) Disposal after 5 April 1985 of asset acquired after 31 March 1982
M bought a freehold factory in December 1983 for £500,000. Further buildings are erected at a cost of £200,000 in May 1984. In February 1991 the factory is sold for £2m. The retail price index (RPI) was re-based in January 1987 from 394.5 to 100 and the values are as follows

December	1983	342.8
May	1984	351.0
February	1991(assumed)	135.3

	£	£
Disposal consideration		2,000,000
Deduct Cost of factory and site	500,000	
Cost of additions	200,000	700,000
Unindexed gain		1,300,000

Indexation allowance
(i) Factory and site
Indexation factor

$$\left(\frac{394.5 \times 135.3}{342.8}\right) - 100 = 55.7\%$$

Indexed rise
£500,000 × 0.557   278,500

(ii) Additions
Indexation factor

$$\left(\frac{394.5 \times 135.3}{351.0}\right) - 100 = 52.1\%$$

Indexed rise £200,000 × 0.521	104,200	382,700
Chargeable gain		£917,300

Note
(*a*)   Alternatively the indexation factors can be calculated using the revised RPI figures given at the beginning of this section so that

December 1983	=	86.9
May 1984	=	89.0
February 1991	=	135.3 (assumed)

Indexation from December 1983 to February 1990 = $\dfrac{135.3 - 86.9}{86.9} = 0.557$

Indexation from May 1984 to February 1990 = $\dfrac{135.3 - 89.0}{89.0} = 0.521$

The examples in this book use this simpler method where relevant.

(B) Disposal after 5 April 1988 of asset acquired before 1 April 1982
X acquired an eighteenth century clock for £4,500 in August 1979. Its price reflected the need for major repairs, which X carried out at a cost of £2,000 in May 1981. He sold the clock for £15,000 in December 1990. The agreed market value of the repaired clock at 31 March 1982 is £8,000. The indexation factor for March 1982 to December 1990 is assumed to be 0.676.

	£	£	£
Disposal consideration	15,000		15,000
Deduct Cost of clock		4,500	
Cost of repairs		2,000	6,500
Deduct Market value 31.3.82	8,000		
Unindexed gain	7,000		8,500
Indexation allowance £8,000 × 0.676	5,408		5,408
Gain after indexation	£1,592		£3,092
Chargeable gain	£1,592		

Notes

(*a*)   In both the calculation using cost and that using 31 March 1982 value indexation is automatically based on 31 March 1982 value. If, however, a greater allowance would have been produced by basing indexation on cost, that would automatically apply instead. If an irrevocable election were to be made under *FA 1988, s 96(5)* for all assets to be treated as sold and reacquired at 31 March 1982, however, indexation must then be based on 31 March 1982 value whether it is beneficial or not. [*FA 1985, s 68(4)(5); FA 1988, 8 Sch 11*].

(*b*)   For disposals after 5 April 1985 and before 6 April 1988, indexation may be based on 31 March 1982 value, but only if the taxpayer claims such treatment. [*FA 1985, s 68(4)(5) as originally enacted*].

(*c*)   The repair expenditure is not disallowed by virtue of *CGTA 1979, s 33* because it would have been treated as capital expenditure for income tax purposes (*Law Shipping Co Ltd v CIR SC/S 1923, 12 TC 621*).

(*d*)   See also 204.1 ASSETS HELD AT 31 MARCH 1982.

(C) Disposal at a loss
M carried out the following transactions in quoted £1 shares in E plc.

		Cost/(proceeds)
		£
16.8.78	Purchased 20,000	44,000
14.2.80	Purchased 30,000	84,000
23.1.84	Sold 10,000	(25,000)
2.2.91	Sold 40,000	(102,000)

The share value at 31 March 1982 was £3. The indexation factor from March 1982 to February 1991 is assumed to be 0.704.

(i) Disposal on 23.1.84

	£
Disposal consideration	25,000
Allowable cost $\dfrac{10,000}{50,000} \times £(44,000 + 84,000)$	25,600
Allowable loss 1983/84	£(600)

(ii) Disposal on 2.2.91

	£	£
Disposal consideration	102,000	102,000
Allowable cost		
($£44,000 + 84,000 - £25,600$)	102,400	
Market value 31.3.82 (40,000 × £3)		120,000
Unindexed loss	400	18,000
Indexation allowance £120,000 × 0.704	84,480	84,480
Loss after indexation	£84,880	£102,480
Allowable loss 1990/91	£84,880	

Note
(*a*)   For disposals before 6 April 1985 (1 April 1985 for companies), the indexation allowance could not be used to increase or create a loss.

(D) Disposals on a no gain/no loss basis: inter-spouse transfers — asset acquired by first spouse before 1 April 1982 [*FA 1982, 13 Sch 2; FA 1985, s 68(7)(7A)(8); FA 1988, s 118(3)(4)*]
Mr N owns agricultural land which he acquired by inheritance in 1977, at a value of £80,000. In May 1983 he gave the land to his wife. In November 1990 Mrs N sells the land for £380,000 to a neighbouring farmer. The agreed market value of the land at 31 March 1982 is £185,000. The indexation factor from March 1982 to November 1990 is assumed to be 0.662.

(i) Disposal in May 1983
Consideration deemed to be such that neither gain nor loss arises.

Indexation factor $\dfrac{84.6 - 79.4}{79.4} = 0.065$

	£
Cost of land to Mr N	80,000
Indexation allowance to May 1983 £80,000 × 0.065	5,200
Cost of land to Mrs N	£85,200

(ii) Disposal in November 1990

	£	£	£
Disposal consideration		380,000	380,000
Cost	85,200		
less indexation allowance on disposal by Mr N	5,200	80,000	
Market value 31.3.82			185,000
Unindexed gain		300,000	195,000
Indexation allowance £185,000 × 0.662		122,470	122,470
Gain after indexation		£177,530	£72,530
Chargeable gain			£72,530

Notes

(*a*)   Having acquired the asset by means of a no gain/no loss disposal, under *CGTA 1979, s 44,* from her husband, who held it at 31 March 1982, Mrs N is deemed to have held the asset at 31 March 1982 for the purpose of the *Finance Act 1988* re-basing provisions and the *Finance Act 1985* provisions under which indexation allowance is computed using value at 31 March 1982. [*FA 1985, s 68; FA 1988, 8 Sch 1*].

(*b*)   See also (E) below and 214.3 MARRIED PERSONS below.

(E) Disposals on a no gain/no loss basis: inter-spouse transfers — asset acquired by first spouse after 31 March 1982

Assume in (D) above, that Mr N had acquired the land in April 1982 (at the same probate value). The indexation factor from May 1983 to November 1990 is assumed to be 0.560.

(i) Disposal in May 1983

Consideration deemed to be such that neither gain nor loss arises.

Indexation factor $\dfrac{84.6 - 84.3}{84.3} = 0.004$

	£
Cost of land to Mr N	80,000
Indexation allowance to May 1983 £80,000 × 0.004	320
Cost of land to Mrs N	£80,320

(ii) Disposal in November 1990

	£
Disposal consideration	380,000
Allowable cost	80,320
Unindexed gain	299,680
Indexation allowance £80,320 × 0.560	44,979
Chargeable gain	£254,701

Notes

(*a*) For disposals before 6 April 1985 (1 April 1985 for companies), there was a 12-month 'waiting period' before indexation applied. [*FA 1982, s 87(2)* (*as originally enacted*)]. Thus, indexation in (i) above runs from April 1983 to May 1983.

(*b*) For further examples on inter-spouse transfers, see (D) above and 214.3 MARRIED PERSONS below.

209.2 SHARE IDENTIFICATION RULES [*FA 1982, s 88, 13 Sch 8–10; FA 1985, 19 Sch*]

(A) General

B has the following transactions in 25p ordinary shares of H plc, a quoted company.

		Cost/(proceeds)
		£
6.6.81	Purchased 500 at £0.85	425
3.11.81	Purchased 1,300 at £0.80	1,040
15.5.82	Purchased 1,000 at £1.02	1,020
8.9.82	Purchased 400 at £1.08	432
1.2.83	Purchased 1,200 at £1.14	1,368
29.7.83	Sold 2,000 at £1.30	(2,600)
8.6.85	Purchased 1,500 at £1.26	1,890
10.12.90	Sold 2,900 at £1.90	(5,510)

The shares stood at £1.00 at 31.3.82.

Indexation factors	March 1982 to December 1990 (assumed)	0.676
	May 1982 to April 1985	0.161
	May 1983 to July 1983	0.008
	April 1985 to June 1985	0.007
	June 1985 to December 1990 (assumed)	0.395

Disposal on 29 July 1983	£
(i) Identify 400 with acquisition on 8.9.82	
Disposal consideration 400 × £1.30	520
Allowable cost	432
Chargeable gain	£88

(ii) Identify 1,200 with acquisition on 1.2.83	
Disposal consideration 1,200 × £1.30	1,560
Allowable cost	1,368
Chargeable gain	£192

(iii) Identify 400 with 400 of acquisition on 15.5.82	
Disposal consideration 400 × £1.30	520
Allowable cost 400 × £1.02	408
Gross gain	112
Indexation allowance £408 × 0.008	3
	£109

Total chargeable gain (1983/84)	£389

Disposal on 10 December 1990

(i)   Establish pools

(a)   New holding

	Shares	Qualifying expenditure £	Indexed pool £
Initial pool (balance of 15.5.82 shares) before indexation	600	612	612
Indexation allowance to initial pool £612 × 0.161			99
Pool at 6.4.85	600	612	711
Indexed rise: April 1985 – June 1985 £711 × 0.007			5
8.6.85 acquisition	1,500	1,890	1,890
	2,100	2,502	2,606
Indexed rise: June 1985 – December 1990 £2,606 × 0.395			1,029
	2,100	£2,502	£3,635

(b)   1982 holding

	Shares	Allowable expenditure £
6.6.81 acquisition	500	425
3.11.81 acquisition	1,300	1,040
	1,800	£1,465

(ii)   Identify 2,100 with new holding

	£
Disposal consideration 2,100 × £1.90	3,990
Allowable cost	2,502
Unindexed gain	1,488
Indexation allowance £3,635 − £2,502	1,133
Chargeable gain	£355

(iii)   Identify 800 with 1982 holding

	£	£
Disposal consideration 800 × £1.90	1,520	1,520
Cost $\dfrac{800}{1,800}$ × £1,465	651	
Market value 31.3.82 $\dfrac{800}{1,800}$ × £1,800		800
Unindexed gain	869	720
Indexation allowance £800 × 0.676	541	541
Gain after indexation	£328	£179
Chargeable gain		£179
Total chargeable gain (1990/91) (£355 + £179)		£534

313

Notes

(*a*)   On share disposals before 6.4.85 (1.4.85 for companies), indexation was onl available from 12 months after the purchase date. Subject to certain specia rules, disposals were identified first with acquisitions within the 12 month preceding disposal (on a first-in, first-out basis) and then with earlier acqu sitions on a last-in, first-out basis.

(*b*)   On share disposals after 5.4.88 identified with shares held at 31.3.82, th *Finance Act 1988* re-basing provisions have effect and indexation i automatically based on the higher of cost and 31.3.82 value. If an irrevocabl election is made under *FA 1988, s 96(5)* for all assets to be treated as dispose of and re-acquired at their market value on 31.3.82, indexation must b based on the 31.3.82 value even if this is less than cost. [*FA 1985, s 68(4)(5) FA 1988, 8 Sch 11*].

(*c*)   On share disposals after 5.4.85 (31.3.85 for companies), but before 6 Apr 1988, identified with shares held at 31.3.82 (not illustrated here), a clair could be made for indexation to be based on 31.3.82 value rather than cost [*FA 1988, s 68(4)(5) as originally enacted*].

(B) Special rules — 'same day' transactions and the 'ten day' rule [*CGTA 1979 s 66; FA 1985, 19 Sch 18*].
C has the following transactions in 25p ordinary shares of J plc.

		Cost/(proceeds £
16.12.84	Purchased 20,000 at £1.92	38,400
5.8.87	Purchased 12,000 at £2.40	28,800
3.4.88	Sold 4,000 at £2.00	(8,000)
4.4.88	Purchased 4,000 at £2.02	8,080
14.9.89	Purchased 5,000 at £2.20	11,000
14.9.89	Sold 1,000 at £2.19	(2,190)
28.2.91	Purchased 2,000 at £2.45	4,900
3.3.91	Purchased 2,000 at £2.48	4,960
8.3.91	Sold 6,000 at £2.75	(16,500)

Holding at 5.4.91 – 34,000

Indexation factors	December 1984 to August 1987	0.124
	August 1987 to April 1988	0.036
	April 1988 to September 1989	0.102
	September 1989 to March 1991 (assumed)	0.171

1987/88

Disposal on 3.4.88
Establish new holding pool

	Shares	Qualifying expenditure £	Indexed pool £
16.12.84 acquisition	20,000	38,400	38,400
Indexed rise: December 1984 — August 1987 £38,400 × 0.124			4,762
5.8.87 acquisition	12,000	28,800	28,800
	32,000	67,200	71,962
Indexed rise: August 1987 — April 1988 £71,962 × 0.036			2,591
	32,000	67,200	74,553
3.4.88 disposal	(4,000)	(8,400)	(9,319)
4.4.88 acquisition	4,000	8,080	8,080
Pool carried forward	32,000	£66,880	£73,314

	£
Disposal consideration	8,000
Cost $\dfrac{4,000}{32,000} \times £67,200$	8,400
Unindexed loss	400

Indexation allowance

$$\frac{4,000}{32,000} \times £74,553 = £9,319$$

£9,319 − £8,400	919
Allowable loss	£1,319

1989/90

(i) Disposal on 14.9.89
Match with acquisitions on the same day

	£
Disposal consideration	2,190
Cost $\dfrac{1,000}{5,000} \times £11,000$	2,200
Allowable loss	£10

Add balance of 14.9.89 acquisition to pool

	Shares	Qualifying expenditure £	Indexed pool £
Pool at 4.4.88	32,000	66,880	73,314
Indexed rise: April 1988 — September 1989 £73,314 × 0.102			7,478
Balance of 14.9.89 acquisition	4,000	8,800	8,800
Pool carried forward	36,000	£75,680	£89,592

(ii) Disposal on 8.3.91
Match first with acquisition on 28.2.91

	£
Disposal consideration 2,000 × £2.75	5,500
Cost 28.2.91	4,900
Chargeable gain	£600

Match next with 3.3.91 acquisition

	£
Disposal consideration 2,000 × £2.75	5,500
Cost 3.3.91	4,960
Chargeable gain	£540

Match finally with new holding pool

	Shares	Qualifying expenditure £	Indexed pool £
Pool at 14.9.89	36,000	75,680	89,592
Indexed rise: September 1989 — March 1991 £89,592 × 0.171			15,320
	36,000	75,680	104,912
Balance of 8.3.91 disposal	(2,000)	(4,204)	(5,828)
Pool carried forward	34,000	£71,476	£99,084

Disposal consideration 2,000 × £2.75	£5,500
Cost $\dfrac{2,000}{36,000} \times £75,680$	4,204
Unindexed gain	1,296

Indexation allowance

$$\frac{2,000}{36,000} \times £104,912 = £5,828$$

£5,828 − £4,204	1,624
Allowable loss	£328

Total chargeable gain 1990/91 (£600 + £540 − £10 − £328)	£802

Notes

(*a*)   Under *CGTA 1979, s 66*, a disposal of securities is matched as far as possible with an acquisition on the same day. It follows that no indexation can be available.

(*b*)   Subject to the overriding rule described in (*a*) above, and for disposals after 5.4.85 (31.3.85 for companies), a disposal of securities is first matched with preceding acquisitions within a ten-day period on a first in/first out basis, and to the extent that they can be so matched, the securities are not pooled and no indexation allowance is due. [*FA 1985, 19 Sch 18*]. Note that no special rules apply where an acquisition *follows* a disposal within the ten-day period and the above rules do not therefore affect a 'bed-and-breakfast' transaction.

209.3 RELEVANT SECURITIES — IDENTIFICATION RULES [*FA 1982, ss 87, 88; FA 1985, s 68*]

X carried out the following transactions in 10% convertible loan stock of A plc. The stock is within the accrued income scheme.

		Cost/(proceeds)
		£
25.11.78	Purchased £5,000 at 95%	4,750
7.4.81	Purchased £4,000 at 92%	3,680
16.7.83	Purchased £3,000 at 94%	2,820
22.9.84	Purchased £3,000 at 95%	2,850
25.1.86	Sold £4,000 at 96%	(3,840)
18.4.90	Sold £6,500 at 100%	(6,500)

The stock was quoted at 91% on 31 March 1982.

Indexation factors	March 1982 to April 1990	0.575
	July 1983 to April 1990	0.467
	July 1984 to January 1986	0.080
	September 1985 to January 1986	0.008

For the purposes of the accrued income scheme, the sale on 18.4.90 is without accrued interest and the rebate amount is £50.

Disposal on 25.1.86

	£
(i) Identify £3,000 with purchase on 22.9.84 (LIFO)	
Disposal consideration £3,000 × 96%	2,880
Allowable cost	2,850
Unindexed gain	30
Indexation allowance £2,850 × 0.008	23
Chargeable gain	£7
(ii) Identify £1,000 with purchase on 16.7.83 (LIFO)	
Disposal consideration £1,000 × 96%	960
Allowable cost £1,000 × 94%	940
Unindexed gain	20
Indexation allowance £940 × 0.080 = £75, restricted to	20
No gain/no loss	Nil
Total chargeable gain 1985/86	£7

Disposal on 18.4.90

(i)   Identify £2,000 of sale with purchase on 16.7.83

	£	£
Disposal consideration £2,000 × 100%		2,000
Rebate amount £50 × $\dfrac{2,000}{6,500}$		15
		2,015
Allowable cost £2,000 × 94%	1,880	
Indexation allowance £1,880 × 0.467	878	2,758
Allowable loss		£743

(ii)   Identify £4,500 of sale with 1982 pool

	£	£
Disposal consideration £4,500 × 100%	4,500	4,500
Rebate amount (£50 − £15)	35	35
	4,535	4,535
Allowable cost $\dfrac{4,500}{9,000}$ × (£4,750 + £3,680)	4,215	
Market value 31.3.82 £4,500 × 91%		4,095
Unindexed gain	320	440
Indexation allowance £4,215 × 0.575	2,424	2,424
Loss after indexation	£2,104	£1,984
Allowable loss		£1,984
Total allowable loss 1990/91 (£743 + £1,984)		£2,727

Notes

(a)   See 22.3 SCHEDULE D, CASE VI in the Income Tax section for income tax effects of the accrued income scheme. The rebate amount arising on a disposal is added to the disposal consideration in the capital gains tax computation. [*CGTA 1979, s 33A*].

(b)   Disposals of securities which fall within the accrued income scheme (most types of loan stock, see *ICTA 1988, s 710*) continue to be identified on or after 6.4.85 in accordance with the rules which applied to disposals of shares and securities before that date (i.e. subject to special rules, on a FIFO basis with acquisitions in the preceding 12 months, and then on a LIFO basis). For disposals of such securities before 28 February 1986, no indexation allowance is due for the first 12 months after acquisition, and indexation cannot create or increase a loss. These restrictions on indexation (and the old identification rules) applied to disposals of gilt-edged securities and qualifying corporate bonds before 2 July 1986; disposals of such securities after 1 July 1986 are exempt from CGT. See also 219 QUALIFYING CORPORATE BONDS below.

(c)   Note the effect of the re-basing provisions of *FA 1988* on the 18.4.90 disposal identified with the 1982 pool. Re-basing creates a loss which is no greater than the loss using cost, and therefore re-basing does apply. Indexation allowance, however, is still based on cost, being greater than 31.3.82 value.

210 Interest on Overpaid Tax

[F(No 2)A 1975, s 47]

210.1 L realised net chargeable gains (after the annual exemption) of £20,000 in 1987/88. An assessment was made on 15 January 1989, charging tax of £6,000. L paid the tax on 30 January 1989. In December 1989, L made a claim under *CGTA 1979, s 115* (rollover relief) and the 1987/88 assessment was reduced to £8,000, with tax payable of £2,400. A repayment of £3,600 was made by payable order issued on 15 January 1990.

Repayment supplement is	£
6.4.89 – 5.7.89 £3,600 at 11.5% $\times \frac{3}{12}$	103.50
6.7.89 – 5.11.89 £3,600 at 12.25% $\times \frac{4}{12}$	147.00
6.11.89 – 5.2.90 £3,600 at 13% $\times \frac{3}{12}$	117.00
	£367.50

Note

(a) The calculation may be made, or checked, using the interest factor tables published from time to time by the Revenue.

Factor for February 1990	2.7196
Factor for April 1989	2.6175
Difference	0.1021
£3,600 × 0.1021 =	£367.56

211 Interest on Unpaid Tax

[*TMA 1970, ss 69, 86–92; F(No 2)A 1975, s 46; FA 1989, s 156(1)*]

211.1 **(A)**

P was assessed to CGT for 1988/89 by a notice of assessment dated 15 November 1989. The amount of tax charged is £45,000. P appeals on 20 November 1989 against the assessment, which is estimated, and applies to postpone payment of £20,000 of the tax charged. The Inspector agrees in writing to the postponement on 5 January 1990 and P pays the agreed amount of £25,000 on 6 March 1990.

The appeal is determined by agreement on 10 May 1990, and a revised notice of assessment is issued on 15 May 1990, charging tax of £29,000. P pays the balance of £4,000 on 5 June 1990.

(i) Tax payment of which is not postponed (£25,000)

Date tax would have been due and payable if no appeal	(D1)	15.12.89
Date tax actually becomes due and payable	(D2)	4.2.90
Table date	(D3)	1.6.90
Reckonable date Because D2 is not later than D3, D2		4.2.90

Interest runs from 4 February 1990 to 6 March 1990

$$£25,000 \times \frac{30}{365} \times 13\%$$

£267.12

(ii) Tax payment of which is postponed (£4,000)

Date tax would have been due and payable if no appeal	(D1)	15.12.89
Date tax actually becomes due and payable	(D2)	14.6.90
Table date	(D3)	1.6.90
Reckonable date Because D2 is later than D3, later of D1 and D3 (i.e. D3)		1.6.90

Interest runs from 1 June 1990 to 5 June 1990

$$£4,000 \times \frac{4}{365} \times 13\%$$

£5.70

Total interest payable

£272.82

(B)
V realised chargeable gains in 1988/89 and was assessed to CGT by an estimated notice dated 15 October 1989. The CGT charged was £8,000. V appealed against the assessment but did not apply for any tax to be postponed, paying the tax due on 1 December 1989. The appeal was determined by the General Commissioners in January 1990, on the basis of computations supplied, which showed the CGT chargeable to be £12,600. A revised notice of assessment was issued on 15 February 1990, and V paid the additional tax of £4,600 on 23 May 1990.

The £4,600 additional tax is treated as if it had been charged by the original assessment. [*TMA 1970, s 86(3)(3A); FA 1989, s 156(1)*].

Date tax would (notionally) have been due and
payable if no appeal   (D1)   1.12.89

Date tax actually becomes due and payable   (D2)   17.3.90

Table date   (D3)   1.6.90

Reckonable date
Because D2 is not later than D3, D2   17.3.90

Interest runs from 17.3.90 to 23.5.90 (67 days)

£4,600 × $\dfrac{67}{365}$ × 13%   £109.77

Suppose that the revised assessment was not issued until
15 June 1990, with V paying the tax of £4,600 on 30 June
1990.

D1 and D3 remain the same as above; D2 becomes 15 July
1990.

Reckonable date
Because D2 is later than D3, later of D1 and D3 (i.e. D3)   1.6.90

Interest runs from 1.6.90 to 30.6.90 (29 days)

£4,600 × $\dfrac{29}{365}$ × 13%   £47.51

212 Land

212.1 SMALL PART DISPOSALS [*CGTA 1979, s 107; FA 1984, s 63(2); FA 1986, s 60*]

C owns farmland which cost £175,000 in May 1982. In February 1989, a small plot of land is exchanged with an adjoining landowner for another piece of land. The value placed on the transaction is £18,000. The value of the remaining estate excluding the new piece of land is estimated at £250,000. In March 1991, C sells the whole estate for £300,000.

Indexation factors   May 1982 to February 1989   0.370
                     February 1989 to March 1991 (assumed)   0.221
                     May 1982 to March 1991 (assumed)   0.673

(i) No *CGTA 1979, s 107 (2)* claim made

(*a*)   *Disposal in February 1989*   £
       Disposal proceeds   18,000

       Allowable cost $\dfrac{18,000}{18,000 + 250,000} \times £175,000$ 11,754

       Unindexed gain   6,246
       Indexation allowance £11,754 × 0.370   4,349

       Chargeable gain 1987/88   £1,897

(*b*)   *Disposal in March 1991*
       Disposal proceeds   300,000
       Allowable cost
       Original land £(175,000 − 11,754)   163,246
       Exchanged land   18,000

                                                                         181,246

       Unindexed gain   118,754
       Indexation allowance
       Original land £163,246 × 0.673   109,864
       Exchanged land £18,000 × 0.221   3,978   113,842

       Chargeable gain 1990/91   £4,912

(ii) Claim made under *CGTA 1979, s 107(2)*

(*a*)   *No disposal in February 1989*
       Allowable cost of original land   175,000
       Deduct disposal proceeds   18,000

       Adjusted allowable cost   £157,000

       Allowable cost of additional land   £18,000

(*b*) *Disposal in March 1991*

	£	£
Disposal proceeds		300,000
Allowable cost		
Original land	157,000	
Additional land	18,000	175,000
Unindexed gain		125,000
Indexation allowance		
Original land £175,000 × 0.673	117,775	
Additional land £18,000 × 0.221	3,978	
	121,753	
Receipt set-off £18,000 × 0.221	3,978	117,775
Chargeable gain		£7,225

Notes

(*a*) For disposals on or after 5 April 1986 a claim under *CGTA 1979, s 107* may be made where the part disposal does not exceed one-fifth of the value of the whole, up to a maximum of £20,000.

(*b*) If the second disposal were also made in 1988/89 no claim under *CGTA 1979, s 107* could be made on the part disposal as proceeds of all disposals in the year would exceed £20,000.

(*c*) If the original land had been held at 31 March 1982 and the part disposal took place after that date, the disposal proceeds, on a claim under *CGTA 1979, s 107(2)*, would be deducted from the 31 March 1982 value for the purpose of the *Finance Act 1988, s 96* re-basing provisions.

212.2 COMPULSORY PURCHASE [*CGTA 1979, ss 108–111, 111A, 111B*]
(A) Rollover where new land acquired
(i) Rollover not claimed

D owns freehold land purchased for £10,000 in 1967. Part of the land is made the subject of a compulsory purchase order. The compensation of £60,000 is agreed on 10 April 1990. The market value of the remaining land is £150,000. The value of the total freehold land at 31 March 1982 was £125,000.

	£	£
Disposal consideration	60,000	60,000
Cost £10,000 × $\frac{60,000}{60,000 + 150,000}$	2,857	
Market value 31.3.82		
£125,000 × $\frac{60,000}{60,000 + 150,000}$		35,714
Unindexed gain	57,143	24,286
Indexation allowance £35,714 × 0.575	20,536	20,536
Gain after indexation	£36,607	£3,750
Chargeable gain		£3,750

(ii) Rollover claimed under *CGTA 1979, s 111A*
If, in (i), D acquires new land costing £80,000 in December 1990, relief may be claimed as follows.

	£
Allowable cost of land compulsorily purchased	35,714
Indexation allowance	20,536
Deemed consideration for disposal	56,250
Actual consideration	60,000
Chargeable gain rolled over	£3,750
Allowable cost of new land (£80,000 − £3,750)	£76,250

(B) Small disposals
(i) No rollover relief claimed
T inherits land in June 1983 at a probate value of £290,000. Under a compulsory purchase order, a part of the land is acquired for highway improvements. Compensation of £30,000 and a further £10,000 for severance, neither sum including any amount in respect of loss of profits, is agreed on 15 April 1990. The value of the remaining land is £800,000. Prior to the compulsory purchase, the value of all the land had been £850,000.

	£
Total consideration for disposal (£30,000 + £10,000)	40,000
Deduct allowable cost $\dfrac{40,000}{40,000 + 800,000} \times £290,000$	13,810
Unindexed gain	26,190
Indexation allowance 0.475 × £13,810	6,560
Chargeable gain	£19,630

(ii) Rollover relief claimed under *CGTA 1979, s 108*
Total consideration for disposal is £40,000, less than 5% of the value of the estate before the disposal. T may therefore claim that the consideration be deducted from the allowable cost of the estate.

Revised allowable cost (£290,000 − £40,000)	£250,000

Note
(*a*)　An indexation adjustment in respect of the amount deducted will be required on a subsequent disposal of the estate (*FA 1982, 13 Sch 4(2)*). For an example of the computation, see 206.4(E) DISPOSAL above.

212.3 **LEASES**

(A) Short leases which are not wasting assets [*CGTA 1979, 3 Sch 1*]

On 31 August 1986, N purchased the remaining term of a lease of commercial premises for £55,000. The lease was subject to a 25-year sub-lease granted on 1 July 1964 at a fixed rental of £1,000 a year. The market rental was estimated at £15,000 a year. The term of the lease held by N is 60 years from 1 April 1962. The value of the lease in 1989, when the sub-lease expired, was estimated at 31 August 1986 as being £100,000. Immediately upon expiry of the sub-lease, N has refurbishment work done at a cost of £50,000 (payable on 30 September 1989), £40,000 of which qualifies as enhancement expenditure. On 31 March 1991, N sells the lease for £200,000.

Indexation factors (assumed) August 1986 to March 1991   0.396
September 1989 to March 1991   0.171

Term of lease at date of expiry of sub-lease   32 years 9 months
Relevant percentage $89.354 + \frac{9}{12} \times (90.280 - 89.354)$ 90.049%

Term of lease at date of assignment   31 years
Relevant percentage   88.371%

	£	£
Disposal consideration		200,000
Deduct allowable cost	55,000	
enhancement costs	40,000	
	95,000	
Less Wasted		
$\dfrac{90.049 - 88.371}{90.049} \times 95,000$	1,770	
		93,230
Unindexed gain		106,770
Indexation allowance		
Cost of lease		
$0.396 \times \dfrac{55,000}{95,000} \times £93,230$	21,374	
Enhancement costs		
$0.171 \times \dfrac{40,000}{95,000} \times £93,230$	6,713	28,087
Chargeable gain		£78,683

Note
(*a*)   The head-lease becomes a wasting asset on the expiry of the sub-lease.

(B) Grant of long lease [*CGTA 1979, 3 Sch 1*]

In 1975, K acquired a long lease by assignment for £22,000. At the time he acquired it, the lease had an unexpired term of 82 years. On 10 April 1990, he granted a 55-year sub-lease for a premium of £100,000 and a peppercorn rent. The value of the reversion plus the capitalised value of the rents is £10,000. The value of the lease at 31 March 1982 was estimated at £55,000.

	£	£
Disposal consideration	100,000	100,000
Cost £22,000 × $\dfrac{100,000}{100,000 + 10,000}$	20,000	
Market value 31.3.82		
£55,000 × $\dfrac{100,000}{100,000 + 10,000}$		50,000
Unindexed gain	80,000	50,000
Indexation allowance £50,000 × 0.575	28,750	28,750
Gain after indexation	£51,250	£21,250
Chargeable gain		£21,250

(C) Grant of short lease [*CGTA 1979, 3 Sch 2, 5; ICTA 1988, s 34*]

L is the owner of a freehold factory which he leases for a term of 25 years commencing in December 1990. The cost of the factory was £100,000 in April 1985. The lease is granted for a premium of £30,000 and an annual rent. The reversion to the lease plus the capitalised value of the rents amount to £120,000. The indexation factor for April 1985 to December 1990 is assumed to be 0.404.

Amount chargeable to income tax

	£
Amount of premium	30,000
Deduct excluded $\dfrac{25-1}{50}$ × £30,000	14,400
Amount chargeable to income tax	£15,600

	£	£
Chargeable gain		
Premium received	30,000	
Deduct charged to income tax	15,600	
		14,400
Allowable cost $\dfrac{14,400}{30,000 + 120,000} \times £100,000$		9,600
Unindexed gain		4,800
Indexation allowance £9,600 × 0.404		3,878
Chargeable gain		£922

Note

(*a*)   The amount chargeable to income tax is not deducted from the amount of premium appearing in the denominator of the apportionment fraction.

(D) Disposal by assignment of short lease: without enhancement expenditure [*CGTA 1979, 3 Sch 1,2*]

X buys a lease for £200,000 on 1 October 1986. The lease commenced on 1 June 1977 for a term of 60 years. X assigns the lease for £300,000 at the end of March 1991. The indexation factor for October 1986 to March 1991 is assumed to be 0.386.

Term of lease unexpired at date of acquisition	50 years 8 months
Relevant percentage	100%
Term of lease unexpired at date of assignment	46 years 2 months
Relevant percentage $98.490 + \frac{2}{12} \times (98.902 - 98.490)$	98.559%

	£	£
Disposal consideration		300,000
Allowable cost	200,000	
Deduct Wasted $\dfrac{100 - 98.559}{100} \times £200,000$	2,882	
		197,118
Unindexed gain		102,882
Indexation allowance £197,118 × 0.386		76,087
Chargeable gain		£26,795

(E) Disposal by assignment of short lease held at 31 March 1982 [*CGTA 1979, 3 Sch 1,2; FA 1988, s 96*].

A buys a lease for £100,000 on 1 March 1981. The lease commenced on 31 March 1971 for a term of 60 years. Its value at 31 March 1982 was estimated at £104,000. On 31 March 1991, A assigns the lease for £240,000. The indexation factor for the period March 1982 to March 1991 is assumed to be 0.719.

(i) The computation without re-basing to 1982 is as follows

Term of lease unexpired at date of acquisition (1.3.81)

	50 years 1 month	
Relevant percentage	100%	
Term of lease unexpired at date of assignment	40 years 0 months	
Relevant percentage	95.457%	

	£	£
Disposal consideration		240,000
Cost	100,000	
Deduct Wasted $\dfrac{100 - 95.457}{100} \times £100,000$	4,543	95,457
Unindexed gain		144,543
Indexation allowance (see (ii) below)		71,625
Gain after indexation		£72,918

(ii) The computation with re-basing to 1982 is as follows

Term of lease unexpired at deemed date of acquisition (31.3.82)

	49 years
Relevant percentage	99.657%
Term of lease unexpired at date of assignment	40 years
Relevant percentage	95.457%

	£	£
Disposal consideration		240,000
Market value 31.3.82	104,000	
Deduct Wasted $\dfrac{99.657 - 95.457}{99.657} \times £104,000$	4,383	99,617
Unindexed gain		140,383
Indexation allowance £99,617 × 0.719		71,625
Gain after indexation		£68,758
Chargeable gain		£68,758

Notes

(*a*)   A is deemed, under *FA 1988, s 96*, to have disposed of and immediately re-acquired the lease on 31 March 1982 at its market value at that date.

(*b*)   Both calculations produce a gain with the re-basing calculation producing the smaller gain. Therefore, re-basing applies. [*FA 1988, s 96(2)(3)(a)*].

(*c*)   Indexation is based, in both calculations, on the assumption that the asset was sold and re-acquired at market value on 31 March 1982 since this gives a greater allowance than if based on original cost as reduced by the wasting asset provisions. [*FA 1985, s 68(4)(5); FA 1988, 8 Sch 11*].

(F) Disposal by assignment of short lease: with enhancement expenditure [*CGTA 1979, 3 Sch 1,2*]

D Ltd acquires the lease of office premises for £100,000 on 1 July 1983. On 1 January 1985, the company contracts for complete refurbishment of the premises at a total cost of £180,000, of which £120,000 can be regarded as capital enhancement expenditure. The work is done at the beginning of January 1985, and the money is payable in equal tranches in March 1985 and May 1985. The lease is for a term of 50 years commencing 1 April 1976. On 1 January 1991, the lease is assigned to a new lessee for £450,000.

Indexation factors (assumed)	July 1983 to January 1991	0.573
	March 1985 to January 1991	0.446
	May 1985 to January 1991	0.410

Term of lease unexpired at date of acquisition   42 years 9 months
Relevant percentage $96.593 + \frac{9}{12} \times (97.107 - 96.593)$ 96.978%

Term of lease unexpired at date of expenditure
incurred   41 years 3 months
Relevant percentage $96.041 + \frac{3}{12} \times (96.593 - 96.041)$ 96.179%

Term of lease unexpired at date of assignment   35 years 3 months
Relevant percentage $91.981 + \frac{3}{12} \times (92.761 - 91.981)$ 92.176%

	£	£	£
Disposal consideration			450,000
Cost of acquisition	100,000		
Deduct Wasted			
$\dfrac{96.978 - 92.176}{96.978} \times 100,000$	4,952	95,048	
Enhancement expenditure	120,000		
Deduct Wasted			
$\dfrac{96.179 - 92.176}{96.179} \times 120,000$	4,994	115,006	210,054
Unindexed gain			239,946
Indexation allowance			
Cost of lease £95,048 × 0.573		˙ 54,463	
Enhancement costs			
March 1985 £57,503 × 0.446		25,646	
May 1985 £57,503 × 0.410		23,576	
			103,685
Chargeable gain			£136,261

Note

(a) The wasting provisions apply to enhancement expenditure by reference to the time when it is first reflected in the nature of the lease; the indexation provisions by reference to the date it became due and payable. [*FA 1982, s 87(5)(b)*].

(G) Sub-lease granted out of short lease: lease premium greater than potential sub-lease premium [*CGTA 1979, 3 Sch 4, 5*]

On 1 November 1988, S purchased a lease of shop premises then having 50 years to run for a premium of £100,000 and an annual rental of £40,000. After occupying the premises for the purposes of his own business, S granted a sub-lease to N Ltd. The sub-lease was for a term of 21 years commencing on 1 August 1990, for a premium of £50,000 and an annual rental of £30,000. It is agreed that, had the rent under the sub-lease been £40,000, the premium obtainable would have been £20,000. The indexation factor for November 1988 to August 1990 is assumed to be 0.171.

Term of lease at date granted	50 years
Relevant percentage	100%
Term of lease at date sub-lease granted	48 years 3 months
Relevant percentage $99.289 + \frac{3}{12} \times (99.657 - 99.289)$	99.381%
Term of lease at date sub-lease expires	27 years 3 months
Relevant percentage $83.816 + \frac{3}{12} \times (85.053 - 83.816)$	84.125%

Premium chargeable on S under Schedule A	£
Amount of premium	50,000
$Deduct \dfrac{21 - 1}{50} \times £50,000$	20,000
	———
Amount chargeable under Schedule A	£30,000

Chargeable gain	
Disposal consideration	50,000
Allowable expenditure	
$£100,000 \times \dfrac{99.381 - 84.125}{100}$	15,256
	———
Unindexed gain	34,744
Indexation allowance $£15,256 \times 0.171$	2,609
	———
Chargeable gain	32,135
Deduct Amount chargeable under Schedule A	30,000
	———
Net chargeable gain	£2,135

(H) Sub-lease granted out of short lease: lease premium less than potential sub-lease premium [*CGTA 1979, 3 Sch 4, 5*]

C bought a lease of a house on 1 May 1987, when the unexpired term was 52 years. The cost of the lease was £20,000, and the ground rent payable is £500 p.a. C then let the house on a monthly tenancy until 30 November 1990 when he granted a 10-year lease for a premium of £5,000 and an annual rent of £8,000. Had the rent under the sub-lease been £500 a year, the premium obtainable would have been £40,000. C does not at any time occupy the house as a private residence. The indexation factor for May 1987 to November 1990 is assumed to be 0.295.

Term of lease at date of acquisition	52 years
Relevant percentage	100%
Term of lease when sub-lease granted	48 years 5 months
Relevant percentage $99.289 + \frac{5}{12} \times (99.657 - 99.289)$	99.442%
Term of lease when sub-lease expires	38 years 5 months
Relevant percentage $94.189 + \frac{5}{12} \times (94.842 - 94.189)$	94.461%

	£
Amount chargeable under Schedule A	
Amount of premium	5,000
Deduct exclusion $\dfrac{10 - 1}{50} \times 5,000$	900
Chargeable under Schedule A	£4,100
Disposal consideration	5,000
Deduct allowable expenditure	
$20,000 \times \dfrac{99.442 - 94.461}{100} \times \dfrac{5,000}{40,000}$	125
Unindexed gain	4,875
Indexation allowance £125 × 0.295	37
Chargeable gain	4,838
Deduct Amount chargeable under Schedule A	4,100
Net chargeable gain	£738

Note

(*a*)   If the amount chargeable under Schedule A exceeded the chargeable gain, the net gain would be nil. The deduction cannot create or increase a loss. [*CGTA 1979, 3 Sch 5(2)*].

213 Losses

213.1 GENERAL

On 30 April 1990 Q sells for £40,000 a part of the land which he owns. The market value of the remaining estate is £200,000. Q bought the land for £300,000 in March 1985.

	£
Disposal consideration	40,000
Allowable cost $\dfrac{40,000}{40,000 + 200,000} \times £300,000$	50,000
Unindexed loss	10,000
Indexation allowance £50,000 × 0.348	17,400
Allowable loss	£27,400

213.2 INTERACTION WITH ANNUAL EXEMPT AMOUNT [*CGTA 1979, s 5(4); FA 1980, s 77; FA 1982, s 80*]

U has the following chargeable gains and allowable losses

	Gains £	Losses £	Net £
1987/88	8,000	11,000	(3,000)
1988/89	800	2,100	(1,300)
1989/90	5,500	—	5,500
1990/91	14,000	2,000	12,000

1987/88

	£
Net chargeable gains	—
Losses carried forward	£3,000

1988/89

	£
Net chargeable gains	—
Allowable losses	£1,300
Losses carried forward (£3,000 + £1,300)	£4,300

1989/90

	£
Chargeable gains	5,500
Deduct losses brought forward (part)	500
Taxable amount (exempt)	£5,000
Losses carried forward (£4,300 − £500)	£3,800

1990/91

	£
Chargeable gains	12,000
Deduct losses brought forward	3,800
Taxable amount	8,200
Deduct exempt amount	5,000
Net chargeable gains	£3,200

213.3 **LOANS TO TRADERS — QUALIFYING CORPORATE BONDS** [*CGTA 1979, ss 136, 136A, 136B; FA 1990, s 84*]

V subscribed on 15 July 1985 for £5,000 unsecured loan stock in W plc, a UK trading company which used the funds raised by the issue for the purposes of its retail trade. The security was issued at £95 per £100 nominal and is a qualifying corporate bond as defined by *FA 1984, s 64*. In 1990, the company went into liquidation, and on 30 June 1990, V makes a claim under *CGTA 1979, s 136A* on the basis that the value of the security had become negligible. The Inspector agrees and V's allowable loss for 1990/91 is the lesser of

(*a*)	the principal outstanding	£5,000
and		
(*b*)	V's acquisition cost	£4,750
	Thus, V's allowable loss is	£4,750

On 1 May 1991, W plc makes a once and for all distribution of £15 per £100 of loan stock, V thus receiving £750.

V has a chargeable gain for 1991/92 of £750.

Notes

(*a*)   The provisions of *CGTA 1979, s 136* (relief in respect of loans to traders) were extended after 14 March 1989 by *FA 1990, s 84* to include debts on security where the security is a qualifying corporate bond. [*CGTA 1979, ss 136A, 136B*].

(*b*)   No indexation allowance is due.

(*c*)   The amount recovered, restricted to the amount of loss claimed, is taxed in the year of recovery.

(*d*)   In the above example, a loss is claimed on the basis that the value of the security has become negligible. [*Sec 136A(3)*]. There are two further conditions under which a loss can be claimed. [*Sec 136A(4)(5)*].

(*e*)   See 219 QUALIFYING CORPORATE BONDS below generally.

213.4 **LOSSES ON SHARES IN UNQUOTED TRADING COMPANIES** [*ICTA 1988, ss 574–576*]

P subscribed for 3,000 £1 ordinary shares in W Ltd, a new trading company, at par in June 1986. In September 1987, P acquired a further 2,000 shares at £1.60 from another shareholder. In December 1990, P sold 3,800 shares at 90p.

Indexation factors	June 1986 to September 1987	0.047
	June 1986 to December 1990 (assumed)	0.361
	September 1987 to December 1990 (assumed)	0.300

333

CGT 213.4 Losses

(i) Establish new holding pool

	Shares	Qualifying expenditure £	Indexed pool £
June 1986 subscription	3,000	3,000	3,000
Indexation to September 1987 £3,000 × 0.047			141
September 1987 acquisition	2,000	3,200	3,200
	5,000	6,200	6,341
Indexed rise: September 1987 to December 1990 £6,341 × 0.300			1,902
	5,000	6,200	8,243
December 1990 disposal	(3,800)	(4,712)	(6,265)
Pool carried forward	1,200	£1,488	£1,978

(ii) The overall capital loss is calculated as follows

	£
Disposal consideration 3,800 × £0.90	3,420
Allowable cost $\dfrac{3,800}{5,000} \times £6,200$	4,712
Unindexed loss	1,292
Indexation allowance $\dfrac{3,800}{5,000} \times £8,243 = £6,265$	
£6,265 − £4,712	1,553
Allowable loss	£2,845

(iii) The loss allowable against income is calculated as follows

Loss referable to 1,800 subscription shares $\dfrac{1,800}{3,800} \times £2,845$	£1,348

	£
Loss restricted to actual loss on the subscription shares	
Disposal consideration 1,800 × £0.90	1,620
Allowable cost 1,800 × £1.00	1,800
Unindexed loss	180
Indexation allowance £1,800 × 0.361	650
Allowable loss for income tax purposes	£830

(iv) The loss not relieved against income remains a capital loss

£2,845 − £830 =	£2,015

Notes

(a) For capital gains tax purposes, the shares merge in a new holding pool, but for the purposes of relief under *ICTA 1988, ss 574–576*, shares disposed of are identified with shares acquired later rather than with shares acquired earlier.

(b) For further examples on this topic, see 10.5 LOSSES in the income tax section and 115.5 LOSSES in the corporation tax section.

214 Married Persons

214.1 ANNUAL EXEMPTION [*FA 1988, s 104*]

Marcus and Joanna are a married couple. In 1990/91 they have gains of £10,000 and £2,000 respectively, and in 1991/92 their gains are £4,000 and £15,000 respectively. The capital gains tax position for the two years is as follows (it is assumed that the annual exemption will remain at £5,000 for 1991/92).

1990/91	Marcus	Joanna
	£	£
Gains	10,000	2,000
Annual exemption (Maximum £5,000 each)	5,000	2,000
Taxable gains	£5,000	Nil

1991/92	Marcus	Joanna
	£	£
Gains	4,000	15,000
Annual exemption (Maximum £5,000 each)	4,000	5,000
Taxable gains	Nil	£10,000

Notes

(*a*) Independent taxation of husband and wife commenced on 6 April 1990. For examples illustrating the old rules for married couples see Tolley's Tax Computations 1989/90.

(*b*) Unused balances of a married person's annual exemption may not be transferred to the spouse, and may not be carried forward by that person to the following year.

214.2 LOSSES [*CGTA 1979, s 5(4); FA 1988, s 104*]

Nigel and Barbara have gains and losses for the years 1990/91 to 1992/93 as follows (it is assumed that the annual exemption remains at £5,000 throughout).

1990/91	Nigel	Barbara
	£	£
Gains/(losses)	10,000	(3,000)
Annual exemption	5,000	—
Taxable gains	£5,000	Nil
Losses carried forward		£3,000

1991/92

	Nigel £	Barbara £
Gains/(losses)	(11,000)	12,000
Losses brought forward		3,000
	(11,000)	9,000
Annual exemption	—	5,000
Taxable gains	Nil	£4,000
Losses carried forward	£11,000	

1992/93

	Nigel £	Barbara £
Gains	6,000	3,000
Losses brought forward	1,000	—
	5,000	3,000
Annual exemption	5,000	3,000
Taxable gains	Nil	Nil
Losses carried forward	£10,000	

Note

(a) For 1990/91 and subsequent years, the losses of a married person cannot be offset against the gains of the spouse.

214.3 INTER-SPOUSE TRANSFERS AND RATES OF TAX [*CGTA 1979, s 44; FA 1988, s 98*]

(A) No inter-spouse transfer

Paul and Heidi are a married couple with total income of £21,000 and £25,000 respectively for 1990/91. On 4 April 1991, Heidi sells a painting which she had acquired in June 1989 at a cost of £5,000. Net sale proceeds amount to £17,000 and the indexation factor for the period June 1989 to April 1991 is assumed to be 0.192. Neither spouse disposed of any other chargeable assets during 1990/91.

Chargeable gain — Heidi

	£
Net proceeds	17,000
Cost	5,000
Unindexed gain	12,000
Indexation allowance £5,000 × 0.192	960
Chargeable gain	£11,040
Annual exemption	5,000
Taxable gain	£6,040

	£
Total income	25,000
Personal allowance	3,005
Taxable income	£21,995

Basic rate band = £20,700, so gain of £6,040 is all taxed at 40%.

Tax payable £6,040 × 40%	£2,416.00

(B) Inter-spouse transfer
The facts are as in (A) above except that in January 1991, Heidi gives the painting to Paul who then makes the sale on 4 April 1991.
Indexation factors (assumed)

June 1989 to January 1991 0.163
January 1991 to April 1991 0.025

Chargeable gain — Heidi

	£
Deemed consideration (January 1991)	5,815
Cost	5,000
Unindexed gain	815
Indexation allowance £5,000 × 0.163	815
Chargeable gain	Nil

Chargeable gain — Paul

	£
Net proceeds (4.4.91)	17,000
Cost (January 1991)	5,815
Unindexed gain	11,185
Indexation allowance £5,815 × 0.025	145
Chargeable gain	11,040
Annual exemption	5,000
Taxable gain	£6,040

	£
Total income	21,000
Personal allowance	(3,005)
Married couple's allowance	(1,720)
Taxable income	£16,275

£4,425 (£20,700 − £16,275) of the basic rate band is unused, so gain of £6,040 is taxed as follows.

£4,425 at 25%	1,106.25
£1,615 at 40%	646.00
Tax payable	£1,752.25
Tax saving compared with (A) above	£663.75

Notes

(*a*) The inter-spouse transfer is deemed to be for such consideration as to ensure that no gain or loss accrues. [*CGTA 1979, s 44*]. Effectively, the consideration is equal to cost plus indexation to date. See 209.1(D)(E) INDEXATION above for further examples.

(*b*) The fact that *CGTA 1979, s 44* remains in force following the introduction of independent taxation enables savings to be made by ensuring that disposals are made by a spouse with an unused annual exemption and/or lower tax rates.

(*c*) An inter-spouse transfer followed by a sale could be attacked by the Revenue as an anti-avoidance device. To minimise the risk, there should be a clear time interval between the two transactions and no arrangements made to effect the ultimate sale until after the transfer. The gift should be outright with no strings attached and with no 'arrangement' for eventual proceeds to be passed to the transferor.

215 Mineral Royalties

215.1 **GENERAL** [*FA 1970, 6 Sch 3–9; ICTA 1988, s 122(1)(b)(3)*]

L Ltd, an investment company, is the holder of a lease of land acquired in 1977 for £66,000, when the lease had an unexpired term of 65 years. In January 1985, L Ltd grants a 10-year licence to a mining company to search for and exploit minerals beneath the land. The licence is granted for £60,000 plus a mineral royalty calculated on the basis of the value of any minerals won by the licensee. The market value of the retained land (exclusive of the mineral rights) is then £10,000. L Ltd receives mineral royalties as follows

	£
Year ended 31 December 1985	10,000
31 December 1986	12,000
31 December 1987	19,000
31 December 1988	29,000
31 December 1989	38,000
31 December 1990	17,000

On 1 January 1991, L Ltd relinquishes its rights under the lease and receives no consideration from the lessor. The lease was valued at £70,000 at 31 March 1982. No election is made under *FA 1988, s 96(5)* (election for 31 March 1982 value). The indexation factor from March 1982 to January 1991 is assumed to be 0.690.

(i) Chargeable gains 1985

		£
(*a*)	Disposal proceeds	60,000
	Allowable cost $\dfrac{60,000}{60,000 + 10,000} \times £66,000$	56,571
	Chargeable gain before indexation	£3,429
(*b*)	$\frac{1}{2} \times £10,000$	£5,000

(ii) Chargeable gains 1986 to 1990

		£
1986	$\frac{1}{2} \times £12,000$	6,000
1987	$\frac{1}{2} \times £19,000$	9,500
1988	$\frac{1}{2} \times £29,000$	14,500
1989	$\frac{1}{2} \times £38,000$	19,000
1990	$\frac{1}{2} \times £17,000$	8,500

(iii) Loss 1991

		£
Proceeds of disposal of lease		Nil
Allowable cost £66,000 − £56,571	note (*a*)	9,429
Unindexed loss		9,429
Indexation allowance £10,000 × 0.690	note (*a*)	6,900
Allowable loss		£16,329

(iv) The loss may be set off against the chargeable gains arising on the mineral royalties as follows

	£
1990 (whole)	8,500
1989 (part)	7,829
	£16,329

Notes

(a) Re-basing to 1982 does not apply, by virtue of *FA 1988, s 96(3)(b)*, as this would increase the loss. If re-basing had applied, the allowable cost would be £10,000, i.e.

$$£70,000 \times \frac{10,000}{60,000 + 10,000} = £10,000$$

For indexation purposes, however, the allowable expenditure is £10,000 as this gives a greater allowance than would be the case if based on cost of £9,429. [*FA 1985, s 68(4)(5); FA 1988, 8 Sch 11*].

(b) Under *ICTA 1988, s 122*, one half of mineral royalties is taxed as income and one half as a chargeable gain. The gain is deemed to accrue in the year of assessment or company accounting period for which the royalties are receivable and is not capable of being reduced by any expenditure or by indexation.

216 Overseas Matters

216.1 **A UK BENEFICIARY OF AN OVERSEAS TRUST** [*FA 1981, s 80; ICTA 1988, s 740(6)*]

(A)

M, resident and domiciled in the UK, is the sole beneficiary of a discretionary settlement administered in the Cayman Islands. The trustees are all individuals resident in the Cayman Islands. The settlement was created in 1973 by M's father, who is resident and domiciled in the UK. For 1986/87 to 1990/91 the trustees have no income but have chargeable gains and allowable losses as follows

	Chargeable gains £	Allowable losses £
1986/87	50,000	60,000
1987/88	80,000	30,000
1988/89	95,000	—
1989/90	—	35,000
1990/91	—	7,000

In 1986/87, M receives a capital payment of £20,000, in 1987/88 he receives £50,000, in 1989/90 £35,000, and in 1990/91 £20,000.

1986/87

		£
Trust gains (£50,000 – £60,000)		—
Capital payment		£20,000
Balance of capital payment carried forward		£20,000
Trust losses carried forward		£10,000

1987/88

		£
Trust gains (£80,000 – £30,000 – £10,000)		£40,000
Capital payment	50,000	
Brought forward	20,000	£70,000
Chargeable gains assessable on M		£40,000
Capital payment carried forward (£70,000 – £40,000)		£30,000

1988/89

	£
Trust gains	£95,000
Capital payment brought forward	£30,000
Chargeable gains assessable on M	£30,000
Trust gains carried forward (£95,000 – £30,000)	£65,000

1989/90

Trust gains	—
Trust gains brought forward	£65,000
Capital payment	£35,000
Chargeable gains assessable on M	£35,000
Trust gains carried forward (£65,000 − £35,000)	£30,000
Trust losses carried forward	£35,000

1990/91

Trust gains	—
Trust gains brought forward	£30,000
Capital payment	£20,000
Chargeable gains assessable on M	£20,000
Trust gains carried forward (£30,000 − £20,000)	£10,000
Trust losses carried forward (£35,000 + £7,000)	£42,000

(B)

T and M are the only beneficiaries under a Jersey settlement set up by their grandfather, who was then domiciled and resident in the UK. None of the trustees is resident in the UK.

T is resident in the UK but M is neither resident nor ordinarily resident in the UK. Both beneficiaries have a UK domicile. In 1989/90, the trustees sell shares realising a chargeable gain of £102,000. No disposals are made in 1990/91. The trustees receive no income.

The trustees advance £60,000 to M in 1989/90. In 1990/91 they advance £60,000 to T and £10,000 to M.

1989/90	£
Trust gains	102,000
Capital payment	60,000
Trust gains carried forward	£42,000

M has chargeable gains of £60,000 but is not subject to CGT.

1990/91	
Trust gains (brought forward)	42,000
Capital payments (£60,000 + £10,000)	70,000
Balance of capital payments carried forward	£28,000

The chargeable gains are apportioned as follows

		£
T	$\dfrac{60,000}{70,000} \times £42,000$	36,000
M	$\dfrac{10,000}{70,000} \times £42,000$ (not assessable)	6,000
		£42,000

The capital payments carried forward are apportioned as follows

T	£60,000 − £36,000	24,000
M	£10,000 − £6,000	4,000
		£28,000

(C)

A Liechtenstein foundation was created in 1952 by a UK resident domiciled in Scotland. None of the trustees is resident in the UK and the trust administration is carried on in Switzerland. The foundation has the following income and chargeable gains.

	Income £	Chargeable gains £
1988/89	15,000	5,000
1989/90	24,000	12,000
1990/91	30,000	3,000

L, who is resident and domiciled in the UK, receives payments of £28,000 in 1988/89 and £50,000 in 1990/91.

	Total £	Income £	Chargeable gains £
1988/89			
Total income/gains	20,000	15,000	5,000
Payment	28,000	15,000	5,000
Balance	Nil	Nil	Nil
Balance of payment	£8,000		
1989/90			
Total income/gains	36,000	24,000	12,000
Payment (balance b/f)	8,000	8,000	—
Balance	£28,000	£16,000	£12,000
1990/91			
Total income/gains	33,000	30,000	3,000
Brought forward	28,000	16,000	12,000
	61,000	46,000	15,000
Payment	50,000	46,000	4,000
Balance	£11,000	—	£11,000

Summary of assessments	Schedule D, Case VI £	Capital gains tax £
1988/89	15,000	5,000
1989/90	8,000	—
1990/91	46,000	4,000

16.2 **COMPANY MIGRATION** [*FA 1988, ss 105, 107*]

Z Ltd is a company incorporated in Ruritania, but regarded as resident in the UK by virtue of its being managed and controlled in the UK. It is the 75% subsidiary of Y plc, a UK resident company. On 1 October 1990, the management and control of Z Ltd is transferred to Ruritania and it thus ceases to be UK resident, although it continues to trade in the UK, on a much reduced basis, via a UK branch.

Details of the company's chargeable assets immediately before 1 October 1990 were as follows.

	Market value	Capital gain after indexation if all assets sold
	£	£
Factory in UK	480,000	230,000
Warehouse in UK	300,000	180,000
Factory in Ruritania	350,000	200,000
Warehouse in Ruritania	190,000	100,000
UK quoted investments	110,000	80,000
Foreign trade investments	100,000	Loss (60,000)

The UK warehouse continues to be used in the UK trade. The UK factory does not and is later sold. On 1 June 1991, the Ruritanian warehouse is sold for the equivalent of £210,000. On 1 October 1992, Y plc sells its shareholding in Z Ltd.

Prior to becoming non-UK resident, Z Ltd had unrelieved capital losses brought forward of £40,000.

The capital gains tax consequences assuming no election under *FA 1988, s 107* are as follows

Chargeable gain accruing to Z Ltd on 1.10.90

	£
Factory (UK)	230,000
Factory (Ruritania)	200,000
Warehouse (Ruritania)	100,000
UK quoted investments	80,000
Foreign trade investments	(60,000)
	550,000
Losses brought forward	40,000
Net gain chargeable to corporation tax	£510,000

The later sale of the UK factory does not attract CGT as the company is non-resident and the factory has not, since the deemed reacquisition immediately before 1.10.90, been used in a trade carried on in the UK through a branch or agency. Similarly, the sale of the overseas warehouse, and of any other overseas assets, is outside the scope of CGT. Any subsequent disposal of the UK warehouse *will* be within the charge to CGT, having been omitted from the deemed disposal on 1 October 1990, due to its being used in a trade carried on in the UK through a branch. On disposal, the gain will be computed by reference to original cost, or 31.3.82 value if appropriate, rather than to market value immediately before 1.10.90 — see also note (*e*).

Y plc will realise a capital gain (or loss) on the sale of its shareholding in Z Ltd on 1.10.92. There are no CGT consequences for Y plc on Z Ltd's becoming non-UK resident.

The capital gains tax consequences if an election is made under *FA 1988, s 107* are as follows

Chargeable gain accruing to Z Ltd on 1.10.90

	£
Factory (UK)	230,000
UK quoted investments	80,000
	310,000
Losses brought forward	40,000
Net gain liable to corporation tax	£270,000

Postponed gain on foreign assets

	£
Factory (Ruritania)	200,000
Warehouse (Ruritania)	100,000
Foreign trade investments	(60,000)
	£240,000

On 1.6.91, a proportion of the postponed gain becomes chargeable as a result of the sale, within six years of Z Ltd's becoming non-resident, of one of the assets in respect of which the postponed gain accrued. The gain chargeable to corporation tax as at 1.6.91 on Y plc is

$$\frac{100,000 \quad \text{(postponed gain on warehouse)}}{300,000 \quad \text{(aggregate of postponed gains)}} \times £240,000 = £80,000$$

On 1 October 1992, in addition to any gain or loss arising on the sale of the shares, Y plc will be chargeable to corporation tax on the remainder of the postponed gain, i.e. on £160,000 (£240,000 − £80,000) by virtue of Z Ltd having ceased to be its 75% subsidiary as a result of the sale of shares.

The position as regards the UK warehouse is the same as if no election had been made.

Notes

(a) The provisions of *FA 1988, s 105* apply where a company ceases to be resident in the UK. By virtue of *FA 1988, s 66, 7 Sch*, all companies incorporated in the UK are, subject to transitional provisions, regarded after 14 March 1988 as UK resident. As such a company cannot therefore cease to be resident, *FA 1988, s 105* can apply only to companies incorporated abroad which are UK resident (subject again to transitional provisions). See also Revenue Statement of Practice SP 1/90 as regards company residence generally.

(b) If, with an election, Z Ltd's allowable losses had exceeded its chargeable gains arising on 1.10.90, the excess could have been allowed against postponed gains at the time when they become chargeable on Y plc, subject to the two companies making a joint election to that effect under *FA 1988, s 107(5)*.

(c) A charge on the deemed disposal of certain chargeable assets can also arise where a company continues to be UK resident, but ceases, by virtue of a double taxation treaty, to be within the charge to UK tax on gains arising on disposal of those assets. [*FA 1988, s 106*]. Where such a company is the 75% subsidiary of a UK resident company, the provisions of *section 107* apply as they apply to gains under *section 105*, thus enabling gains on foreign assets to be postponed.

(d)   *FA 1988, ss 130–132* contain management provisions designed to secure payment of all outstanding tax liabilities on a company becoming non-UK resident. See also Revenue Statement of Practice SP 2/90.

(e)   If the UK warehouse ceases to be a chargeable asset by virtue of Z Ltd's ceasing to carry on a trade in the UK through a branch or agency, there will be a deemed disposal at market value at that time, under *FA 1989, s 127.* See 216.3 below.

16.3 NON-RESIDENTS CARRYING ON TRADE, ETC. THROUGH UK BRANCH OR AGENCY [*CGTA 1979, s 12; FA 1989, ss 126–128*]

X, who is non-resident in the UK, practises abroad as a tax consultant and also practises in the UK through a London branch. The assets of the UK branch include premises bought in 1983 for £50,000 and a computer also acquired in 1983 for £20,000 on which a 100% first-year capital allowance was claimed. On 31 January 1991, the computer ceases to be used in the UK branch and is immediately shipped abroad, and on 28 February 1991, X closes down the UK branch. He sells the premises in June 1991 for £98,000.

Relevant market values of the assets are as follows

		£
Computer,	at 14 March 1989	10,000
	at 31 January 1991	9,000
Premises,	at 14 March 1989	75,000
	at 28 February 1991	95,000
Indexation factors March 1989 to January 1991 (assumed)		0.195
	March 1989 to February 1991 (assumed)	0.205

The UK capital gains tax consequences are as follows

		£	£
Computer			
Market value 31.1.91			9,000
Deduct market value 14.3.89		10,000	
Less capital allowances claimed	note (f)	1,000	9,000
			—
Indexation allowance £9,000 × 0.195			1,755
Allowable loss			£1,755

	£
Premises	
Market value 28.2.91	95,000
Deduct market value 14.3.89	75,000
Unindexed gain	20,000
Indexation allowance £75,000 × 0.205	15,375
Chargeable gain	£4,625

Net chargeable gains 1990/91 (£4,625 − £1,755) note (e)	£2,870

Notes

(*a*)   X is within the charge to UK capital gains tax for disposals after 13 March 1989 by virtue of his carrying on a profession in the UK through a branch or agency. Previously, the charge applied only to non-residents carrying on *trade* in this manner. X is deemed to have disposed of (with no capital gains tax consequences) and reacquired immediately before 14 March 1989 all chargeable assets used in the UK branch at market value, so that any subsequent CGT charge will be by reference only to post-13 March 1989 gains. [*CGTA 1979, s 12; FA 1989, s 126*].

(*b*)   There is a deemed disposal, at market value, of the computer on 31 January 1991 as a result of its ceasing to be a chargeable asset by virtue of its becoming situated outside the UK. [*FA 1989, s 127(1)*].

(*c*)   There is a deemed disposal, at market value, of the premises on 28 February 1991 as a result of the asset ceasing to be a chargeable asset by virtue of X's ceasing to carry on a trade, profession or vocation in the UK through a branch or agency. [*FA 1989, s 127(3)*]. See also note (*g*) below.

(*d*)   There are no UK CGT consequences on the actual disposal of the premises in June 1991.

(*e*)   X's net gains will be covered by the £5,000 annual exemption, assuming he has no other UK gains, including any arising from deemed disposals under the above rules, for 1990/91.

(*f*)   Where a chargeable asset has qualified for capital allowances and a loss accrues on its disposal, the allowable expenditure is restricted, under *CGTA 1979, s 34*, by the net allowances given, which in this example amount to £11,000 (first-year allowance £20,000 less balancing charge £9,000 arising on the asset's ceasing to be used in the trade). The view taken in this example is that £10,000 of those allowances relates to expenditure which is not allowable for CGT, being the difference between cost of £20,000 and 14 March 1989 value of £10,000, and that only the remaining £1,000 of allowances needs to be deducted from allowable expenditure; the purpose of *CGTA 1979, s 34* is to restrict losses and not to turn losses into gains.

(*g*)   *FA 1989, s 127(3)* (see note (*c*) above) does not apply, on a claim under *ICTA 1970, s 273A*, in relation to an asset where a non-UK resident company transfers its trade (carried on through a UK branch or agency) to a UK resident group company. The asset is deemed to be transferred at no gain/no loss. [*ICTA 1970, s 273A; FA 1990, s 70*].

216.4 **TRANSFER OF ASSETS TO NON-RESIDENT COMPANY** [*ICTA 1970, s 268A; FA 1977, s 42*]

Q Ltd, a UK resident company, carries on business in a foreign country through a branch there. In July 1986, it is decreed that all enterprises in that country be carried on by locally resident companies. Q Ltd forms a wholly-owned subsidiary R and transfers all the assets of the branch to R wholly in consideration for the issue of shares. The assets transferred, all of which were held at 31 March 1982, include the following

	Value	Chargeable gains
	£	£
Goodwill	100,000	95,000
Freehold land	200,000	120,000
Plant (items worth more than £3,000)	50,000	20,000
Other assets	150,000	—
	£500,000	£235,000

In March 1987, there is a compulsory acquisition of 50% of the share capital of R for £300,000. The value of the whole shareholding is then £750,000.

In June 1990, R is forced to sell its freehold land to the government.

Q Ltd's capital gains position is as follows

1986

The gain of £235,000 is deferred. The allowable cost of the shares in R is £500,000.

1987

	£
Consideration on disposal	300,000
Add	
Proportion of deferred gain £235,000 × $\dfrac{300,000}{750,000}$	94,000
	394,000
Deduct	
Cost of shares sold	250,000
Chargeable gain	£144,000

1990

	£	
Proportion of deferred gain chargeable		
Gain arising $\dfrac{120,000}{235,000}$ × £235,000	120,000	
Less one-half exempt (*FA 1988, 9 Sch 3*)	60,000	£60,000
Balance of gain still held over (£235,000 − £94,000 − £120,000)		£21,000

349

217 Partnerships

217.1 ASSETS [*CGTA 1979, s 60*]

G, H and I trade in partnership. They share capital in the ratio 5:4:3. Land occupied by the firm is sold on 15 April 1990 for £78,000, having been acquired for £30,000 in 1973. The agreed market value of the land at 31 March 1982 is £60,000. G has elected under *FA 1988, s 96(5)* for his share of partnership assets held on 31 March 1982 to be treated as disposed of and re-acquired at their market value on that date.

The position without re-basing to 1982 is as follows

	G ($\frac{5}{12}$) £	H ($\frac{4}{12}$) £	I ($\frac{3}{12}$) £
Disposal consideration	32,500	26,000	19,500
Cost	12,500	10,000	7,500
Unindexed gain	20,000	16,000	12,000
Indexation allowance £60,000 × 0.575	14,375	11,500	8,625
Gain after indexation	£5,625	£4,500	£3,375

The position with re-basing to 1982 is as follows

	G ($\frac{5}{12}$) £	H ($\frac{4}{12}$) £	I ($\frac{3}{12}$) £
Disposal consideration	32,500	26,000	19,500
Market value 31.3.82	25,000	20,000	15,000
Gain after indexation	7,500	6,000	4,500
Indexation allowance (as above)	14,375	11,500	8,625
Loss after indexation	£6,875	£5,500	£4,125
Chargeable gain/(Allowable loss)	£(6,875)	Nil	Nil

Note

(a) It is understood that the Inland Revenue take the view that an individual partner's election under *FA 1988, s 96(5)* in respect of his personal assets does not extend to his share of partnership assets and *vice versa*, this being by virtue of *section 96(7)*. As regards the disposal illustrated in the above example, it would clearly be to each partner's advantage to make the election in respect of his share of partnership assets, but there is no statutory requirement for each partner to make the election.

217.2 CHANGES IN SHARING RATIOS

J and K have traded in partnership for several years, sharing capital and income equally. The acquisition costs and 31 March 1982 values of the chargeable assets of the firm are as follows

	Cost £	31.3.82 value £
Premises	60,000	150,000
Goodwill	10,000	50,000

The assets have not been revalued in the firm's balance sheet. On 1 June 1990, they admit L to the partnership, and the sharing ratio is J 35%, K 45% and L 20%.

J and K are regarded as disposing of part of their interest in the firm's assets to L as follows

	£	£
J		
Premises		
Deemed consideration		
£60,000 × (50% − 35%)	9,000	
Add indexation allowance (see below)	13,410	
Total deemed consideration	22,410	
Allowable cost	9,000	
Unindexed gain	13,410	
Indexation allowance (50% − 35%) × £150,000 × 0.596	13,410	—
Goodwill		
Deemed consideration		
£10,000 × (50% − 35%)	1,500	
Add indexation allowance (see below)	4,470	
Total deemed consideration	5,970	
Allowable cost	1,500	
Unindexed gain	4,470	
Indexation allowance (50% − 35%) × £50,000 × 0.596	4,470	—
Chargeable gain/allowable loss		**Nil**
K		
Premises		
Deemed consideration		
£60,000 × (50% − 45%)	3,000	
Add indexation allowance (see below)	4,470	
Total deemed consideration	7,470	
Allowable cost	3,000	
Unindexed gain	4,470	
Indexation allowance (50% − 45%) × £150,000 × 0.596	4,470	—

		£	£
Goodwill			
Deemed consideration			
£10,000 × (50% − 45%)		500	
Add indexation allowance (see below)		1,490	
Total deemed consideration		1,990	
Allowable cost		500	
Unindexed gain		1,490	
Indexation allowance (50% − 45%) × £50,000 × 0.596		1,490	—
Chargeable gain/allowable loss			Nil

The allowable costs (inclusive, in L's case, of indexation allowance to June 1990) of the three partners are now

		Freehold land	Goodwill
		£	£
J		21,000	3,500
K		27,000	4,500
L	note(*c*)	29,880	7,960

Notes

(*a*)   The treatment illustrated above is taken from Revenue Statement of Practice SP D12 (17.1.75), para. 4 as extended by SP 1/89. Each partner's disposal consideration is equal to his share of current balance sheet value of the asset concerned plus, for disposals after 5 April 1988, indexation allowance, and each disposal treated as producing no gain and no loss.

(*b*)   As the deemed disposals are no gain/no loss disposals, re-basing to 1982 is prevented from applying by *FA 1988, s 96(3)(d)*. The incoming partner, having acquired his share in the assets by means of a no gain/no loss disposal after 31 March 1982 is regarded as having held the asset at that date for the purposes of re-basing on a subsequent disposal (Revenue Statement of Practice SP 1/89).

(*c*)   L's allowable costs comprise 20% of original cost, plus indexation allowance to date based on 20% of 31 March 1982 value.

217.3 **ACCOUNTING ADJUSTMENTS**

A, B and C trade in partnership. They share income and capital profits equally. The firm's only chargeable asset is its premises which cost £51,000 in 1983. C, who is 59, decides to retire. The remaining partners agree to share profits equally. Before C retires (in May 1990), the premises are written up to market value in the accounts, estimated as £81,000. C does not receive any payment from the other partners on his retirement.

The capital gains tax consequences are
On retiring, C is regarded as having disposed of his interest in the firm's premises for a consideration equal to his share of the then book value.

		£
Disposal consideration	$\frac{1}{3}$ × £81,000	27,000
Acquisition cost	$\frac{1}{3}$ × £51,000	17,000
Unindexed gain		£10,000

A and B will each be treated as acquiring a $\frac{1}{6}$ ($\frac{1}{2}$ × $\frac{1}{3}$) share in the premises, at a cost equal to one half of C's disposal consideration. Their acquisition costs are then

		A	B
		£	£
Cost of original share	$\frac{1}{3}$ × £51,000	17,000	17,000
Cost of new share	$\frac{1}{2}$ × £27,000	13,500	13,500
Total		£30,500	£30,500

Notes

(a) If the asset had been held at 31.3.82, $\frac{1}{3}$ of its market value at that date would be substituted for $\frac{1}{3}$ of cost in C's capital gains tax computation, assuming that re-basing to 1982 applied. Indexation would be based on the higher of $\frac{1}{3}$ of cost and $\frac{1}{3}$ of 31.3.82 value.

(b) If C retires for reasons of ill-health, he may be entitled to retirement relief. See 220 RETIREMENT RELIEF.

217.4 CONSIDERATION OUTSIDE ACCOUNTS

D, E and F are partners in a firm of accountants who share all profits in the ratio 7:7:6. G is admitted as a partner in May 1990 and pays the other partners £10,000 for goodwill. The new partnership shares are D $\frac{3}{10}$, E $\frac{3}{10}$, F $\frac{1}{4}$ and G $\frac{3}{20}$. The book value of goodwill is £18,000, its cost on acquisition of the practice from the predecessor in 1983.

The partners are treated as having disposed of shares in goodwill as follows

	£	£
D		
$\frac{7}{20} - \frac{3}{10} = \frac{1}{20}$		
Disposal consideration		
Notional $\quad \frac{1}{20} \times £18,000$	900	
Actual $\quad \frac{7}{20} \times £10,000$	3,500	
		4,400
Allowable cost $\frac{1}{20} \times £18,000$		900
Unindexed gain		£3,500
E		
$\frac{7}{20} - \frac{3}{10} = \frac{1}{20}$		
Disposal consideration (as for D)		4,400
Allowable cost (as for D)		900
Unindexed gain		£3,500
F		
$\frac{6}{20} - \frac{1}{4} = \frac{1}{20}$		
Disposal consideration		
Notional $\quad \frac{1}{20} \times £18,000$	900	
Actual $\quad \frac{6}{20} \times £10,000$	3,000	
		3,900
Allowable cost		900
Unindexed gain		£3,000
G's allowable cost of his share of goodwill is therefore		
Actual consideration paid		10,000
Notional consideration paid $\frac{3}{20} \times £18,000$		2,700
		£12,700

Note

(a) In practice, the above calculations must be adjusted for indexation allowance which is added to the notional consideration and deducted from the unindexed gain—see 217.2 above and Revenue Statement of Practice SP 1/89.

217.5 SHARES ACQUIRED IN STAGES

Q is a partner in a medical practice. The partnership's only chargeable asset is a freehold house used as a surgery. The cost of the house to the partnership was £3,600 in 1960 and it was revalued in the partnership accounts to £50,000 in 1985. Q was admitted to the partnership in June 1963 with a share of $\frac{1}{6}$ of all profits. As a result of partnership changes, Q's profit share altered as follows

1968 $\frac{1}{5}$
1977 $\frac{1}{4}$
1990 $\frac{3}{10}$

For capital gains tax, Q's allowable cost of his share of the freehold house is calculated as follows

		£	
1963	$\frac{1}{6} \times £3,600$		£600
1968	$(\frac{1}{5}-\frac{1}{6}) \times £3,600$	120	
1977	$(\frac{1}{4}-\frac{1}{5}) \times £3,600$	180	
1990	$(\frac{3}{10}-\frac{1}{4}) \times £50,000$	2,500	£2,800

Notes

(a)   The pre- and post-6.4.65 costs are not pooled.

(b)   On Q's acquisition of an increased share of the property in 1990, any partner with a reduced share will be treated as having made a disposal and thus a chargeable gain. The re-basing rules of *FA 1988, s 96* will apply to the disposal (subject to the usual comparison with the gain or loss without re-basing).

217.6 PARTNERSHIP ASSETS DISTRIBUTED IN KIND

R, S and T are partners sharing all profits in the ratio 4:3:3. Farmland owned by the firm is transferred to T for future use by him as a market gardening enterprise separate from the partnership business. No payment is made by T to the other partners but a reduction is made in T's future share of income profits. The book value of the farmland is £5,000, its cost in 1983, but the present market value is £15,000.

		£
R		
Deemed disposal consideration	$\frac{4}{10} \times £15,000$	6,000
Allowable cost	$\frac{4}{10} \times £5,000$	2,000
Unindexed gain		£4,000
S		
Deemed disposal consideration	$\frac{3}{10} \times £15,000$	4,500
Allowable cost	$\frac{3}{10} \times £5,000$	1,500
Unindexed gain		£3,000
T		
Partnership share	$\frac{3}{10} \times £5,000$	1,500
Market value of R's share		6,000
Market value of S's share		4,500
Allowable cost of land for future disposal		£12,000

355

218 Private Residences

218.1 **PERIODS OF OWNERSHIP QUALIFYING FOR EXEMPTION AND LET PROPERTY EXEMPTION** [*CGTA 1979, ss 101, 102; FA 1980, s 80; FA 1984, s 63(3); FA 1988, 8 Sch 8*]

(A)

P sold a house on 1 July 1990 realising an otherwise chargeable gain of £36,667. The house was purchased on 1 February 1977 and was occupied as a residence until 30 June 1982 when P moved to another residence, letting the house as residential accommodation. He did not re-occupy the house prior to its sale.

	£
Gain on sale	36,667
Deduct Exempt amount under main residence rules	
$\dfrac{3m + 2y}{8y\ 3m} \times £36,667$	10,000
	26,667
Deduct Let property exemption (maximum £20,000)	10,000
Net chargeable gain	£16,667

Notes

(a)   The final period of 2 years of ownership is always included in the exempt period of ownership.

(b)   For disposals after 5 April 1988, period of ownership for the exemption calculation does not include any period before 31 March 1982. This applies regardless of whether the gain has been calculated by reference to cost or to 31 March 1982 value under the re-basing rules.

(c)   The gain attributable to the letting is exempt to the extent that it does not exceed the lesser of £20,000 and the gain otherwise exempt (£10,000).

(B)

Q bought a house on 1 August 1980 for £40,000 and used it as his main residence. On 10 February 1982, he was sent by his employer to manage the Melbourne branch of the firm and continued to work in Australia until 4 August 1986, the whole of his duties being performed outside the UK. The house was let during that period. Q took up residence in the house once again following his return to the UK, but on 30 November 1987 moved to Switzerland for health reasons, and again let the property. He returned to the UK in October 1990, but did not reside in the house at any time prior to its being sold on 30 November 1990 for £150,000. The house had a market value of £50,000 at 31 March 1982 and the indexation factor for the period March 1982 to November 1990 is assumed to be 0.662.

Computation of gain before applying exemptions

	£	£
Disposal consideration	150,000	150,000
Cost	40,000	
Market value 31.3.82		50,000
Unindexed gain	110,000	100,000
Indexation allowance £50,000 × 0.662	33,100	33,100
Gain after indexation	£76,900	£66,900
Gain before applying exemptions		£66,900

The gain is reduced by the main residence exemptions as follows

Period of ownership (excluding period before 31.3.82)		8y 8m
Exempt periods since 31.3.82:		
31.3.82 – 30.11.87	5y 8m	
1.12.88 – 30.11.90 (last two years)	2y 0m	7y 8m

	£
Gain as above	66,900

Deduct Exempt amount under main residence rules

$\dfrac{\text{7y 8m}}{\text{8y 8m}} \times £66,900$	59,181
	7,719
Deduct Let property exemption (maximum £20,000)	7,719
Net chargeable gain	Nil

Notes

(a) For disposals after 5 April 1988, periods of ownership before 31 March 1982 are excluded in applying the main residence exemptions. This is the case even if re-basing to 1982 does not apply. [*CGTA 1979, s 102(4); FA 1988, 8 Sch 8*].

(b) The period spent in Australia (regardless of its length but excluding that part of it before 31 March 1982) counts as a period of residence as Q worked in an employment all the duties of which were performed outside the UK and used the house as his main residence at some time before and after this period of absence. [*CGTA 1979, s 102(3)(b)*].

(c) The period spent in Switzerland would have been exempt, having not exceeded three years, but the exemption is lost as Q did not occupy the property as a main residence at any time after this period. [*CGTA 1979, s 102(3)(a)*].

(d) The last two years of ownership are always exempt providing the property has been used as the owner's only or main residence at some time during the period of ownership, and for this purpose, period of ownership is not restricted to the period after 30 March 1982. [*CGTA 1979, ss 101, 102(1)(2)*].

(e) The let property exemption is the lesser of the gain attributable to the period of letting, the gain otherwise exempt (£59,181 in this example) and £20,000. It cannot create or increase a loss, and it is only available if the property is let as residential accommodation. [*FA 1980, s 80; FA 1984, s 63(3)*].

CGT 218.1   Private Residences

(C)

R owns a property which he acquired on 1 June 1982 and uses as his main residence. He lets part of the house to students. Although the tenants have separate facilities for cooking, washing, etc., their accommodation is not self-contained and cannot, for example, be separately accessed from the street. On 30 September 1990, R sells the house, making an otherwise chargeable gain of £60,000. It is agreed with the inspector that the let portion of the house represented approximately $\frac{2}{5}$ of the whole.

	£
Gain on sale	60,000
Deduct Exempt amount $-\frac{3}{5} \times$ £60,000	36,000
	24,000
Deduct Let property exemption	20,000
Chargeable gain	£4,000

Notes

(*a*)   The let property exemption is limited to the lower of £36,000 (the amount otherwise exempt) and £20,000.

(*b*)   If the tenants had merely been lodging with the owner and living as members of his own family, the whole of the gain would have been exempt under normal principles and the let property exemption would not apply. If, on the other hand, they occupied self-contained accommodation within the same building, that accommodation would be treated as a separate residence fully chargeable to CGT, with the remainder of the property being fully exempt under the private residence rules. See Revenue Statement of Practice SP 14/80.

218.2 **ELECTION FOR MAIN RESIDENCE** [*CGTA 1979, s 101(5)*]

S purchased the long lease of a London flat on 1 June 1984. He occupied the flat as his sole residence until 31 July 1986 when he acquired a property in Shropshire. Both properties were thereafter occupied as residences by S until the lease of the flat was sold on 28 February 1991, realising an otherwise chargeable gain of £75,000.

The possibilities open to S are

(i) Election for flat to be treated as main residence throughout

Exempt gain   £75,000

(ii) Election for Shropshire property to be treated as main residence from 31.7.86 onwards

Exempt gain £75,000 × $\dfrac{\text{2y 2m + 2y}}{\text{6y 9m}}$ £46,296

(iii) Election for London flat to be treated as main residence up to 28 February 1989, thereafter the Shropshire property

Exempt gain £75,000 × $\dfrac{\text{2y 2m + 2y 7m + 2y}}{\text{6y 9m}}$ £75,000

Note

(*a*)   Election (iii) is the most favourable, provided it could have been made, in respect of the London flat, by 31 July 1988, and by 28 February 1991 in respect of the Shropshire property. Note that the last two years' ownership of the London flat is an exempt period in any case. The advantage of (iii) over (i) is that the period of ownership 1 March 1989 to 28 February 1991 of the Shropshire property will be treated as a period of residence as regards any future disposal of that property. It is understood that current Revenue practice is that the *initial* election must be made within two years of acquisition of the second property, although the legislation is not clear on this point.

219 Qualifying Corporate Bonds

[*FA 1984, s 64, 13 Sch; FA 1989, s 139*]

219.1 IDENTIFICATION RULES [*FA 1982, s 88; FA 1985, s 68*]

(A)

A carried out the following transactions in B 8% loan stock (a qualifying corporate bond)

		£
12.6.84	Purchase £1,000	850
6.8.85	Purchase £1,200	960
21.10.85	Purchase £500	450
5.6.86	Sale £600	(400)
25.9.90	Sale £1,500	(1,600)

For the purposes of the accrued income scheme, the sale on 5.6.86 is without accrued interest and the sale on 25.9.90 is with accrued interest. The rebate amount on the 5.6.86 sale is £3 and the accrued amount on the 25.9.90 sale is £29.

Disposal on 5.6.86	£
Proceeds	400
Add rebate amount	3
	403

Cost
Identify sale with £600 purchased on 6.8.85

$$\frac{600}{1,200} \times £960 \qquad\qquad 480$$

Allowable loss   £77

Disposal on 25.9.90

The disposal is exempt from CGT as it occurs after 1.7.86. It will, however, give rise to an income tax charge on the £29 accrued amount.

Notes

(*a*) In general, the normal rules of identification for shares and securities which applied before 6 April 1985 (1 April 1985 for companies) continued to apply after those dates to qualifying corporate bonds. See 209.3 INDEXATION above. However, where there was a disposal at a loss followed by a reacquisition and this was not covered by *F(No 2)A 1975, s 58* (applicable only to companies), the gilt-edged security identification rules of *CGTA 1979, s 70* were extended to qualifying corporate bonds. No identification rules are needed for disposals after 1 July 1986, as such disposals are exempt.

(*b*) See 22.3 SCHEDULE D, CASE VI in the Income Tax section for the income tax effects of the accrued income scheme.

(*c*) See also 213.3 LOSSES above for allowable losses arising on qualifying corporate bonds in certain circumstances.

(B)

B has the following transactions in 5% unsecured loan stock issued in 1983 by F Ltd. No shares or securities in F Ltd have ever been quoted on the UK Stock Exchange or Unlisted Securities Market.

		£
11.11.83	Purchase £2,000	1,800
10.7.84	Gift from wife £1,000 (original cost £900)	—
30.9.84	Purchase £2,000	1,700
5.6.90	Sale £4,000	(3,300)

Apart from the gift on 10.7.84, all acquisitions were arm's length purchases. B's wife acquired her £1,000 holding on 11.11.83.

For the purposes of the accrued income scheme, the sale is without accrued interest and the rebate amount is £10. The stock is a corporate bond in relation to disposals after 13 March 1989 — see note (*a*).

Under the rules for matching relevant securities in *FA 1982, s 88* (see 209.3 INDEX-ATION above), the stock disposed of is identified with acquisitions as follows.

(i) Identify £2,000 with purchase on 30.9.84 (LIFO)

	£
Disposal consideration £3,300 × $\frac{2,000}{4,000}$	1,650
Add rebate amount £10 × $\frac{2,000}{4,000}$	5
	1,655
Allowable cost	1,700
Unindexed loss	£45

The loss is *not* allowable as the £2,000 stock purchased on 30.9.84 is a qualifying corporate bond (note (*a*)).

(ii) Identify £1,000 with acquisition on 10.7.84

	£
Disposal consideration £3,300 × $\frac{1,000}{4,000}$	825
Add rebate amount £10 × $\frac{1,000}{4,000}$	2
	827
Allowable cost	900
Unindexed loss	£73

The loss, increased by indexation allowance, is allowable as the stock acquired on 10.7.84 is not a qualifying corporate bond (note (*b*)).

(iii) Identify £1,000 with purchase on 11.11.83

	£
Disposal consideration £3,300 × $\frac{1,000}{4,000}$	825
Add rebate amount £10 × $\frac{1,000}{4,000}$	3
	828
Allowable cost £1,800 × $\frac{1,000}{2,000}$	900
Unindexed loss	£72

The loss, increased by indexation allowance, is allowable as the stock acquired on 11.11.83 is not a qualifying corporate bond (note (*c*)).

Notes

(*a*) For disposals after 13 March 1989, *FA 1984, s 64(2)(a)* was repealed by *FA 1989, s 139, 17 Sch Part VII*. The effect of this is that unquoted securities can be corporate bonds. It is assumed in this example that the securities in question satisfy *FA 1984, s 64(2)(b)(c)*. Although, as noted in (A) above, no identification rules are required for disposals after 1 July 1986 of qualifying corporate bonds, such rules must be applied to corporate bonds where some acquisitions qualify and others do not.

In this case, the acquisition on 30.9.84 is a qualifying corporate bond as it was acquired after 13 March 1984 otherwise than as a result of an excluded disposal. [*FA 1984, s 64(4)(b)*].

(*b*) The acquisition on 10.7.84 was the result of an excluded disposal, being a no gain/no loss transfer between spouses where the first spouse had acquired the stock before 14 March 1984. It is therefore not a qualifying corporate bond. [*FA 1984, s 64(4)(b)(5)*].

(*c*) Securities acquired before 14 March 1984 cannot be qualifying corporate bonds in the hands of the person who so acquired them.

(*d*) See also 213.3 LOSSES above for allowable losses arising on qualifying corporate bonds in certain circumstances.

219.2 REORGANISATION OF SHARE CAPITAL [*FA 1984, 13 Sch 7, 8, 10; FA 1985, s 67; FA 1990, s 85*]

D holds 5,000 £1 ordinary shares in H Ltd. He acquired the shares in April 1982 by subscription at par. On 1 August 1985, he accepts an offer for the shares from J plc. The terms of the offer are one 25p ordinary share of J plc and £50 J plc 10% unsecured loan stock (a qualifying corporate bond) for each H Ltd ordinary share. Both the shares and the loan stock are listed on the Stock Exchange. In December 1990, D sells £100,000 loan stock at its quoted price of £105 per cent.

The value of J plc ordinary shares at 1 August 1985 is £9.52 per share and the loan stock is £99.20 per cent. The indexation factor for April 1982 to August 1985 is 0.178.

The cost of the H Ltd shares must be apportioned between the J plc ordinary shares and loan stock.

	£
Value of J plc shares	
5,000 × £9.52	47,600
Value of J plc loan stock	
£250,000 × 99.2%	248,000
	£295,600

Allowable cost of J plc shares

$$\frac{47,600}{295,600} \times £5,000 \qquad £805$$

Allowable cost of J plc loan stock

$$\frac{248,000}{295,600} \times £5,000 \qquad £4,195$$

Chargeable gain on H Ltd shares attributable to J plc loan stock to date of exchange

	£
Deemed disposal consideration	248,000
Allowable cost	4,195
Unindexed gain	243,805
Indexation allowance £4,195 × 0.178	747
Deferred chargeable gain	£243,058

Deferred chargeable gain accruing on disposal of loan stock

Loan stock sold (nominal)	£100,000
Total holding of loan stock before disposal (nominal)	£250,000

Deferred chargeable gain accruing in 1990/91

$$\frac{100,000}{250,000} \times £243,058 \qquad\qquad £97,223$$

Notes

(a)   The gain on the securities is exempt (as the disposal occurs after 1.7.86) except for that part which relates to the gain on the previous holding of H Ltd shares. [*FA 1984, 13 Sch 10; FA 1985, s 67*]. There will also be income tax consequences under the accrued income scheme. See 22.3 SCHEDULE D, CASE VI in the Income Tax section.

(b)   The qualifying corporate bond is treated as acquired at the date of the reorganisation, so even if the original shares had been held at 31 March 1982, the re-basing provisions of *FA 1988, s 96* could *not* apply on the subsequent disposal, after 5 April 1988, of the loan stock. However, where the original shares are acquired before 31 March 1982, the reorganisation takes place before 6 April 1988, and the qualifying corporate bonds are disposed of after 5 April 1988, the deferred chargeable gain is halved. [*FA 1988, 9 Sch 3*].

(c)   The H Ltd shares exchanged for J plc ordinary shares are dealt with as if *CGTA 1979, ss 79–81* applied in the normal way. See 223.1 SHARES AND SECURITIES below.

220 Retirement Relief

[FA 1985, ss 69, 70, 20 Sch; FA 1987, s 47; FA 1988, s 110]

220.1 EXTENT OF RELIEF

(A) General provisions

N had been the proprietor of a newsagent's business for more than ten years. In December 1990, when N was 61, he sold the whole of the business to a national group for £320,000. The consideration under the agreement and the cost of the relevant assets were

	Cost £	Consideration £
Freehold shop	7,000	240,000
Flat over shop (occupied throughout by N as main residence)	6,500	30,000
Goodwill	600	30,000
Trading stock	10,500	12,000
Fixtures and fittings (one item over £6,000)	12,800	8,000
		£320,000

Chargeable gains and allowable losses (after indexation, and re-basing to 1982 where appropriate) are

	£
Freehold shop	162,160
Goodwill	17,020
Fixture	(980)
Aggregate	£178,200

Retirement relief is calculated as follows

Gain subject to relief	178,200
Maximum available for 100% relief	
Qualifying period — 10 years	
$\dfrac{10}{10} \times £125,000$	(125,000)
Maximum available for 50% relief	
£178,200 − £125,000 = £53,200	
£53,200 × $\frac{1}{2}$	(26,600)
Chargeable gain	£26,600

Notes

(a) For disposals after 5 April 1988, the exemption is extended to one half of gains between £125,000 and £500,000 these limits being reduced by reference to qualifying periods of less than ten years.

(b) The flat over the shop is exempt from capital gains tax as it has been N's main residence throughout the period.

(B) Retirement from business on ill-health grounds and relief restricted by reference to qualifying period [*FA 1985, s 69(1)–(3), 20 Sch 13*]

After giving up salaried employment in June 1984 at the age of 51, R purchased a small philately business. In June 1990, R finds he is unable to continue running the business because of ill-health and sells for the following amounts.

	Proceeds	Chargeable gain (after indexation)
	£	£
Premises	110,000	66,000
Goodwill	30,000	22,800
Fixtures and fittings (none over £6,000)	8,000	—
Stock	25,000	—
		£88,800

Retirement relief is given as follows

	£
Gains eligible for relief	88,800

Maximum available for 100% relief
Qualifying period — 6 years

$$\frac{6}{10} \times £125,000 \qquad\qquad (75,000)$$

Maximum available for 50% relief

$$\frac{6}{10} \times £500,000 = £300,000$$

£88,800 (being less than £300,000) − £75,000 = £13,800

£13,800 × ½	(6,900)
Chargeable gain	£6,900

Note

(*a*)   Relief is given where an individual has retired below the age of 60 on ill-health grounds provided the Board are satisfied that he has ceased work and is likely to remain permanently incapable of that kind of work. Claims for relief on the grounds of ill-health must be made to the Board within two years after the end of the year of assessment of the relevant disposal. [*FA 1985, 20 Sch 1, 5(2)(4)*].

(C) Operative date — ceasing to be a full-time working director [*FA 1985, s 69(5)(7), 20 Sch 1*]

Q gave up full-time work at 60 in June 1990 when she had been a director of Q Ltd, her family company, for five years. She continued as a director, working three mornings per week until January 1991 when she sold her 40% shareholding in Q Ltd realising a chargeable gain of £270,000.

CGT 220.1   Retirement Relief

Retirement relief is given as follows

	£
Gain eligible for relief	270,000

Maximum available for 100% relief
Qualifying period — 5 years

$$\frac{5}{10} \times £125,000 \qquad\qquad (62,500)$$

Maximum available for 50% relief

$$\frac{5}{10} \times £500,000 = £250,000$$

£250,000 − £62,500 = £187,500
£187,500 × ½   (93,750)

Chargeable gain	£113,750

Note

(a)   If an individual ceases to be a full-time working director of a company but remains a director and works an average of ten hours per week in a technical or managerial capacity until the date of disposal, the operative date is deemed to be the date of ceasing to be a full-time working director.

(D) Share for share exchange — relief available [*FA 1985, 20 Sch 2*]
In November 1990, D, aged 67, accepts an offer to exchange his 60% holding of 1,200 shares in C Ltd for shares in M plc on the basis of 10 for 1. He has been a full-time working director of C Ltd for 15 years. He receives 12,000 shares in M plc valued at £168,000. The holding in C Ltd cost £5,000 in 1971.
D elects not to treat the new shares and the holding disposed of as the same asset under *CGTA 1979, s 78*.
The market value of the shares on 31 March 1982 is agreed at £100,000. The indexation factor to November 1990 is assumed to be 0.662.
C Ltd had no non-business assets.

The chargeable gain is calculated as follows

	£	£
Disposal consideration	168,000	168,000
Cost	5,000	
Market value 31.3.82		100,000
Unindexed gain	163,000	68,000
Indexation allowance £100,000 × 0.662	66,200	66,200
Gain after indexation	£96,800	£1,800
Gain subject to retirement relief		1,800
Retirement relief available (maximum £125,000 at 100% and £375,000 at 50%)		1,800
Chargeable gain		Nil

Note

(a)   The base cost for the new shares is £168,000.

220.2 GAINS QUALIFYING FOR RELIEF
(A) Non-business chargeable assets [FA 1985, 20 Sch 6, 7, 12]

P Ltd carries on a trade of printing and bookbinding. Its directors include C who owns 40% of the issued share capital. In December 1990, on reaching the age of 63, C gives his shares to his sister. At the date of transfer, the company's assets are valued as follows

	£	£	Market value £	Cost £
Leasehold printing works			190,000	50,000
Goodwill			60,000	—
Stocks of materials			80,000	75,000
Plant				
Printing presses No 1	8,000			3,000
No 2	8,500			3,500
No 3	6,500	23,000		2,000
Typesetter		10,500		15,000
Binding machine		16,500		12,000
Small tools, type etc.		7,000		10,000
Office fixtures and fittings (items under £6,000)		9,000	66,000	15,000
Shares in associated publishing company			60,000	40,000
Cash at bank and in hand			7,500	—
Debtors			11,500	—

The chargeable gain arising on the shares given to C's sister is £75,000.

The value of the company's chargeable assets is as follows

	Business £	Non-business £
Leasehold	190,000	—
Goodwill	60,000	—
Plant (£23,000 + £10,500 + £16,500)	50,000	—
Shares	—	60,000
	£300,000	£60,000

Gain eligible for retirement relief is therefore

$$£75,000 \times \frac{300,000}{300,000 + 60,000} \qquad £62,500$$

Note

(a) Chargeable assets are all assets other than those on which any gain accruing on a disposal immediately before the end of the qualifying period would not be a chargeable gain.

(B) Shares in holding company — group holding non-business assets. [*FA 1985, 20* *Sch 6, 8, 12*]

D, aged 60, gives 30% of his shares in the family holding company N Ltd to his son. The business of manufacturing and distributing double glazing units is carried on through two subsidiaries X Ltd and Y Ltd. At the date of disposal in November 1990, the market value of the assets of the group are as follows.

	Assets	Chargeable assets Business	Non-business
	£	£	£
N Ltd			
Leasehold of factory	150,000	150,000	
Investment in subsidiaries			
X (100%)	60,000		
Y (60%)	40,000		
Quoted shares	10,000		10,000
X Ltd (100% owned)			
Plant	32,000	32,000	
Stock, debtors and cash	18,000		
		£182,000	£10,000
Y Ltd (60% owned)			
Freehold shop (half let)	50,000	25,000	25,000
Plant and machinery	15,000	15,000	
Stock, debtors and cash	9,000		
		£40,000	£25,000
60% thereof		£24,000	£15,000
Total		£206,000	£25,000

The chargeable gain on the gift of shares is £57,750.

The gain eligible for retirement relief is therefore

$$£57,750 \times \frac{206,000}{206,000 + 25,000} = £51,500$$

Notes

(a)   A shareholding in another member of the family trading group is not counted as a chargeable asset.

(b)   Chargeable business and non-business assets of a part-owned subsidiary are reduced in proportion to the share capital owned.

(c)   It is assumed that none of the items of plant and machinery are covered by the chattel exemption in *CGTA 1979, s 128*.

(C) Associated disposal by trustees [*FA 1985, s 70(3)–(5), 20 Sch 13*]
B has carried on a business for more than ten years in premises held by a family trust in which he has a life interest of 40%.
In May 1990 B, who is then 64, sells the business, realising a chargeable gain of £98,000. The trustees sell the property in April 1991, at a chargeable gain of £89,000.

Disposal by B

	£
Chargeable gain	98,000
Retirement relief (100%)	(98,000)
Chargeable gain	Nil
Disposal by trustees	
Chargeable gain	89,000
Gain subject to retirement relief: 40% × £89,000 = £35,600	
Relief available at 100% £(125,000 − 98,000)	(27,000)
Relief available at 50% £(35,600 − 27,000)	(4,300)
Chargeable gain	£57,700

Notes

(*a*) For the purposes of calculating the maximum available retirement relief, a trustees' disposal is regarded as a qualifying disposal by the beneficiary. If disposals by trustees and a beneficiary are made on the same day, relief is given first to the gain by the beneficiary.

(*b*) The qualifying period of full-time working must end not more than one year before the trustees' disposal. If the trustees' sale were deferred to June 1991, no relief would be allowable except at the Board's discretion.

(D) Associated disposal — restriction for non-business use, qualifying period and rent [*FA 1985, 20 Sch 10*]
In May 1990, X, who had been a full-time working director for 10 years and was aged 62, sold his qualifying holding of shares in W Ltd realising a chargeable gain of £90,000. The company had, since 1980, used a warehouse acquired by X personally in 1975. It was agreed that the company would vacate the property (for which it paid a rent of 75% market rate) after six months. X then sold the warehouse realising a chargeable gain of £31,500.

Disposal of shares

	£
Chargeable gain	90,000
Retirement relief (100%)	(90,000)
	Nil

	£
Disposal of warehouse	
Chargeable gain	31,500
Gain subject to retirement relief	

(i)   Proportion of business use

$$\frac{10 \text{ years}}{15 \text{ years}} \times £31,500 = \underline{£21,000}$$

(ii)   Qualifying period of ownership

$$\frac{10}{10\frac{1}{2}} \times £21,000 = \underline{£20,000} \quad \text{note } (b)$$

(iii)   Proportion rent free
      25% × £20,000 = £5,000

Balance of relief available (at 100%) £(125,000 − 90,000) = £35,000

	£
Retirement relief (restricted to £5,000 × 100%)	5,000
Chargeable gain	£26,500

Notes

(a)   Restricted retirement relief is available where the asset has not been used for business purposes throughout the period of ownership or where the individual was not concerned in carrying on the trade during part of the period of use in the business or where rent has been paid for the use of the asset. The part qualifying for relief is that which appears just and reasonable to the Board. The above computation shows one way in which the Board might interpret 'just and reasonable'.

(b)   For the final six months of use in the business, W Ltd was not X's family company.

(E) Partnerships [*FA 1985, s 69(8), 20 Sch 10*]
U, V and W trade in partnership. They have shared income and capital in the ratio 5:3:2 since 1970. On 30 April 1990, V retires aged 63 after 30 years as a partner and receives a lump sum of £35,000 from the other partners. He also transfers to the firm, for £120,000, office premises which it has occupied for business purposes, paying an annual rent to V of £3,000. The open market rent for the property is £5,000. V's chargeable gain is £82,000. The book values of the firm's chargeable assets are as follows.

Freehold depot   £40,000 (cost on 1.5.83)
Goodwill   £10,000 (valuation on 31.3.82)

Of the £35,000, £25,000 is expressed to relate to V's interest in the freehold depot, £5,500 to goodwill and £4,500 to other assets.

Chargeable gains eligible for retirement relief are

		£	£	£
Freehold depot	Consideration	25,000		
	Allowable cost $\frac{3}{10} \times$ £40,000	12,000		
Unindexed gain			13,000	
Indexation allowance £12,000 × 0.478			5,736	
				7,264
Goodwill	Consideration	5,500		
	Allowable cost $\frac{3}{10} \times$ £10,000	3,000		
Unindexed gain			2,500	
Indexation allowance £3,000 × 0.575			1,725	
				775

Office premises
Chargeable gain   £82,000

Fraction eligible

$$\frac{5,000 \text{ (market rent)} - 3,000 \text{ (actual rent)}}{5,000 \text{ (market rent)}}$$

$$+ \frac{\frac{3}{10} \times 3,000 \text{ (partner's share of actual rent)}}{5,000 \text{ (market rent)}} = \frac{29}{50}$$

	47,560
	£55,599

Notes

(a)   The whole of the £55,599 attracts 100% retirement relief. V is therefore chargeable only on the non-eligible part of the gain on the office premises of £34,440 (£82,000 − £47,560).

(b)   Where rent, but at less than market rent, is paid by the partnership, *FA 1985, 20 Sch 10* gives relief for a 'just and reasonable' amount of the gain. The formula shown above is one possible interpretation which, it is believed, would normally be accepted by the Revenue.

(c)   See (D) above for restriction of relief where an asset has not been used for business purposes throughout the period of ownership.

CGT 220.2 Retirement Relief

(F) Capital distribution [*FA 1985, s 69(1)(2)(4), 20 Sch 11, 12(5)(6)*].

At 61, M decides to put his trading company into voluntary liquidation. He holds all the share capital and has been a working director for 20 years. In November 1990, the company sold off machinery for £7,000. The company ceases to trade in February 1991 and in November 1991 the liquidator pays M a cash distribution of £15,000 and transfers the lease of its premises to him after settling all debts and taxation liabilities.

M's chargeable gain on disposal of his shares is £40,000.

At cessation, the company's assets (at market value) were

	Assets	Chargeable Business	Chargeable Non-business
	£	£	£
Lease of premises	25,000	25,000	
Flat over premises (let)	5,000		5,000
Plant, fixtures	13,000	13,000	
Stock, debtors, cash	19,000		

M elects under *FA 1985, 20 Sch 12(6)* to substitute the machinery sold in November 1990 for the proceeds of its sale held at cessation in order to increase the proportion of business chargeable assets.

The chargeable gain is calculated as follows

	£
Gain on disposal	40,000

Allowable for retirement relief

$$\frac{25,000 + 13,000 + 7,000}{25,000 + 13,000 + 7,000 + 5,000} \times £40,000 = \underline{£36,000}$$

Restricted to cash portion of distribution   note (*b*)

$$\frac{15,000}{15,000 + 25,000} \times £36,000 \qquad \qquad \underline{13,500}$$

Chargeable gain	£26,500

Notes

(*a*) The liquidator's distribution must be within one year of the date of cessation of business or such longer period as the Board allows.

(*b*) No retirement relief is available on that part of the gain attributable to the proportion of the capital distribution represented by chargeable business assets. [*FA 1985, 20 Sch 11*].

(*c*) It is assumed that no item of the plant and fixtures is covered by the chattel exemption of *CGTA 1979, s 128*.

220.3 **AMOUNT OF RELIEF**
(A) Aggregation of earlier business periods [*FA 1985, 20 Sch 14*]
A sold the hotel he had owned and run for ten years in July 1982. In January 1983 he reinvested £65,000 in a similar business, rolling over the earlier chargeable gain of £50,000. When he was 61 in January 1991, the hotel was severely damaged by fire and A decided to retire. He received £250,000 from the insurance company and £60,000 for the sale of the land. The indexation factor for the period January 1983 to January 1991 is assumed to be 0.625.

	£	£
Disposal proceeds — sale of land	60,000	
— insurance monies	250,000	
		310,000
Cost	65,000	
Less deferred gain × $\frac{1}{2}$ note (*b*)	25,000	
		40,000
		270,000
Indexation allowance £40,000 × 0.625		25,000
		245,000

Maximum retirement relief available at 100% £125,000
Restricted by qualifying period

$$\frac{8 + 1\frac{1}{2}}{10} \times £125,000 \times 100\% \qquad\qquad 118,750$$

126,250

Maximum retirement relief available at 50%:

$$£500,000 \times \frac{9\frac{1}{2}}{10} = £475,000 - £118,750 = £356,250$$

£245,000 − £118,750 = £126,250 × 50%   63,125

Chargeable gain   £63,125

Notes
(*a*)   The two businesses carried on in the ten-year qualifying period are aggregated but the qualifying period is restricted by the gap between the ownership of the two businesses.

(*b*)   See 204.2 ASSETS HELD ON 31 MARCH 1982 above for relief in respect of gains deferred after 31 March 1982 and before 6 April 1988 and attributable, wholly or partly, to assets held on 31 March 1982.

(B) Earlier disposal [*FA 1985, 20 Sch 15; FA 1988, s 110(3)–(5)*]
Y gave shares in his family trading company to his children on his 61st birthday in September 1990 realising a chargeable gain of £110,000. He had been a full-time working director for 8 years. The gain was eligible in full for retirement relief.

Retirement relief was given as follows

	£
Gain eligible for relief	110,000
Maximum available for 100% relief	

$$\frac{8}{10} \times £125,000 \times 100\% \qquad (100,000)$$

Maximum available for 50% relief

$$\frac{8}{10} \times £500,000 = £400,000 - £100,000 = £300,000$$

	£
£110,000 − £100,000 = £10,000 × 50%	(5,000)
Chargeable gain	£5,000

In September 1991, Y gives his remaining 30% holding to his children. The gain on the gift is £50,000.

Retirement relief is given as follows

		£
Gain eligible for relief		50,000
Maximum available for 100% relief		

$$\frac{10}{10} \times £125,000 = \qquad £125,000$$

	£	
Deduct Relief already given at 100%	100,000	(25,000)
Maximum available for 50% relief		

$$\frac{10}{10} \times £500,000 = £500,000 - £125,000 = \qquad 375,000$$

	£	
Deduct (Relief already given £5,000) × 2 =	10,000	
	£365,000	
Restricted to (£50,000 − £25,000) £25,000 × 50%		(12,500)
Chargeable gain		£12,500

(C) Married persons — aggregation of spouses' qualifying periods — transfer on death [*FA 1985, 20 Sch 16*]
R acquired her late husband's 30% shareholding in X Ltd on his death in June 1982. She took over the office he had held for many years as a full-time working director until, at the age of 63, she sold her shares in June 1990 incurring a chargeable gain of £139,000.

The chargeable gain is calculated as follows	£
Gain eligible for relief	139,000
Maximum available for 100% relief	

$$\frac{8 + 2}{10} \times £125,000 \times 100\% \qquad\qquad (125,000)$$

Maximum available for 50% relief

$$\frac{8 + 2}{10} \times £500,000 = £500,000 - £125,000 = £375,000$$

£139,000 − £125,000 = £14,000 × 50%	(7,000)
Chargeable gain	£7,000

Note
(*a*)   Written election must be made within two years after the end of the year of assessment in which the disposal occurs for the qualifying period to be extended by the spouse's qualifying period.

(D) Married persons — aggregation of spouses' qualifying periods — lifetime transfer [*FA 1985, 20 Sch 16*]

In May 1983, J, who was 65 that month, gave 40% of the shares in Y Ltd to his son realising a chargeable gain of £20,000. He had been a full-time working director for 12 years. His wife G, aged 54, already held 20% of the share capital and both she and the son became full-time directors. Later that year, J's health failed and he transferred his remaining 40% holding to G who continued as a director until November 1990 when she sold her shares to her son realising a chargeable gain of £115,000.

Gift by J to son	£
Gain eligible for relief	20,000
Retirement relief available (maximum £50,000)	20,000
Chargeable gain	Nil

Disposal by G

No election to aggregate qualifying periods

Gain eligible for relief   115,000

Maximum available for 100% relief

$$\frac{7\frac{1}{2}}{10} \times £125,000 \qquad\qquad\qquad (93,750)$$

Maximum available for 50% relief

$$\frac{7\frac{1}{2}}{10} \times £500,000 = £375,000 - £93,750 = £281,250$$

£115,000 − £93,750 = £21,250 × 50%   (10,625)

Chargeable gain   £10,625

Election made to aggregate qualifying periods   £

Gain eligible for relief   115,000

Maximum available for 100% relief

$$\frac{10}{10} \times £125,000 = \qquad\qquad 125,000$$

Deduct Relief at 100% previously given   20,000   (105,000)

Maximum available for 50% relief

$$\frac{10}{10} \times £500,000 = £500,000 - £125,000 = £375,000$$

£115,000 − £105,000 = £10,000 × 50%   (5,000)

Chargeable gain   £5,000

The election is beneficial.

221 Rollover Relief

Cross-reference. See also 204.2 ASSETS HELD ON 31 MARCH 1982 for relief under *FA 1988,*
s 97, 9 Sch for certain gains accruing before 31 March 1982.

[CGTA 1979, ss 115–121]

221.1 NATURE OF RELIEF
(A)

N Ltd commenced a manufacturing business on 1 April 1982, having held no fixed
assets before that date. It makes the following disposals and acquisitions of assets
during the company's accounting periods ended 31 December 1988, 31 December
1989 and 31 December 1990.

	Asset	Bought/ (sold) £	Chargeable gains £
1.10.88	Freehold depot	18,000	—
12.12.88	Leasehold warehouse	(50,000)	28,000
19.6.89	Business formerly carried on by another company		
	Goodwill	20,000	—
	Freehold factory unit	90,000	—
1.2.90	Land adjacent to main factory, now surplus to requirements	(40,000)	19,000
8.9.90	Industrial mincer (obsolete)	(30,000)	5,000
1.11.90	Extension to new factory	35,000	—

(i) The gain on the leasehold warehouse may be rolled over against the following

	Cost £		Gain £
Freehold depot	18,000	$\dfrac{18,000}{50,000} \times £28,000$	10,080
Goodwill	20,000	$\dfrac{20,000}{50,000} \times £28,000$	11,200
Freehold factory (part)	12,000	$\dfrac{12,000}{50,000} \times £28,000$	6,720
	£50,000		£28,000

(ii) The gain on the surplus land may be rolled over as follows

Freehold factory (part)	£40,000	Gain rolled over	£19,000

(iii) The gain on the industrial mincer may be rolled over as follows

Extension to new factory (part)	£30,000	Gain rolled over	£5,000

CGT 221.1   Rollover Relief

The position at 31 December 1990 is therefore as follows

	£
Freehold depot	
Cost	18,000
Deduct gains rolled over	10,080
Allowable cost	£7,920
Goodwill	
Cost	20,000
Deduct gains rolled over	11,200
Allowable cost	£8,800
Freehold factory	
Cost	90,000
Deduct gains rolled over (£6,720 + £19,000)	25,720
Allowable cost	£64,280
Extension to new factory	
Cost	35,000
Deduct gains rolled over	5,000
Allowable cost	£30,000

Notes

(*a*)   The expenditure still available to match against disposal proceeds is

Extension to factory (£35,000 − £30,000)   £5,000

The expenditure is available only against disposals up to 31 October 1991.

(*b*)   There is no statutory rule prescribing the way in which the gain on an asset must be rolled over against a number of different assets. In (i) the chargeable gain has been rolled over rateably to the costs of the items which is understood to reflect the Revenue's view on the method of apportionment.

378

(B)

L Ltd carries on a vehicle repair business. In December 1990 it sells a workshop for £90,000 net of costs. The workshop had cost £45,000 inclusive in April 1984. A new workshop is purchased for £144,000 in January 1991 and sold for £168,000 in January 1993.

Indexation factors (assumed)   April 1984 to December 1990   0.502
                                                January 1991 to January 1993   0.210

L Ltd claims rollover of the chargeable gain.

	£
Allowable cost of original workshop	45,000
Indexation allowance £45,000 × 0.502	22,590
	67,590
Actual disposal consideration	90,000
Chargeable gain rolled over	£22,410
Cost of new workshop	144,000
Deduct amount rolled over	22,410
Deemed allowable cost	£121,590
Disposal consideration, replacement workshop	168,000
Allowable cost	121,590
Unindexed gain	46,410
Indexation allowance £121,590 × 0.210	25,534
Chargeable gain	£20,876

221.2 PARTIAL RELIEF

(A)

G carries on an accountancy practice. In March 1990, he agrees to acquire the practice of another sole practitioner, who is about to retire. As part of the acquisition, G pays £20,000 for goodwill. In January 1991, G moves to new premises, acquiring the remaining 70 years of a 99-year lease for £50,000. The sale of his former office realises £80,000, and a chargeable gain of £59,000 arises.

	£	£
Amount of proceeds of disposal of old office		80,000
Costs against which gains can be rolled over		
Goodwill	20,000	
Lease	50,000	
	——	
		70,000
Chargeable gain not rolled over		£10,000
Chargeable gain rolled over (£59,000 − £10,000)		£49,000
Allowable cost of assets		
Goodwill	20,000	
Gain rolled over $\dfrac{20,000}{70,000} \times £49,000$	14,000	
	——	
		£6,000
Lease	50,000	
Gain rolled over $\dfrac{50,000}{70,000} \times £49,000$	35,000	
	——	
		£15,000

Note

(a)   There is no statutory direction as to apportionment of chargeable gains to items of expenditure, so that, say, £20,000 could have been rolled over against the cost of goodwill and £29,000 against the cost of the lease. The Revenue are understood to take the view that the apportionment must be made on the above basis.

(B) Partial business use

N carries on a consultancy business from commercial premises formerly used as a shop. N has owned the property since 1 July 1973, but it was let until 1 September 1986 when N moved in following the expiry of the lease held by the former tenant. The property cost £8,000. On 1 February 1991, N sells the property for £100,000, moving to a new office a long lease of which he acquires for £60,000 and which is wholly used for his business. The value at 31 March 1982 of the property sold was £43,000. The indexation factor for March 1982 to February 1991 is assumed to be 0.704.

For rollover relief purposes, N is treated as having disposed of two separate assets, one representing his occupation and professional use of the property, the other his ownership of it as an investment. In practice, the proceeds and chargeable gain may be allocated by a simple time apportionment.

Business use

$$\text{Proceeds} \,£100,000 \times \frac{4y\ 5m}{8y\ 10m} \quad \text{note } (c) \qquad\qquad\qquad £50,000$$

Chargeable gain

$$[£100,000 - £43,000 - (£43,000 \times 0.704)] = £26,728 \times \frac{4y\ 5m}{8y\ 10m} \qquad £13,364$$

Notes

(a)   The proceeds attributable to business use are less than the cost of the new office, so that the whole of the chargeable gain attributable to business use is rolled over. The allowable cost of the new office is then £46,636 (£60,000 – £13,364).

(b)   The balance of the chargeable gain, £13,364 (£26,728 – £13,364) is not eligible for rollover.

(c)   The time apportionment, for disposals after 5 April 1988, takes into account only the period of ownership after 30 March 1982. [*CGTA 1979, s 115(7A); FA 1988, 8 Sch 9*].

(d)   Re-basing to 1982 will clearly apply to the computation of the gain as it produces a gain lower than that which would have been produced by using cost as opposed to 31.3.82 value.

221.3 WASTING ASSETS

(A)

H Ltd carries on a motor agency trade. On 30 October 1990 it sells one of its branches to another company as a going concern. The purchaser pays H Ltd £20,000 for the unexpired term of the showroom lease and £18,000 for goodwill. Chargeable gains of £6,000 arise on disposal of the lease, and £15,000 on goodwill. H Ltd opens a new branch in June 1991, having purchased for £30,000 the remaining term of a lease which expires on 31 December 2005.

The most beneficial method of computing the hold over is

	Proceeds £	Chargeable gain held over £
Goodwill (whole)	18,000	15,000
Lease (part)	12,000	nil
Cost of new lease	£30,000	£15,000

Notes

(a) The gain on the old lease remains chargeable because it is less than the amount of the proceeds not reinvested (£20,000 − £12,000 = £8,000).

(b) There is no statutory formula for deciding which gains are to be held over where more than one asset has been disposed of. It is usually beneficial to consider first the asset on which the chargeable gain is higher in proportion to the disposal proceeds (the goodwill in the above example).

(B)

C Ltd, a manufacturing company, sells an item of fixed plant, acquired after 30 March 1982, for £30,000 in 1986. A chargeable gain of £7,200 arises. In 1988, the company buys storage facilities on a 20-year lease for £40,000. In 1990, an extension to the company's freehold factory is completed at a cost of £25,000.

The position is as follows

(i) The company may claim holdover of the £7,200 chargeable gain in 1986, against the cost of the lease.

(ii) In 1990, part of the chargeable gain can be rolled over against the cost of the factory extension, as follows

	£
Expenditure available for rollover	25,000
Maximum capable of rollover	
£7,200 − (£30,000 − £25,000)	2,200
Adjusted base cost of extension	£22,800

Notes

(a) The balance of the chargeable gain, £5,000 (£7,200 − £2,200) may continue to be held over against the cost of the lease, either until it crystallises or until further rollover is possible.

(b) Had the company not claimed holdover against the cost of the lease, a claim against the cost of the extension in 1990 would not have been possible, as the expenditure was incurred outside the normal time limit.

222   Settlements

222.1   ANNUAL EXEMPTIONS AND RATES OF TAX [*CGTA 1979, s 5, 1 Sch 6(1)(2); FA 1988, s 98*]

The trustees of the E settlement, created in 1962, realise chargeable gains and allowable losses as follows

	Chargeable gain/ (allowable loss) £
1986/87	(2,300)
1987/88	800
1988/89	4,200
1989/90	2,450
1990/91	5,000

The trust is not an accumulation or discretionary settlement, nor does the settlor have an interest therein (see notes (*a*) and (*b*)).

The trustees' capital gains tax liability is computed as follows

	£
1986/87	
Taxable amount	Nil
Losses carried forward	£2,300
1987/88	
Net chargeable gains	800
Losses brought forward	—
Taxable amount (covered by annual exemption)	£800
CGT	Nil
Losses carried forward	£2,300
1988/89	
Net chargeable gains	4,200
Losses brought forward	1,700
Taxable amount (covered by annual exemption)	£2,500
CGT	Nil
Losses carried forward (£2,300 − £1,700)	£600
1989/90	
Net chargeable gains	2,450
Losses brought forward	—
Taxable amount (covered by annual exemption)	£2,450
CGT	Nil
Losses carried forward	£600

	£
1990/91	
Net chargeable gains	5,000
Losses brought forward	600
Taxable amount	£4,400
CGT at 25% on £(4,400 − 2,500)	£475
Losses carried forward	Nil

Notes

(a) If the trust had been an accumulation or discretionary settlement (within the meaning of *FA 1988, s 100(2)*), the rate of tax applicable to the net gain of £1,900 for 1990/91 would have been 35%, giving a liability of £665. [*FA 1988, s 100(1)*].

(b) If the settlor had an interest in the settlement (as defined by *FA 1988, 10 Sch 2*) at any time during 1990/91, the gain of £4,400 (after deducting losses but before deducting the annual exemption) would be chargeable on the settlor and not on the trustees. His own annual exemption of £5,000 could be set against the gain, if not used against his own gains. Any tax payable may be recovered from the trustees. See also 222.2 below. [*FA 1988, s 109, 10 Sch*].

222.2 **SETTLEMENT IN WHICH SETTLOR HAS AN INTEREST** [*FA 1988, s 109, 10 Sch*]

In 1989, Henry, a UK resident, settled £25,000 on trust to his wife for her life with the remainder to his adult daughter absolutely. The trustees are resident in the UK. For 1989/90, the trustees make disposals on which they incur losses of £200. For 1990/91, they realise gains of £2,900 and losses of £700. Henry has personal gains of £4,000 for 1990/91 with no losses brought forward. Henry's taxable income for 1990/91 is £30,000 and he is therefore liable to tax at 40%.

Henry's capital gains tax liability for 1990/91 is calculated as follows

		£	£
Personal gains			4,000
Settlement gains		2,900	
Deduct Losses		700	
		2,200	
Deduct Losses b/f		200	2,000
			6,000
Deduct Annual exemption			5,000
Gain liable to CGT			£1,000
CGT payable at 40%			£400.00
CGT recoverable from trustees	note (a)		£400.00

Notes

(a)   The settlement gains are regarded as forming the highest part of the total amount on which Henry is liable to CGT. His personal gains are therefore fully covered by the annual exemption and the whole of the liability relates to the settlement gains; it is thus fully recoverable from the trustees. [*FA 1988, 10 Sch 5*].

(b)   If either Henry or his wife died during 1990/91, or if they ceased to be married during that year, the *Finance Act 1988* provisions would not apply and the settlement gain of £2,200 (before deducting losses brought forward) would be covered by the trustees' annual exemption of £2,500, with losses of £200 carried forward to 1991/92. [*FA 1988, 10 Sch 3*].

222.3   **CREATION OF A SETTLEMENT** [*CGTA 1979, s 53; FA 1981, s 86*]

(A)

In December 1990, C transfers to trustees of a settlement for the benefit of his children 10,000 shares in W plc, a quoted company. The value of the gift is £80,000. C bought the shares in 1978 for £20,000 and their value at 31 March 1982 was £35,000. The indexation factor for March 1982 to December 1990 is assumed to be 0.676.

	£	£
Deemed disposal consideration	80,000	80,000
Cost	20,000	
Market value 31.3.82		35,000
Unindexed gain	60,000	45,000
Indexation allowance £35,000 × 0.676	23,660	23,660
Gain after indexation	£36,340	£21,340
Chargeable gain		£21,340
Trustees' allowable cost		£80,000

Note

(a)   If the transfer is a chargeable lifetime transfer for inheritance tax purposes, or would be one but for the annual inheritance tax exemption, C may elect under *CGTA 1979, s 147A* (inserted by *FA 1989, 14 Sch 4*) to roll the gain over against the trustees' base cost of the shares. The trustees do not join in any such election.

(B)

In March 1991 H settles farmland on trust for himself for life, with interests in reversion to his children. The land cost £20,000 in 1969 and its agreed values are £60,000 at 31 March 1982 and £120,000 at the date of transfer. H's interest in possession in the settled property is valued at £90,000. The indexation factor from March 1982 to the date of disposal is assumed to be 0.719.

The chargeable gain is computed as follows

	£	£
Deemed disposal proceeds	120,000	120,000
Cost	20,000	
Market value 31.3.82		60,000
Unindexed gain	100,000	60,000
Indexation allowance £60,000 × 0.719	43,140	43,140
Gain after indexation	£56,860	£16,860
Chargeable gain		£16,860

Notes

(a) The value of H's interest in the settled property is ignored and the transfer is not treated as a part disposal.

(b) For as long as H has an interest in the settlement the provisions of *FA 1988, s 109, 10 Sch* will apply to any settlement gains, with the effect that they will be chargeable on the settlor and not on the trustees. See 222.2 above.

222.4 **PERSON BECOMING ABSOLUTELY ENTITLED TO SETTLED PROPERTY**
[*CGTA 1979, s 54*]
(A)

M is a beneficiary entitled to an interest in possession in settled property, under a settlement made by her mother. The trustees exercise a power of appointment to advance capital to M, and transfer to her a house valued at £80,000. The house was acquired by the trustees by gift from the settlor in 1983, when its value was £45,000. No election was made to roll over the settlor's gain against the trustees' base cost.

The trustees realise an unindexed gain of £35,000 (£80,000 – £45,000) on the advancement of capital to M.

Notes

(a) An indexation allowance is available to the trustees and will be based on their deemed acquisition cost of £45,000.

(b) If the house had previously been occupied by M as her private residence with the permission of the trustees, then all or part of the gain would be exempt under *CGTA 1979, s 104*.

(B)

F, who is a beneficiary under a discretionary settlement, realises chargeable gains of £40,000 on share transactions in May 1990. In June 1990, the trustees exercise a discretion to advance capital to F and do so by transferring to him ordinary shares purchased for £50,000. The shares have a value of £30,000 at the date of transfer. The trustees have no chargeable gains for 1990/91.

The consequences are

(i) The shares cease to be settled property, and the trustees realise an allowable loss, subject to indexation, of £20,000 (£50,000 – £30,000).

(ii) The loss, subject to indexation, is then available to F to set off against his chargeable gain of £40,000 in 1990/91.

222.5 **TERMINATION OF LIFE INTEREST ON DEATH** [*CGTA 1979, s 55*]

(A)

K is entitled to an interest in possession under a settlement. The settled property consists of shares and cash. On K's death, L takes a life interest in succession to K. K dies on 1 December 1990, when the shares are valued at £200,000. The trustees' allowable cost in respect of the shares is £40,000.

On K's death, the trustees are deemed to have disposed of and immediately reacquired the shares for £200,000, thus uplifting the CGT base cost, but no chargeable gain then arises.

(B)

In 1967, E created a settlement for the benefit of his children M and N, then aged 10 and 12, transferring an investment property valued at £10,000 to the trustees. The terms of the settlement were that M and N should each become entitled to an interest in possession in a half share of the trust's income at age 25, with capital vesting in equal shares at age 40. In 1982, N assigned his interest to an unrelated party for £35,000, its then market value. In 1990, N dies and the interest terminates. The value of a half share of the property is then £65,000.

On N's death, the life interest terminates. There is no effect on the trustees as N was no longer the person entitled to the life interest within the meaning of *CGTA 1979, s 55*.

Notes

(a)   No chargeable gain arises on the disposal by N of his interest. [*CGTA 1979, s 58*].

(b)   The third party may claim an allowable loss on extinction of the interest. For an example of the computation if the interest is a wasting asset, see WASTING ASSETS 225.3 below.

223 Shares and Securities

Cross-references. See also 203 ASSETS HELD ON 6 APRIL 1965, 204 ASSETS HELD ON 31 MARCH 1982, 209 INDEXATION and 219 QUALIFYING CORPORATE BONDS.

223.1 REORGANISATION OF SHARE CAPITAL — VALUATION OF DIFFERENT CLASSES OF SHARE ON SUBSEQUENT DISPOSAL [*CGTA 1979, ss 77–81*]

(A) Unquoted shares — reorganisation on or before 31 March 1982

W has since 1968 owned shares in L Ltd, an unquoted trading company. W subscribed for 5,000 £1 ordinary shares at par, and has not made any disposals. In November 1980, L Ltd offered ordinary shareholders two 7% preference shares for each five ordinary shares held. The full price payable was £1 for each preference share, on allotment. W took up his entitlement, paying £2,000 for his 2,000 preference shares. In July 1990, W sells his preference shares at £1.08 each (total £2,160) to another shareholder. The sale price is the full market value. The value of W's ordinary shares at that time is £4 (total £20,000).

The total values of the ordinary and preference shares at 31.3.82 were £10,000 and £2,100 respectively and the indexation factor for the period March 1982 to July 1990 is assumed to be 0.608.

The calculation, without re-basing to 1982, is

	£
Disposal consideration	2,160

$$\text{Cost} \ (£5,000 + £2,000) \times \frac{2,160}{2,160 + 20,000}$$

	£
	682
Unindexed gain	1,478
Indexation allowance £2,100 × 0.608	1,277
Gain after indexation	£201

The calculation, with re-basing to 1982, is

	£
Disposal consideration	2,160
Market value 31.3.82	2,100
Unindexed gain	60
Indexation allowance (as above)	1,277
Loss after indexation	£1,217
Chargeable gain/(allowable loss)	Nil

As one calculation produces a gain and the other a loss, the transaction is treated as giving rise to no gain and no loss. [*FA 1988, s 96*].

Notes

(a)   On a subsequent disposal of the ordinary shares, the allowable cost would be £6,318 (£5,000 + £2,000 − £682) or, if re-basing applied, £10,000. In either case, indexation would be based on £10,000.

(*b*)   If an irrevocable election under *FA 1988, s 96(5)* were made for all assets to be treated as disposed of and reacquired at their market value on 31 March 1982, the loss of £1,217 would be allowable. However, as the election must extend to, broadly speaking, all assets held at 31 March 1982, it should not be made unless likely to prove beneficial overall.

(*c*)   The above is one interpretation of how the re-basing rules would apply to a reorganisation before 31 March 1982. The *Finance Act 1988* provisions do not deal with this subject. This interpretation takes the view that, as there is a deemed disposal and reacquisition on 31 March 1982 for re-basing purposes, the assets deemed to have been reacquired are separate assets and no longer have to be treated as a single asset; there is therefore no need for any apportionment. One alternative treatment would be to apportion the 31.3.82 values of ordinary and preference shares as follows:

$$(£2,100 + £10,000) \times \frac{2,160}{2,160 + 20,000} = £1,179$$

This, however, seems the less logical approach and is not beneficial to the taxpayer in this example, although it may be beneficial in some cases.

(B) Unquoted shares — reorganisation after 31 March 1982
Assume the facts to be as in (A) above except that the reorganisation took place in November 1982 rather than in 1980. The indexation factor for the period November 1982 to July 1990 is assumed to be 0.544.

The calculation, without re-basing to 1982, is

	£
Disposal consideration	2,160

	£
Cost (£5,000 + £2,000) × $\dfrac{2,160}{2,160 + 20,000}$	682
Unindexed gain	1,478
Indexation allowance (see below)	699
Gain after indexation	£779

The calculation, with re-basing to 1982, is

	£
Disposal consideration	2,160

	£
(31.3.82 value £10,000 + cost £2,000) × $\dfrac{2,160}{2,160 + 20,000}$	1,170
Gain before indexation	990

Indexation allowance $\dfrac{10,000}{12,000} \times £1,170 \times 0.608 = £593$

$\dfrac{2,000}{12,000} \times £1,170 \times 0.544 = 106$

	699
Gain after indexation	£291
Chargeable gain	£291

CGT 223.1 Shares and Securities

Notes

(a) On a subsequent disposal of the ordinary shares, their cost would be £6,318 (£5,000 + £2,000 − £682) or, if re-basing applied, £10,830 (£10,000 + £2,000 − £1,170). In either case, indexation would be based on £10,830.

(b) If the original holding was itself acquired after 31 March 1982, there would be no question of re-basing.

(C) Quoted shares — reorganisation on or before 31 March 1982

Assume the shares held by W in (A) above were all quoted shares. On the first day of dealing after the reorganisation the ordinary shares were quoted at £1.50 (total £7,500) and the preference shares at £1.02 (total £2,040). The calculation on the disposal of the preference shares is as follows

The calculation, without re-basing to 1982, is

	£
Disposal consideration	2,160

$$\text{Cost } (\pounds5,000 + \pounds2,000) \times \frac{2,040}{2,040 + 7,500} \qquad 1,497$$

Unindexed gain	663
Indexation allowance £2,100 × 0.608	1,277
Loss after indexation	£614

The calculation, with re-basing to 1982, is

	£
Disposal consideration	2,160
Market value 31.3.82	2,100
Unindexed gain	60
Indexation allowance (as above)	1,277
Loss after indexation	£1,217
Allowable loss	£614

Re-basing does not apply (in the absence of an election under *FA 1988, s 96(5)*) as it cannot be used to increase a loss. [*FA 1988, s 96*].

Notes

(a) On a subsequent disposal of the ordinary shares, the allowable cost would be £5,503 (£5,000 + £2,000 − £1,497) or, if re-basing applied, £10,000. In either case, indexation would be based on £10,000.

(b) See note (c) to (A) above, which applies to this example with the substitution, for the fraction therein quoted, of the fraction:

$$\frac{2,040}{2,040 + 7,500}$$

(D) Quoted shares — reorganisation after 31 March 1982
If the facts were as in (C) above, except that the reorganisation took place after 31 March 1982, the calculation would proceed along the same lines as (B) above, but substituting the fraction used in (C) for that used in (B).

If the original holding was itself acquired after 31 March 1982, there would be no question of re-basing.

(E) Shares held at 6.4.65
F purchased 20,000 T plc ordinary shares (which are quoted on the Stock Exchange) on 1 January 1964 for £15,000.
The value of the shares on 6 April 1965 was 80p per share. F sold 2,000 of the shares on 1 August 1968, having elected for pooling of shares other than fixed interest preference shares. On 1 August 1979, T plc made a rights issue of one 6% £1 preference share for every two ordinary shares, the full price of £1 being payable on allotment. F took up his entitlement of 9,000 shares, paying £9,000. On the first business day after the rights issue, ordinary shares in T plc had a market value of £2.30, and the value of preference shares was 94p. In March 1991, F sold the preference shares for £1.90 per share. The indexation factor for March 1982 to March 1991 is assumed to be 0.719. The preference shares and ordinary shares were quoted at 95p and £2.40 respectively on 31.3.82.

The calculation, without re-basing to 1982, is

	£
Disposal consideration (9,000 at £1.90)	17,100
Allowable cost (6.4.65 value)	

$$[(18,000 \times £0.80) + £9,000] \times \frac{9,000 \times 0.94}{(9,000 \times 0.94) + (18,000 \times 2.30)} \qquad 3,970$$

	£
Unindexed gain	13,130
Indexation allowance £(9,000 × £0.95) × 0.719	6,147
Gain after indexation	£6,983

The calculation, with re-basing to 1982, is

	£
Disposal consideration	17,100
Market value at 31.3.82 (9,000 at 95p)	8,550
Unindexed gain	8,550
Indexation allowance (as above)	6,147
Gain after indexation	£2,403
Chargeable gain	£2,403

Note
(a)   As regards the second calculation, see also (note (c) to (A) above.

(F) Shares held at 6.4.65: effect of election for pooling at 1965 value

W purchased 1,000 £1 ordinary shares in N plc, a quoted company, in 1962. The cost was £3,000. The shares had a market value on 5 April 1965 of £3.20 per share. In 1966, he purchased a further 2,000 ordinary shares in N plc for £2.50 per share, and in 1968 he bought 2,000 3% convertible preference shares in the company for 98p per share. In 1977, N plc made a rights issue of 3% convertible preference shares to ordinary shareholders, on the basis of 1 preference share per two ordinary shares, at a price of £1.01. On the first dealing day after the reorganisation, N plc ordinary shares were quoted at £5.50 and preference shares at £1.03. In September 1990, W sold 1,500 preference shares for £1,200. He had already made an election to pool pre-7.4.65 fixed interest securities on another disposal. The indexation factor for March 1982 to September 1990 is assumed to be 0.636. The preference shares and ordinary shares were quoted at 96p and £6.50 respectively on 31.3.82.

The calculation, without re-basing to 1982, is

(i)   The 1,000 ordinary shares purchased in 1962 are linked with 500 preference shares acquired on the rights issue. The allowable cost (6 April 1965 value) of these 500 preference shares is therefore computed as follows

$$[(1{,}000 \times £3.20) + (500 \times £1.01)] \times \frac{500 \times 1.03}{(500 \times 1.03) + (1{,}000 \times 5.50)} \qquad £317$$

(ii) The 2,000 ordinary shares purchased in 1966 are linked with 1,000 preference shares acquired on the rights issue. The allowable cost of these 1,000 preference shares is computed as follows

$$[(2{,}000 \times £2.50) + (1{,}000 \times £1.01)] \times \frac{1{,}000 \times 1.03}{(1{,}000 \times 1.03) + (2{,}000 \times 5.50)} \qquad £515$$

(iii) The 2,000 preference shares purchased in 1968 have an allowable cost of £1,960

The chargeable gain on the disposal of preference shares is calculated as follows

	£
Disposal consideration	1,200
Allowable cost (£317 + £515 + £1,960) × $\frac{1{,}500}{3{,}500}$	1,197
Unindexed gain	3
Indexation allowance £(1,500 × 0.96) × 0.636	916
Loss after indexation	£913

The calculation, with re-basing to 1982, is

The chargeable gain on the disposal of preference shares is calculated as follows

	£
Disposal consideration	1,200
Market value 31.3.82 (3,500 × 0.96) × $\frac{1{,}500}{3{,}500}$	1,440
Unindexed loss	240
Indexation allowance (as above)	916
Loss after indexation	£1,156

The outcome is

Allowable loss   £913

Notes

(a)   The preference shares are pooled as a result of the 1965 election even though the original ordinary shares are not so pooled. [*CGTA 1979, 5 Sch 6*].

(b)   As regards the re-basing calculation, see also note (c) to (A) above.

223.2 BONUS ISSUES [*CGTA 1979, ss 77–79, 81*]

(A) Bonus of same class

In October 1985, Y plc makes a scrip issue of one ordinary share for every 10 held. L holds 5,000 ordinary shares, which he acquired in May 1982 for £6,000, and therefore receives 500 shares in the bonus issue. In October 1990, L sells 3,000 of his shares for £4,500.

Indexation factors   May 1982 to April 1985 (actual)   0.161
                     April 1985 to October 1990 (assumed)   0.381

New holding	Shares	Qualifying expenditure £	Indexed pool £
May 1982 acquisition	5,000	6,000	6,000
Indexed rise: May 1982 – April 1985			
£6,000 × 0.161			966
Pool at 6.4.85	5,000	6,000	6,966
October 1985 bonus issue	500		
Indexed rise: April 1985 – October 1990			
£6,966 × 0.381			2,654
	5,500	6,000	9,620
October 1990 disposal	(3,000)	(3,273)	(5,247)
Pool carried forward	2,500	£2,727	£4,373

Calculation of chargeable gain	£
Disposal consideration	4,500
Allowable cost $\dfrac{3,000}{5,500} \times £6,000$	3,273
Unindexed gain	1,227

Indexation allowance

$$\frac{3,000}{5,500} \times £9,620 = £5,247$$

£5,247 – £3,273	1,974
Allowable loss	£747

Note

(a)   If the original shares had been held on 31 March 1982 with a value of, say, £6,500 on that date, the allowable cost of the 3,000 shares sold, applying the re-basing provisions of *FA 1988, s 96*, would be

$$\frac{3,000}{5,500} \times £6,500 = £3,545$$

Re-basing could not, however, increase the allowable loss, unless an election under *FA 1988, s 96(5)* were made.

(B) Bonus of different class

After 5 April 1982 and before 6 April 1985, R bought 2,000 'A' shares in T plc for £3,800. The value of the indexed pool immediately before 6 April 1985 was £4,460. In June 1985 R bought a further 500 'A' shares for £800. In October 1985 T plc made a bonus issue of 2 'B' shares for each 5 'A' shares held, and R received 1,000 'B' shares, valued at £1.20 each (total value £1,200) on the first dealing day after the issue. On the same day the 'A' shares were quoted at £2 each (total value £5,000). In December 1990 R sells his 1,000 'B' shares for £1,500.

Indexation factors		
April 1985 to June 1985 (actual)		0.007
June 1985 to October 1985 (actual)		0.002
October 1985 to December 1990 (assumed)		0.392

New holding – 'A' shares

	Shares	Qualifying expenditure £	Indexed pool £
Pool at 6.4.85	2,000	3,800	4,460
Indexed rise: April 1985 to June 1985			
£4,460 × 0.007			31
June 1985 acquisition	500	800	800
	2,500	4,600	5,291
Indexed rise: June 1985 to October 1985			
£5,291 × 0.002			11
	2,500	4,600	5,302
October 1985 bonus issue of 'B' shares: transfer proportion of expenditure and indexed pool to 'B' shares (see notes)		(890)	(1,026)
Pool of 'A' shares carried forward	2,500	£3,710	£4,276

New holding – 'B' shares

	Shares	Qualifying expenditure £	Indexed pool £
October 1985 bonus issue: proportion of pools transferred from 'A' shares holding	1,000	890	1,026
Indexed rise: October 1985 to December 1990			
£1,026 × 0.392			402
	1,000	890	1,428
December 1990 disposal	1,000	890	1,428
	—	—	—

Calculation of chargeable gain on disposal of 'B' shares	£
Disposal consideration	1,500
Allowable cost (as allocated)	890
Unindexed gain	610
Indexation allowance £1,428 − £890	538
Chargeable gain	£72

Notes

(a)   The interaction between the reorganisation rules and the *FA 1985* indexation rules is not clear, but it is understood that the above and the note below are in accordance with the present view of the Inland Revenue.

(b)   The bonus issue of the 'B' shares results in a decrease in the expenditure attributable to the 'A' shares and is thus understood to be an operative event within the meaning of *FA 1985, 19 Sch 13*. Although *CGTA 1979, s 78* specifies that the 'A' and 'B' shares are to be regarded as a single asset, the 'B' shares cannot be part of the same 'new holding' as the 'A' shares as only shares of the same class can form a 'new holding'. [*FA 1985, 19 Sch 6*]. The proportion of the indexed pool allocated to the 'B' shares is determined in the same way as qualifying expenditure.

$$\text{Proportion of qualifying expenditure } £4,600 \times \frac{1,200}{1,200 + 5,000} \qquad £890$$

$$\text{Proportion of indexed pool } £5,302 \times \frac{1,200}{1,200 + 5,000} \qquad £1,026$$

(c)   See also 223.1(A)–(D) above for reorganisations affecting shares held on 31 March 1982. If, in this example, the 'B' shares had been issued before 31.3.82 and held on that date, their full market value at that date would appear to be deductible on a disposal after 5.4.88 to which the re-basing rules of *FA 1988, s 96* applied.

(C) Pre-6 April 1965 holdings

L plc is a company whose shares have been quoted since 1955. In 1960, C purchased 5,000 £1 ordinary shares at a total cost of £6,300. On 6 April 1965, the shares had a market value of £1.10 per share. In 1969, the company made a bonus issue of three 3% preference shares for every 20 ordinary shares held. C received 750 preference shares, which were also quoted. The market values of the ordinary and preference shares on the first day of dealing after the bonus issue were £1.40 and 95p respectively. In December 1990, C sells 2,000 of the ordinary shares for £18,000. The indexation factor for March 1982 to December 1990 is assumed to be 0.676. The ordinary shares and preference shares were quoted at £2.75 and £1.50 respectively on 31.3.82.

(i) 6.4.65 value of ordinary shares, as adjusted for scrip issue

$$£1.10 \times 5,000 \times \frac{5,000 \times £1.40}{(5,000 \times £1.40) + (750 \times £0.95)} \qquad £4,992$$

(ii) Historic cost of ordinary shares, as adjusted

$$£6,300 \times \frac{5,000 \times £1.40}{(5,000 \times £1.40) + (750 \times £0.95)} \qquad \underline{£5,718}$$

(iii) 31.3.82 value of ordinary shares

$$£2.75 \times 5,000 \qquad \underline{£13,750}$$

The chargeable gain is

	£	£	£
Disposal consideration	18,000	18,000	18,00
Market value 6.4.65 $\frac{2,000}{5,000} \times £4,992$	1,997		
Cost $\frac{2,000}{5,000} \times £5,718$		2,287	
Market value 31.3.82 $\frac{2,000}{5,000} \times £13,750$			5,50
Unindexed gain	16,003	15,713	12,50
Indexation allowance £5,500 × 0.676	3,718	3,718	3,71
Gain after indexation	£12,285	£11,995	£8,78
Chargeable gain			£8,78

Note

(*a*)   The allowable costs of the preference shares (which are deemed to have bee acquired with the ordinary shares in 1960) are

(i)	6.4.65 value (£5,500 − £4,992)	£508
(ii)	Historic cost (£6,300 − £5,718)	£582
(iii)	31.3.82 value (750 × £1.50)	£1,125

223.3 **RIGHTS ISSUES** [*CGTA 1979, ss 35, 73(1), 79(3), 80*]
(A) Rights issue of same class
W plc is a quoted company which in June 1985 makes a rights issue of one £1 ordinary share for every eight £1 ordinary shares held, at £1.35 payable on allotment. V, who holds 16,000 £1 ordinary shares purchased in May 1982 for £15,000, takes up his entitlement in full, and is allotted 2,000 shares. In December 1990, he sells 6,000 of his shares for £10,000.

Indexation factors		
May 1982 to April 1985 (actual)		0.161
April 1985 to June 1985 (actual)		0.007
June 1985 to December 1990 (assumed)		0.395

New holding	Shares	Qualifying expenditure £	Indexed pool £
May 1982 acquisition	16,000	15,000	15,000
Indexed rise: May 1982 – April 1985 £15,000 × 0.161			2,415
Pool at 6.4.85	16,000	15,000	17,415
Indexed rise: April 1985 – June 1985 £17,415 × 0.007			122
June 1985 rights issue	2,000	2,700	2,700
	18,000	17,700	20,237
Indexed rise: June 1985 – December 1990 £20,237 × 0.395			7,994
			28,231
December 1990 disposal	(6,000)	(5,900)	(9,410)
Pool carried forward	12,000	£11,800	£18,821

Calculation of chargeable gain	£
Disposal consideration	10,000
Allowable cost $\dfrac{6,000}{18,000} \times £17,700$	5,900
Unindexed gain	4,100
Indexation allowance	
$\dfrac{6,000}{18,000} \times £28,231 = £9,410$	
£9,410 − £5,900	3,510
Chargeable gain	£590

(B) Rights issue of different class
At 6.4.85, A's 'new holding' of 6,000 quoted £1 ordinary shares in S plc has a pool of expenditure of £7,800 and an indexed pool of £9,200. In October 1985, S plc made a rights issue of one 50p 'B' share for every five £1 ordinary shares held, at 60p payable in full on application. A took up his entitlement in full, acquiring 1,200 'B' shares. On the first dealing day after issue, the 'B' shares were quoted at 65p and the £1 ordinary shares at £1.50. A sells his 'B' shares in March 1991 for £840.

| Indexation factors | April 1985 to October 1985 (actual) | 0.009 |
| | October 1985 to March 1991 (assumed) | 0.428 |

New holding — ordinary shares

	Shares	Qualifying expenditure £	Indexed pool £
Pool at 6.4.85	6,000	7,800	9,200
Indexed rise: April 1985 to October 1985 £9,200 × 0.009			83
October 1985 rights issue of 'B' shares	—	720	720
	6,000	8,520	10,003
Transfer proportion of expenditure and indexed pool to 'B' shares note (b)		(680)	(798)
Pool of ordinary shares carried forward	6,000	£7,840	£9,205

New holding—'B' shares

	Shares	Qualifying expenditure	Indexed pool
October 1985 rights issue: proportion of pools transferred from ordinary shares holding	1,200	680	798
Indexed rise: October 1985 to March 1991 £798 × 0.428			341
	1,200	680	1,139
March 1991 disposal	(1,200)	(680)	(1,139)
	—	—	—

Calculation of chargeable gain on disposal of 'B' shares

	£
Disposal consideration	840
Allowable cost (as allocated)	680
Unindexed gain	160
Indexation allowance £1,139 − £680	459
Allowable loss	£299

Notes

(a)   The interaction between the reorganisation rules and the *FA 1985* indexation rules is not clear, but it is understood that the above and the note below are in accordance with the present view of the Inland Revenue.

(b)   The rights issue is an operative event within the meaning of *FA 1985, 19 Sch 13* and results in a decrease in the expenditure attributable to the ordinary shares. Although *CGTA 1979, s 78* specifies that the ordinary shares and the 'B' shares are to be regarded as a single asset, the 'B' shares cannot be part of the same 'new holding' as the ordinary shares as only shares of the same class can form a 'new holding'. [*FA 1985, 19 Sch 6*]. The proportion of the indexed pool allocated to the 'B' shares is determined in the same way as qualifying expenditure.

Proportion of qualifying expenditure

$$£8,520 \times \frac{1,200 \times 0.65}{(1,200 \times 0.65) + (6,000 \times 1.50)} \qquad £680$$

Proportion of indexed pool

$$£10,003 \times \frac{1,200 \times 0.65}{(1,200 \times 0.65) + (6,000 \times 1.50)} \qquad \text{£798}$$

(C) Rights issue of same class: disposal out of new holding and 1982 holding
G holds 75,000 25p ordinary shares in C plc, acquired as follows

Date	Number of shares acquired	Cost £
22.5.80	20,000	0.80
5.11.83	15,000	1.10
14.9.84	40,000	1.00

In May 1985, C made a rights issue of one ordinary share for every five held, at 95p payable in full on application. G took up his rights in full (15,000 ordinary shares). He sells 80,000 shares in December 1990 for £2.40 per share. The shares were quoted at 90p on 31.3.82.

Indexation factors		
March 1982 to December 1990 (assumed)	0.676
November 1983 to April 1985 (actual)	0.094
September 1984 to April 1985 (actual)	0.052
April 1985 to May 1985 (actual)	0.005
May 1985 to December 1990 (assumed)	0.398

New holding	Shares	Qualifying expenditure £	Indexed pool £
5.11.83 acquisition	15,000	16,500	16,500
Indexed rise: November 1983 to April 1985			
£16,500 × 0.094			1,551
14.9.84 acquisition	40,000	40,000	40,000
Indexed rise: September 1984 to April 1985			
£40,000 × 0.052			2,080
Pool at 6.4.85	55,000	56,500	60,131
Indexed rise: April 1985 to May 1985			
£60,131 × 0.005			301
May 1985 rights issue	11,000	10,450	10,450
	66,000	66,950	70,882
Indexed rise: May 1985 to December 1990			
£70,882 × 0.398			28,211
	66,000	66,950	99,093
December 1990 disposal	(66,000)	(66,950)	(99,093)
	—	—	—

1982 holding

	Shares	Cost £	Market value 31.3.82 £
22.5.80 acquisition	20,000	16,000	18,000
May 1985 rights issue	4,000	3,800	3,800
	24,000	19,800	21,800
December 1990 disposal	(14,000)	(11,550)	(12,717
Pool carried forward	10,000	£8,250	£9,083

Calculation of chargeable gain £
(i) Identify 66,000 shares sold with new holding
Disposal consideration 66,000 × £2.40 | 158,40
Allowable cost | 66,95
Unindexed gain | 91,45
Indexation allowance £99,093 − £66,950 | 32,14
Chargeable gain | £59,30

(ii) Identify 14,000 shares with 1982 holding

Without re-basing to 1982

£
Disposal consideration 14,000 × £2.40 | 33,60

Cost $\dfrac{14,000}{24,000} \times £19,800$ | 11,55

Unindexed gain | 22,05
Indexation allowance (see below) | 7,98
Gain after indexation | £14,07

With re-basing to 1982

£
Disposal consideration | 33,60

Allowable expenditure $\dfrac{14,000}{24,000} \times £21,800$ | 12,71

Unindexed gain | 20,88
Indexation allowance

$£12,717 \times \dfrac{18,000}{21,800} \times 0.676$ | £7,098

$£12,717 \times \dfrac{3,800}{21,800} \times 0.398$ | 882

| | 7,98

Gain after indexation | £12,90

Chargeable gain | £12,90

Total chargeable gain £59,307 + £12,903 | £72,21

400

Note

(a)   The 1982 holding cannot be increased by an 'acquisition', but can be increased by a rights issue as this is not treated as involving an acquisition. [*CGTA 1979, s 79; FA 1985, 19 Sch 7*].

223.4   COMPANY AMALGAMATIONS [*CGTA 1979, ss 85, 87, 88*]

(A) Takeover by quoted company

S was a shareholder in N Ltd, an unquoted company. He subscribed for his 10,000 50p ordinary shares at 60p per share in 1975 and the shares were valued at £3 each at 31.3.82. In July 1984, the shareholders accepted an offer by a public company M plc for their shares. Each ordinary shareholder received one £1 ordinary M plc share plus 25p cash for every two N Ltd shares held. S acquired 5,000 M plc shares and received cash of £1,250. The M plc shares were valued at £6 each at the time of the acquisition. In March 1991, S sells 2,000 of the M shares for £27,000.

Indexation factors   March 1982 to July 1984 (actual)   0.122
                                   March 1982 to March 1991 (assumed)   0.719

(i) On the merger in 1984/85, S makes a disposal only to the extent that he receives cash

	£
Disposal consideration	1,250
Allowable cost $\dfrac{1,250}{1,250 + 30,000} \times £6,000$	240
Gross gain	1,010
Indexation allowance £240 × 0.122	29
Chargeable gain	£981

Note

(a)   Alternatively, S could elect to have the consideration deducted from his allowable cost, as the amount received is less than 5% of the total value of his shares.

(ii) The chargeable gain on disposal in 1990/91 is

Without re-basing to 1982

	£
Consideration for disposal of M plc shares	27,000
Allowable cost $(6,000 - 240) \times \dfrac{2,000}{5,000}$	2,304
Unindexed gain	24,696
Indexation allowance (see below)	8,283
Gain after indexation	£16,413

With re-basing to 1982

	£
Disposal consideration (as above)	27,000

Market value 31.3.82

$$£30,000 \times \frac{30,000}{30,000 + 1,250} \times \frac{2,000}{5,000} \qquad 11,520$$

Unindexed gain	15,480
Indexation allowance £11,520 × 0.719	8,283
Gain after indexation	£7,197

Chargeable gain	£7,197

Notes

(a) An asset acquired after 31 March 1982 the value of which derived from an asset held on that date is deemed to have been held on 31 March 1982 for the purpose of the re-basing provisions. [*FA 1988, 8 Sch 5*].

(b) Where there has been a part disposal after 31 March 1982 and before 6 April 1988 of an asset held on the earlier of those dates, and this is followed by a disposal after 5 April 1988 to which re-basing applies, the re-basing rules are deemed to have applied to the part disposal. [*FA 1988, 8 Sch 4*].

(B) Takeover by unquoted company
Y Ltd, a small unquoted company, is taken over in June 1985 by another unquoted company, C Ltd. The terms of the acquisition are that holders of £1 ordinary shares in Y Ltd receive ten £1 ordinary shares and five £1 deferred shares in C Ltd per ten ordinary shares held.
B acquired his holding of 500 Y Ltd shares on the death of his wife in May 1982, at probate value of £10,000. In January 1991, B sells his 2,500 C Ltd deferred shares for £4,500. The value of the C Ltd ordinary shares he holds is then £25,000. The indexation factor for May 1982 to January 1991 is assumed to be 0.645.

	£
Disposal consideration	4,500

$$\text{Allowable cost } \frac{4,500}{4,500 + 25,000} \times £10,000 \qquad 1,525$$

Unindexed gain	2,975
Indexation allowance £1,525 × 0.645	984
Chargeable gain	£1,991

The allowable cost of the C Ltd ordinary shares is (£10,000 − £1,525)	£8,475

(C) Takeover before 1 April 1982
S was the sole shareholder in R Ltd. (One share is held by a nominee for S.) He subscribed for 5,000 £1 ordinary shares at par in 1967. In July 1981, he accepted an offer for his shares from N plc, a substantial quoted public group. The terms accepted by S were that he would receive one ordinary and five 10% preference shares in N plc for each of his shares in R Ltd. On the first day after the takeover on which the shares are dealt in, N ordinary shares have a market value of £8.50 and the value of the preference shares is £1.02, a value maintained at 31.3.82. In September 1990, S sold 10,000 of the preference shares for 99p a share. The indexation allowance for March 1982 to September 1990 is assumed to be 0.636.

(i) Allowable cost of N plc ordinary shares (assuming no re-basing to 1982)

$$£5,000 \times \frac{5,000 \times £8.50}{(5,000 \times £8.50) + (25,000 \times £1.02)} \qquad £3,125$$

(ii) Allowable cost of N plc preference shares (assuming no re-basing to 1982)

£5,000 − £3,125   £1,875

(iii) Calculation without re-basing to 1982

	£
Disposal consideration	9,900
Allowable cost $\frac{10,000}{25,000} \times £1,875$	750
Unindexed gain	9,150
Indexation allowance $10,000 \times £1.02 \times 0.636$	6,487
Gain after indexation	£2,663

(iv) Calculation with re-basing to 1982

	£
Disposal consideration	9,900
Market value 31.3.82 $\frac{10,000}{25,000} \times (25,000 \times £1.02)$	10,200
Unindexed loss	300
Indexation allowance £10,200 × 0.636	6,487
Loss after indexation	£6,787

(v) Outcome
Chargeable gain/(allowable loss)   Nil

As one calculation produces a gain and the other a loss, the transaction is treated, in the absence of an election under *FA 1988, s 96(5)*, as producing no gain and no loss. [*FA 1988, s 96*].

Note
(*a*)   See also 223.1(A) (note (*c*)) above.

(D) Takeover involving issue of qualifying corporate bond
See 219.2 QUALIFYING CORPORATE BONDS for example.

(E) Earn-outs
K owns 10,000 ordinary shares in M Ltd, which he acquired for £12,000 i
December 1987. In July 1990, the whole of the issued share capital of M Ltd wa
acquired by P plc. Under the terms of the takeover, K receives £2 per share plus th
right to further consideration up to a maximum of £1.50 per share depending o
future profit performance. The initial consideration is receivable in cash, but th
deferred consideration is to be satisfied by the issue of shares in P plc. In Decembe
1991, K duly receives 2,000 ordinary shares valued at £6 per share in full settleme
of his entitlement. The right to future consideration is valued at £1.40 per share i
July 1990. The indexation factor for the period December 1987 to July 1990
assumed to be 0.236 and that for the period July 1990 to December 1991 assumed t
be 0.151.

**Without a claim by K under Inland Revenue extra-statutory concession D27 th
position would be**

1990/91

	£	£
Disposal proceeds 10,000 × £2	20,000	
Value of rights 10,000 × £1.40	14,000	34,000
Cost	12,000	
Indexation allowance		
£12,000 × 0.236	2,832	14,832
Chargeable gain		£19,168

1991/92

	£
Disposal of rights to deferred consideration	
Proceeds 2,000 PQR shares @ £6	12,000
Deemed cost of acquiring rights	14,000
Unindexed loss	2,000
Indexation allowance £14,000 × 0.151	2,114
Allowable loss	£4,114
Cost for CGT purposes of 2,000 PQR shares	£12,000

On a claim under extra-statutory concession D27, the position would be

1990/91

	£
Proceeds (cash) (as above)	20,000
Cost £12,000 × $\dfrac{20,000}{20,000 + 14,000}$	7,059
Unindexed gain	12,941
Indexation allowance £7,059 × 0.236	1,666
Chargeable gain	£11,275
Cost of rights for CGT purposes (£12,000 − £7,059)	£4,941

1991/92

The shares in P plc stand in the place of the right to deferred consideration and will be regarded as having been acquired in July 1990 for £4,941. No further gain or loss arises until a disposal of the shares takes place.

Notes

(*a*)   Under Inland Revenue extra-statutory concession D27 (26 April 1988), on a claim by the vendor, the right to deferred consideration is treated as a security within the meaning of *CGTA 1979, s 82(3)(b)* and the gain on the original shares held over against the value of the new shares.

(*b*)   Various conditions must be satisfied for a claim to be admitted. In particular, the deferred consideration must be wholly in the form of shares or debentures, although the immediate consideration may be in cash, and as a consequence of the right being treated as a security, the conditions of *CGTA 1979, s 85* must be satisfied as regards the disposal of the original shares.

(*c*)   The concession applies to all cases where the liability on the disposal of the original shares had not been finally determined at 26 April 1988. The concession also contains some transitional provisions in respect of certain rights acquired before that date.

(*d*)   See 206.3(B)(C) DISPOSAL above for deferred consideration generally.

223.5 SCHEMES OF RECONSTRUCTION OR AMALGAMATION [*CGTA 1979, s 86*]
N Ltd carries on a manufacturing and wholesaling business. In 1987, it was decided that the wholesaling business should be carried on by a separate company. Revenue clearance under *CGTA 1979, s 88* was obtained, and a company R Ltd was formed which, in consideration for the transfer to it by N Ltd of the latter's wholesaling undertaking, issued shares to the shareholders of N Ltd. Each holder of ordinary shares in N Ltd received one ordinary share in R Ltd for each N Ltd share he held. W, who purchased his 2,500 N shares for £10,000 in 1984, received 2,500 R shares. None of the shares involved is quoted. In August 1990, W sells 1,500 of his N shares for £6 each, a total of £9,000, agreed to be their market value. The value of W's remaining N shares is also £6 per share, and the value of his R shares is £4.50 per share.

	£
Disposal consideration	9,000

Allowable cost $£10,000 \times \dfrac{9,000}{9,000 + (1,000 \times £6) + (2,500 \times £4.50)}$ 3,429

Unindexed gain	£5,571

Note

(*a*)   If the original shares had been held on 31 March 1982, the above fraction would be applied to their 31.3.82 value for the purposes of the re-basing calculation under *FA 1988, s 96*.

223.6 **CONVERSION OF SECURITIES** [*CGTA 1979, s 82*]

N bought £10,000 8% convertible loan stock in S plc, a quoted company, in 1972 The cost was £9,800 and the stock stood at par at 31.3.82. In June 1983, N exercisec his right to convert the loan stock into 'B' ordinary shares of the company, on the basis of 50 shares for £100 loan stock, and acquired 5,000 shares. In July 1990, N sells 3,000 of the shares for £2.50 each. The indexation factor for March 1982 to July 1990 is assumed to be 0.608.

	£	£
Disposal consideration	7,500	7,50(
Cost $\dfrac{3,000}{5,000} \times £9,800$	5,880	
Market value 31.3.82 $\dfrac{3,000}{5,000} \times £10,000$		6,00(
Unindexed gain	1,620	1,50(
Indexation allowance £6,000 × 0.608	3,648	3,648
Loss after indexation	£2,028	£2,148
Allowable loss	£2,028	

Note

(*a*)   For re-basing purposes, the shares acquired on the conversion in 1983 are deemed to have been acquired on the original acquisition of the loan stock in 1972, by virtue of *CGTA 1979, s 82*.

223.7 **CAPITAL DISTRIBUTIONS**

(A) [*CGTA 1972, s 72*]

T holds 10,000 ordinary shares in a foreign company M SA. The shares were bought in April 1982 for £80,000. In February 1991, M SA has a capital reconstruc tion involving the cancellation of one-fifth of the existing ordinary shares in consideration of the repayment of £10 to each shareholder per share cancelled. T's holding is reduced to 8,000 shares, valued at £96,000. The indexation factor for April 1982 to February 1991 is assumed to be 0.670.

	£
Disposal consideration (2,000 × £10)	20,000
Allowable cost $\dfrac{20,000}{20,000 + 96,000} \times £80,000$	13,793
Unindexed gain	6,207
Indexation allowance £13,793 × 0.670	9,241
Allowable loss	£3,034
The allowable cost of the remaining shares is £80,000 − £13,793	£66,207

(B) Sale of rights [*CGTA 1979, ss 72, 73*]

X is a shareholder in K Ltd, owning 2,500 £1 ordinary shares which were purchased for £8,000 in September 1983. K Ltd makes a rights issue, but X sells his rights without taking them up. He realises £500 on the sale. The shares are valued at £12,000 in May 1990 when X sells the rights.

Indexation factors	September 1983 to April 1985	0.101
	April 1985 to May 1990	0.332

New holding of K £1 ordinary shares	Shares	Qualifying expenditure £	Indexed pool £
September 1983 acquisition	2,500	8,000	8,000
Indexed rise: September 1983 to April 1985 £8,000 × 0.101			808
Pool at 6.4.85	2,500	8,000	8,808
Indexed rise: April 1985 to May 1990 £8,808 × 0.332			2,924
	2,500	£8,000	£11,732

(i)   IF X chooses, the capital distribution need not be treated as a disposal, as the £500 received for the rights amounts to less than 5% of £12,000. The £500 is then deducted from the allowable cost of the shares and from the indexed pool, leaving balances of £7,500 (cost) and £11,232 (indexed pool).

(ii)   Otherwise X is treated as having made a part disposal

	£
Disposal proceeds	500
Allowable cost $\dfrac{500}{500 + 12,000} \times £8,000$	320
Unindexed gain	180
Indexation allowance $£11,732 \times \dfrac{500}{500 + 12,000} = 469$	
£469 − £320	149
Chargeable gain	£31

The allowable cost of the shares is then reduced to £7,680 (£8,000 − £320) and the balance on the indexed pool to £11,263 (£11,732 − £469).

(iii) Say the original 2,500 shares had been acquired for £8,000 in September 198[] and had a market value of £8,400 at 31 March 1982. The indexation factor f[] the period March 1982 to May 1990 is 0.589. Assume that X does not clai[] that the distribution should not be treated as a disposal.

	£	£
Disposal proceeds	500	50[]
Cost (see (ii) above)	320	
Market value 31.3.82		
$\dfrac{500}{500 + 12,000} \times £8,400$		33[]
Unindexed gain	180	16[]
Indexation allowance £336 × 0.589	198	19[]
Loss after indexation	£18	£3[]
Allowable loss	£18	

(C) Distributions in a liquidation — unquoted shares

The shareholders of N Ltd, an unquoted company, resolve that the company be p[] into liquidation, and a liquidator is appointed on 1 July 1988. An interim distrib[] tion of 60p per share is made on 1 April 1989, and a final distribution of 3p p[] share is made on 1 April 1990. The liquidator's estimates of the share value are

1.4.89	2p
1.4.90	Nil

S subscribed for 10,000 £1 ordinary shares at par on 30 June 1962. He does not ele[] for 6.4.65 value to be used instead of time apportionment. The shares were value[] at £4,000 at 31.3.82.

Indexation factors	March 1982 to April 1989	0.439
	March 1982 to April 1990	0.575

His allowable losses are as follows

1988/89

(i) Without re-basing to 1982

	£
Disposal consideration 10,000 × £0.60	6,000
Cost £10,000 × $\dfrac{6,000}{6,000 + 200}$	9,677
Unindexed loss	3,677
Indexation allowance £9,677 × 0.439	4,248
Loss before time apportionment	£7,925
Time apportionment £7,925 × $\dfrac{24\text{y }0\text{m}}{26\text{y }9\text{m}}$	7,110
Loss after time apportionment and indexation	£7,110

(ii) With re-basing to 1982

	£
Disposal consideration	6,000
Market value 31.3.82 £4,000 × $\dfrac{6,000}{6,000 + 200}$	3,871
Unindexed gain	2,129
Indexation allowance (as above)	4,248
Loss after indexation	£2,119

(iii) Outcome

Allowable loss	£2,119

1989/90

(i) Without re-basing to 1982

	£
Disposal consideration £10,000 × £0.03	300
Cost £10,000 − £9,677	323
Unindexed loss	23
Indexation allowance £323 × 0.575	186
Loss before time apportionment	£209
Time apportionment £209 × $\dfrac{24\text{y } 0\text{m}}{26\text{y } 9\text{m}}$	188
Loss after time apportionment and indexation	£188

(ii) With re-basing to 1982

	£
Disposal consideration	300
Market value 31.3.82 £4,000 − £3,871	129
Unindexed gain	171
Indexation allowance (as above)	186
Loss after indexation	£15

(iii) Outcome

Allowable loss	£15

Notes

(*a*)   The time apportionment fraction is calculated at the time of the first distribution. See Revenue Statement of Practice D3.

(*b*)   The High Court ruled in July 1990, overturning a decision of the Special Commissioners, that time apportionment should be applied to the gain *after* indexation (*Smith v Schofield C/D*, [*1990*] *STC 602*). The position is thus restored, pending any appeal by the taxpayer in the above-mentioned case, to that set out in Revenue Statement of Practice SP 3/82.

224 Underwriters

224.1 PREMIUMS TRUST FUND GAINS AND LOSSES

Q is a member of the P syndicate and for 1987/88 he is allocated £2,000 of the £10,000 capital loss on the premiums trust fund (syndicate losses). Chargeable gains and allowable losses for 1987/88 are

	Gain/(loss)
	£
Personal investments	10,000
Special reserve fund	(3,000)
Lloyd's deposits	1,200

Q's capital gains tax position is as follows

Original 1987/88 assessment

Gains on personal investments	10,000
Net losses on Lloyds non-syndicate investments (i.e. £3,000 loss – £1,200 gain)	1,800
	8,200
Annual exemption	6,600
Taxable amount	£1,600
CGT payable £1,600 at 30%	£480

The revised position following agreement of syndicate losses is

Chargeable gains	(£10,000 + £1,200)	11,200
Allowable losses	(£3,000 + £2,000)	5,000
		6,200
Annual exemption (maximum £6,600)		6,200
Taxable amount		Nil
CGT payable		Nil
Repayment due		£480

225 Wasting Assets

Cross-reference. See also 212.3 LAND.

225.1 GENERAL [*CGTA 1979, ss 37–39*]

(A)

V bought an aircraft on 31 May 1986 at a cost of £90,000 for use in his air charter business. It has been agreed that V's non-business use of the aircraft amounts to one-tenth, on a mileage basis, and capital allowances and running costs have accordingly been restricted for income tax purposes. On 1 February 1991, V sells the aircraft for £185,000. The aircraft is agreed as having a useful life of 20 years at the date it was acquired. The indexation factor for May 1986 to February 1991 is assumed to be 0.383.

	£
Amount qualifying for capital allowances	
Relevant portion of disposal consideration $\frac{9}{10} \times$ £185,000	166,500
Relevant portion of acquisition cost $\frac{9}{10} \times$ £90,000	81,000
Unindexed gain	85,500
Indexation allowance £81,000 × 0.383	31,023
Chargeable gain	£54,477

		£
Amount not qualifying for capital allowances		
Relevant portion of disposal consideration $\frac{1}{10} \times$ £185,000		18,500
Relevant portion of acquisition cost		
$\frac{1}{10} \times$ £90,000	9,000	
Deduct Wasted £9,000 $\times \dfrac{4y\ 8m}{20y}$	2,100	6,900
Gain		£11,600

The whole of the £11,600 is exempt.

	£
The total chargeable gain is therefore	£54,477

Note

(*a*) Gains on tangible moveable property which are wasting assets not qualifying for capital allowances are exempt (and any losses would not be allowable). [*CGTA 1979, s 127*].

411

(B)
Imagine the facts to be as in (A) above except that the date of acquisition was 3
May 1981. The 31.3.82 value of the aircraft was £92,000 and the indexation facto
for the period March 1982 to February 1991 is assumed to be 0.704.

**The gain on the part qualifying for capital allowances (the remainder being exemp
as in (A) above) is as follows**

	£	£
Relevant portion of disposal consideration	166,500	166,50
Relevant portion of acquisition cost	81,000	
Relevant portion of 31.3.82 value $\frac{9}{10} \times £92,000$		82,80
Unindexed gain	85,500	83,70
Indexation allowance £82,800 × 0.704	58,291	58,29
Gain after indexation	£27,209	£25,40
Chargeable gain		£25,40

Note
(a)   Note that machinery and plant qualifying for capital allowances is exclude
from any election under *FA 1988, s 96(5)* (election to treat all assets a
disposed of and re-acquired at their market value at 31.3.82). [*FA 1988, 8 Sc*
12]. However, the general re-basing provisions can apply.

225.2 **OPTIONS** [*CGTA 1979, ss 37, 38, 138; FA 1980, s 84*]

Cross-reference. See also 206.5 DISPOSAL above.

(A) Unquoted shares
On 1 July 1988, R grants C an option to purchase unquoted shares held by R. Th
cost of the option is £600 to purchase 10,000 shares at £5 per share, the option to be
exercised by 31 December 1990. On 1 September 1990 C assigns the option to V
for £500. The indexation factor for July 1988 to September 1990 is assumed to b
0.217.

	£	£
Disposal consideration		500
Acquisition cost	600	
Deduct Wasted £600 × $\frac{26}{30}$	520	80
Unindexed gain		420
Indexation allowance £80 × 0.217		17
Chargeable gain		£403

(B) Traded options
On 1 December 1990, C purchases 6-month options on T plc shares for £1,000. Two weeks later, he sells the options, which are traded on the Stock Exchange, for £1,200.

	£
Disposal consideration	1,200
Allowable cost	1,000
Chargeable gain	£200

Note
(*a*)   The wasting asset rules do not apply to traded options. [*CGTA 1979, s 138*].

225.3 **LIFE INTERESTS** [*CGTA 1979, s 37(1)(d)*]
(A)
N is a beneficiary under a settlement. On 30 June 1982, when her actuarially estimated life expectancy was 40 years, she sold her life interest to an unrelated individual, R, for £50,000. N dies on 31 December 1995, and the life interest is extinguished. The indexation factor for June 1982 to December 1995 is assumed to be 1.300.

	£	£
Disposal consideration on death of N		Nil
Allowable cost	50,000	
Deduct wasted		
$\dfrac{\text{13y 6m}}{\text{40y}} \times £50,000$	16,875	
		33,125
Unindexed loss		33,125
Indexation allowance £33,125 × 1.300		43,063
Allowable loss 1995/96		£76,188

Note
(*a*)   The amount of the cost wasted is computed by reference to the predictable life, not the actual life, of the wasting asset.

(B)
Assume the facts to be as in (A) above except that the sale of the life interest was on 30 June 1981, N's life expectancy at that date was 40 years, and N died on 31 December 1994. Assume the indexation factor to be 1.207 for the period March 1982 to December 1994, and that the value of the life interest was still £50,000 at 31 March 1982.

Calculation without re-basing

	£
Unindexed loss (as in (A) above)	33,125
Indexation allowance (see below)	40,746
Loss after indexation	£73,871

CGT 225.3 Wasting Assets

Calculation with re-basing

	£	£
Disposal consideration		Nil
Market value 31.3.82	50,000	
Deduct wasted		
$£50,000 \times \dfrac{12\text{y 9m} \quad (31.3.82 - 31.12.94)}{39\text{y 3m} \quad (\text{life expectancy at } 31.3.82)}$	16,242	
		33,758
Unindexed loss		33,758
Indexation allowance £33,758 × 1.207		40,746
Loss after indexation		£74,504
Allowable loss 1994/95		£73,871

Note

(*a*) The second of the above calculations is an interpretation of how the wasting assets provisions interact with the re-basing provisions of *FA 1988, s 96*. Where, by virtue of the re-basing rules, an asset is deemed to have been disposed of and re-acquired at its market value on 31 March 1982, that market value must be reduced in accordance with the period of ownership *after* that date and the predictable life of the wasting asset *at* that date.

Inheritance Tax

301 Accumulation and Maintenance Trusts

[IHTA 1984, s 71]

301.1 On 1 January 1981 G settled £50,000 on trust equally for his great nephews and nieces born before 1 January 1999. The beneficiaries were to take life interests at age 18, income being accumulated for minor beneficiaries. By 1999 G had three great nephews and nieces, A (his brother's grandson) born in 1976 and B and C (his sister's grandsons) born in 1991 and 1996 respectively. The settlement was valued at £150,000 on 1 January 2006.

On 1 January 2006 the settlement fails to qualify as an accumulation and maintenance settlement as more than 25 years have elapsed since the date of settlement and the beneficiaries do not have a common grandparent. A has an interest in possession in one third as he is over 18, but the remaining two thirds which is held equally for B and C is not subject to an interest in possession. There will be a charge to IHT on two thirds.

The rate of tax is the aggregate of

0.25% for each of the first	40 quarters	10%
0.20% for each of the next	40 quarters	8%
0.15% for each of the next	20 quarters	3%
	100	21%

The IHT charge is 21% $\times \frac{2}{3} \times$ £150,000 = £21,000

Note

(*a*)   There was no charge to IHT on A becoming entitled to an interest in possession in one third on his eighteenth birthday in 1994.

302 Agricultural Property

[IHTA 1984, ss 115–124B; FA 1986, 19 Sch 22]

302.1 **RELIEF FOR TRANSFERS AFTER 9 MARCH 1981**
(A) Relief given at 50% *[IHTA 1984, ss 116(1)(2)(7), 124A(1)(3)]*
A was a farmer for many years using for that trade 200 acres of land. On 1 July 1990 he transferred all the land to his son at a time when its agricultural value was £1,000 per acre and its open market value £1,500 per acre. He had not used his annual exemption for 1990/91. A died on 6 September 1993. His son had farmed continuously since the gift.

The value of the gift for inheritance tax purposes before relief is

	£
200 acres at £1,500 per acre	£300,000

The transfer subject to tax is

(i)	Agricultural value of land is £200,000	
	50% thereof	100,000
(ii)	Non-agricultural value of land	100,000
		200,000
Deduct Annual exemption		3,000
Value transferred by PET becoming chargeable on death		£197,000

Notes

(*a*)   Relief is at 50% as the transferor, immediately before the transfer, enjoyed the right to vacant possession and the land was farmed by the son between the date of the gift and A's death.

(*b*)   Annual exemptions are deducted after deducting the agricultural relief.

(*c*)   Business property relief may be available in respect of the £100,000 excess of the open market value over the agricultural value.

(*d*)   IHT will be charged at 80% of full rates as A died more than 3 but not more than 4 years after the gift.

(B) Transfer after 14 March 1983 where land is held tenanted under an agricultural lease. *[IHTA 1984, s 116(1)(2)(7)]*
A is the freehold owner of agricultural land which at current vacant possession value is estimated to be valued at £850,000. On 29 September 1982, he enters into an agricultural tenancy with a farming partnership comprising his two sons and his grandson for a full market rental of £25,000 p.a. The tenanted value is estimated at £500,000.
A dies on 1 October 1990 when the tenanted value of the land has risen to £600,000.

	£
Transfer at death (tenanted valuation)	600,000
Deduct Agricultural property relief 30% × £600,000	180,000
IHT payable on	£420,000

IHT 302.1   Agricultural Property

Note

(*a*)   No IHT charge arises on the grant of the lease to the partnership on the basis that it is for full consideration. [*IHTA 1984, s 16*].

(C)

Assume the facts are as in (B) above except that A did not die but, on 1 October 1990, gave the tenanted land to the trustees of a discretionary settlement for his remaining grandchildren when it was valued at £640,000. He arranged for the capital gain on the gift to be held over but paid the IHT on the transfer at lifetime rates. He has not used his annual exemption for the current or previous years.

	£
Value transferred	640,000
30% agricultural relief	192,000
	448,000
Annual exemptions	6,000
Chargeable transfer (subject to grossing-up)	£442,000

Note

(*a*)   The IHT attributable to the value of the asset on the original chargeable transfer (as varied on the subsequent death of the transferor or otherwise) will be an allowable deduction for CGT purposes on the disposal of the property by the trustees, but not so as to create an allowable loss. [*CGTA 1979, s 147A(7); FA 1989, 14 Sch 4*].

(D) Interaction with capital gains tax

A discretionary settlement has 400 acres of tenanted agricultural land. On 30 September 1990, the trustees appoint the agricultural land to a beneficiary who then becomes absolutely entitled to the land. 30% agricultural relief is available. The value of the 400 acres as tenanted is £450,000. The trustees fail to pay the capital gains tax due of £60,000 by 1 December 1992 and the beneficiary is assessed and pays the liability.

	£
Value transferred	450,000
Agricultural relief 30%	135,000
	315,000
Capital gains tax	60,000
Chargeable transfer (subject to grossing-up)	£255,000

Notes

(*a*)   An election may be made for the CGT to be held over. [*CGTA 1979, s 147A(1)–(5); FA 1989, 14 Sch 4*].

(*b*)   If the trustees fail to pay all or part of the capital gains tax within twelve months of the due date, an assessment may be made on the beneficiary [*CGTA 1979, s 59*] and the amount of such tax borne by the donee is treated as reducing the value transferred. The beneficiary must become absolutely entitled to the property to obtain the relief. [*IHTA 1984, s 165*].

(E) Transitional relief [*IHTA 1984, s 116(2)–(4)*]
Q owns 1200 acres of tenanted agricultural land, acquired before 10 March 1981 and let to a partnership in which he is a partner. The land is valued at £833 per acre.

On a chargeable transfer in December 1990, without transitional relief

	£
Value of 1200 acres land (tenanted)	999,600
30% relief on 1200 acres worth £999,600	299,880
Chargeable transfer (subject to grossing-up)	£699,720

On a chargeable transfer in December 1990, with transitional relief

	£
Value of 1200 acres land (tenanted)	999,600
Relief	
50% on 1000 acres worth £833,000	(416,500)
30% on 200 acres worth £166,600	(49,980)
Chargeable transfer (subject to grossing-up)	£533,120

302.2 SHARES ETC. IN AGRICULTURAL COMPANIES [*IHTA 1984, ss 122, 123*]
AC Ltd is an agricultural company of which A owns 60% of the shares.

	£
The company owns	
4,000 acres of land — agricultural value	4M
Other trading assets (net)	2M
Total value of company	£6M
A's shareholding is valued at	£4.5M

All necessary conditions for relief are satisfied.

If A were to die in November 1990 the position would be as follows

	Total Value £	Land £	Other Assets £
Value of assets of company	£6M	£4M	£2M
Value of shares, split in same proportions	4.5M	£3M	£1.5M
Agricultural relief (50% of £3M)	(1.5M)		
Business relief (50% of £1.5M)	(0.75M)		
Chargeable to IHT	£2.25M		

Notes

(*a*)   Part of the value transferred is attributable to the agricultural value of agricultural property so agricultural property relief is available. [*IHTA 1984, s 122*].

(*b*)   The legislation appears to require that both agricultural property relief and business property relief be given, each against its appropriate part of the value. [*IHTA 1984, s 114*]. See also 304 BUSINESS PROPERTY. When some of the land owned by the company is tenanted, attracting only 30% relief, the total relief given will be less than would be the case if business property relief were given on the whole value.

303 Anti-Avoidance

303.1 ASSOCIATED OPERATIONS [*IHTA 1984, s 268*]

(A)

H owns a set of four Chippendale chairs valued, as a set, at £6,000. Individually they would be valued at only £1,000, although a pair would be worth £2,500 and three £4,000.

He gives one chair to his son each year over four years, during which time all values increase at 10% p.a. (simple). In the fifth year A dies.

	£	£
Year 1		
Value of four chairs	6,000	
Deduct value of three	4,000	
Value transferred		2,000
Year 2		
Basic computation ignoring the associated operations rule		
Current value of three chairs	4,400	
Deduct value of two	2,750	
Value transferred	£1,650	
Revised to take account of associated operations rule		
Current value of four chairs	6,600	
Deduct value of two	2,750	
	3,850	
Deduct value transferred in Year 1	2,000	
		1,850
Year 3		
Current value of four chairs	7,200	
Deduct value of one	1,200	
	6,000	
Deduct value transferred in Years 1 and 2	3,850	
		2,150
Year 4		
Current value of four chairs	7,800	
Deduct value tranferred in Years 1, 2 and 3	6,000	
Value transferred		1,800
Total values transferred		£7,800

Note

(*a*)   The normal rule would be that the transfer of value is the loss to the donor's estate, as in Year 1. However, if a series of transfers are treated as associated operations, the transfer is treated as if made at the time of the latest transfer reduced by the value transferred by the earlier transfers.

(B)

If in (A) above H had wished to give away the chairs over two years instead of four, he might first have given two chairs to his wife, so that each could give the son one chair each year.

Year 1	£	£
(i) Value transferred by husband		
Value of two chairs (as half of a set of		
four linked by the related property rule)	3,000	
Deduct value of one chair (as half of a pair)	1,250	
		1,750
(ii) Value transferred by wife		
(similar calculation)		1,750
Year 2		
(i) Value transferred by husband,		
applying the associated operation rule		
Current value of four chairs	6,600	
Deduct value transferred in Year 1 by		
H to son	1,750	
Value transferred		4,850
Total values transferred		£8,350

Note

(*a*)   In this case, the total of the values transferred can exceed the value of the assets, although it must be doubtful whether the Inland Revenue would seek to apply the full rigours of the section unless the transfer by the wife in Year 1 had fallen within her annual exemptions, or she had survived seven years so that the gift was exempt.

304 Business Property

[*IHTA 1984, ss 103–114, 269; FA 1987, s 58, 8 Sch*]

304.1 RELEVANT BUSINESS PROPERTY

(A) Shares or securities

A has owned for many years 60,000 shares in X Ltd, an unquoted company, whose issued share capital is 100,000 shares of £1 each. All shares carry full voting rights. A gifts to his son 20,000 shares in June 1990, a further 20,000 in June 1991 and the remaining 20,000 in June 1992. The son agrees to pay any IHT on all gifts. A dies in March 1996, at which time his son still owns the shares. A has not made any previous transfers of value other than £3,000 in 1989/90. It is assumed that IHT rates do not change.

The value of holdings at all three dates of transfer were as follows

60% holding	£10 per share
40% holding	£4 per share
20% holding	£3 per share

First gift	£	£
Value of holding before transfer	600,000	
Value of holding after transfer	160,000	
Reduction in value of estate	440,000	
Deduct buisiness property relief (50%) note (*b*)	220,000	
	220,000	
Deduct annual exemption	(3,000)	
PET becoming chargeable transfer on death	£217,000	
IHT payable at 40% of full rates (death between 5 and 6 years after gift)		14,240
Second gift		
Value of holding before transfer	160,000	
Value of holding after transfer	60,000	
Reduction in value of estate	100,000	
Deduct business property relief (50%) note (*b*)	50,000	
	50,000	
Deduct annual exemption	(3,000)	
PET becoming chargeable on death	£47,000	
IHT payable at 60% of full rates (death between 4 and 5 years after gift)		11,280
		c/f £25,520

		£
		b/f 25,520
Third gift		
Value of shares transferred	60,000	
Deduct business property relief (30%) note (*b*)	18,000	
	42,000	
Deduct annual exemption	(3,000)	
PET becoming chargeable on death	£39,000	
IHT payable at 80% of full rates		
(death between 3 and 4 years after gift)		12,480
Total IHT payable		£38,000

Notes

(*a*)   If A had made a single gift of his entire holding in June 1990, the computation would be as follows

Value of gift	600,000
Deduct business property relief (50%)	(300,000)
	300,000
Deduct annual exemption	(3,000)
PET becoming chargeable transfer on death	£297,000
IHT payable at 40% of full rates	£27,040
Saving in IHT	£10,960

(*b*)   Business property relief on the first transfer is 50% as the gift was made from a controlling interest. On the second transfer, 50% relief is due as the gift was from a holding yielding more than 25% of the voting rights. The third transfer satisfies neither of these criteria and relief is therefore at only 30%.

(B) Shares in a holding company with a non-qualifying subsidiary

A owns 85% of the share capital of H Ltd, which has two wholly owned subsidiary companies S Ltd and P Ltd. H Ltd and S Ltd are trading companies and P Ltd is a property investment company. The issued share capital of H Ltd is 100,000 ordinary shares of £1 each valued at £8 per share. The values of the issued shares in S Ltd and P Ltd are £250,000 and £300,000 respectively.

A gives 10,000 shares in H Ltd to his son in August 1990. He has already made chargeable transfers using up his basic exemptions. His son agrees to pay any IHT. A dies in January 1994, at which time his son still owns the shares.

	£	£
Value of gift		80,000
Deduct business property relief 50% × £80,000	40,000	
Less 50% × 80,000 × $\dfrac{300,000}{800,000}$	15,000	
		25,000
PET becoming chargeable transfer on death		£55,000

423

IHT 304.1 Business Property

(C) Land used by a business

M has for many years owned a factory used in the business of Q Ltd, of which he has control. In September 1990, M gives the factory to his son S when its value is £275,000. He has made no previous chargeable transfer, but made a gift of £3,000 in 1989/90. M dies in October 1991, when the factory is being used for business purposes by S's partnership. S agreed to pay any IHT on the gift.

	£
Value of gift	275,000
Deduct business property relief (30%)	82,500
	192,500
Deduct annual exemption	(3,000)
PET becoming chargeable transfer on death	£189,500
IHT payable at full rates (death within 3 years)	£28,600

Notes

(a)   If M wishes also to dispose of shares in Q Ltd by sale or gift after which he would no longer have control, he should give the factory to his son before disposing of the shares, or else the business property relief would not be available.

(b)   If the factory had been used by Q Ltd at the date of M's death, no business property relief would be available on the gift since the factory would not be relevant business property in S's hands at the date of death.

(D) Land and buildings owned by trustees

X died in 1974 leaving a life interest in factory premises to his son A, with remainder to his grandsons B and C. A occupies the premises for the purposes of his trade, rent-free. In September 1990 A gives up his life interest when the value of the premises is £260,000. B and C agree to pay any IHT. A has already made chargeable transfers using up his annual exemptions. A dies in November 1992, when the factory is still being used in the trade which was then being carried on by B and C in partnership.

	£
Value of gift	260,000
Deduct business property relief (30%)	(78,000)
PET becoming chargeable transfer on death	£182,000
IHT payable at full rates (death within 3 years)	£25,600

305   Calculation of Tax

305.1 **POTENTIALLY EXEMPT TRANSFERS** [*IHTA 1984, ss 3, 3A, 7*]

On 1 May 1990 A gave £50,000 to his daughter D, and on 1 May 1993 he gave £78,000 to his son S. Both D and S agreed to pay any IHT due on the gifts.

On 7 March 1998 A died, leaving his estate, valued at £300,000 equally to D and S. A had made no other transfers apart from chargeable transfers of £76,000 during 1988/89.

Gift on 1 May 1990

The gift is a PET, which becomes exempt since A does not die within seven years of the date of the gift. No IHT is payable.

Gift on 1 May 1993

This PET becomes chargeable since A dies between 4 and 5 years after the gift. IHT is payable by S following the death at 60% of full rates on the basis of the Table of rates in force in 1997/98.

The cumulative total of chargeable transfers in the seven years prior to the gift is £76,000 (1988/89), since the transfer on 1 May 1990 is an exempt transfer.

	£	£
Gift		78,000
Deduct annual exemptions 1993/94	3,000	
1992/93	3,000	
		6,000
		£72,000

IHT on £72,000 charged in band £76,000 to £148,000 (assuming no change in the rates)

	£
76,001–128,000 at nil%	—
128,001–148,000 at 40%	8,000
	£8,000
IHT payable at 60% of full rates — £8,000 at 60%	£4,800

Death 7 March 1998

The chargeable transfers in the seven years prior to death comprise only the gift on 1 May 1992 of £72,000.

IHT on death on estate of £300,000 chargeable in band £72,000 to £372,000

	£
72,001–128,000 at nil%	—
128,001–372,000 at 40%	97,600
IHT payable	£97,600

Notes

(*a*)   If A directs in his will that, despite the earlier agreement, any IHT due on the gift to S is to be borne by his estate, this amounts to a pecuniary legacy to S of the amount of the tax. The reduction in A's estate by the transfer is unchanged at £78,000 as is the tax of £4,800. The legacy is paid out of the death estate of £300,000 with previous chargeable transfers of £72,000. Since the whole of the estate is liable on death the IHT remains at £97,600.

(*b*)   If S has not by 1 April 1999 paid the IHT of £4,800 due on the gift from A, the personal representatives of A become liable for the tax as it has not been paid by S within 12 months after the end of the month in which A died. The IHT due remains £4,800 since the gross chargeable transfer is £72,000. A had no liability for the tax at the time the transfer was made and the reduction in value to his estate was, therefore, the amount of the gift to S, £78,000. The personal representatives have a right under general law to reimbursement for the tax from S. To the extent that reimbursement is probable, the tax is not a deduction from the estate. Since the personal representatives can claim reimbursement from the half estate due to S, no deduction will be given. Tax on the estate remains, therefore, at £97,600. [*IHTA 1984, ss 199, 204; FA 1986, 19 Sch 28*]. If S had not benefited under A's will so that no assets were available to reimburse the personal representatives, the tax due of £4,800 might fall to be met from the estate.

305.2   **NET CHARGEABLE TRANSFER** [*IHTA 1984, ss 3, 3A, 7*]

   (A)

On 13 July 1990 B gave £138,000 to his nephew N, who agreed to pay any IHT on the gift. On 24 December 1990 B settled £160,000 on discretionary trusts for his great-nephews and nieces, paying the IHT himself.

On 9 August 1996 B died with an estate worth £50,000, having made no other gifts.

Gift 13 July 1990

This PET becomes chargeable since B dies between 6 and 7 years after the gift. The annual exemption for 1990/91, and that brought forward from 1989/90 are, however, set against the chargeable transfer on 24 December 1990.

IHT is charged on the transfer at 20% of full rates.

	£
IHT on gift	
1–128,000 at nil%	—
128,001–138,000 at 40%	4,000
	£4,000

IHT payable by N at 20% of full rates 20% × £4,000	£800

Gift 24 December 1990

The gift to the discretionary trust is a chargeable transfer; net since B is to pay the IHT. At the time the gift is made the PET on 13 July 1990 is treated as exempt, and the annual exemptions for 1990/91 and 1989/90 are set against the chargeable transfer.

IHT is charged at half of full rates.

	£	£
Gift		160,000
Deduct annual exemptions 1990/91	3,000	
1989/90	3,000	
		6,000
Net chargeable transfer		154,000
IHT thereon		
0–128,000	—	
128,001–154,000 at 25%	6,500	
IHT payable on gift	£6,500	6,500
Gross chargeable transfer		£160,500

B's death occurs between 5 and 6 years after the gift, so the tax on the chargeable transfer is revised to the IHT payable at 40% of full rates. The PET on 13 July 1990 becomes chargeable, so IHT is charged on the gross chargeable transfer of £160,500 in the bracket £138,001 to £298,500.

	£
138,001–298,500 at 40%	64,200
IHT at 40% of £64,200	25,680
Less paid on chargeable lifetime transfer	6,500
Additional IHT payable following death	£19,180

Death 9 August 1996
Chargeable transfers in the seven years prior to death amount to £298,500, so IHT is charged on the death estate of £50,000 in the bracket £298,501 to £348,500.

IHT payable	
298,501–348,500 at 40%	£20,000

(B)
Facts are as in (A) above except that B died on 9 August 1997.

The PET on 13 July 1990 is exempt and thus not cumulated when reworking the IHT on the chargeable transfer on 24 December 1990 or on death.

Gift 24 December 1990

IHT on gift, as before	£6,500

Following B's death between 6 and 7 years after the gift, IHT is reworked at 20% of full rates.

	£
0–128,000	—
128,001–160,500 at 40%	13,000
	£13,000

	£
IHT at 20% of £13,000	2,600
Less IHT paid on chargeable lifetime transfer	6,500
IHT payable following death	Nil

Death 9 August 1997
Chargeable transfers in the previous 7 years amount to £160,500 so IHT is charged on the death estate of £50,000 in the bracket £160,501 to £210,500.

IHT payable	
160,501–210, 500 at 40%	£20,000

Note
(*a*) No IHT is repayable in respect of the chargeable transfer on 24 December 1990, even though the IHT on death is less than the IHT originally paid on the gift.

305.3 TRANSITIONAL PROVISIONS [*FA 1986, 19 Sch 31*]

On 1 March 1986 C gave his daughter £80,000 and paid the tax due on the gift. On 1 November 1988 C gave his son £88,000.
C died on 6 January 1992, with an estate of £120,000, which passed equally to his children. C had made no other gifts.

Gift 1 March 1986
The gift is a net chargeable transfer for CTT purposes.

	£	£
Gift		80,000
Deduct annual exemptions 1985/86	3,000	
1984/85	3,000	
		6,000
Net chargeable transfer		74,000
Tax thereon		
1–67,000	—	
67,001–74,000 at 17.647%	1,235	
Tax payable	£1,235	1,235
Gross chargeable transfer		£75,235

Although C died between 5 and 6 years after the gift, so that IHT would be revised to 40% of full rates under the provisions applying after 17 March 1986, there is no revision to the tax payable since the chargeable transfer was before 18 March 1986 and was more than 3 years before death.

Gift 1 November 1988
The PET becomes chargeable since C dies between 3 and 4 years after the gift.

	£
Gift	88,000

	£	
Deduct annual exemptions 1988/89	3,000	
1987/88	3,000	
		6,000
		£82,000

The cumulative total of gross chargeable transfers is £75,235, so IHT is charged at 80% of Table rates for 1991/92 in the bracket £75, 236 to £157,235.

	£	£
Tax thereon (assuming no changes in rates)		
75,236–128,000 at nil%	—	
128,001–157,235 at 40%	11,694	
	£11,694	
IHT payable at 80% of full rates 80% × £11,694		£9,355

Death
IHT is charged on the estate of £120,000 at full rates, in the bracket £157,236 to £277, 235.

Tax thereon

157,236–277,235 at 40%	£48,000

305.4 PARTLY EXEMPT TRANSFERS [*IHTA 1984, ss 36–42*]
(A) Where the only chargeable part of a transfer is specific gifts which do not bear their own tax
A, a widow, dies on 8 June 1990. Her estate is valued at £258,000 and her will provides for a tax-free legacy to her nephew of £148,000 and the residue of her estate to the National Trust. A had made no chargeable transfers during her lifetime.

Gross-up tax-free legacy at 'death' rates

	£	
Tax-free legacy	148,000	
Tax thereon		
0–128,000	—	
128,001–148,000 at 66.66%	13,333	
	£13,333	13,333
Grossed-up legacy		£161,333

IHT 305.4   Calculation of Tax

Calculation of net residuary estate	£
Value of estate	258,000
Deduct gross value of legacy	(161,333)
Residue	£96,667

Allocation of estate at death	
Nephew	148,000
National Trust	96,667
Tax	13,333
	£258,000

(B) As (A) above but with lifetime transfers

The facts are as in (A) above except that A made a gift on 7 December 1983 to her cousin of £80,000 which has not previously been disclosed. The executors agree to pay tax on the gift.

The revised calculations are as follows

	£	£
Tax on lifetime gift		
Gift made 7 December 1983		80,000
Deduct annual exemption for current year		
(1983/84)	3,000	
annual exemption for previous year		
(1982/83)	3,000	
		(6,000)
Chargeable transfers (net)		74,000
Tax thereon at lifetime rates applicable at 7.12.83		
0–60,000	—	
60,001–74,000 at 17.647%	2,470	
Tax payable by executors	£2,470	2,470
Gross cumulative chargeable transfer		£76,470

Revised calculation at 8 June 1990	
Previous gross chargeable transfers	76,470
Deduct tax thereon at current death scale	—
Net lifetime transfers	76,470
Add tax-free legacy	148,000
Total net transfers	224,470
Add tax to gross-up	64,313
Total gross transfers	288,783
Deduct gross lifetime transfers	(76,470)
Gross equivalent of tax-free legacy	£212,313

Allocation of estate at death	£
Original estate	258,000
Deduct CTT on lifetime transfer	2,470
	£255,530

Nephew	148,000
Tax	64,313
National Trust (residue)	43,217
	£255,530

(C) Where tax-free specific gifts are not the only chargeable gifts

A dies on 1 January 1991 leaving a widow, son and nephew. His estate is valued at £500,000 before deduction of business property relief of £50,000 and his will provides for a tax-free legacy to his son of £160,000, a legacy to the nephew of £15,000 bearing its own tax, a bequest to charity of £25,000, with the residue shared three-quarters by his widow and one-quarter by the son. A had made no previous chargeable transfers.

Allocation of business property relief [*FA 1986, s 105*]

Since the will made no specific gifts of the business property, the business property relief is apportioned between the specific gifts i.e. each gift is multiplied by

$$\frac{\text{Estate less business property relief}}{\text{Estate before business property relief}}$$

Son $£160,000 \times \dfrac{450,000}{500,000} = £144,000$

Nephew $£15,000 \times \dfrac{450,000}{500,000} = £13,500$

Charity $£25,000 \times \dfrac{450,000}{500,000} = £22,500$

Hypothetical chargeable estate	£	£	£
Tax-free legacy to son			144,000
Tax thereon			
0–128,000		Nil	
128,001–144,000 at 66.666%		10,667	10,667
			154,667
Legacy to nephew			13,500
			168,167
Chargeable residue			
Gross estate		450,000	
Deduct gross legacies	168,167		
charity	22,500		
		(190,667)	
		£259,333	
Son's one-quarter share			64,833
Hypothetical chargeable estate			£233,000

IHT 305.4   Calculation of Tax

Hypothetical chargeable estate — calculation of assumed tax rate

Tax on £233,000   £42,000

Assumed rate $\dfrac{42,000}{233,000} \times 100 = 18.026\%$

Re-gross tax-free legacy to son using assumed rate

$£144,000 \times \dfrac{100}{100 - 18.026}$ £175,66⬚

Calculate chargeable estate and tax thereon

Grossed-up value of tax-free legacy		175,66⬚
Legacy to nephew		13,50⬚
		189,16⬚
Chargeable residue		
Gross estate		450,000
Deduct gross legacies	189,165	
charity	22,500	
		(211,665)
		£238,335
Son's one-quarter share		59,58⬚
Chargeable estate		£248,74⬚

Tax on estate		
0–128,000		—
128,001–248,749 at 40%		48,300
		£48,300

Estate rate is $\dfrac{48,300}{248,749} \times 100 = 19.417\%$

432

Distribution of estate		£
Specific legacies — son		144,000
— nephew		13,500
— charity		22,500
		180,000

Tax on nephew's legacy
(£13,500 at 19.417% = £2,621
to be borne by nephew)

Tax on son's legacy of	£144,000	
Gross at assumed rate (18.026%)	£175,665	
£175,665 at 19.417%		34,109
Legacies plus tax thereon		£214,109
Gross estate		450,000
Deduct legacies plus tax		(214,109)
Residue		£235,891

Allocation of estate		
Widow (three-quarters of residue)		176,918
Son (one-quarter of residue)	58,973	
Tax on son's share		
£58,973 at 19.417%	11,451	
	47,522	
Specific legacy	144,000	
		191,522
Legacies to nephew and charity		36,000
Tax borne by residue £(34,109 + 11,451)		45,560
		£450,000

306 Charities

[IHTA 1984, s 70]

306.1 **PROPERTY LEAVING TEMPORARY CHARITABLE TRUSTS**
   (A) Gross payment to beneficiaries
   On 1 January 1971 A settled £100,000 on temporary charitable trusts. The income and capital were to be applied for charitable purposes only for a period of 25 years from the date of settlement, and thereafter could be applied for charitable purposes or to or for the settlor's grandchildren. On 1 January 1996 the trustees paid £50,000 to charity and the balance of the settlement, valued at £75,000, to the three grandchildren.

The relevant period is the period from 13 March 1975 to 1 January 1996, i.e. 83 complete quarters, and the amount on which tax is charged is £75,000 gross.

The rate of tax is

	%
0.25% for 40 quarters	10.00
0.20% for 40 quarters	8.00
0.15% for 3 quarters	0.45
	18.45%

IHT payable is 18.45% × £75,000 = £13,837

(B) Net payment to beneficiaries
Assume the same facts as in (A) above except that the trustees apply £75,000 net for the settlor's three grandchildren, and the balance to charity.

The rate of tax is, as before, 18.45%

IHT payable is $\dfrac{18.45}{100 - 18.45} \times £75,000 = £16,968$

The gross payment to the beneficiaries is £75,000 + £16,968 = £91,968.

07 Close Companies

HTA 1984, ss 94–98, 102]

7.1 VALUE TRANSFERRED

The ordinary shares of companies A and B are held as follows (in January 1991)

	A	B
Individuals X	80%	
Y	20%	
Z		10%
Company A		90%

Company B is non-resident and Z is domiciled in the UK. Company A sells a property valued at £220,000 to a mutual friend of X and Y for £20,000. The following month, company B sells a foreign property worth £100,000 to X for £90,000.

Company A

	£
The transfer of value is £220,000 − £20,000	200,000

Apportioned to X	80% × £200,000	160,000
Y	20% × £200,000	40,000
		£200,000

Company B

The transfer of value of £10,000 is apportioned

To X	80% × 90% × £10,000	7,200
	Deduct increase in X's estate	10,000
		—
To Y	20% × 90% × £10,000	1,800
To Z	10% × £10,000 note (c)	1,000
		£2,800

Notes

(a) If the sale by company A were to X (or Y), there would be no apportionment because the undervalue would be treated as a net distribution, thus attracting income tax.

(b) On the sale by company B, X would not be liable to income tax.

(c) If Z were not domiciled in the UK, his share of the transfer of value would not be apportioned to him. [*IHTA 1984, s 94(2)(b)*].

307.2 **CHARGE ON PARTICIPATORS**

Assume the values transferred by X, Y and Z in 307.1 above and that X and Y ha~
each made previous chargeable transfers of £150,000 since January 1984, using u
their annual exemptions for 1989/90.

Company A

	X	Y	Z
	£	£	£
Value transferred	160,000	40,000	
Annual exemption	(3,000)	(3,000)	
	157,000	37,000	
Tax (25% of net)	39,250	9,250	
Gross transfer	£196,250	£46,250	
IHT	£39,250	£9,250	

Company B

	X	Y	Z
Value transferred	7,200	1,800	1,0(
Deduct increase in X's estate	(10,000)	—	—
		1,800	1,0(
Deduct annual exemption		—	1,0(
		1,800	—
Tax (25% of net)		450	
Gross transfer		£2,250	
IHT		£450	

Note

(*a*)   Although it is understood that the Inland Revenue would follow this meth(
of calculation, there is an alternative view which follows the exact wording ·
IHTA 1984, s 94(1). This view is that the grossing-up should take pla·
before the increase in X's estate is deducted. In the above example, it mak·
no difference as the gross transfer would still be less than the increase in X
estate. But suppose that X held 90% of the ordinary shares in Company /
His value transferred would then be £8,100 (90% × 90% × £10,000) and th·
alternative method would proceed as follows.

	£
Value transferred	8,100
Tax (25% of net)	2,025
	10,125
Deduct increase in X's estate	(10,000)
	£125
IHT thereon at 20%	£25

307.3 ALTERATION OF SHARE CAPITAL

In January 1991 the share capital of company H, an investment company, is owned by P and Q as follows

P   600
Q   400
          ─────
          1,000 ordinary £1 shares

The shares are valued at £10 per share for P's majority holding and £4 per share for Q's minority holding.

The company issues 2,000 shares at par to Q and the shares are then worth £3.50 per share for Q's majority holding and £1.50 per share for P's minority holding. P has previously made chargeable transfers in excess of £150,000 since January 1984.

The transfer of value for P is

	£
Value of holding previously	6,000
Value of holding now	900
Decrease in value	5,100
Tax (25% of net)	1,275
Gross transfer	£6,375
IHT thereon at 20%	£1,275

Notes

(a)   P's transfer of value is *not* a potentially exempt transfer. [*IHTA 1984, s 98(3)*].

(b)   An alternative charge may arise under *IHTA 1984, s 3(3)* (omission to exercise a right) but the transfer would be a potentially exempt transfer and only chargeable if P died within seven years.

308 Deeds Varying Dispositions on Death

[IHTA 1984, ss 17, 142]

308.1 A died in December 1990 leaving his estate of £188,000 to his wife absolutely. His wife, having an index-linked widow's pension, agreed with her sons, B and C, that they could benefit from the estate to the extent of £128,000 in equal shares, i.e. £64,000 each.

A had made no chargeable transfers before his death.

	£
Exempt transfer to widow	£60,000
Transfer to B	64,000
Transfer to C	64,000
	£128,000
IHT payable	Nil

Note

(a)   If A's widow died 5 years later when her estate was valued at £148,000, IHT would be £8,000. If no deed of family arrangement had been made on A's death and his widow's estate was, as a result, £276,000, the IHT payable on her death would have been £59,200. The disclaimer has thus saved IHT of £51,200 (ignoring any increase in value in the funds originally intended for the children and assuming no changes in the rates of IHT).

09 Double Taxation Relief

HTA 1984, s 159]

09.1 UNILATERAL RELIEF
(A) Where property is situated in an overseas territory only

A, domiciled in England, owns a holiday home in Spain valued at £138,000 which he gives to his son in July 1990. He is liable to Spanish gifts tax of, say, £750. He has made no previous transfers and does not use the home again at any time before his death in February 1995.

	£	£
Market value of holiday home		138,000
Annual exemption 1990/91	(3,000)	
1989/90	(3,000)	
		(6,000)
Chargeable transfer		£132,000
IHT payable at 60% of full rates by son (death between 4 and 5 years after gift)		960
Unilateral relief for foreign tax		(750)
IHT borne		£210

Note
(*a*) If the overseas tax suffered exceeds the UK liability before relief, there will be no IHT payable but the excess will not be repayable.

(B) Where property is situated in both the UK and an overseas territory

M, of English domicile, owns company shares which are regarded as situated both in the UK and country X under the rules of the respective countries. On M's death in June 1990 the shares pass to M's son S. The UK IHT amounts to £5,000 before unilateral relief. The equivalent tax liability arising in country X amounts to £2,000.

Applying the formula $\dfrac{A}{A + B} \times C$

Where A = amount of IHT
B = amount of overseas tax
C = smaller of A and B

the unilateral relief available is

$$\frac{5,000}{5,000 + 2,000} \times £2,000 = £1,429$$

IHT payable = £5,000 − £1,429 = £3,571

(C) Where tax is imposed in two or more overseas territories on property situated in the UK and each of those territories

Assume the facts in (B) above except that a third country imposes a tax liability on the death as the shares are regarded as also situated in that country.

UK IHT before unilateral relief	£5,000
Tax in country X	£2,000
Tax in country Y	£400

Unilateral relief for IHT

$$\frac{5,000}{5,000 + 2,000 + 400} \times (2,000 + 400) = £1,622$$

IHT payable £5,000 − £1,622 = £3,378

(D) Where tax in one overseas territory is relieved against another overseas territory's tax

Assume the same facts as in example (C) above except that country X allows credit for tax paid in country Y.

Unilateral relief for IHT

$$\frac{5,000}{5,000 + (2,000 - 400) + 400} \times £((2,000 - 400) + 400) = £1,429$$

IHT payable £5,000 − £1,429 = £3,571

310   Exempt Transfers

310.1   ANNUAL GIFTS [*IHTA 1984, ss 19, 20, 57; FA 1986, 19 Sch 5*]

(A) General

T made gifts to his son of £2,000 on 1 June 1990 and £5,000 on 1 May 1991. On 9 November 1990 T had given £20,000 to a discretionary trust for his children and grandchildren. T had made no other gifts since 6 April 1990, but had used his annual exemptions in each year up to and including 1989/90. T died on 13 February 1996.

The gifts on 1 June 1990 and 1 May 1991 are potentially exempt transfers (PETs) which become chargeable since T died within seven years of each gift.

The gift on 9 November 1990 is a chargeable transfer. For the purpose of allocating the annual exemption only, the PET on 1 June 1990 is treated as having been made later in 1990/91 than any transfer of value in that year which is not a PET.

1990/91	£
1 June 1990 Gift to son — PET becoming chargeable	£2,000
9 November 1990 Gift to trust	20,000
Deduct 1990/91 annual exemption	3,000
Chargeable transfer	£17,000

1991/92	£
1 May 1991 Gift to son — PET becoming chargeable	5,000
Deduct 1991/92 annual exemption	3,000
Chargeable	£2,000

(B)

The facts are as in (A) above, except that the gift into settlement was made on 9 November 1991.

The gifts on 1 June 1990 and 1 May 1991 are PETs which become chargeable by reason of T's death. As they are treated as exempt until then, the 1990/91 and 1991/92 annual exemptions are initially available against the chargeable transfer on 9 November 1991. Although for the purpose of allocating the annual exemptions the chargeable transfer is treated as made earlier in 1991/92 than the PET on 1 May 1991, it is preceded by the PET on 1 June 1990.

	£	£
Initial position		
1991/92		
9 November 1991 Gift to trust		20,000
Deduct annual exemptions 1991/92	3,000	
1990/91	3,000	
		6,000
Chargeable transfer		£14,000

Revised position on T's death

1990/91

	£
1 June 1990 Gift to son	2,000
Deduct 1990/91 annual exemption (part)	2,000
Chargeable gift	—

1991/92

	£
1 May 1991 Gift to son	£5,000

		£
9 November 1991 Gift to trust		20,000
Deduct annual exemptions 1991/92	3,000	
1990/91 (balance)	1,000	
		4,000
Revised chargeable transfer		£16,000

310.2 NORMAL EXPENDITURE OUT OF INCOME [*IHTA 1984, s 21*]

A wife pays annual life assurance premiums on a policy in favour of her son. The annual income of her husband and herself is

	£
Husband's salary	25,000
Wife's salary	5,005
	£30,005

The wife's disposable income is

	£
Salary	5,005
Basic rate tax (personal allowance £3,005)	500
Personal income	£4,505

Notes

(*a*)   Depending on her lifestyle, the wife is probably able to show that she has sufficient income to justify a 'normal expenditure' gift of a £1,000 premium paid annually (and therefore habitual).

(*b*)   If the wife was also accustomed to pay personally for an annual holiday costing £2,500, it might be difficult to show that the payment was made out of income.

311 Gifts with Reservation

[FA 1986, s 81, 20 Sch; SI 1987/1130]

311.1 **(A) Reservation released within 7 years before death**
On 19 June 1987 D gave his house to his grandson G, but continued to live in it alone paying no rent. The house was valued at £100,000. On 5 May 1990 D remarried, and went to live with his new wife F. G immediately moved into the house, which was then valued at £148,000.
On 3 January 1995 D died, leaving his estate of £200,000 equally to his grand-daughter H and his wife F.

Gift 19 June 1987
As the gift was made more than seven years before death, it is a PET which has become exempt.

5 May 1990 release of reservation
The release of D's reservation is a PET which becomes chargeable by reason of D's death between 4 and 5 years later. IHT is charged at 60% of full rates on the basis of the Table of rates in force at the time of death on the value of the house at the date of release of reservation.

	£	£
Gift		148,000
Deduct annual exemptions 1990/91	3,000	
1989/90	3,000	
		6,000
Chargeable transfer		£142,000
Tax thereon (assuming no change in rates)		
0–128,000 at nil%	—	
128,001–142,000 at 40%	5,600	
	£5,600	
IHT payable at 60% of full rates, 60% × £5,600 =		£3,360

Death 3 January 1995
IHT is charged at full rates on the chargeable estate of £100,000 (£100,000 passing to the wife is exempt) in the bracket £142,000 to £242,000.

Tax thereon

142,001–242,000 at 40%	£40,000

(B) Reservation not released before death
The facts are as in (A) above except that the gift was on 19 June 1989 when the house was valued at £138,000, that D remained in his house on remarriage, and that G did not move in until D's death. The house was valued at £160,000 on 3 January 1995.

Gift 19 June 1989
This is a potentially exempt transfer which becomes chargeable by reason of D's death within seven years.

Death 3 January 1995

As the reservation had not been released at the date of D's death, D is treated as beneficially entitled to the house, which thus forms part of his chargeable estate on death.

A double charge would arise by virtue of the house being the subject of a PET and a part of the chargeable estate on death. *The Inheritance Tax (Double Charges Relief) Regulations 1987 [SI 1987/1130]* provide relief as follows.

First calculation under Reg 5(3)(a)

Charge the house in the death estate and ignore the PET.

	£
Chargeable estate	
Free estate passing to H	100,000
House	160,000
	£260,000

There are no chargeable transfers within the previous seven years.

	£
IHT payable	
First £128,000	—
£128,001 – 260,000 at 40%	52,800
	£52,800

Second calculation under Reg 5(3)(b)

Charge the PET and ignore the value of the house in the death estate.

	£	£
Gift 19 June 1989		138,000
Deduct annual exemptions 1989/90	3,000	
1988/89	3,000	
		6,000
Chargeable transfer		£132,000
Tax thereon		
0–128,000		
128,001–132,000 at 40%	1,600	
	£1,600	
IHT payable at 40% of full rates, 40% × £1,600 =	£640	

	£
Chargeable estate on death (excluding house)	100,000
IHT payable in the bracket £132,001 to £232,000	
£132,001–232,000 at 40%	£40,000
Total IHT payable	£40,640

The first calculation yields the higher amount of tax (£52,800), so tax is charged by reference to the value of the gift with reservation in the estate, ignoring the PET.

312 Interest on Tax

[IHTA 1984, s 233; FA 1989, s 178; SI 1989, No 1002]

312.1 B died on 10 February 1991. The executors made a payment on account of IHT of £90,000 on 30 June 1991 on delivery of the account. The final notice of determination was raised by the Capital Taxes Office on 19 June 1992 in the sum of £102,500. The rate of interest is assumed to be 11%.

Date of chargeable event (death)	10 February	1991
Date on which interest starts to accrue	1 September	1991

	£
IHT payable	102,500
Payment made on account 30 June 1991	90,000
Balance due	£12,500

Assessment raised by Capital Taxes Office 19 June 1992
Interest payable (1.9.91 to 19.6.92)

£12,500 at 11% for 291 days	£1,096

Note
(a)   Further interest may be charged if payment of the balance is not made promptly.

312.2 F gave his holiday home in Cornwall to his granddaughter G on 7 August 1990. On 23 May 1994 F died. He had made no use of the property at any time after 7 August 1990. G made a payment of £15,000, on account of the IHT due, on 1 January 1995. The liability was agreed at £17,000, and the balance paid, on 17 February 1995.

Date of PET	7 August	1990
Date on which PET becomes chargeable	23 May	1994
Date on which IHT is due	1 December	1994

	£
IHT payable	17,000
Payment made on account 1 January 1995	15,000
Balance due	£2,000

Interest payable

On £17,000 from 1.12.94 – 1.1.95	
£17,000 at 11% for 31 days	159
On £2,000 from 1.1.95 – 17.2.95	
£2,000 at 11% for 47 days	28
Total interest payable	£187

313 Liability for Tax

313.1 **LIFETIME TRANSFERS** [*IHTA 1984, ss 199(1), 204(2)(3)(5)(6)*]
(A) Transferor
A settled £78,000 on discretionary trusts in December 1990, having previously made chargeable transfers on 31 March 1990 totalling £136,000 so that his IHT rate is 20%.

A's liability is as follows	£
Gift	78,000
Deduct 1990/91 annual exemption	3,000
	£75,000
Grossed at 20%	£93,750
IHT thereon at 20%	£18,750

(B) Transferee
In example (A) above A pays only £10,000 of IHT and defaults on the balance of £8,750, so that the trustees become liable as transferee.

The trustees' liability is not however £8,750 but is as follows	£
Original gross	93,750
Deduct IHT unpaid	8,750
Revised gross	£85,000
IHT thereon at 20%	17,000
Deduct Paid by A	10,000
Now due from trustees	£7,000

(C) Person in whom property is vested
In January 1991 C transferred to trustees of a discretionary trust shares in an unquoted property company worth, as a minority holding, £50,000. However the transfer deprives C of control of the company with the result that the value of his estate is reduced by £210,000. His IHT rate is 20%.

C's liability is as follows	
Net loss to him	£210,000
Grossed at 20%	£262,500
IHT thereon at 20%	£52,500

C fails to pay so that the trustees become liable, as follows

	£
Original gross	262,500
Deduct unpaid IHT	52,500
	£210,000
IHT thereon at 20%	£42,000

Notes

(*a*)   The trustees' liability cannot exceed the value of the assets which they hold, namely the proceeds of sale of the shares, less any CGT and costs incurred since acquisition, plus any undistributed income in their hands.

(*b*)   If the trustees have already distributed net income of £2,000 to D who is liable to pay further tax, at higher rates, of £154, D can be made to pay IHT of £1,846, being the net benefit received by him.

313.2 **TRANSFERS ON DEATH** [*IHTA 1984, ss 200(1)(3), 204(1)–(3)(5), 211*]
Personal representatives of E, who died on 30 September 1990, received the following assets

	£
Free personal property	78,000
Land bequeathed to F (which, under the terms of the Will, bears its own IHT)	26,000
Private residence, bequeathed to spouse	50,000

A trust in which E had a life interest was valued at £104,000. Under the will of E, legacies of £15,000, each free of IHT, were given to F and G and the residue was left to H. E had made no chargeable transfers during his lifetime.

	Persons liable	£	IHT £
IHT is borne as to			
Chargeable transfer			
Free personal property	PR's	78,000	12,000
Land bequeathed to F	F	26,000	4,000
Private residence to spouse	—	Exempt	Nil
Trust fund	Trustees	104,000	16,000
		£208,000	£32,000
The residue left to H is as follows			
Free personal property			78,000
Deduct IHT		12,000	
Legacies to F and G		30,000	42,000
			£36,000

Note

(*a*)   If the will had not directed that the IHT on the land bequeathed to F be borne by F, the IHT would be payable out of residue. [*IHTA 1984, s 211*].

313.3 **LIFETIME TRANSFER WITH ADDITIONAL LIABILITY ON DEATH** [*IHTA 1984, ss 131, 199(2), 201(2), 204(4)*]

(A)

On 31 December 1990, H, who had made no earlier chargeable transfers other than to utilise his annual exemptions for 1990/91 and earlier years, transferred £145,000 into a discretionary trust and, a month later, settled an asset worth £20,000 into the same trust. H paid the appropriate IHT. On 30 June 1994, H died.

The trustees become liable to further IHT as follows

	£	£
Original net gift	£145,000	£20,000
Grossed-up at half of full rates	£149,250	£25,000
IHT (paid by H)	£4,250	£5,000
IHT at 80% of death rates applicable in June 1994 on original gross (death between 3 and 4 years after gifts)	6,800	8,000
Deduct paid originally by H	4,250	5,000
Now due from trustees	£2,550	£3,000

Note

(*a*)   The additional IHT on death is calculated using the rates in force at the date of death. If the IHT at the new death rates, as tapered, is less than the IHT paid on the original chargeable transfer, there will be no repayment.

(B)

The second gift in (A) above had fallen in value to £18,000 by the time of H's death.

The trustees may claim to reduce the IHT payable to follows

	£
Original gross gift	25,000
Deduct drop in value (£20,000 − £18,000)	2,000
Revised gross	£23,000
IHT thereon at 80% of death rate applicable in June 1994	7,360
Deduct paid by H	5,000
	£2,360

Note

(*a*)   If the asset had fallen in value to £10,625 or less, so that the revised gross became £15,625 or less and the IHT at 80% of death rates £5,000 or less, the trustees would have no liability because H had already paid IHT of £5,000.

313.4 **POTENTIALLY EXEMPT TRANSFER BECOMING CHARGEABLE
ON DEATH**
[*IHTA 1984, ss 199, 201, 204; FA 1986, 19 Sch 26–28*]
On 19 May 1990 M gave N £144,000. M died on 3 August 1993 having made no
other gifts.

	£
Gift	144,000
Deduct annual exemptions 1990/91	(3,000)
1989/90	(3,000)
	£138,000

The IHT at 80% of full rates on the gift to N is payable by N on 1 March 1994.

	£
First £128,000 at nil	—
Next £10,000 at 40%	4,000
	£4,000

IHT payable by N 80% × £4,000 = £3,200

Notes
(*a*)   If N has not paid the IHT due of £3,200 by 1 March 1995 the personal representatives of M are liable, although their liability cannot exceed the death
estate of M. The amount is a deductible liability from the estate only to the
extent that reimbursement from N cannot be obtained.

(*b*)   See also 305.1 CALCULATION OF TAX for liability to tax on potentially exempt
transfers.

449

314 Life Assurance Policies

[IHTA 1984, ss 21, 167]

314.1 A has paid premiums of £2,000 p.a for 6 years on a policy on his own life. He gives the policy to his son B. The market value of the policy at the date of gift is £11,000. A also pays annual premiums of £2,000 on a policy on his life written in favour of his son.

Assignment of policy
The gift is valued either at
(i)   market value (£11,000), or
(ii)   the accumulated gross premiums paid (£12,000) if greater.

Annual premiums
The annual premium is regarded as an annual gift of £2,000 *less* the life assurance relief (if available and not restricted) of $12\frac{1}{2}\%$, i.e. a gift of £1,750.

Notes
(*a*)   The gifts are PETs. The assignment of the policy will only become chargeable if A dies within seven years, and only the annual premiums paid within seven years of A's death will be chargeable.

(*b*)   Exemptions available for reduction of the chargeable transfer on assignment include the annual exemption and the marriage exemption.

(*c*)   The normal expenditure exemption may be available to A for premiums paid and the annual exemption may also be claimed to exempt the gift in whole or in part.

(*d*)   Normal expenditure relief is not available when a policy and annuity have been effected on a back-to-back basis (with certain exceptions).

315 Mutual Transfers

[FA 1986, s 104; SI 1987/1130]

315.1 POTENTIALLY EXEMPT TRANSFERS AND DEATH

A, who has made no previous transfers of value other than to use his annual exemptions for 1989/90 and 1990/91, makes a gift of £138,000 to B on 1 July 1990. On 15 July 1991 and 20 January 1992, he makes gifts of £106,000 and £55,000 respectively into a discretionary trust and the trustees pay the IHT due of £6,000 on the later transfer. On 2 January 1993, B dies and the 1990 gift is returned to A by virtue of B's Will. On 4 April 1994, A dies. His taxable estate on death is valued at £400,000 which includes the 1990 gift returned to him in 1993 which is still valued at £138,000.

First calculation under Reg 4(4)(a)

The gift in 1990 is a PET and would normally become a chargeable transfer by virtue of A's death within seven years of making the gift. However, for the purpose of this calculation, it is ignored and the returned gift is charged as part of A's death estate.

Additional tax due on chargeable lifetime transfers

	£
Gift on 15 July 1991	106,000
Deduct 1991/92 annual exemption	3,000
	103,000
Gift on 20 January 1992	55,000
	£158,000

IHT at death rates on £158,000	12,000
IHT paid	6,000
Additional IHT payable by trustees	£6,000

Tax on death estate of £400,000 charged at 40%

IHT payable note *(a)*	£160,000

Total IHT payable as consequence of death (£6,000 + £160,000)   £166,000

Second calculation under Reg 4(4)(b)

The 1989 gift is charged as a PET but the returned gift is ignored in the death estate.

The tax due on PET of £138,000 at death rates

	£
0–128,000	Nil
128,001–138,000 at 40%	4,000
	£4,000

IHT payable at 80% of full rates
(death between 3 and 4 years after gift)   £3,200

Tax due on chargeable lifetime transfers of £158,000 (after annual exemption)
charged at 40%

	£
IHT payable	63,200
IHT paid	6,000
Additional IHT payable	£57,200

Tax on death estate of £262,000 charged at 40%
IHT payable   £104,800

Total IHT payable as consequence of death
(£3,200 + £57,200 + £104,800)   £165,200

The first calculation gives the higher amount of tax, so the PET is ignored and the
returned gift included in the death estate, the tax liabilities being as in the first calculation above.

Note
(a)   Quick succession relief under *IHTA 1984, s 141* (see 319.1 below) might be
      due in respect of the returned PET by reference to any tax charged on that
      PET in connection with B's death. If, as a result of such relief, the first calcu-
      lation produces a lower tax charge than the second, then the second calcula-
      tion will prevail, i.e. the PET will be charged and the returned gift ignored in
      the death estate.

315.2   CHARGEABLE TRANSFERS AND DEATH
C, who had made no other transfer of value, gifted £156,000 on 31 May 1986 into
discretionary trust, on which IHT of £13,750 was paid. On 5 October 1986, he gave
D a life interest in shares worth £85,000; IHT of £19,500 was paid. On 3 January
1991, C makes a PET of £30,000 to E. On 31 December 1992, D dies and the settled
shares return to C, the settlor (no tax charge arises on D's death). On 10 August
1993, C dies; his death estate is valued at £260,000 which includes the shares
returned from D, now worth £60,000.

First calculation under Reg 7(4)(a)
The gift in October 1986 is ignored and the returned shares included as part of the
taxable estate on death.
No additional tax arises on the May 1986 lifetime transfer of £150,000 (after annual
exemptions) as it was made more than seven years before death.
Tax due on PET of £30,000 made in January 1991 charged in band
£150,001–180,000.

£30,000 at 40% = £12,000.

Tax on death estate of £260,000 charged in band £30,001–290,000 (the gift to the discretionary trust having fallen out of cumulation)

	£	£
30,001–128,000	Nil	
128,001–290,000 at 40%	64,800	64,800

Total IHT payable as consequence of death
(£12,000 + £64,800) (but see note (*a*) below)   £76,800

Second calculation under Reg 7(4)(b)
The October 1986 gift is charged and the returned shares are excluded from the taxable estate on death.
Additional tax due on October 1986 transfer as a result of death — charged in band £150,001 to £235,000.

150,001–235,000 at 40%	£34,000

IHT payable at 20% of full rates	
(death between 6 and 7 years after gift)	6,800
IHT paid £19,500, but credit restricted to	6,800
Additional IHT	Nil

Tax due on PET of £30,000 charged in band £235,001–265,000.

£30,000 at 40%	£12,000

Tax on death estate of £200,000 charged in band £115,001–315,000.

115,001–128,000	Nil	
128,001–315,000 at 40%	74,800	£74,800

Total IHT payable as consequence of death (£12,000 + £74,800)   £86,800

The second calculation gives the higher amount of tax so the returned gift is excluded from the death estate, the tax liabilities being as in the second calculation above.

Note
(*a*)   If the first calculation had given the higher amount, a credit for IHT would have been due, restricted to the lower of

(i)   the IHT paid on the lifetime transfer (i.e. £19,500); and

(ii)   the IHT attributable to the returned shares on death, calculated as follows:

$$\text{Estate rate } \frac{64,800}{260,000} = 24.923\%$$

£60,000 × 24.923% = £14,954

The IHT actually payable as a consequence of death would have been £61,846 (£76,800 − £14,954).

316 National Heritage

[*IHTA 1984, ss 30–35, 57A, 77–79, 207, 2 Sch 5, 6, 4 Sch, 5 Sch; FA 1987, s 59, 9 Sch*]

316.1 CONDITIONALLY EXEMPT TRANSFERS AFTER 6 APRIL 1976

(A) Chargeable event during lifetime of relevant person

C, who has made previous chargeable transfers during 1986 of £230,000, makes a conditionally exempt gift of property in February 1987. In October 1990, the property is sold for £500,000 and capital gains tax of £100,000 is payable.

		£
Cumulative total of previous chargeable transfers of relevant person		230,000
Net sale proceeds of conditionally exempt property	500,000	
Deduct capital gains tax payable	(100,000)	
Chargeable transfer		400,000
Revised cumulative total for relevant person		£630,000

Inheritance tax payable (by reference to lifetime rates in October 1990)

£400,000 at 20% =   £80,000

(B) Chargeable event after relevant person is dead

D died in April 1984 leaving a taxable estate of £350,000 together with conditionally exempt property valued at £600,000 at the breach in October 1990.

	£
Value of relevant person's estate at death	350,000
Value of conditionally exempt property at date of breach	600,000
	£950,000

Inheritance tax payable (by reference to full rates applicable in October 1990).

£600,000 at 40% =   £240,000

Note

(a)   As the chargeable event occurs after tax is reduced by the substitution of a new table of rates, the new rates are used.

(C) Multiple conditionally exempt transfers

D died in December 1979 leaving a conditionally exempt property to his son E. D's taxable estate at death was £230,000. In 1986 E gave the property to his daughter F. F gave the necessary undertakings so this transfer was also conditionally exempt. In December 1990 F sold the property for its market value of £500,000 and paid capital gains tax of £80,000. During 1984 E had made chargeable transfers of £20,000 and he has made no other transfers.

	£	£
Value of relevant person's estate at death		230,000
Net sale proceeds of conditionally exempt property	500,000	
Deduct capital gains tax	80,000	
Chargeable transfer		420,000
		£650,000

Inheritance tax payable by F

£420,000 at 40% =	£168,000

Previous cumulative total of E	20,000
Add chargeable transfer	420,000
E's revised cumulative total	£440,000

Notes

(*a*)   There have been two conditionally exempt transfers within the period of 30 years ending with the chargeable event in December 1990. The Inland Revenue may select either D or E as the 'relevant person' for the purpose of calculating the tax due. The IHT liability will be higher if D is selected. [*IHTA 1984, ss 33(5), 78(3)*].

(*b*)   As F receives the proceeds of sale, she is the person liable to pay the IHT. [*IHTA 1984, s 207(1)*].

(*c*)   Although the IHT is calculated by reference to D's cumulative total, it is E whose cumulative total is adjusted as he made the last conditionally exempt transfer of the property. [*IHTA 1984, s 34(1)*].

(*d*)   As the chargeable event occurs after a reduction in the rates of tax, the new rates are used to calculate the tax payable. [*IHTA 1984, 2 Sch 5*].

316.2 CONDITIONALLY EXEMPT TRANSFERS ON DEATH BEFORE 7 APRIL 1976

Chargeable event more than 3 years after death

B died on 31 December 1975 leaving a taxable estate of £100,000 together with a conditionally exempt painting valued at £50,000. In June 1990 the painting was sold for £110,000.

		£
Value of deceased's taxable estate		100,000
Value of exempt property at date of chargeable event	note (*a*)	110,000
		£210,000
Recalculated IHT liability	note (*b*)	£90,750

IHT payable on conditionally exempt property

$$£90,750 \times \frac{110,000}{210,000} \qquad £47,536$$

No further liability accrues to the estate of the deceased.

Notes

(*a*) The value of the exempt property will be reduced by any capital gains tax chargeable in respect of the sale. [*CGTA 1979, s 147(8)*].

(*b*) The IHT liability is calculated using rates in force at the date of death.

316.3 CHARGE TO TAX

Tax credit [*IHTA 1984, s 33(7)*]

Property inherited in 1982 from A's estate by B, who gave the necessary under-takings so that the property is conditionally exempt, is given in December 1990 by B to C. B dies in March 1991. C agrees to pay any inheritance tax arising from the transfer but does not wish to give the necessary undertakings, so a chargeable event arises.

	£
A's estate at date of death in 1982	180,000
B's cumulative chargeable transfers at date of chargeable event in December 1990 (all in 1989/90)	58,000
Value of property at date of chargeable event	250,000

Inheritance tax on chargeable event (subject to tax credit)

	£
Value of A's estate at date of death	180,000
Value of property at date of chargeable event	250,000
	£430,000

Inheritance tax payable £250,000 at 40% =	£100,000

Inheritance tax on B's gift

Cumulative total of previous transfers		58,000
Value of property gifted	250,000	
Deduct available annual exemption	3,000	247,000
		£305,000

Inheritance tax arising on gift of £247,000	£70,800

Tax credit

IHT on B's gift		70,800
IHT on chargeable event	100,000	
Deduct tax credit	(70,800)	
		29,200
Total inheritance tax borne		£100,000

316.4 SETTLEMENTS — EVENTS AFTER 8 MARCH 1982

(A) Chargeable events following conditionally exempt occasions

A, who is still alive, settled property and investments on discretionary trusts in September 1980, conditional exemption being granted in respect of designated property. In April 1990, the designated property was appointed absolutely to beneficiary C who gave the necessary undertakings for exemption to continue. However, in February 1991, C sold the property for £113,000 net of costs, suffering a capital gains tax liability of £20,000. At the time of C's sale, A had made chargeable transfers of £40,000 all in 1989/90.

	£
Cumulative total of previous chargeable transfers of relevant person	40,000
Net sale proceeds of conditionally exempt property	93,000
	£133,000

Inheritance tax payable by C

£88,000 at nil	—	
£5,000 at 20%	1,000	
£83,000	£1,000	£1,000

Notes

(a)   A is the relevant person in relation to the chargeable event as he is the person to effect the only conditionally exempt transfer *and* the person who is settlor in relation to the settlement in respect of which the only conditionally exempt occasion arose. [*IHTA 1984, ss 33(5), 78(3)*].

(b)   The Inland Revenue have discretion to select either the conditionally exempt transfer (by A to the trustees) in 1979 or the conditionally exempt occasion (from the trustees to C) in 1990 as the 'last transaction' for the purposes of determining who is the relevant person. A is the relevant person regardless of which is selected but the Inland Revenue is more likely to choose the earlier transfer as this will result in a greater amount of tax being collected. [*IHTA 1984, ss 33(5), 78(3)(4)*].

(c)   The chargeable amount of £83,000 does not increase either A's cumulative total or that of the trustees for the purpose of calculating the IHT liability on any subsequent transfers. As the last conditionally exempt transaction before the chargeable event was a conditionally exempt occasion rather than a conditionally exempt transfer, the provisions of *IHTA 1984, s 34* (which allow for an increase in the cumulative total) do not apply. [*IHTA 1984, s 78(6)*].

(B) Exemption from the ten-year anniversary charge [*IHTA 1984, s 79*]
Trustees own National Heritage property for which the necessary undertakings have been given and the property has been designated by the Treasury. The property was settled in July 1974 and is the sole asset of the trust. No appointments or advances of capital have been made. On 30 October 1994, there is a breach of the undertakings. At this date the property is valued at £150,000.

Ten-year anniversary charge
There is no liability in 1984 or 1994.

Breach in October 1994

Value of property at time of event   £150,000

The relevant period is the period from 13 March 1975 to 30 October 1994 i.e. 78 complete quarters.

The rate of tax is

	%
0.25% for 40 quarters	10.00
0.20% for 38 quarters	7.60
	17.60%

IHT payable is 17.6% × £150,000 = £26,400

316.5 **MAINTENANCE FUNDS FOR HISTORIC BUILDINGS** [*IHTA 1984, 2 Sch 6, Sch 8, 12–14*]

On 1 January 1986 P settled £500,000 in an approved maintenance fund for hi historic mansion during the lives of himself and his wife, W. On 1 January 2001, th date of death of W, the fund, which has been depleted by extensive repairs to th mansion, is valued at £300,000. £100,000 is transferred to the National Trust, whic also accepts the gift of the mansion, and the balance is paid to P's grandson G. had died in February 1991, his taxable estate and lifetime transfers chargeable o death amounting to £118,000.

No IHT is payable on the £100,000 paid to the National Trust, but the balanc passing to G is liable to IHT at the higher of a tapered scale rate (the 'first rate') an an effective rate calculated by reference to P's estate (the 'second rate'). [*IHT 1984, 4 Sch 12–14*].

First rate

The property was comprised in the maintenance fund for 15 years, i.e. 60 quarters

The scale rate is

	%
0.25% for each of the first 40 quarters	10
0.20% for each of the next 20 quarters	4
	14%

Second rate

The effective rate is calculated, using half Table rates applying on 1 January 2001 as if the chargeable amount transferred had been added to the value transferred b P on his death and had formed the highest part of it. Half Table rates are use because the fund was set up in P's lifetime. (It is assumed that Table rates do nc change.)

	£
£10,000 at nil	—
£190,000 at 20%	38,000
£200,000	£38,000

The effective rate is $\dfrac{38,000}{200,000} \times 100\% =$ 19%

As the second rate (19%) is higher than the first rate (14%) the second rate is used

IHT payable is £200,000 at 19% =   £38,000

317   Partnerships

IHTA 1984, s 10(1)]

17.1 A, B and C (A's son) carry on a business in partnership sharing profits 60:25:15. The partnership deed provides that on the death or retirement of a partner, goodwill shall accrue to the continuing partners for no payment. The present value of goodwill is £100,000.
Profit sharing ratios are varied on 1 January 1991 and become 40:35:25.

If there had merely been a reduction of 10% in A's share and a corresponding increase in his son's, the Inland Revenue might claim that there was gratuitous intent and that the transfer was not one which would have been made between parties at arm's length. If that claim succeeded, the transfer would be as follows

	£
Value of goodwill transferred 10% of £100,000	10,000
Deduct business property relief (50%)	5,000
Transfer of value	£5,000

However, since there is also a transfer from A to B, it seems more likely that this is a bona fide commercial arrangement under which one partner gives up a share of profits to the others in return for their acceptance of greater responsibility. If so, no transfer of value would arise.
The transfer will, in any case, be a PET, and only become chargeable if A dies within seven years. Business property relief will be available provided C remains in the partnership, so that the goodwill is a business asset.

318 Payment of Tax

[IHTA 1984, ss 227, 228, 234; FA 1986, 19 Sch 31; SI 1989, No 1002]

318.1 PAYMENT BY INSTALMENTS ON TRANSFER OR DEATH

(A)

F died on 17 December 1990 leaving a free estate of £250,000 including £75,000 i respect of a controlling interest, in the share capital of an unquoted trading com pany, valued at £150,000 on which business property relief at 50% is available. A election is made to pay inheritance tax on unquoted shares by 10 equal yearl instalments.

Inheritance tax on free estate	£
On first £128,000	Nil
On next £122,000 at 40%	48,800
£250,000	£48,800

IHT applicable to unquoted shares

$$\frac{75,000}{250,000} \times £48,800 \qquad 14,640$$

1st instalment due 1.7.91	£1,464
2nd instalment due 1.7.92	£1,464

Notes

(*a*)   Even if the shares did not give F control of the company, the tax due could b paid by instalments as they attract more than 20% of the tax payable o death.

(*b*)   Instalments continue to be paid at yearly intervals for 10 years or until th shares are sold when all unpaid IHT becomes payable.

(*c*)   Interest is payable on each instalment from the day it falls due. If payment are made on time, no interest is payable.

(B)

On 1 December 1990 G gave his 60% holding in an unquoted trading company to his son S who agreed to pay any IHT on the transfer. The shareholding was valued at £100,000. G had made prior chargeable transfers of £98,000, had already used his 1989/90 and 1990/91 annual exemptions, and he died on 31 December 1994.

S elected to pay the IHT by 10 yearly instalments and paid the first on 1 August 1995, and the second on 1 September 1996. On 1 December 1996 he sold the shareholding, and paid the balance of the IHT outstanding on 1 February 1997. It is assumed that the rate of interest on unpaid tax is 11%.

Inheritance tax on gift

	£
Value of shareholding	100,000
Deduct business property relief at 50%	50,000
PET becoming chargeable on death	£50,000

IHT payable in the band £98,001–£148,000

	£
£98,001–128,000	Nil
£128,001–148,000 at 40%	8,000
	£8,000

Total IHT payable at 60% of full rates (death between 4 and 5 years after gift)	£4,800

1st instalment due 1.7.95	480	
Interest at 11% from 1.7.95 to 1.8.95		
$\frac{31}{365} \times £480 \times 11\%$	4	
		484
2nd instalment due 1.7.96	480	
Interest at 11% from 1.7.96 to 1.9.96		
$\frac{62}{365} \times £480 \times 11\%$	9	
		489
Balance due on sale on 1.12.96	3,840	
Interest at 11% from 1.12.96 to 1.2.97		
$\frac{62}{365} \times £3,840 \times 11\%$	72	
		3,912
Total IHT and interest		£4,885

319 Protective Trusts

319.1 FORFEITURE BEFORE 12 APRIL 1978 [*IHTA 1984, s 73*]

In 1951 X left his estate on protective trusts for his son Z. On 1 January 1978
attempted to assign his interest and the protective trusts determined. On 1 Ma
1983 the trustees advanced £25,000 to Z to enable him to purchase a flat. At th
same time, they also advanced £10,000 (net) to his granddaughter D. On 1 Marc
1991 Z died and the trust fund, valued at £50,000, passed equally to his grand
children absolutely.

1 May 1983
There is no charge to IHT on the payment to Z, but a charge arises on the payme
to D.
The relevant period is the period from the determination of the protective trus
(1 January 1978) to 1 May 1983 i.e. 21 complete quarters.

The rate of tax is 0.25% for each of 21 quarters   5.25%

IHT payable is $\dfrac{5.25}{100 - 5.25} \times £10,000 = £554$

The gross payment is £10,554

1 March 1990
There is a charge to IHT when the trust vests on the death of Z. 52 comple
quarters have elapsed since the protective trusts determined.

The rate of tax is

	%
0.25% for each of the first 40 quarters	10.0
0.20% for each of the next 12 quarters	2.4
	12.4%

IHT payable is 12.4% × £50,000 = £6,200

19.2 **FORFEITURE AFTER 11 APRIL 1978** [*IHTA 1984, s 88*]

Assume the same facts as in 319.1 above but that Z attempted to assign his interest on 1 January 1980.

1 May 1983
There is no charge to IHT on the payment to Z who is treated as beneficially entitled to an interest in possession under the trust. The payment to D is a chargeable transfer. Tax is charged at Z's personal cumulative rate of tax so that if he had made no previous transfers, the payment would be covered by his nil rate tax band. If the payment had been made after 16 March 1987, it would have been a potentially exempt transfer.

1 March 1990
There is a charge to IHT when the trust vests on the death of Z, calculated by aggregating £50,000 with all other chargeable property passing on his death and applying the normal death rates.

320 Quick Succession Relief

[IHTA 1984, s 141]

320.1 TRANSFERS AFTER 9 MARCH 1981

On 1 January 1991 A died with a net estate valued at £128,000. In December 198■ he had received a gift from B of £20,000 on which B paid the tax. B had made prio■ transfers of £60,000 all during the year to 5 April 1986, in addition to using up hi■ basic exemptions for 1984/85 and 1985/86.

A was also entitled to an interest in possession in the whole of his father's estate His father had died in February 1988 with a net estate of £80,000 on which the IH■ paid was £3,000. On A's death, the property passed to A's sister and was valued a■ £75,000. A had made no previous transfers and left his estate to his brother.

	£
Free estate	128,00■
Settled property	75,00■
Taxable estate	£203,00■

IHT on an estate of £203,000 = £30,000

Quick succession relief

Gift by B to A	20,00■
Deduct annual exemption	3,00■
Net chargeable transfer	£17,00■

	Gross	Tax	Net
Previous transfers	60,000	Nil	60,00■
This transfer	18,059	1,059	17,00■
Total	£78,059	1,059	£77,00■

Tax paid by B	£1,05■

The gift from B was made more than four but not more than five years before deat■ so the quick succession relief is at 20%.

$$QSR = 20\% \times £1,059 \times \frac{17,000}{18,059}$$ £19■

Interest in possession in father's will trust	£
Net estate before tax	80,000
Tax	3,000
Net estate after tax	£77,000

A's death was more than two but not more than three years after his father's so the relief is at 60%.

$$QSR = 60\% \times £3,000 \times \frac{77,000}{80,000} \qquad £1,733$$

Tax payable on death of A	£	£
IHT on an estate of £203,000		30,000
Deduct QSR		
On gift from B	199	
On father's estate	1,733	
		1,932
IHT payable		£28,068

$$\text{On free estate } \frac{128,000}{203,000} \times £28,068 \qquad £17,698$$

$$\text{On settled property } \frac{75,000}{203,000} \times £28,068 \qquad £10,370$$

Notes

(*a*) The relief applies to the *chargeable* transfer from B to A, so the exempt part of the transfer (the £3,000 annual exemption) is excluded.

(*b*) The relief is given only by reference to the tax charged on the part of the value received by the donee (i.e. the net transfer). Thus the tax paid must be apportioned by applying the fraction 'net transfer received divided by gross transfer made'.

321 Settlements with Interests in Possession

[IHTA 1984, ss 49(1), 51(1), 52(1), 54A, 54B, 57; F (No 2) A 1987, s 96, 7 Sch]

321.1 TERMINATION OF AN INTEREST IN POSSESSION

A had an interest in possession in a settlement valued at £100,000 with remainder t his son S. On 1 July 1990, A released his life interest to S in consideration of S marriage on 2 July 1990. A had made no gifts since 5 April 1990 but had used h annual exemptions prior to that date. His cumulative total of chargeable transfe at 5 April 1990 was £56,000, and these had all been made since 1 July 1983. A die on 30 June 1991.

The release of A's life interest is a potentially exempt transfer which become chargeable by reason of A's death within seven years. The charge is at full rate with no tapering relief as the transfer took place within three years before death.

	£	£
Value of property		100,00
Exemptions		
Annual	3,000	
In consideration of marriage	5,000	
		8,00
Chargeable transfer		£92,00

	Gross £	Tax £	Net £
Cumulative total b/f	56,000	—	56,00
Chargeable transfer	92,000	8,000	84,00
	£148,000	£8,000	£140,00

Tax payable by trustees as a consequence of A's death			£8,00

Notes

(*a*)   The annual gifts exemption and the exemption of gifts in consideration c marriage apply if notice is given to the trustees by the donor within 6 month of the gift. This requirement seems to apply even though the gift is poter tially exempt when made.

(*b*)   The tax payable is computed by reference to the transferor's cumulative tot of chargeable transfers within the previous seven years, and the chargeab transfer forms part of his cumulative total carried forward.

321.2 POTENTIALLY EXEMPT TRANSFER TO INTEREST IN POSSESSION TRUS — ANTI-AVOIDANCE PROVISIONS *[IHTA 1984, ss 54A, 54B; F (No 2) A 1987 7 Sch]*

B transferred £100,000 on 1 October 1990 into an interest in possession trust wher his brother C is the life tenant. On 31 August 1993, C released his life interest, the valued at £116,000, to a discretionary settlement in favour of his children. B cumulative chargeable transfers at 1 October 1990 amounted to £230,000. B wa still alive on 31 August 1993, at which date C's cumulative chargeable transfers amounted to £68,000 and he had not used his annual exemptions for 1992/93 and 1993/94. It is assumed that there is no change in IHT rates between October 1990 and August 1993.

The transfer by B in October 1990 is a potentially exempt transfer which will not become chargeable unless B dies before 1 October 1997.

The transfer by C is a chargeable lifetime transfer which is charged at lifetime rates i.e. one half of death rates, taking into account cumulative transfers of £68,000. If, however, a higher tax liability would be produced by substituting B's cumulative transfers at the time of his PET for those of C at the time of his transfer, this takes precedence over the normal calculation.

Normal calculation

	£	£
Value transferred by C on 31 August 1993		116,000
Deduct annual exemptions 1993/94	3,000	
1992/93	3,000	6,000
		£110,000

IHT on £110,000 is charged in the band £68,001 to £178,000.

	£
68,001–128,000	Nil
128,001–178,000 at 20%	10,000
	£10,000

Calculation under Section 54A

Value transferred by C on 31 August 1993, after exemptions as above	£110,000

IHT on £110,000 is charged in the band £230,001 to £340,000.

230,001–340,000 at 20%	£22,000

IHT payable is therefore £22,000.

Notes

(*a*) C's cumulative chargeable transfers following the gift in August 1993 will be £178,000 (*not* £340,000).

(*b*) If B dies after 31 August 1993 and before 1 October 1997, the IHT liability of £22,000 may increase. For example, B's cumulative chargeable transfers at 1 October 1990 may increase due to his having made other PETs prior to that date but within seven years of death. If the IHT liability had been determined under normal rules because this produced a liability greater than that produced by a calculation under *IHTA 1984, s 54A*, such liability could not be affected by the death of B. [*IHTA 1984, s 54B(1)*].

322 Settlements without Interests in Possession

Note
In all examples in this chapter, where the value of trust property is given, it is assumed that this does not include any undistributed and unaccumulated income. Such income is not treated as a taxable trust asset. (Revenue Statement of Practice SP 8/86).

322.1 **RATE OF TEN-YEAR ANNIVERSARY CHARGE**
(A) **Post-26 March 1974 settlements** [*IHTA 1984, ss 64, 66*]
On 1 May 1980 S settled £150,000 net, £100,000 to be held on discretionary trust and £50,000 in trust for his brother B for life. At the date of the transfer S had a cumulative total of chargeable transfers of £48,000. £20,000 (gross) was advanced from the discretionary trusts to C on 1 March 1988.

The property held on discretionary trusts was valued at £155,000 on 1 May 1990.

On 1 January 1995 B died, when the property subject to his interest in possession was valued at £95,000. The whole trust property was valued at £300,000 on 1 May 2000 of which £105,000 derived from B's fund. The trustees had made no advances other than that to C.

It is assumed that rates of tax do not change.

1 May 1990 Ten-year anniversary charge

		£
Assumed chargeable transfer		
(i)	value of relevant property immediately before the ten-year anniversary	155,000
(ii)	value, at date of settlement, of property which was not, and has not become, relevant property	50,000
(iii)	value, at date of settlement of property in related settlement	—
		£205,000

Assumed transferor's cumulative total		
(i)	value of chargeable transfers made by settlor in seven-year period ending on date of settlement	48,000
(ii)	amounts on which proportionate charges have been levied in ten years before the anniversary	20,000
		68,000
(iii)	amounts of distribution payments in period 1 May 1980 to 9 March 1982	—
		£68,000

	Gross £	Tax £
Assumed cumulative total	68,000	—
Assumed transfer	205,000	29,000
	£273,000	£29,000

Effective rate of tax $\dfrac{29,000}{205,000} \times 100 = \underline{14.146\%}$

Ten-year anniversary charge

The IHT payable is at 30% of the effective rate on the relevant property

IHT payable = 30% × 14.146% × £155,000 = £6,578

1 May 2000 Ten-year anniversary charge

		£
Assumed chargeable transfer		
(i)	value of relevant property immediately prior to the ten-year anniversary	300,000
(ii)	value at date of settlement of property which was not and has not become relevant property	—
(iii)	value at date of settlement of property in related settlement	—
		£300,000

		£
Assumed transferor's cumulative total		
(i)	value of chargeable transfers made by settlor in seven-year period ending on date of settlement	48,000
(ii)	amounts on which proportionate charges have been levied in ten years before the anniversary	—
		£48,000

	Gross £	Tax £
Assumed cumulative total	48,000	—
Assumed transfer	300,000	44,000
	£348,000	£44,000

Effective rate of tax $\dfrac{44,000}{300,000} \times 100 = \underline{14.667\%}$

Ten-year anniversary charge

Of the relevant property, £105,000 had not been relevant property throughout the period 1 May 1990–1 January 1995, i.e. 18 complete quarters.

IHT payable

At 30% × 14.667%	= 4.4%	on £195,000	8,580
At 30% × 14.667%	= 4.4%		
Less 18/40 × 30% × 14.667%	= 1.98%		
	2.42%	on £105,000	2,541
Total IHT payable			£11,121

(B) Pre-27 March 1974 settlements [*IHTA 1984, ss 64, 66*]

On 1 June 1970 T settled property on discretionary trusts. The trustees made the following advances (gross) to beneficiaries

1.1.74	H	£10,000
1.1.77	B	£20,000
1.1.81	C	£48,000
1.1.86	D	£40,000
1.1.92	E	£68,000

On 1 June 1990 the settled property was valued at £175,000 and on 1 June 2000 £180,000.

It is assumed that rates of tax do not change.

1 June 1990 Ten-year anniversary charge

Assumed chargeable transfer		
Value of relevant property		£175,000

Assumed transferor's cumulative total

(i)	Aggregate of distribution payments made between 1 June 1980 and 9 March 1982	48,000	
(ii)	Aggregate of amounts on which proportionate charge arises between 9 March 1982 and 1 June 1990	40,000	£88,000

	Gross £	Tax £
Assumed cumulative total	88,000	—
Assumed chargeable transfer	175,000	27,000
	£263,000	£27,000

$$\text{Effective rate of tax} = \frac{27,000}{175,000} \times 100 = \underline{15.429\%}$$

Ten-year anniversary charge

The IHT payable is at 30% of the effective rate on the relevant property.
IHT payable = 30% × 15.429% × £175,000 = £8,100

1 June 2000 Ten-year anniversary charge

Assumed chargeable transfer	
Value of relevant property	£180,000

Assumed transferor's cumulative total	
Aggregate of amount on which proportionate charge arises between 1 June 1990 and 1 June 2000	£68,000

	Gross £	Tax £
Assumed cumulative total	68,000	—
Assumed chargeable transfer	180,000	24,000
	£248,000	£24,000

$$\text{Effective rate of tax} = \frac{24,000}{180,000} \times 100 = \underline{13.333\%}$$

Ten-year anniversary charge
The IHT payable is at 30% of the effective rate on the relevant property.

IHT payable = 30% × 13.333% × £180,000 = £7,200

322.2 RATE OF PROPORTIONATE CHARGE BEFORE THE FIRST TEN-YEAR ANNIVERSARY
(A) Post-26 March 1974 settlements [*IHTA 1984, ss 65, 68*]
On 1 April 1981 M settled £60,000 (net) on discretionary trusts. His cumulative total of chargeable transfers (gross) prior to the settlement was £113,000. On 3 December 1989 he added £20,000 (net), having made no chargeable transfers since 1 April 1981.

On 11 October 1989 the trustees had advanced £40,000 to N, and on 1 May 1990 the trustees distributed the whole of the remaining funds equally to P and Q. The remaining funds were valued at £110,000, of which £88,000 derived from the original settlement, and £22,000 from the addition.

11 October 1989 proportionate charge

It is assumed that rates of tax do not change.

Assumed chargeable transfer
(i)	Value of property in the settlement at date of settlement	60,000
(ii)	Value at date of settlement of property in related settlement	—
(iii)	Value at date of addition of property added	—
		£60,000

Assumed transferor's cumulative total
Value of chargeable transfers made by settlor in seven-year period ending on date of settlement   £113,000

	Gross £	Tax £
Assumed cumulative total	113,000	—
Assumed transfer	60,000	9,000
	£173,000	£9,000

$$\text{Effective rate of tax} = \frac{9,000}{60,000} \times 100 = \underline{15\%}$$

Appropriate fraction
The number of complete quarters that have elapsed between the date of settlement, 1 April 1981, and the advance on 11 October 1989 is 34.

IHT 322.2 Settlements without Interests in Possession

IHT is charged at the appropriate fraction of the effective rate on the property advanced.

$$\text{IHT payable} = 30\% \times \frac{34}{40} \times 15\% \times £40,000$$

$$= 3.825\% \times £40,000$$
$$= £1,530$$

Had the advance of £40,000 been net, the IHT payable would be

$$\frac{3.825}{100 - 3.825} \times £40,000 = £1,591$$

and the gross advance would be £41,591

1 May 1990 proportionate charge

As property has been added to the settlement, the effective rate of tax is recalculated.

Assumed chargeable transfer	£
(i) Value of property in settlement at date of settlement	60,00
(ii) Value at date of settlement of property in related settlement	—
(iii) Value at date of addition of property added	20,00
	£80,00

Assumed transferor's cumulative total
Value of chargeable transfers made by settlor in
seven-year period ending on date of settlement £113,00

	Gross £	Tax £
Assumed cumulative total	113,000	—
Assumed transfer	80,000	13,00
	£193,000	£13,00

$$\text{Effective rate of tax} = \frac{13,000}{80,000} \times 100 = 16.25\%$$

Appropriate fraction
The number of complete quarters that have elapsed between the date of settlement, 1 April 1981, and the advance on 1 May 1990 is 36.

The number of complete quarters that elapsed between the date of settlement, 1 April 1981, and 3 December 1989, the date on which property was added, was 34

The IHT is charged at the appropriate fraction of the effective rate on the property advanced

£

$$30\% \times \frac{36}{40} \times 16.25\% \qquad\qquad \text{on} \quad \text{£88,000} = \qquad\qquad\qquad 3,861$$

$$30\% \times \frac{(36 - 34)}{40} \times 16.25\% \qquad \text{on} \quad \underline{\text{£22,000}} = \qquad\qquad\qquad 54$$

$$\underline{\text{£110,000}}$$

IHT payable on advance of £110,000   <u>£3,915</u>

(B) Settlor dies within 7 years of settlement — post-26 March 1974 settlement
On 1 July 1990 T settled £160,000 net on discretionary trusts. His only other transfer had been a gift of £50,000 to his brother B on 1 June 1990. On 7 March 1992 the trustees advanced £70,000 to B, who agreed to pay any IHT due.
On 30 August 1994 T died.

Proportionate charge 7 March 1992
At the time of the advance, T had made no chargeable transfers in the seven years prior to the settlement (the gift to B being a PET).

Assumed chargeable transfer
  Value of property in the settlement
  at the date of settlement   <u>£160,000</u>

Assumed transferor's cumulative total   <u>£Nil</u>

Tax on an assumed transfer of £160,000 =   <u>£6,400</u>

$$\text{Effective rate of tax} = \frac{6{,}400}{160{,}000} \times 100 = 4\%$$

Appropriate fraction
The number of complete quarters that have elapsed between the date of the settlement, 1 July 1990, and the advance on 7 March 1992 is 6.
IHT is charged at the appropriate fraction of the effective rate on the property advanced.

$$\text{IHT} = 30\% \times \frac{6}{40} \times 4\% \times \text{£70,000}$$

$$= 0.18\% \times \text{£70,000}$$
$$= \text{£126}$$

On the settlor's death within seven years the PET on 1 June 1990 becomes a chargeable transfer. The annual exemptions are still set against the chargeable transfer to the settlement. There will be additional IHT payable by the trustees on the creation of the settlement, and additional IHT payable by B on the advance to him.

The gross gift to the settlement (allowing for two years' annual exemptions) was

	Gross £	Tax £	Net £
	128,000	—	128,000
	32,500	6,500	26,000
	£160,500	£6,500	£154,000

Additional IHT is payable to increase the charge to 60% of full rates (death between 5 and 6 years after gift), with a previous chargeable transfer to B of £50,000

	Gross £	Tax £	Net £
Prior transfer	50,000	—	50,000
	160,500	33,000	127,500
	£210,500	£33,000	£177,500

	£
IHT at 60% of full rates 60% × £33,000	19,800
Deduct paid on lifetime chargeable transfer	6,500
Additional IHT payable	£13,300

The additional IHT is payable by the trustees, reducing the value of property settled to £160,000 – £13,300 = £146,700

The IHT on the advance to B is recalculated

Assumed chargeable transfer	£146,700

Assumed transferor's cumulative total
    Chargeable transfers made by the
    settlor in 7 years prior to the
    settlement (gift 1 June 1990)
	£50,000

	Gross £	Tax £
Assumed cumulative total	50,000	—
Assumed transfer	146,700	13,740
	£196,700	£13,740

$$\text{Effective rate of tax} = \frac{13,740}{146,700} \times 100 = 9.366\%$$

The appropriate fraction is $\frac{6}{40}$(unchanged).

$$\text{IHT borne} = 30\% \times \frac{6}{40} \times 9.366\% \times £70,000$$
$$= 0.4215\% \times £70,000$$
$$= £295$$

	£
IHT borne	295
Deduct already paid	126
IHT payable	£169

(C) Pre-27 March 1974 settlements [*IHTA 1984, ss 65, 68*]

A discretionary trust was set up on 1 June 1969.

The following advances (gross) have been made by the trustees

	£
1 May 1981 to V	50,000
1 June 1982 to W	80,000
1 April 1990 to X	40,000

1 June 1982 proportionate charge on advance to W

Assumed chargeable transfer	
Property advanced	£80,000

Assumed transferor's cumulative total	
Distribution payments between 26 March 1974 and	
9 March 1982	£50,000

	Gross	Tax
	£	£
Assumed cumulative total	50,000	—
Assumed transfer	80,000	13,375
	£130,000	£13,375

$$\text{Effective rate of tax} = \frac{13,375}{80,000} \times 100 = 16.719\%$$

Assuming that W is domiciled in the UK on 1 June 1982, the CTT payable on the advance will be calculated at 20% of the effective rate.

CTT payable = 20% × 16.719% × £80,000 = £2,675

If W had not been UK domiciled, CTT would have been payable at 30% of the effective rate.

CTT payable = 30% × 16.719% × £80,000 = £4,012

1 April 1990 proportionate charge on advance to X

	£	£
Assumed chargeable transfer		
Property advanced		£40,000

		£	£
Assumed transferor's cumulative total			
(i)	distribution payments in period 1 April 1979 to 9 March 1982	50,000	
(ii)	amounts on which proportionate charge is payable in period 10 March 1982–1 April 1989	80,000	£130,000

477

	Gross £	Tax £
Assumed cumulative total	130,000	400
Assumed transfer	40,000	8,000
	£170,000	£8,400

$$\text{Effective rate of tax} = \frac{8,000}{40,000} \times 100 = \underline{20\%}$$

IHT payable on advance to X is calculated at 30% of the effective rate.

IHT payable = 30% × 20% × £40,000 = £2,400

322.3 **RATE OF PROPORTIONATE CHARGE BETWEEN TEN-YEAR ANNIVERSARIES** [*IHTA 1984, ss 65, 69*]

On 1 January 1980 G settled £50,000 (net) on discretionary trusts. His cumulative total of chargeable transfers at that date was £58,000. On 1 January 1990 the funds were valued at £110,000, no advances having been made. On 1 February 1992 the trustees advanced £30,000 (gross) to H. On 1 January 1993 G added £60,000 to the settlement, having made cumulative chargeable transfers in the previous seven years of £30,000. On 1 February 1994 the trustees advanced £40,000 to F from the funds originally settled.

It is assumed that rates of tax do not change.

1 February 1992 advance to H
8 complete quarters have elapsed since the ten-year anniversary charge so the appropriate fraction is 8/40ths. The rate of tax is therefore 8/40ths of the rate at which IHT was charged on the last ten-year anniversary.

Tax would have been charged at the last ten-year anniversary as follows

Assumed chargeable transfer		£
(i)	value of relevant property immediately before the ten-year anniversary	110,000
(ii)	value, at date of settlement, of property which was not, and has not become, relevant property	—
(iii)	value at date of settlement of property in related settlement	—
		£110,000

Assumed transferor's cumulative total		£
(i)	value of chargeable transfers made by settlor in seven-year period ending on date of settlement	58,000
(ii)	amounts on which proportionate charges have been levied in ten years before the anniversary	—
(iii)	amounts of distribution payments in period 1 January 1979 to 9 March 1982	—
		£58,000

	Gross £	Tax £
Assumed cumulative total	58,000	—
Assumed transfer	110,000	8,000
	£168,000	£8,000

Effective rate $= \dfrac{8,000}{110,000} \times 100 = \underline{7.273\%}$

Rate of tax at ten-year anniversary $= 30\% \times 7.273\% = \underline{2.182\%}$

Therefore rate of tax on advance to H
$$= 8/40 \times 2.182\%$$
IHT payable $= 8/40 \times 2.182\% \times £30,000 = \underline{£131}$

1 February 1994 advance to F
Since property has been added to the settlement, a hypothetical rate of tax at the previous ten-year anniversary must be recalculated as if the added property had been added prior to the anniversary.

	£	Gross £	Tax £
Assumed cumulative total		58,000	—
Assumed transfer			
property at anniversary	110,000		
added property	60,000	170,000	20,000
		£228,000	£20,000

Effective rate $= \dfrac{20,000}{170,000} \times 100 = \underline{11.765\%}$

Rate of tax that would have been charged at the ten-year anniversary
$$= 30\% \times 11.765\%$$
$$= \underline{3.530\%}$$

The advance to F took place 16 complete quarters after the ten-year anniversary. The rate of tax is $16/40 \times 3.530\% = \underline{1.412\%}$

If the advance to F was £40,000 gross

IHT payable $\quad = £40,000 \times 1.412\% = \underline{£565}$

If the advance to F was £40,000 net

IHT payable $\quad = \dfrac{1.412}{100 - 1.412} \times £40,000 = \underline{£573}$

The gross distribution would then be £40,573.

323 Transfers on Death

323.1 **POTENTIALLY EXEMPT TRANSFER FOLLOWED BY LOAN FROM DONEE TO DONOR** [*FA 1986, ss 103, 104; SI 1987/1130, reg 6*]

X gives cash of £133,000 to Y on 1 November 1990. On 20 December 1990, Y makes a loan of £133,000 to X. On 31 May 1991, X makes a gift of £20,000 into a discretionary trust. X dies on 15 April 1996, his death estate is worth £200,000 before deducting the liability of £133,000 to Y which remains outstanding. X has made no lifetime transfers other than those specified, except that he has used his annual exemptions for all relevant years. It is assumed that rates of tax do not change.

First calculation under Reg 6(3)(a)

The transfer of £133,000 in November 1990 is a PET which becomes chargeable by virtue of X's death within seven years. However, for the purpose of this calculation the PET is ignored but no deduction is allowed against the death estate for the outstanding loan.

No IHT is due in respect of the chargeable transfer in May 1991 as it is covered by the Nil rate band.

The estate of £200,000 is charged in the band £20,001 to £220,000.

	£
20,001–128,000	Nil
128,001–220,000 at 40%	36,800
IHT due	£36,800

Second calculation under Reg 6(3)(b)

The PET in November 1990 is charged on death in the normal way and the loan is deducted from the death estate.

The PET is charged in the band £0 to £133,000.

	£
0–128,000	Nil
128,001–133,000 at 40%	2,000
	£2,000

IHT at 40% of full rates (death between 5 and 6 years after transfer)	£800

Additional tax is due on the chargeable transfer in May 1990, £20,000 is charged in the band £133,001 to £153,000.

20,000 at 40%	£8,000

IHT at 60% of full rates (death between 4 and 5 years after transfer)	£4,800

Tax is charged on the death estate of £67,000 (£200,000–133,000) in the band £153,001 to £220,000.

153,001–220,000 at 40%	£26,800

Total IHT due (£800 + 4,800 + 26,800)	£32,400

The first calculation gives the higher amount of tax, so the PET is ignored and no deduction is allowed against the death estate.

Note

(*a*)   If X had made more than one PET to Y and the total PETs exceeded the amount of the loan, only those PETs equalling the amount of the loan are ignored for the purpose of the first calculation above, later PETs being disregarded in preference to earlier ones.

324 Trusts for Disabled Persons

[*IHTA 1984, ss 74, 89*]

324.1 **PROPERTY SETTLED BEFORE 10 MARCH 1981**

In 1967 Q settled £50,000 in trust mainly for his disabled son P, but with power to apply property to his daughter S. On 1 January 1991 the trustees advanced £5,000 gross to S on her marriage.

There will be a charge to IHT on the payment to S.

The relevant period is the period between 13 March 1975 and 1 January 1991, i.e. 63 complete quarters.

The rate of IHT is the aggregate of

0.25% for each of the first	40 quarters	10.00%
0.20% for each of the next	23 quarters	4.60%
	63	14.60%

IHT payable is £5,000 × 14.60% = £730

324.2 **PROPERTY SETTLED AFTER 9 MARCH 1981**

Assume the facts in 324.1 above except that the settlement was made on 1 July 1982.

If the trust secures that not less than half the settled property which is applied during P's life is applied for his benefit, then P is treated as beneficially entitled to an interest in possession in the settled property. The transfer to S is a potentially exempt transfer which may become chargeable in the event of P's death within seven years of the transfer. The gift in consideration of marriage exemption applies (£1,000 on a gift from brother to sister) subject to the required notice.

Otherwise, the trust is discretionary and the IHT liability, if any, would be calculated under the rules applying to SETTLEMENTS WITHOUT INTERESTS IN POSSESSION (322).

325 Trusts for Employees

[IHTA 1984, s 72]

325.1 **POSITION OF THE TRUST**

A qualifying trust for employees of a close company was created on 1 July 1980. On 4 May 1990, £15,000 is paid to a beneficiary who is a participator in the close company and holds not less than 5% of the issued ordinary shares. On 4 August 1992, the whole of the remaining fund of £100,000 ceases to be held on qualifying trusts.

4 May 1990
There is a charge to IHT. The relevant period is the period from 1 July 1980 to 4 May 1990 i.e. 39 complete quarters.

The rate of tax is

0.25% for 39 quarters = 9.75%

IHT payable is $\dfrac{9.75}{100 - 9.75} \times £15,000 = £1,620$

1 July 1980
There is no liability at the ten-year anniversary.

4 August 1992
There is a charge to IHT. The relevant period is the period from 1 July 1980 to 4 August 1992 i.e. 48 complete quarters.

The rate of tax is

0.25% for 40 quarters = 10.00
0.20% for 8 quarters = 1.60
                         ——
                        11.60%

IHT payable is £100,000 × 11.60% = £11,600

326 Valuation

326.1 **LAND SOLD WITHIN THREE YEARS OF DEATH**
[*IHTA 1984, ss 190–198*]
(A)
A (a bachelor) died owning four areas of land
   (i)   10 acres valued at death £20,000
   (ii)   15 acres valued at death £30,000
   (iii) 20 acres valued at death £30,000
   (iv)   30 acres valued at death £40,000

He also owned a freehold house valued at death at £50,000.
In the three years following his death his executors sold land areas (ii) and (iii) for £26.000, after paying fees of £1,000 on the sale, and £28,000, after paying fees of £1,500 on the sale, respectively. His executors retained areas (i) and (iv) but sold the freehold house 1 year after death for £51,000 after £2,000 expenses.

The following revisions must be calculated on a claim under IHTA 1984, Part VI, Chapter IV

	£	
Gross sale proceeds of house	53,000	
Deduct probate value	50,000	£3,000
Gross sale proceeds of land area (ii)	27,000	
Deduct probate value	30,000	£(3,000)
Gross sale proceeds of land area (iii)	29,500	
Deduct probate value	30,000	£(500)

Notes
(*a*)   The sale of area (iii) is disregarded as the loss on sale (before allowing for expenses) is less than 5% of £30,000 (£1,500) and is also lower than £1,000. [*IHTA 1984, s 191*].

(*b*)   The overall allowable reduction on all sales is therefore nil even though there is a loss after expenses of £5,000.

(B) Further purchases of land
A died owning a house and a seaside flat.
At death the valuations were

	£
House	50,000
Flat	30,000
	£80,000
In the year following death, sales realised (gross)	
House proceeds	45,000
Flat proceeds	26,000
	£71,000

1 month after the sale of the house, the executors bought a town house for the widow for £40,000 (excluding costs).

Initially relief is due of £(80,000 − 71,000)   £9,000

Recomputation of relief

$$\text{Appropriate fraction} = \frac{\text{Purchase price}}{\text{Selling price}} = \frac{40,000}{71,000}$$

	House £	Seaside Flat £
Original value at death	50,000	30,000
Sale price	45,000	26,000
Loss on sale	£5,000	£4,000
Sale price	45,000	26,000
Add appropriate fraction of loss on sales $\frac{40}{71}$	2,817	2,254
Revised value for IHT	£47,817	£28,254
Total	£76,071	

The relief, initially £9,000, is thus reduced to £3,929 (£80,000 − £76,071).

326.2 RELATED PROPERTY
(A) General [*IHTA 1984, s 161*]
On the death of a husband on 31 October 1990, the share capital of a private company was held as follows

	Shares	
Issued capital	10,000	
Husband	4,000	40%
Wife	4,000	40%
Others (employees)	2,000	20%
	10,000	100%

The value of an 80% holding is £80,000, while the value of a 40% holding is £24,000. In his will, the husband left his 4,000 shares to his daughter.

The related property rules apply to aggregate the shares of
Husband	4,000
Wife	4,000
Related property	8,000 shares

Chargeable transfer on legacy to daughter
IHT value of 8,000 shares (80%)   £80,000

IHT value attributed to legacy of husband's shares (4,000)   £40,000
(Subject to business property relief if appropriate)

(B) Sale of related property within three years after death [*IHTA 1984, s 176*]
The facts are as in (A) above but there was no specific legacy of the 4,000 shares to his daughter and the husband's executors sold them to an unconnected third party for £28,000 within 3 years of the death in the course of winding up the estate.

The executors could claim that the value be reduced to £24,000 by ignoring the related property rule. However, the IHT and CGT effects both require consideration, especially when business property relief is involved, as follows

	IHT £	CGT £
As related property		
Value	40,000	40,000
Deduct business property relief (50%)	20,000	
IHT payable on	£20,000	
Proceeds of sale		28,000
CGT loss (subject to indexation)		£(12,000)
As unrelated property		
Value	24,000	24,000
Deduct business property relief (50%)	12,000	
IHT payable on	£12,000	
Proceeds of sale		28,000
CGT gain (subject to indexation)		£4,000

Note
(a)   A claim would save IHT on £8,000 but would convert a CGT loss of £12,000 into a gain of £4,000 (subject to adjustment for the indexation allowance).

326.3 SHARES AND SECURITIES

Quoted shares sold within twelve months after death [*IHTA 1984, ss 178–189*]

An individual died on 30 June 1990 and included in his estate was a portfolio of quoted investments. The executors sold certain investments within twelve months of death. The realisations were as follows

	Probate Value £	Gross Sales £
Share A	7,700	7,200
Share B	400	600
Share C	2,800	2,900
Share D	13,600	11,600
Share E	2,300	2,300
Share F	5,700	5,100
Share G	19,400	17,450
Share H	8,500	8,600
	£60,400	55,700
Commission, stamp duty etc.		2,750
Net proceeds of sale		£53,000

Within two months of the date of the last sale they purchased a new holding for £1,750.

The executors would initially be able to claim a reduction of £60,400 less £55,750 .... £4,650

After the purchase, the reduction is restricted as follows

$$\text{Relevant proportion} = \frac{\text{Reinvestment}}{\text{Total sales}} = \frac{1,750}{55,750}$$

Original relief restricted by

$$\frac{1,750}{55,750} \times £4,650 = £146$$

Total relief £4,650 less £146 .... £4,504

Notes

(*a*)   No costs of selling investments may be deducted from the sale proceeds.

(*b*)   The probate value of each of the investments sold will be adjusted, both for CGT and IHT purposes, to the gross sale proceeds plus the relevant proportion of the fall in value. Thus the probate value of share A will be revised from £7,700 to

$$£7,200 + \left(\frac{1,750}{55,750} \times (7,700 - 7,200) \right) = £7,216$$

(*c*)   Although excluded from computation of the loss on sale for inheritance tax purposes, costs of selling are deductible from realisations in calculating the CGT proceeds.

327 Woodlands

[IHTA 1984, ss 114(2), 125–130, 208, 226(4), 2 Sch 4]

327.1 TAX CHARGE

(A)

A died owning woodlands valued at £275,000 being land valued at £200,000 and trees growing on the land valued at £75,000. The woodlands passed to his son D. The marginal IHT rate applicable was 55% but the executors elected to exclude the value of the trees from the taxable estate on A's death. D died 5 years later leaving the woodlands to trustees for his grandchildren. They were then valued at £400,000 being land at £250,000 and trees at £150,000. The rate of tax which would have applied to the value of trees on D's death was 40%, but once again the executors elected to exclude the value of the trees from his estate.

The trustees sold the woodlands for £500,000, including trees valued at £180,000, 4 years later.

The IHT on the trees is payable when the trees are sold. The trustees of the settlement pay IHT at what would have been the marginal rate on D's death had the tax scale at the time of the sale applied on D's death, e.g. 40% on £180,000 (the proceeds of sale) = £72,000.

Note

(*a*) If D had gifted the land (with the trees) just before his death, the IHT would have become payable on the trees at what would have been the marginal rate on A's death had the scale at the time of the gift applied on A's death, on the value of the trees at the date of the gift. IHT would also have been payable on D's lifetime transfer (this being a PET but becoming chargeable by virtue of D's death shortly afterwards) but the value transferred by this transfer would have been reduced by the deferred IHT charge.

(B)

B died in 1981 leaving woodlands, including growing timber valued at £100,000, to his daughter C. The executors elected to exclude the value of the timber from the taxable estate on B's death. B had made prior transfers of £50,000 and his taxable estate (excluding the growing timber) was valued at £210,000.

On 1 February 1991 C gave the woodlands to her nephew N, when the land was valued at £318,000 and the growing timber at £125,000. N agreed to pay any IHT on the gift. C died in January 1995, and had made no prior transfers other than to use her annual exemptions each year.

IHT on B's death

No IHT is payable on the growing timber until C's disposal when tax is charged on the net value at that time. The rates are those which would have applied (using the death scale applying on 1 February 1991) if that value had formed the highest part of B's estate on death. The tax is payable on 1 September 1991.

Deferred IHT payable £125,000 at 40% =   £50,000

IHT on C's lifetime transfer

IHT is payable on C's gift to N as C died within 7 years of the gift. The deferred IHT is deducted from the value transferred.

	£
Value of land and timber	443,000
Deduct deferred IHT	50,000
Chargeable transfer	£393,000

IHT at death rates	
On first £128,000	—
On next £265,000 at 40%	106,000
£393,000	£106,000

IHT payable at 80% of full rates (death between 3 and 4 years after gift)	£84,800

Total IHT payable

Deferred IHT	50,000
Lifetime transfer	84,800
	£134,800

Note

(*a*) In the above calculations it has been assumed that the woodlands were not run as a business either at the time of B's death or at the time of C's gift. If C had been running the woodlands as a business, business property relief would be available on her gift to N provided N also ran the woodlands as a business, but would be given after the credit for the deferred IHT.

	£
Value of land and timber	443,000
Deduct deferred IHT	50,000
	393,000
Deduct business property relief at 50%	196,500
Chargeable transfer	£196,500

IHT payable	
On first £128,000	—
On next £68,500 at 40%	27,400
£196,500	£27,400

IHT payable at 80% of full rates (death between 3 and 4 years after gift)	£21,920

Value Added Tax

401 Bad Debt Relief

-[FA 1990, s 11]

401.1 PART PAYMENTS AND MUTUAL SUPPLIES

W Ltd has supplied goods to A Ltd. The sales ledger reveals the following amount due

Invoice	Gross £	Net £	VAT £
16159 dated 31.7.90	487.39	423.82	63.57
15874 dated 12.7.90	364.19	364.19	—
14218 dated 12.6.90	238.04	238.04	—
14104 dated 10.6.90	256.59	223.12	33.47
	1,346.21	£1,249.17	£97.04
Less paid on account on 14104	100.00		
Amount due from A Ltd	£1,246.21		

A Ltd was, however, used by W Ltd for delivery work and there is one unpaid invoice for £143.75.

The bad debt relief claimable is as follows

	£
Amount due from A Ltd	1,246.21
Less amount due to A Ltd	143.75
Debt due from A Ltd	£1,102.46

The debt is attributed to

	Gross £	VAT £
Invoice 16159	487.39	63.57
Invoice 15874	364.19	—
Invoice 14218	238.04	—
Invoice 14104 (part)	12.84	1.67*
	£1,102.46	65.24

The amount of bad debt relief claimable is £65.24

$$* \frac{12.84}{256.58} \times £33.47 = £1.67$$

Notes

(*a*)   The relief can only be claimed after two years has elapsed following the date of supply and after the debt has been written off as a bad debt in the supplier's accounts. It can be claimed after 31 March 1991 for supplies made after 31 March 1989 and is subject to Regulations to be made in 1991.

(*b*)   The debt is first attributed to the latest outstanding invoices. Where payments on account are specifically allocated by the customer, this allocation must be followed. General payments on account must be first allocated to earliest supplies.

(*c*)   For supplies made before 1 April 1989, A Ltd would have had to be formally insolvent for a bad debt relief claim to be made. The set-off of mutual supplies had to be made for VAT purposes whether or not the debt could be so set off under insolvency law.

402 Capital Goods

402.1 **THE CAPITAL GOODS SCHEME** [*SI 1985/886, Regs 37A–37E; SI 1989/2355*
C & E Leaflet 700/2/90]
On 1 July 1990, A Ltd, a partly exempt business, acquired the freehold of a fiv
storey office block for £750,000 plus VAT of £112,500. The premises are used as th
head office administration block for the whole company. Due to cash flow prob
lems, the company subleases one floor for one year with effect from 1 January 199
without exercising the option to tax. The building is sold on 1 October 1997 for £1.
million to a company which only makes exempt supplies. Again the option to tax i
not exercised.

A Ltd's partial exemption year runs to 31 March. Its claimable percentage of non
attributable input tax is as follows.

Year ended	
31 March 1991	80%
31 March 1992	90%
31 March 1993	75%
31 March 1994	60%
31 March 1995	75%
31 March 1996	85%
31 March 1997	90%
31 March 1998	95%

The input tax position is as follows

Year ended 31 March 1991 (Interval 1)
Initial input tax claim £112,500 × 80% = £90,00

Year ended 31 March 1992 (Interval 2)
Additional input tax claimed from C & E

$$\frac{112,500}{10} \times (90 - 80)\% =$$ £1,12.

Year ended 31 March 1993 (Interval 3)
Input tax repayable to C & E

$$\frac{112,500}{10} \times (80-75)\% =$$ (£562.5

Year ended 31 March 1994 (Interval 4)
Adjustment percentage for the year

$$\frac{(275 \times 60\%) + (90 \times 80\% \times 60\%) + (90 \times 20\% \times 0\%)}{365} = 57.04\%$$

Input tax repayable to C & E

$$\frac{112,500}{10} \times (80 - 57.04)\% =$$ (£2,58:

Year ended 31 March 1995 (Interval 5)
Adjustment percentage for the year

$$\frac{(275 \times 80\% \times 75\%) + (275 \times 20\% \times 0\%) + (90 \times 75\%)}{365} = 63.70\%$$

Input tax repayable to C & E

$$\frac{112,500}{10} \times (80 - 63.70)\% = \qquad\qquad\qquad\qquad\qquad (\text{£}1,833.75)$$

Year ended 31 March 1996 (Interval 6)
Additional input tax claimed from C & E

$$\frac{112,500}{10} \times (85 - 80)\% = \qquad\qquad\qquad\qquad\qquad \text{£}562.50$$

Year ended 31 March 1997 (Interval 7)
Additional input tax claimed from C & E

$$\frac{112,500}{10} \times (90 - 80)\% = \qquad\qquad\qquad\qquad\qquad \text{£}1,125.00$$

Year ended 31 March 1998 (Interval 8)
Additional tax claimed from C & E

$$\frac{112,500}{10} \times (95 - 80)\% = \qquad\qquad\qquad \text{£}1,687.50$$

Adjustment in respect of Intervals
9 and 10
Input tax repayable to C & E

$$2 \times \frac{112,500}{10} \times (80 - 0)\% = \qquad\qquad\qquad \text{£}18,000.00$$

$$(\text{£}16,312.50)$$

Notes

(*a*)   The adjustment period for buildings is normally ten years.

(*b*)   During the period of the sublease, as the option to tax has not been exercised, one floor of the building (20%) is used for the purposes of making exempt supplies. The claimable percentage of non-attributable input tax must be restricted on a day-to-day basis to allow for this.

(*c*)   For the interval in which the building is sold, the adjustment is calculated in the normal way as if it had been used for the whole of the interval. This applies whether it was sold on the first or last day of the interval. For the remaining intervals, the recovery percentage is nil as the option to tax has not been exercised and the supply of the building is therefore exempt.

(*d*)   If the option to tax had been exercised on the sale of the building, then in Interval 8, instead of input tax of £18,000 being repayable to C & E in respect of Intervals 9 and 10, further input tax would have been claimable of

$$2 \times \frac{112,500}{10} \times (100 - 80)\% = \text{£}4,500$$

On the other hand, VAT of £225,000 would have been chargeable on the sale which would not have been recoverable by the exempt company, increasing the effective price to £1,725,000 which might not have been acceptable.

403 Catering

403.1 **SPECIAL METHOD FOR CATERERS** [*SI 1972/1148, Reg 10; C & E Leafle*
709/2/87]
A fish bar sells both fried fish and chips and wet fish and seafoods. It also has
small restaurant. It is impractical for the owner to keep a record of each sale. H
can, however, note his zero-rated supplies over a limited period and for a represen
tative month the results are

	£
	£
Receipts from wet fish rounds	724
Shops sales of wet fish and seafoods	285
Sundries (cold leftovers)	28
	£1,037
Overall gross takings	£7,580

At the end of a given quarterly tax period gross takings total £24,016.28.

Standard-rated percentage is

$$\frac{(7,580 - 1,037)}{7,580} \times 100 = 86\%$$

Standard-rated sales for the tax period are

£24,016.28 × 86%	20,654.00
Add cost of standard-rated goods taken	
for own consumption (say)	54.50
	£20,708.50
Output tax = £20,708.50 × $\frac{3}{23}$	£2,701.11

Notes

(*a*)   It is essential that the local VAT office is advised of any percentage and tha
the figure is reviewed at least once a year, over a different period. The figur
must be reviewed immediately if the pattern of trade changes.

(*b*)   There is no legislation governing the way in which any estimate of standard
rated sales should be made.

04 Hotels and Holiday Accommodation

04.1 **LONG STAY ARRANGEMENTS IN HOTELS ETC.** [*VATA 1983, 4 Sch 9; FA 1986, s 11; C & E Leaflet 709/3/86*]

S stays for five weeks at a hotel, arriving on Monday evenings and leaving on Friday mornings. The hotel normally prints all bills in tax-inclusive form: it does not offer reduced rates to long-stay guests. A typical charge is £40 per night, including breakfast, broken down as

	£	Gross £			£	VAT £
Breakfast		3.45	@ $\frac{3}{23}$			0.45
Facilities	7.31		@ $\frac{3}{23}$		0.95	
Accommodation	29.24		@ $\frac{3}{23}$		3.81	
		36.55	@ $\frac{3}{23}$			4.76
		£40.00				£5.21

For 'long stay' guests, no VAT is due on accommodation and the charge is broken down as

	£	Gross £			£	VAT £
Breakfast		3.45	@ $\frac{3}{23}$			0.45
Facilities	8.16		@ $\frac{3}{23}$		1.06	
Accommodation	28.39		Nil		—	
		36.55	@ $\frac{3}{103}$			1.06
		£40.00				£1.51

The charge for S is therefore made up as follows

	Gross £	VAT £	Net £
20 Breakfasts	69.00	9.00	60.00
16 Facilities	116.96	15.20	101.76
4 Facilities (long stay)	32.64	4.24	28.40
16 Accommodation	467.84	60.96	406.88
4 Accommodation (long stay)	113.56	—	113.56
	£800.00	£89.40	£710.60

Notes

(a) The tax exclusive charge for facilities is shown at the 20% minimum, hence the fraction

$$\frac{15 \times \text{facilities element}\%}{100 + (15 \times \text{facilities element}\%)} = \frac{15 \times 20\%}{100 + (15 \times 20\%)} = \frac{3}{103}$$

At a specialist hotel, such as a health farm, the charge for facilities could be as high as 40% and the VAT fraction would then be correspondingly higher.

(b) The taxable turnover of a hotel with many long stay guests is very different from its gross takings. It may not therefore need to apply for registration.

405 Input Tax

405.1 **NON-BUSINESS ACTIVITIES** [*VATA 1983, s 14(2)(3)(4); C & E Notice 700, par 36, Appendix J*]

A cathedral receives income not only by way of grants and donations, but als through the sale of books, cards and light refreshments in its bookcentre and coffe shop. For the first quarter its total income is £34,671.49 of which £11,246.22 grants and donations. VAT on purchases directly attributable to religious activitie is £217.95, VAT on purchases related to the bookcentre and coffee shop is £738.9: VAT on general repairs, maintenance and overheads is £2,185.27.

Input tax is calculated as follows	£
VAT on purchases related to business activities	738.95
Add proportion of VAT on general repairs etc.	
$\dfrac{(34,671.49 - 11,246.22)}{34,671.49} \times £2,185.27$	1,476.44
	£2,215.39

Notes

(*a*)   VAT on purchases directly attributable to religious activities (non-business is not input tax and cannot be recovered.

(*b*)   The calculation continues in the same way, quarter by quarter, until the ta year end when an annual adjustment is made by applying the same calcu lation to the total figures for the year.

(*c*)   There is no UK legislation covering the apportionment of VAT to arrive a input tax. If computations based on times, attendance, floor areas, etc. pro duce a fairer result, they can be used. Prior approval of Customs and Excis is, however, required.

(*d*)   If some element of business income arises from exempt supplies, input ta may have to be further apportioned to arrive at deductible input tax. See 40 PARTIAL EXEMPTION.

06 Land and Buildings

06.1 SELF-SUPPLY [*VATA 1983, 6A Sch 5, 6; FA 1989, 3 Sch 6(2)*]

D plc carries on a partially exempt business. It decides to build new offices on a plot of land which it acquired some years ago for £20,000. Construction commenced in September 1990 and the building was completed and the offices ready for occupation on 1 March 1991. The company can deduct 10% of its input tax for the quarter to 31 March 1991 under the partial exemption rules (see 408 PARTIAL EXEMPTION below).

D plc is deemed to make a taxable supply to itself of an amount equal to the cost of the land plus the standard-rated supplies made to it in connection with the construction, which amount to £800,000, all of which is incurred in the quarter to 31 March 1991. The effect on the company's VAT position for the quarter to 31 March 1991 is as follows

Output tax		£
£20,000 × 15%		3,000
£800,000 × 15%		120,000
£820,000	Output tax	£123,000

Deductible input tax		
On self-supply:		
£820,000 × 15% × 10%		12,300
Actual input tax:		
£800,000 × 15%		120,000
	Deductible input tax	£132,300

Notes

(*a*) There is no restriction on deductibility of the actual input tax suffered as it is attributable to a taxable supply, i.e. the self-supply.

(*b*) The input tax on the self-supply is not regarded as attributable to the self-supply and must therefore be restricted under the partial exemption rules. [*SI 1985/886, Reg 30B; SI 1989/1302*].

(*c*) The self-supply rules illustrated in this example apply to construction commencing after 31 July 1989 of non-residential and non-charitable buildings.

406.2 RENTS — ELECTION TO WAIVE EXEMPTION [*VATA 1983, 6A Sch 2–4; F 1989, 3 Sch 6(2); C & E Notice 742B, paras 40–52*]

A has for many years rented an office to B for £1,200 a quarter, payable in advan at the beginning of January, April, July and October. A issues invoices ten da before each due date. A elects to have the rents standard-rated from 1 Augu 1989. VAT will be due as follows:

Tax point	Standard-rated rent	VAT
	£	£
1.8.89	400*	60
21.9.89	600**	90
22.12.89	600**	90
22.3.90	600**	90
21.6.90	1,000***	150
21.9.90 and quarterly thereafter	1,200	180

*   Half of rent for August and September
**   Half of rent for the quarter
*** Half of rent for July and all of rent thereafter

Notes

(*a*)   Only half of the rents relating to the period 1.8.89–31.7.90 are taxable.

(*b*)   The purpose of electing to waive exemption on rents is to prevent input t from being non-deductible owing to the existence of exempt supplies.

(*c*)   It is assumed in this example that the terms of the lease do not prevent from increasing the rent by the VAT charged. If this is prohibited, the ta able rents would have to be treated as VAT inclusive. Output tax for the fir quarter above would then be £52.17 (£400 × $\frac{3}{23}$) with similar calculations f subsequent quarters until such time as the landlord is able to increase ren on a rent review.

407   Motor Cars

[C & E Notice 700, Appendix C]

407.1   VAT ON SCALE CHARGE FOR PRIVATE FUEL
[FA 1986, s 9, 6 Sch]

L Ltd provides its employees with cars and pays all day-to-day running expenses, including the cost of any petrol used for private motoring. Each employee submits a monthly return showing opening and closing mileage, together with fuel and servicing receipts for the period. The monthly mileage must be split between business and private.

T, the sales director, has a 2,000cc car and puts in a monthly claim showing 1,468 miles split 1,048 business and 420 private. He supports this with petrol bills totalling £66.20 and a service invoice for £48.88 (£42.50 plus VAT £6.38). The company prepares monthly VAT returns.

The company will code the expenses claim as follows

Debit		£
Servicing		42.50
Fuel £66.20 × $\frac{20}{23}$	57.57	
Scale charge note (a)	6.52	
		64.09
Input VAT — on service	6.38	
— on petrol £66.20 × $\frac{3}{23}$	8.63	
		15.01
		£121.60

Credit		
Expenses reimbursed to T		
£66.20 + £48.88		115.08
Output VAT		6.52
		£121.60

Notes

(a) As from 6 April 1987, a fuel benefit scale is used to assess a VAT charge where any petrol or other motor fuel is provided by registered traders for private journeys made by employees, directors, partners or proprietors. The monthly scale charge for 1987/88 to 1990/91 for a 2,000cc car used for less than 1,500 business miles is £50. The VAT charge is therefore £50 × $\frac{3}{23}$ = £6.52

(b) If T travels 1,500 business miles or more in the month the scale charge is reduced by 50%.

408 Partial Exemption

408.1 **STANDARD METHOD** [*SI 1985/886, Regs 29–33; SI 1987/510; SI 1989/1302; C &*
Notice 706].

In a tax year, X Ltd makes the following supplies

	Total supplies (excl VAT) £	Standard rated supplies (excl VAT) £	Exempt supplies £
First quarter	442,004	392,286	49,718
Second quarter	310,929	266,712	44,217
Third quarter	505,867	493,614	12,253
Fourth quarter	897,135	876,387	20,748
	£2,155,935	£2,028,999	£126,936

Input tax for the year is analysed as follows

	Attributable to taxable supplies £	Attributable to exempt supplies £	Remaining input tax £	Total input tax £
First quarter	36,409	4,847	11,751	53,007
Second quarter	20,245	311	5,212	25,768
Third quarter	34,698	1,195	10,963	46,856
Fourth quarter	69,707	5,975	9,357	85,039
	£161,059	£12,328	£37,283	£210,670

C & E's recommended way of calculating recoverable input tax in the remainin
input tax is

$$\text{Remaining input tax} \times \frac{\text{VAT attributable to taxable supplies}}{\text{Total input tax}}$$

First quarter

	£	£
Input tax attributable to taxable supplies	36,409	

Proportion of remaining input tax deductible

$$£11,751 \times \frac{36,409}{53,007} =$$

8,071

c/f 44,48

	£	£
		b/f 44,480

Second quarter

Input tax attributable to taxable supplies   20,245

Proportion of remaining input tax deductible

$£5,212 \times \dfrac{20,245}{25,768} =$ 4,095

24,340

The value of exempt input tax is
£1,428 (311 + [5,212 − 4,095]). As this is less than
both £500 per month on average and 25% of total
input tax, all input tax in the quarter is recoverable.

Deductible input tax   25,768

Third quarter

Input tax attributable to taxable supplies   34,698

Proportion of remaining input tax deductible

$£10,963 \times \dfrac{34,698}{46,856} =$ 8,118

42,816

Fourth quarter

Input tax attributable to taxable supplies   69,707

Proportion of remaining input tax deductible

$£9,357 \times \dfrac{69,707}{85,039} =$ 7,670

77,377

£190,441

Annual adjustment

At the end of the tax year the company carries out
an annual adjustment.

Input tax attributable to taxable supplies   161,059

Proportion of remaining input tax deductible

$£37,283 \times \dfrac{161,059}{210,670} =$ 28,503

Deductible input tax for year   189,562
Deducted over the four quarters   190,441

Under declaration to be paid to Customs & Excise   £879

408.2 **SPECIAL METHOD** [*SI 1985/886, Regs 29–33, 36; SI 1987/510; SI 1989/1302 C & E Notice 706*]

The facts are the same as in 408.1 above except that C & E allow X Ltd to use special method and calculate the proportion of remaining input tax attributable t taxable supplies by the formula

$$\text{remaining input tax} \times \frac{\text{value of taxable supplies}}{\text{value of all supplies}}$$

		£
First quarter		
Input tax attributable to taxable supplies	36,409	
Proportion of remaining input tax deductible		
$£11{,}751 \times \dfrac{392{,}286}{442{,}004} =$	10,429	
		46,83
Second quarter		
Input tax attributable to taxable supplies	20,245	
Proportion of remaining input tax deductible		
$£5{,}212 \times \dfrac{266{,}712}{310{,}929} =$	4,471	
	24,716	

The value of exempt input tax is
£1,052 (311 + [5,212 − 4,471]). As this is less than
both £500 per month on average and 25% of total
input tax, all input tax in the quarter is recoverable.

		£
Deductible input tax		25,76
Third quarter		
Input tax attributable to taxable supplies	34,698	
Proportion of remaining input tax deductible		
$£10{,}963 \times \dfrac{493{,}614}{505{,}867} =$	10,697	
		45,39
Fourth quarter		
Input tax attributable to taxable supplies	69,707	
Proportion of remaining input tax deductible		
$£9{,}357 \times \dfrac{876{,}387}{897{,}135} =$	9,141	
		78,84
		£196,84

Annual adjustment
At the end of the tax year the company
carries out an annual adjustment.

	£
Input tax attributable to taxable supplies	161,059

Proportion of remaining input tax deductible

$$£37,283 \times \frac{2,028,999}{2,155,935} =$$ 35,088

Deductible input tax for year	196,147
Deducted over the four quarters	196,849

Under declaration to be paid to Customs & Excise	£702

409 Records

409.1 **ADJUSTMENTS OF ERRORS ON INVOICES** [*C & E Notice 700, para 69*]
F sells a vast range of foodstuffs. Due to a programming error some wholesale
packs of citric acid are incorrectly invoiced as zero-rated 'lemon flavouring'. The
company decides not to raise supplementary invoices.

The following adjustment is required

	£
Citric acid sales	1,725.00
VAT charged	64.70
	£1,789.70
£1,789.70 × $\frac{3}{23}$=	233.44
Less VAT charged	(64.70)
Additional tax payable	£168.74

Note

(*a*) With many computer systems it is difficult to raise invoices or credit notes for
VAT only. It is essential to ensure that any tax amount will appear in the cor-
rect position on the documentation and will be posted by the system to the
VAT account.

410 Retail Schemes

VATA 1983, 7 Sch 2(3); SI 1972/1148; C & E Notice 727 and C & E Leaflet 727/6/87]

410.1 **RETAIL SCHEME A** [*C & E Leaflet 727/7/87*]
K has a small shop selling standard-rated sweets and cigarettes only. At the end of his tax period, the gross takings are £14,285.21.

Output tax is calculated as follows

£14,285.21 $\times \frac{3}{23}$ =   £1,863.29

Note
(*a*)   The method of calculation is the same for all tax periods.

410.2 **RETAIL SCHEME B** [*C & E Leaflet 727/8/87*]
K expands his confectionery and tobacco business by the acquisition of a news-round. At the end of his tax period the gross takings are £18,714.55 and the expected selling prices of newspapers and magazines purchased total £8,154.27.

Standard-rated sales are calculated as follows

	£
Gross takings	18,714.55
Less expected selling prices of zero-rated items	(8,154.27)
	£10,560.28

Output tax = £10,560.28 $\times \frac{3}{23}$ £1,377.43

Notes
(*a*)   The method of calculation is the same for all tax periods.

(*b*)   Scheme B can only be used if zero-rated sales do not exceed 50% of gross takings in a year.

(*c*)   If K were to charge for delivery and show the charge separately on his news-paper bills, the charge would be standard-rated. Any standard-rated charge is simply included in gross takings.

(*d*)   Scheme B cannot be used for supplies of catering.

410.3 **RETAIL SCHEME B1** [*C & E Leaflet 727/8A/87*]

K is eligible to use Scheme B1. When he starts to use the scheme, his opening stoc of zero-rated goods, valued at expected selling price, is £2,250.00. For his first fou quarters, the relevant details are

Gross takings	Expected selling price of zero-rated goods purchased	Output tax
£	£	£
18,714.55	8,154.27	1,377.43
20,726.40	11,667.67	1,181.57
20,855.88	10,124.75	1,399.71
22,649.04	11,008.62	1,518.32
£82,945.87	£40,955.31	£5,477.03

Output tax for each quarter is calculated using the principle illustrated in 410. above. Stock of zero-rated goods at the end of the fourth period, valued a expected selling price, is £3,440.80.

The annual adjustment is as follows

	£	£
Gross takings		82,945.8
Less opening zero-rated stock	2,250.00	
expected selling prices of zero-rated items received	40,955.31	
	43,205.31	
Less closing zero-rated stock	3,440.80	39,764.5
		£43,181.3

	£
Output tax = £43,181.36 × $\frac{3}{23}$	£5,632.3
Output tax previously calculated	5,477.0
Additional tax payable with return for fourth quarter	£155.3

Notes

(*a*)   The closing stock figure is used as the opening stock figure for the next year.

(*b*)   The restriction in 410.2 (note (*b*)) above does not apply to Scheme B1.

410.4 **RETAIL SCHEME B2** [*C & E Leaflet 727/8B/87*]

K further expands his business to include the sale of paperback novels. At the end of his tax period the gross takings are £25,668.52. The costs of purchases for resale are: newspapers and magazines £8,245.44 and books £1,418.50.

Standard-rated sales are calculated as follows

	£	£
Gross takings		25,668.52
Less cost of newspapers/magazines	8,245.44	
Add fixed mark-up 33%	2,721.00	(10,966.44)
cost of books	1,418.50	
Add fixed mark-up 40%	567.40	(1,985.90)
		£12,716.18

Output tax = £12,716.18 × $\frac{3}{23}$ £1,658.63

Notes

(*a*)   The method of calculation is the same for all tax periods.

(*b*)   The fixed mark-ups for various types of goods are listed in *C & E Leaflet 727/8B/87*.

(*c*)   For a retailer to be eligible to use Scheme B2, his taxable turnover (standard- and zero-rated and inclusive of VAT) must not exceed £500,000 per year.

410.5 **RETAIL SCHEME C** [*C & E Leaflet 727/9/87*]

K, whose annual taxable turnover will not exceed £90,000, is eligible to use the Scheme C fixed mark-up of $15\frac{1}{2}$% applicable to his trade classification 8214. At the end of his tax period the total cost, including VAT, of sweets and cigarettes bought for retailing is £9,524.06.

Standard-rated sales are calculated as follows

	£
Cost of standard-rated goods for resale	9,524.06
Add fixed mark-up of $15\frac{1}{2}$%	1,476.23
	£11,000.29

Output tax = £11,000.29 × $\frac{3}{23}$ £1,434.82

Notes

(*a*)   The method of calculation is the same for all periods.

(*b*)   If K was to charge for standard-rated services (e.g. window advertising), sell standard-rated goods he had produced himself (e.g. home-made toffee and fudge) or make supplies of catering, these would have to be dealt with outside the scheme. Taxable turnover outside the scheme counts towards the £90,000 per annum turnover limit for this scheme.

410.6 **RETAIL SCHEME D** [*C & E Leaflet 727/10/87*]

K is eligible to use Scheme D. His figures for the four quarterly periods in a tax year are

	Cost of standard-rated goods for resale (incl VAT)	Total cost of goods for resale (incl VAT)	Gross takings
	£	£	£
First quarter	9,429	15,701	18,714.55
Second quarter	10,418	17,840	21,316.51
Third quarter	9,972	15,919	18,899.29
Fourth quarter	7,076	11,293	13,149.61
	£36,895	£60,753	£72,079.96

First quarter

Standard-rated sales are

$$\frac{9,429}{15,701} \times £18,714.55 = \qquad £11,238.74$$

Output tax = £11,238.74 × $\frac{3}{23}$ = 　　　　　　　　　　1,465.92

By similar calculations output tax in the remaining quarters is

Second quarter	1,623.67
Third quarter	1,544.21
Fourth quarter	1,074.69
	£5,708.49

Annual adjustment

To allow for seasonal variations, K must now look at his year as a whole. Standard-rated sales are

$$\frac{36,895}{60,753} \times £72,079.96 = \qquad £43,773.81$$

Output tax = £43,773.81 × $\frac{3}{23}$ = 　　　　　　　　　　£5,709.63

As he has computed tax of only £5,708.49 for his quarterly returns, he must therefore add £1.14 to the amount of VAT payable for his fourth quarter, which then becomes £1,075.83 (£1,074.69 + £1.14).

Notes

(*a*) If K was to charge for any services (e.g. newspaper deliveries) he would have to account for these services outside the scheme. Similarly, if he was to supplement his income by the sale of any goods he had produced himself (e.g. home-grown vegetables) he would, even where the goods are zero-rated, have to deal with them outside the scheme. Supplies of catering must also be dealt with outside the scheme.

(*b*) The annual taxable turnover limit for this scheme is £500,000.

(*c*) The annual adjustment must be made on a specified date in each year; the first such adjustment may cover less than a full year.

410.7 RETAIL SCHEME E [*C & E Leaflet 727/11/87*]

M owns a shop through which she sells a wide range of herbs and spices (zero-rated). She also does a small trade in ancillary items such as salt pots, pepper mills etc. (standard-rated). She decides to use Scheme E and the value of her standard-rated opening stock, based on tax-inclusive retail prices, is £465.78.

The expected selling prices of standard-rated items purchased are

First period	£184.45
Second period	£108.75

First period

Standard-rated sales are

	£
Opening stock of standard-rated items	465.78
Additional standard-rated purchases	184.45
	£650.23

Output tax = £650.23 × $\frac{3}{23}$	£84.81

Second period

Output tax = £108.75 × $\frac{3}{23}$	£14.18

Notes

(*a*)   After the first period, opening stock is ignored.

(*b*)   On ceasing to use Scheme E, credit may be taken for any tax paid on standard-rated goods in stock at that time.

(*c*)   Supplies of services or catering must be dealt with outside the scheme.

VAT 410.8 Retail Schemes

410.8 **RETAIL SCHEME E1** [*C & E Leaflet 727/11A/87*]
M. in 410.7 above, is eligible to use Scheme E1. She sells pepper mills at £2.99
each. At the beginning of her tax period, she has 150 mills in stock. She buys 144
during the tax period and has a stock of 174 at the end of the period.

Her standard-rated sales of pepper mills are

Opening stock	150
Add purchases	144
	294
Less closing stock	174
Sales	120

Takings 120 × £2.99	£358.80

Output tax £358.80 × $\frac{3}{23}$	£46.80

This calculation must be repeated for each line of standard-rated goods supplied to
arrive at the total output tax for the period. A line is taken to be any goods supplied
that have the same unit selling price including VAT.

410.9 **RETAIL SCHEME F** [*C & E Leaflet 727/12/87*]
N Ltd is a market garden selling flowers, vegetables and fruit. It also sells gardening
books and magazines. Due to the product mix and the fact that much of the sales
volume is from own-produced goods, the company splits takings at the time of sale
using multi-button tills. At the end of its tax period the *standard-rated* gross takings
are totalled at £26,094.74.

Output tax = £26,094.74 × $\frac{3}{23}$	£3,403.66

Note
(*a*)   The method of calculation is the same for all tax periods.

410.10 **RETAIL SCHEME G** [*C & E Leaflet 727/13/87*]
P has a supermarket selling a broad mix of standard-rated and zero-rated goods.
His annual taxable turnover exceeds £500,000 and he elects to use Scheme G
despite its 'uplift'. He values opening stock of all goods (at cost, including VAT) at
£51,742. The value of the standard-rated lines (at cost, including VAT) is £30,458.

His trading figures are

	Standard-rated goods received for resale (incl VAT)	Total goods received for resale (incl VAT)	Gross takings
	£	£	£
First quarter	66,002	109,909	131,002.45
Second quarter	72,926	124,879	149,216.24
Third quarter	69,807	111,431	132,295.74
Fourth quarter	79,186	127,719	152,047.24

	Standard-rated (incl VAT) £	Total (incl VAT) £	
First quarter			
Opening stock	30,458	51,742	
First quarter goods	66,002	109,909	
Standard-rated sales are	£96,460	£161,651	

$$\frac{96,460}{161,651} \times £131,002.45 \qquad\qquad £78,171.47$$

Output tax = £78,171.47 $\times \frac{3}{23} \times \frac{9}{8}$ £11,470.81

	Standard-rated (incl VAT)	Total (incl VAT)	
Second quarter			
Opening stock	30,458	51,742	
First quarter goods	66,002	109,909	
Second quarter goods	72,926	124,879	
Standard-rated sales are	£169,386	£286,530	

$$\frac{169,386}{286,530} \times £149,216.24 \qquad\qquad £88,211.15$$

Output tax = £88,211.15 $\times \frac{3}{23} \times \frac{9}{8}$ £12,944.03

	Standard-rated (incl VAT)	Total (incl VAT)	
Third quarter			
Opening stock	30,458	51,742	
First quarter goods	66,002	109,909	
Second quarter goods	72,926	124,879	
Third quarter goods	69,807	111,431	
Standard-rated sales are	£239,193	£397,961	

$$\frac{239,193}{397,961} \times £132,295.74 \qquad\qquad £79,515.87$$

Output tax = £79,515.87 $\times \frac{3}{23} \times \frac{9}{8}$ £11,668.09

	Standard-rated (incl VAT)	Total (incl VAT)	
Fourth quarter			
First quarter goods	66,002	109,909	
Second quarter goods	72,926	124,879	
Third quarter goods	69,807	111,431	
Fourth quarter goods	79,186	127,719	
Standard-rated sales are	£287,921	£473,938	

$$\frac{287,921}{473,938} \times £152,047.24 \qquad\qquad £92,369.87$$

Output tax = £92,369.87 $\times \frac{3}{23} \times \frac{9}{8}$ £13,554.27

Notes

(a) For the fifth quarter, the method of calculation continues as for the fourth quarter above, the first period goods being dropped and the fifth period added to produce a rolling average across the year.

(b) If P was to supply any services (e.g. shoe repairs), sell goods he had produced himself (e.g. fresh bread) or make supplies of catering, he would, even if they were zero-rated, have to deal with them outside the scheme.

(c) If it had proved impossible to take stock when the scheme started, P could have used instead the values of goods purchased in the previous three months.

(d) Where standard-rated purchases represent a very significant proportion of the total, it is vital to check that the scheme calculations do not yield an output tax figure greater than gross takings times $\frac{3}{23}$.

410.11 **RETAIL SCHEME H** [*C & E Leaflet 727/14/87*]

Z Ltd has a number of superstores spread across the country and can analyse all purchases of stock for resale. Having decided to use Scheme H, the accountant calculates that the expected selling price (ESP), including VAT, of all goods received, made and grown for resale in the previous quarter was £42,648,510. Of this, £17,184,289 represented standard-rated lines. (Alternatively, a complete stocktake could have been made and the tax-inclusive selling prices of goods in stock for resale used instead of the previous quarter's figures.)

Trading figures are

	ESP of standard-rated goods received etc. for resale (incl VAT) £	Total ESP of goods received etc. for resale (incl VAT) £	Gross takings £
First quarter	12,891,658	36,905,859	41,584,617
Second quarter	18,703,932	41,641,326	38,718,265
Third quarter	20,609,199	52,818,703	43,740,861
Fourth quarter	18,463,685	46,235,087	55,619,817

	Standard-rated (incl VAT) £	Total (incl VAT) £
First quarter		
Previous quarter	17,184,289	42,648,510
First quarter	12,891,658	36,905,859
	————	————
Standard-rated sales are	£30,075,947	£79,554,369

$\dfrac{30,075,947}{79,554,369} \times £41,584,617$ £15,721,283

Output tax = £15,721,283 × $\frac{3}{23}$ £2,050,602.13

	£	£
Second quarter		
Previous quarter	17,184,289	42,648,510
First quarter	12,891,658	36,905,859
Second quarter	18,703,932	41,641,326
	£48,779,879	£121,195,695

Standard-rated sales are

$$\frac{48,779,879}{121,195,695} \times £38,718,265 \qquad\qquad £15,583,658$$

Output tax = £15,583,658 × $\frac{3}{23}$ £2,032,651.04

	£	£
Third quarter		
Previous quarter	17,184,289	42,648,510
First quarter	12,891,658	36,905,859
Second quarter	18,703,932	41,641,326
Third quarter	20,609,199	52,818,703
	£69,389,078	£174,014,398

Standard-rated sales are

$$\frac{69,389,078}{174,014,398} \times £43,740,861 \qquad\qquad £17,441,879$$

Output tax = £17,441,879 × $\frac{3}{23}$ £2,275,027.70

	£	£
Fourth quarter		
First quarter	12,891,658	36,905,859
Second quarter	18,703,932	41,641,326
Third quarter	20,609,199	52,818,703
Fourth quarter	18,463,685	46,235,087
	£70,668,474	£177,600,975

Standard-rated sales are

$$\frac{70,668,474}{177,600,975} \times £55,619,817 \qquad\qquad £22,131,453$$

Output tax = £22,131,453 × $\frac{3}{23}$ £2,886,711.26

Notes

(a)   For the fifth quarter, the method of calculation continues as in the fourth period above, the first quarter's figures being dropped and the fifth quarter's added to produce a rolling average across the last year.

(b)   All supplies of services or catering must be dealt with outside the scheme.

410.12 **RETAIL SCHEME J** [*C & E Leaflet 727/15/87*]
The S Co-operative Society deals in foodstuffs and dry goods. It also offers funeral
services. The Society decides to use Scheme J and the accountant calculates the
opening stock figures for all lines at expected resale prices, including VAT. This
amounts to £1,357,508, including standard-rated lines totalling £859,340. Figures
do not include any lines within the funeral service department.

Trading figures are

	ESP of standard-rated goods received etc. for resale (incl VAT)	Total ESP of goods received etc. for resale (incl VAT)	Gross takings excluding services
	£	£	£
First quarter	1,256,659	2,895,779	3,627,690
Second quarter	1,474,486	3,071,845	2,421,526
Third quarter	1,061,542	2,464,812	2,615,816
Fourth quarter	1,233,948	3,150,680	3,014,216
			£11,679,248

At the end of the fourth quarter the stock figures are again calculated for all lines at
expected resale prices, including VAT. This amounts to £1,246,219, including standard-rated lines totalling £772,656. Figures do not include any items within the
funeral services department.

	Standard-rated (incl VAT)	Total (incl VAT)	
	£	£	£
First quarter			
Opening stock	859,340	1,357,508	
Purchases	1,256,659	2,895,779	
	£2,115,999	£4,253,287	

Standard-rated sales are

$$\frac{2,115,999}{4,253,287} \times £3,627,690 \qquad £1,804,766$$

Output tax = £1,804,766 × $\frac{3}{23}$ 235,404.26

Second quarter			
Opening stock	859,340	1,357,508	
First quarter	1,256,659	2,895,779	
Second quarter	1,474,486	3,071,845	
	£3,590,485	£7,325,132	

Standard-rated sales are

$$\frac{3,590,485}{7,325,132} \times £2,421,526 \qquad £1,186,934$$

Output tax = £1,186,934 × $\frac{3}{23}$ 154,817.47

c/f £390,221.73

	£	£	£
			b/f 390,221.73

Third quarter

	£	£	
Opening stock	859,340	1,357,508	
First quarter	1,256,659	2,895,779	
Second quarter	1,474,486	3,071,845	
Third quarter	1,061,542	2,464,812	
	£4,652,027	£9,789,944	

Standard-rated sales are

$$\frac{4,652,027}{9,789,944} \times £2,615,816 \qquad £1,242,994$$

Output tax = £1,242,994 × $\frac{3}{23}$ 162,129.65

Fourth quarter

	£	£	
Opening stock	859,340	1,357,508	
First quarter	1,256,659	2,895,779	
Second quarter	1,474,486	3,071,845	
Third quarter	1,061,542	2,464,812	
Fourth quarter	1,233,948	3,150,680	
	£5,885,975	£12,940,624	

Standard-rated sales are

$$\frac{5,885,975}{12,940,624} \times £3,014,216 \qquad £1,371,000$$

Output tax = £1,371,000 × $\frac{3}{23}$ 178,826.09

£731,177.47

Annual adjustment

	£	£	
Opening stock	859,340	1,357,508	
First quarter	1,256,659	2,895,779	
Second quarter	1,474,486	3,071,845	
Third quarter	1,061,542	2,464,812	
Fourth quarter	1,233,948	3,150,680	
Closing stock	(772,656)	(1,246,219)	
	£5,113,319	£11,694,405	

Standard-rated sales are

$$\frac{5,113,319}{11,694,405} \times £11,679,248 \qquad £5,106,692$$

Output tax = £5,106,692 × $\frac{3}{23}$ £666,090.26

Over the year, the Society has shown output tax of £731,177.47 on its quarterly returns. It must therefore deduct £65,087.21 from the output tax for the fourth quarter, which thus becomes £113,738.88 (£178,826.09 – £65,087.21).

Notes

(*a*)   For the fifth quarter the calculations begin again using the closing stock figures as opening stock for the new year.

(*b*)   This scheme is potentially very accurate but the product mix in stocks can be very different from the mix in day-to-day purchases, resulting in large over-declaration adjustments at the year end. There are two accepted adaptations, one where the stock adjustment is carried out period by period (so that no annual adjustment is required), the other where opening stocks are ignored until the final period of the year.

(*c*)   All supplies of services and catering must be dealt with outside the scheme.

411 Self-Supply

Cross reference. See also 406.1 LAND AND BUILDINGS

411.1 **STATIONERY** [*SI 1981/1741, Reg 14; SI 1985/886, Reg 30B; SI 1989/1302; C & E Leaflet 706/1/87*]

R Ltd acquires a small printing business and decides to produce its own office stationery. In the quarter to 31 December 1990 it incurs £1,584.61 input tax on printing paper, inks, press repairs etc. and values its self-supplies as

	Net £	VAT £
Standard-rated	7,845.21	1,176.78
Zero-rated	428.79	—
	£8,274.00	£1,176.78

For partial exemption purposes the company uses a special method agreed with C & E. In the quarter it receives £2,035,352 from exempt supplies and £379,412 (net) from taxable supplies. It breaks down the related input tax as follows

Attributable to exempt supplies	£1,014.27
Attributable to taxable supplies	£10,428.55
Non-attributable (office overheads)	£88.61

The deductible percentage is

$$\frac{379,412}{2,035,352 + 379,412} \times 100 = 15.7\%$$

Deductible input tax is

	£
VAT on goods and services for use in manufacture of stationery	1,584.61
VAT on taxable supplies	10,428.55
VAT on self-supplies £1,176.78 × 15.7%	184.75
VAT on overheads £88.61 × 15.7%	13.91
	£12,211.82

Against this figure of £12,211.82 the company must show output tax of £1,176.78, as well as the output tax due on taxable supplies of £379,412.

Notes

(*a*) For simplicity, all tax on self-supplies has been shown as non-attributable and apportioned accordingly. The company should, however, attribute its self-supplies as far as possible to either exempt or taxable outputs.

(*b*) After 31 July 1989, the value of self-supplies must be excluded from the computation of the deductible percentage. Previously, this value could be included in both numerator and denominator, giving a higher percentage.

412 Valuation

412.1 **SETTLEMENT DISCOUNTS** [*VATA 1983, 4 Sch 4, 5*]

T offers settlement discounts of $3\frac{3}{4}$% for seven days and $2\frac{1}{2}$% for thirty days. He wishes to raise an invoice for 250 jigsaw puzzles at £0.50 exclusive of VAT.

VAT is calculated as follows	£
250 Jigsaw puzzles at £0.50	125.00
Less $3\frac{3}{4}$% discount	(4.69)
	£120.31
VAT at 15%	£18.05

The invoice reads

250 jigsaws @ £0.50	125.00
VAT	18.05
	£143.05

Notes

(*a*) VAT is calculated using the highest rate of discount offered whether or not the discount is actually taken by the customer.

(*b*) Discount terms must be clearly stated. The invoice should state 'VAT strictly net' or 'Amount payable in seven days £138.36 [£143.05 − £4.69], amount payable in thirty days £139.92 [£143.05 − ($2\frac{1}{2}$% × £125.00)]'.

Table of Statutes

Table of Statutes

Table of Statutes

Table of Statutes

Table of Statutes

Table of Statutes

Statutory Instruments

Index

This index is referenced to chapter and paragraph number within the five main sections of the book. The entries in bold capitals are chapter headings in the text.

Index

Index

D

Death
See Transfers on death
Debenture interest   **CT 118.1**
DECEASED ESTATES   **IT 4**
    absolute interest   IT 4.1
    limited interest   IT 4.2
DEEDS VARYING DISPO-
   SITIONS ON DEATH   **IHT 308**
Deep discount securities   **IT 20.2;**
     CT 118.1
Deep gain securities   **IT 20.3**
Deferment of chargeable gain
   See Hold-over reliefs and Rollover
    relief
Deferred consideration
     CGT 206.3(B)(C); 223.4(E)
Dependent subsidiaries   **IT 25.2(B)**
Depreciatory transactions   **CGT 202.5**
Directors' remuneration (unpaid)
     CT 118.1
Disabled persons, trusts for   **IHT 324**
Discounts on early settlement **VAT 412.1**
Discretionary trusts
   See Settlements without
    interests in possession
DISPOSAL   **CGT 206**
    allowable expenditure   CGT 206.1
   —effect of capital
    allowances   CGT 206.1(B)
   capital sums derived from
    assets   CGT 206.3
   —deferred consideration
     CGT 206.3(B)(C); 223.4(E)
   compulsory acquisition of
    land   CGT 212.2
   connected persons   CGT 202.4
   options   CGT 206.5; 225.2
   part disposal   CGT 206.2; 206.3(A);
     207.1(C); 212.1;
     212.2
   —small part disposals of land
     CGT 212.1
   premiums payable under
    leases   IT 18.3
     CGT 212.3
   receipt of compensation   CGT 206.4;
     212.2
   —capital sum exceeding
    allowable expenditure   206.4(D)
   —compulsory acquisition   CGT 212.2
   —indexation allowance
     CGT 206.4(E)

   —part application of capital
    sum received   CGT 206.4(C
   —restoration using insurance
    moneys   CGT 206.4(B
   value passing out of shares
     CGT 202.1; 202.2; 202.3
Domicile
   See Residence and Domicile
Double charges relief   **IHT 311.1(B)**
     315; 323.1
DOUBLE TAX RELIEF   **IT 5**
     CT 107
     IHT 309
   allocation of charges and ACT
     CT 107.2
   limits on   IT 1.1(B); 5.1
     CT 107.1
   measure of relief   IT 5.1
     CT 107.1
   underlying tax, relief for   CT 107.1(B
   unilateral relief   IT 5.1
     CT 107.1; 107.2
     IHT 309.1
Dredging, allowance for   **IT 3.5**
Dwelling house, gains on   **CGT 218**

E

Earn-outs   **CGT 223.4(E**
Emoluments
   See Schedule E—Emoluments
Employee share schemes   **IT 25**
Employees, trusts for   **IHT 325**
Employments
   See Schedule E—Emoluments
Enterprise zones   **IT 3.6(D**
Entertainers and sportsmen,
   non-resident   **IT 13.1**
EXEMPTIONS AND RELIEFS
     CGT 207
   dwelling house   CGT 218
   qualifying corporate bonds   CGT 219
   tangible movable asset   CGT 207.1
Exempt supplies (VAT)
   See Partial exemption
EXEMPT TRANSFERS   **IHT 310**
   annual gifts   IHT 310.1; 321.1
   —termination of an interest
    in possession   IHT 321.1
   gifts in consideration
    of marriage   IHT 321.1; 324.2
   normal expenditure out of
    income   IHT 310.2

Index

Index

Index

Index

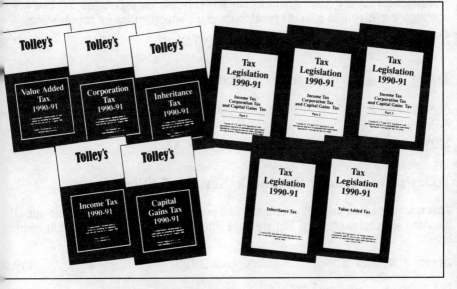

CURRENT TITLES FROM
Tolley

Tolley's Purchase and Sale of a Private Company's Shares (Fourth Edition)

This practical guide to the maze of technically complex tax legislation and case law is designed to highlight both the problems and the opportunities for tax planning.

220 pages   Order code PSPCS4   £24.9

Tolley's Practical Guide to Company Acquisitions

A wide ranging review of all the considerations, including legal aspects, tax planning accounting requirements and employment responsibilities.

220 pages   Order code TPGCA2   £29.9

Tolley's Employment Handbook (Seventh Edition)

This practical guide to employment law and practice has been updated to include all the latest legislative changes, including the Employment Act 1990 and recent case law.

Approx 450 pages   Order code EHB7   £19.9

Tolley's Payroll Handbook (Fourth Edition)

Written by specialists in the field, this title covers the entire field of the payroll activities of an organisation and deals with the legal, financial and administrative problems of payroll managers and departments.

Approx 330 pages   Order code PH4   £29.9

Tolley's Social Security and State Benefits 1990-91

This latest edition has been completely updated to take account of all important changes to the law and includes the changes brought about by the Social Security Act 1990.

Approx 530 pages   Order code SS90   £24.9

Tolley's Health and Safety at Work Handbook (Third Edition)

Published in association with the Royal Society for the Prevention of Accidents this definitive work is a comprehensive guide to the law and practice relating to health and safety at work.

Approx 250 pages   Order code HSW3   £39.9

NEW TITLES

olley's Director's Handbook

eveloped from material in the highly successful Tolly's Company Law, this practical ork provides a concise and accessible guide to all aspects, both legal and dministrative, of a director's work.

pprox 200 pages   Order code DH1   £24.95
vailable Now

olley's Drafting Contracts of Employment

his is a practical guide to drafting terms and conditions for contracts of employment d service agreements for use in the UK and includes useful precedents.

pprox 200 pages   Order code DCE1   £24.95
vailable Now

olley's Tax on Takeovers

formation from Tolley's Tax Planning is brought together in one handy reference urce for both vendor and purchaser.

0 pages   Order code TOT1   £19.95
vailable December

olley's Corporate Insolvency Handbook

his specialist work combines a mass of useful information and provides a detailed alysis of practical problems in one convenient source of reference.

pprox 350 pages   Order code CIH1   £27.95
vailable December

olley's Guide to Statutory Sick Pay & tatutory Maternity Pay

his new book, developed from the text of Tolley's Guide to Statutory Sick Pay and olley's Guide to Statutory Maternity Pay, provides a comprehensive explanation for th employers and employees.

pprox 160 pages   Order Code SMSSP1   £22.95
vailable December

SPECIAL OFFER

ompany Secretary's Review Survey of Company Car Schemes 1990

he tenth edition of this successful title is based on questionnaires returned by a large nple of UK organisations of all sizes enabling those involved in fleet management to ake useful comparisons with those of other companies.

0 pages   Order code CCS90   A4 Paperback

Special Offer Price until 1 January 1990 £32.50

Normal Price £37.50

Tolley
HOTLINE

081-686 0115

The above Hotline number is a direct line to our Customer Liaison staff and can be used for a faster, more convenient service when ordering any Tolley publication.

(Outside office hours an answering machine is in operation)

Tolley Publishing Co. Ltd.,
Tolley House, 2 Addiscombe Road, Croydon, Surrey, CR9 5AF

Tolley Publications

TAXATION PUBLICATIONS

Tax Reference Annuals

Tolley's Income Tax 1990-91 £22.95
Tolley's Corporation Tax 1990-91 £18.95
Tolley's Capital Gains Tax 1990-91 £19.95
Tolley's Inheritance Tax 1990-91 £16.95
Tolley's Value Added Tax 1990-91 £19.95
Tolley's National Insurance Contributions 1990-91 £23.95

Tolley's Tax Legislation Series

Income Tax, Corporation Tax and Capital Gains Tax
Legislation 1990-91 (in 3 parts) £25.95
Inheritance Tax Legislation 1990-91 £10.95
Value Added Tax Legislation 1990-91 £14.95
NIC Legislation 1990-91 £13.95

Tolley's Looseleaf Tax Service

Tolley's Tax Service Income Tax, Corporation Tax
and Capital Gains Tax (4 binders) £295.00
Tolley's Inheritance Tax Service £75.00
Tolley's Value Added Tax Service (2 binders) £175.00

Other Annual Tax Books

Tolley's Taxwise I 1990-91 (IT/CT/CGT) £18.95
Tolley's Taxwise II 1990-91 (IHT/VAT/Trusts/
Planning/Management £15.95
Tolley's Capital Allowances 3rd Edition £21.95
Tolley's Estate Planning 3rd Edition £21.95
Tolley's Official Tax Statements 1990-91 £26.95
Tolley's Tax Cases 1990 £21.95
Tolley's Tax Computations 1990-91 £25.95
Tolley's Tax Data 1990-91 £9.95
Tolley's Tax Guide 1990-91 £18.95
Tolley's Tax Office Addresses 1990 £5.95
Tolley's Tax Planning 1991 (2 volumes) £46.95
Tolley's Tax Tables 1990-91 £6.95
Tolley's Taxation in the Channel Islands and Isle of
Man 1991 £15.95
Tolley's Taxation in the Republic of Ireland 1990-91
£16.95
Tolley's VAT Planning 1991 £22.95
Tolley's VAT Cases 1990 £44.95

Other Tax Books

Tolley's Capital Gains Tax Base Date Prices
31st March 1982 (Revised Issue 1989) £25.00
Tolley's Guide to the VAT Compliance and Penalty
Provisions 2nd Edition £12.95
Tolley's Tax Appeals to the Commissioners £14.95
Tolley's Property Taxes 3rd Edition £24.95
Tolley's Retirement Relief £12.95
Tolley's Roll-over and Hold-over Reliefs £19.95
Tolley's Schedule E: Taxation of Employments
£24.95
Tolley's Re-basing of Capital Gains Tax to 1982
£19.95
Tolley's Stamp Duties and Stamp Duty Reserve Tax
£19.95 (2nd Edition)
Tolley's Personal Tax and Investment Strategy £24.95
Tolley's Tax Havens £35.00
Tolley's Tax Compliance and Investigations £24.95
Tolley's Tax Planning for New Businesses
3rd Edition £15.95

Tolleys Taxation of UK Trusts £24.95
Tolley's Taxation of Insolvent Companies £9.95
Tolley's Taxation of Lloyd's Underwriters £29.95
Tolley's Taxation of Marriage and Marriage
Breakdown £14.95
Tolley's VAT Compliance and Investigations £22.95
Tolley's VAT on Construction, Land and Property
£16.95
Tolley's Purchase and Sale of a Private Company's
Shares 4th Edition £25.95

LEGAL PUBLICATIONS

Company Law and Practice

Tolley's Company Law (looseleaf) £49.95
Tolley's Companies Legislation 1st Edition £19.95
Tolley's Index to Companies Legislation Companies
Act 1989 Edition £9.95
Tolley's Practical Guide to Company Acquisitions
2nd Edition £45.00
Tolley's Company Secretary's Handbook £tba
Tolley's Directors Handbook £24.95

Employment Law and Social Security

Tolley's Employment Handbook 7th Edition £19.95
Tolley's Drafting Contracts of Employment £24.95
Tolley's Health and Safety at Work Handbook
3rd Edition £39.95
Tolley's Payroll Handbook 4th Edition £29.95
Tolley's Social Security and State Benefits 1990-91
£24.95
Tolley's Guide to Statitory Sick Pay and Maternity
Pay £22.95

Insolvency

The Bankruptcy (Scotland) Act 1985 - A Practical
Guide £17.95
Tolley's Receivership Manual 3rd Edition £21.95
Tolley's Corporate Insolvency Handbook £24.95

BUSINESS PUBLICATIONS

Accounting and Finance

Tolley's Charities Manual (looseleaf) £tba
Tolley's Companies Accounts Check List 1990 £9.95
per pack of 5 (inc VAT)
Tolley's Government Assistance for Businesses
2nd Edition £14.95
Tolley's Workbook on Financial Accounting £10.95
Tolley's Workbook on Statistics £9.95
Tolley's Commercial Loan Agreements £29.95
Tolley's Sources of Corporate Finance £tba
Tolley's Accounting for Pension Costs £24.95

Pensions

Tolley's Personal Pensions and Occupational
Pension Schemes: An Employer's Guide £10.95
Tolley's Pension Scheme Model Annual Report £7.0
Tolley's Small Self-Administered Pension Schemes
£16.95
Pension Fund Surpluses £7.50
The Actuary in Practice £14.95
Your New Pensions Choice 3rd Edition £3.50

Survey

CSR Survey of Company Car Schemes 1990 £37.50

You may order any of these titles, or obtain a copy of the Tolley catalogue, by telephoning 081-686 0115

Order form

To: Tolley Publishing Company Ltd., Tolley House, 2 Addiscombe Road, Croydon, Surrey CR9 5AF England. Telephone: 081-686 9141

Please send me the following book(s), as shown below. I understand that if, for any reason, I am not satisfied with my order and return the book(s) in saleable condition within 21 days, Tolley will refund my money in full.

If you wish to place a standing order for any book(s) and obtain the benefits of the Tolley Subscriber Service, please tick the relevant standing order box(es). All books placed on standing order are sent post-free within the U.K. Please add 5% towards postage and packing if not placed on standing order.

Title	Price per copy	No. of copies	Standing order	Amount £
			☐	
			☐	
			☐	
			☐	
			☐	
			☐	

Plus VAT (if applicable)

Plus 5% postage and packing (if applicable)

Total £

Cheque is enclosed for total amount of order £ _____

Please debit Access/Visa* account number

 Signature _____

*Please delete as necessary

Please send me a copy of the full Tolley catalogue ☐

Name† _____

Firm _____

Position _____

Address† _____

_____ Post Code _____

Telephone No _____ Date _____
†If paying by credit card, please enter name and address of cardholder

Registered No. 729731 England VAT No. 243 3583 67   Code 262

Tolley